# One Woman's World
## By
### Wendy J. Levenfeld

To Dr. Nye -

I can't thank you enough for all
of your care.
I hope you enjoy "One Woman's World."

Wendy Levenfeld

For Drew...as always and forever

# Author's Note

For many years I have been writing a weekly column appearing in Northwest Indiana newspapers; the *Michigan City News Dispatch*, the *LaPorte Herald Argus* and *The Northwest Indiana Times*. This book contains my first 300 columns. They are presented in order of publication as many are time-specific to events that occurred in the United States and in the world.

In the first column, my hopes for this endeavor and the subject matter I choose to write about are delineated. To date, I have received well over 3,000 emails from readers. I never imagined that the column would run for so long or that it would be read by so many. For this I am truly grateful.

I hope you enjoy reading the columns and should you want to contact me or find out more about me and what I do, please visit my website www.wendylevenfeld.com.

# Table of Contents

# 2008

# The Wizards of Wall Street

Some of you may know me as the Executive Director of the Sinai Forum Presented by Purdue University North Central. Some may know me as Drew's wife; he is a former "County Attorney" of LaPorte County. Or perhaps you know me because my daughter Mari Jae was one of the valedictorians of LaPorte High School in 1999, or from hearing me yell my lungs out at every Slicer Football Game when my son, Rory, was the star Middle Line-backer in 2000.

But no doubt most of you don't know me at all.

I hope this weekly column will change that!

Let's start by establishing a few facts. I am not an expert anything, although I do believe that I am relatively bright, read quite a lot and have a genuine passion for movies and theatre. I am not a politician through I am a bit of a political "junkie." I am not a financier, but am unafraid to wonder (often out loud, actually quite loudly) WHAT IS GOING ON? I am not a health care professional yet, like most of you, I have faced serious medical situations. And I am not an Oreo cookie though often I feel like the cream filling wedged between the chocolate top (parents) and the chocolate bottom (children).

I am a daughter, a wife, a mother and a woman who loves her family, her country and her world. I am often puzzled by what I see around me and I write about it. If I am tickled by a situation I write about it. If I am angry...you got it, I write about it.

Like today. I heard today that we, the tax payers, are going to be asked by our elected government officials to spend trillions of dollars (yes that is with a T, trillions) to bail the Wizards of Wall Street out of this economic mess they've created.

9

Whose brilliant idea was it to give loans to people who clearly could not afford them? Who hog-tied the financial institutions and forced them to bundle those loans and resell them at HUGE profits? It doesn't take a rocket scientist to know that you don't increase a credit line when the card member isn't even making the minimum payments on the existing credit limit.

Why should we, the majority of people who know that one should live within one's means have to pay to bail out the Wizards of Wall Street?

It's been a long time since I've been into children's books but aren't most wizards bad? Even Toto pulled away the curtain exposing the fraud...HE WAS A DOG and got it!

That moniker "Wizards of Wall Street," should have tipped us off a long time ago.

Now, our government wants to throw a ton of money at the financial problems. This reminds me of the parents (you all know them) who think that if they give their children money, they are good parents. One such parent told me "I can't say no to my kids." Hell, I said no all the time! Sometimes you have to say no; no to your kids and no to the "Wall Street Wizards." I am tempted to send my own version of Parenting 101 to Washington. Do you think they will read it?

Read it or not, I just hope they will take some time. Where is all the urgency? It took years to get us into this mess, what makes anyone think it can be solved in a few days? Lest we forget about another, some would say rush to action that is costing lives and trillions of dollars. Wow, we might just have to borrow even more from the Chinese! Don't get me started on that...

Anyway, I hope you will join me on this weekly journey through my world. C'mon, it's going to be fun. Come along into "One Woman's World."

# We Need a New Election Recipe

What a week it has been. Did you see the Presidential debate? Are you following this whole "bailout thing?" And on top of everything else Paul Newman died! Can things get much worse?

Maybe I'm just a simple Midwestern woman, but it seems to me the lessons I learned from my grandmother in the kitchen should be applied to our government. If a recipe is fundamentally bad, toss it. If you can play with the ingredients, fix it.

So, how to begin? Who can sort through all the political rhetoric? Does anyone have a real plan? I can't remember an election where there was so much doubt about both candidates. And the distortions on both sides, so much mud-slinging, what are we to believe? Does anyone realize that with this proposed bailout plan our National Debt will soar to 11 ½ trillion dollars? This is the greatest challenge for our next president. But which one to elect? Our election process is bad, time to toss it!

We need a new recipe for electing a president. The current process has become a nightmare lasting eons from which we cannot awake. And what do we really know (or can believe) about how either candidate is going to fix things? It's all so complicated...or is it?

O.K. Here is part of my solution. Let's call it "Wendy's Simple yet Satisfying Election Creation."

1. Presidential campaigns are limited to six months: three for the primaries and three for the general election. If a candidate can't effectively communicate his/her stances, opinions, game plans in six months, they should not be President. (Ingredients: qualified candidates)
2. No candidate or campaign is allowed to say anything about an opponent. Let the media do the hatchet jobs.

Rather the candidate can only define his/her vision, describing the various relevant situations and explaining how they will deal with them. Position papers on all of the vital issues of the day must be posted and let the public take some responsibility for reading them. (Ingredients: voter responsibility with a pinch of journalistic integrity)

3. No money can be accepted by any candidate. Media outlets must provide "service announcements" anyway, so let them be position statements by the candidates and debates between the candidates...remember they can only talk about what they will do, no attacking their opponent. (Ingredients: responsible media)

4. Finally, average out the millions that all of those PAC's, Corporations and Washington Insiders have donated to political campaigns for the past 5 elections and make them give it annually to pay down the national debt until it is eliminated. (Ingredients: Corporate/Special Interest Group's responsibility with a dash of humility)

So, what do you think? I've been told that I am naïve and it could never work. But why? We have been adding too much sugar to the mix for years and I say it is time to limit it to one or two teaspoons instead of 11 ½ trillion cups!

# The Aw Shucks Factor

Timing is everything, thus my dilemma. Having just begun this column three weeks ago at a time of political contention and in the midst of the most far-reaching financial crisis this country has experienced in decades, I find myself in a creative quandary. Do I follow my gut and write about the "Aw Shucks" factor exposed by Sara Palin in the V.P. debate and risk everyone thinking that politics is all that I write about? I am not a political commentator! Nor am I affiliated with either of the political parties. I am an independent who will not endorse either party or either candidate. I am a writer who writes about what's around me, what affects me and hopefully what affects you. With these extraordinary political times I find that this is what is affecting me and by your response to my two previous columns, it's affecting you as well. So, I cannot, in good conscience, keep my mouth (or my pen) silent about Sarah Palin's performance in last Thursday's Vice Presidential debate. So, here we go.

Governor Palin's great appeal has been described as her enthusiastically plain-spoken manner and the fact that she is your average "hockey Mom." To which I reply, "Aw shucks." Do I want average to potentially be the leader of the free world? Do you? It reminds me of an experience Drew and I had when we had moved and invited our new Rabbi to dinner. He showed up in Bermuda shorts and proceeded to fall asleep on our couch after the meal. When the evening was over, and he had left, we discussed this whole new "casual approach" to life we have all drifted into over the past couple of decades. I don't want "casual" or "average" in my spiritual leaders any more than I want them in my political leaders. I want a President who communicates effectively with a depth of intelligence greater than my own, who will inspire me to do better, to be better. I want them to lead by example, someone better than me, someone smarter than me; someone experienced and savvy enough to surround themselves with the "best and the brightest" to fill in the gaps of knowledge within their own personal experiences. Whether it be John McCain finding the best minds to deal with the economy or Barack Obama seeking sage advice from seasoned veterans on foreign policy issues; I want a President who knows his limitations and who will then surround himself with the best advisors in those areas. I don't want someone as my President who is like those that sit around my kitchen table having coffee (no offense intended towards my friends) or who falls asleep on my couch wearing Bermuda shorts!

And I'm gonna give a shout out ta all a ya readers out there and tell ya with a big wink...I don't want me as my president! I feel that I deserve someone better...don't you?

# The Lost Art of Language

Over two centuries ago a relatively small group of rebels crafted a nation. The brilliant wordsmith Thomas Jefferson compiled the thoughts and dreams for the nation they envisioned and authored a document so far reaching, so creatively worded, so skillfully executed that it has not only survived these two centuries but remains to this day every bit as relevant, every bit as purposeful, every bit as creative as it was when first penned.

Did you happen to see the HBO mini-series "John Adams?" It is based on the wonderful book of the same title by David McCullough. The majority of his research came from the actual letters written between John and his wife Abigail. In many instances McCullough quotes directly from their letters. Beautiful prose, descriptive and filled with emotion and purpose gave us all insight into not only that extraordinary relationship, but provided a detailed account of just how our nation came to be.

Letters. Letters between a husband and wife; what an extraordinary concept. Language. Language not devised to convey a thought in the fewest words possible but rather to lay open one's emotions, illuminate one's thoughts in a phrase, a sentence, a paragraph.

What has happened to "the Art of the English Language?" With computers that spell check and grammar check, text messaging and e-mailing that abbreviates not only words but whole sentences as well (don't they realize that it might take the reader more time to figure out what the abbreviations mean than it would take to just write the word out!) We have lost the art of language, and I for one mourn that loss. Real communication has been replaced by 30 second sound bites.

At a parent-teacher conference some years ago, when I stated my concern about my children's lack of spelling ability and somewhat less than legible penmanship, I was informed that "it is a new world" and since all "written material" must be done on the computer, and there is, of course, spell-check and grammar check, my concerns were unwarranted.

Unwarranted? What if there is an inter-galactic computer glitch? What if all power is inexplicably interrupted, satellites neutralized and (heaven forbid) we are unable to use our computers, our PDA's and our cell phones? How, oh how would we survive? What a scary scenario that is.

And how sad is that?

Are we all able to craft a sentence in at least a legible handwriting? Can we convey sentiment and depth of forethought in our language? Do we ever take the time, to give some thought to not only what we say but how we say it?

Does it have to take a catastrophic technical communication failure for us to realize that we have lost something precious? We have lost something beautiful given to us by those that came before.

I think our forefathers left us more than just the legacy of our governmental system. I think they left us a legacy of language that we have failed miserably to maintain.

# Debates, Powell and Responsibility

As I write this there are 15 more days until Election Day. I don't know if I can take any more. How about you? Did you see the final debate? I thought both men were pretty good...and pretty bad.

When it was over I heard many "fact checks" on all of the news stations about the validity of what both candidates said during the debate. Both men fudged on many of the points they made about themselves and about their opponent. What good is hearing from the candidates if they don't tell the truth? Both candidates base some of their statistics on reports from "think tanks." Please, can anyone tell me the difference between a think tank and a group of like-minded supporters skewing the data to make it come out in their guy's favor? A smart statistician can make most numbers say just about anything they want.

So, I'm choosing to totally ignore the debates.

What I can't ignore is my obligation to be an informed citizen. We are so blessed to live in this Republic having the rights and freedoms we all take for granted. But living in a country where we're free to disagree with the government, argue with those having dissimilar ideas and pray in whatever manner meets our spiritual needs comes with responsibilities. If we don't work at our democracy one day we just may lose it.

Did you hear Colin Powell's endorsement on Sunday? Whether or not you agree with his choice of candidate, I defy anyone to argue with the brilliance of his presentation about how he came to his decision. He explained in detail how diligently he pursued the facts about each man's candidacy. He stressed that he didn't come to his decision easily. But, while he does have significant political muscle, he is after all just one voter. His vote carries no more weight in the election than yours or mine.

So how do we decide for whom to vote? It would be nice if we all could have direct conversations with the candidates as Powell did, but of course we can't. What we can do is research McCain's and Obama's actual positions on the issues. Not by reading some blog, not by searching websites that have no safeguards against falsehoods and deception, not by listening to network political talking heads; rather we can go to the candidates' websites and read for ourselves their position papers. We can then be the judges as to where they stand on the issues that are important to us. By not relying on the deceptive rhetoric permeating both campaigns, like Colin Powell, we too can flex our political muscle.

Yes, it is time for us to do some work for democracy instead of just reaping its benefits. An uneducated vote is just as bad, if not worse, than not voting at all.

If we don't take the time to do our homework for this election, we certainly shouldn't have the right to complain about the presidency that will result from it.

# The Important Meeting

I sat in the park on one of those gloriously perfect late
September days with which God surprises us just when
we're sure fall has firmly placed its heavy feet on our
hearts heralding the onslaught of winter to come.
Leaves above beginning to turn, children screeching with
delight as they slide down the shining, silvery path into
mother's waiting arms, lovers, old and young, holding
hands or arm-in-arm whispering, nuzzling their passion
into accepting ears; I sat observing, reveling in the
simplicity of it all.

A formation of geese, long necks stretched pointing their
way, streaked through the sun brightened sky above. I
wondered for a moment what it would be like to fly. Is
there somewhere within their feather bedecked breasts
where they sense, where they feel the miracle of flight?

As I sat I thought about how long it had been since I
had taken the time, stolen the time from my hectic daily
routine to do the seemingly forbidden. I was nearly
overwhelmed by the unthinkable decadence of sitting in
the park "doing nothing."

There came a pigeon elegantly strutting toward me.
Right in the middle of the sidewalk he strode. He'd
sidestep to avoid walkers coming toward him. Regally,
haughtily he stared at the interlopers as they passed.
Side-to-side his head swiveled surveying his domain. His
mantle of brilliant green around his neck reflected,
shimmered majestically in the sunlight set off by the
grey tunic of body feathers.

I sat.

Why are these birds considered dirty, urban menaces?
Around me I saw soggy, dirty cigarette butts having
been thoughtlessly scattered by the dominant species of
this land and abandoned synthetic coffee cups discarded
with their double low- fat lattes seeping into the ground

around where they had been carelessly tossed. I guessed that anything not worth washing could be casually discarded without much conscience.

I watched the pigeon and wondered why any creature would prefer to walk, no matter how elegantly, when they could fly. Oh to fly, I imagined how glorious that would be.

The bird stopped in front of the bench upon which I sat. I looked at him. He looked at me. I cocked my head. He mirrored my movement. I moved my head from left to right. He too did likewise. There was a moment, a brief, mystical moment, when I knew, intrinsically knew that this bird, this lovely misunderstood creature found disgusting by many, ignored by most; had sympathy for me. I smiled and to my amazement my pigeon friend lowered his head slowly as if in a slow motion curtsy.

A cell phone rang in the distance. I glanced toward the ring then begrudgingly looked at my watch. A deep sigh emerged from me, unexpected, startling me. I then saw that the bird had moved on.

Many minutes later when I reached my office, the receptionist, a usually pleasant young woman, asked me "Where have you been? You forgot your cell again."

I replied as I closed my office door behind me "I had a very important meeting."

# What Has Happened?

I have reached an age where I find myself looking back through nostalgic eyes on a time when "things were better." What has happened to common courtesy, good manners and that now seeming taboo concept of respect for parents, teachers and other persons of authority? Have we strayed so far from the common human decency which once seemed an integral thread in our life's tapestry?

My husband says it's our generation's fault. In school we fought to dress as we pleased, talk as we pleased; we started calling teachers by their first names. We took part in protests, marches and insisted on change. Many of us then raised our children in a "new, relaxed" home. We were their friends. We let things slide. Life became casual. And the media fueled the fire consuming our past values. Instead of Rob and Laura having separate twin beds in their bedroom, everything from prime time dramas to daytime soaps have steamy, suggestive sex scenes and shocking violence for our children to watch. Song lyrics, electronic games, movie dialogue and our new found instant access to everything stokes the flames further. We are bombarded daily with everyone's personal plights, "U-Tubed" into everyone's bedroom, barraged with mass e-mails...the 21st century equivalent of brainwashing!

I remember my shock when at dinner after the first day of school (my children were in high school) both kids began talking about who was pregnant, who had a baby and who was not in school because of it. Forget the moral implications for the purpose of this argument; what struck me was how normal, how acceptable it all seemed to my children.

How did this happen?

And it is not just the kids. I wrote a book about very bad people doing very bad things and who spoke using very bad language. It was a "based on fact" novel for which I did a lot of research. I had interviews, in prisons, with convicted drug dealers and murderers. For more than a year I was immersed in their world.

When asked now if I was scared, my answer always surprises those asking. What was truly frightening was when my Mom read the proofs of the book, her first comment was "it's good but did you have to use all of that dirty language?" I was stunned. I had become so used to the way they spoke, the words they used, I hadn't even thought that it would be shocking to read. I had become numbed to the perversion.

And I am afraid that we have all been numbed into thinking that our political process with all of the dirt and sleaze, is O.K. because "that's politics."

By the time this goes to press we all should know who has become the President-elect. Both candidates have run on the "change issue." I hope our next president will lead us into the 21st century with not only the charge of changing government, but with a vision and strength and example to help us all change our lives.

# Presidential "Take"

We finally have a President Elect. The campaigning has come to an end. I can stop flipping the channels, stop going to suggested web-sites trying to find some/any insight into the candidates that would help me make a decision about who to vote for (and none-too-soon for I feared developing carpal tunnel syndrome if it had gone on much longer). And I "went cold turkey" giving up politics for a week in the hope that my obsession with this race would abate. I even curbed my almost uncontrollable desire to talk about this campaign with perfect strangers on the street.

In all honesty I have to tell you...it hasn't worked! I am left with the realization that indeed I am a political junkie and I had better just deal with it!

So here is my take. I feel very badly for John McCain. He was not only running against a man, he was running against history. He found himself opposing a "different face" both literally and figuratively at a time when our nation was ready and willing to really vote for change. To be honest, I wasn't sure this could happen. Perhaps I wasn't ready to realize that this presidential race really was different. See, in my entire voting life, I have not been able to "vote for a candidate." I have never felt the passion for a candidate that I have been told others have felt. I have always voted against the man I really couldn't stand.

What a very sad admission. I have never known the enthusiasm that I saw on the Obama supporters' faces, the pure joy in the young peoples' eyes streaming with tears as the cameras scanned that amazing gathering in Grant Park after the results were in. I truly envy those that had it, felt it.

And then I heard him speak that night. While I have always been impressed with his oratory skills, I have to admit, the President Elect blew me away with his speech that night. It wasn't until that moment that I began to understand, yes even to feel, that perhaps things had changed and that more change might be possible. Oh how I hate when I have to admit I am turning into a cynical old lady! But truly I hadn't believed until that speech.

And I think that John McCain's concession speech was his best of the campaign (why are concession speeches always so much better than the campaign speeches?) I believed him when he asked that we all support this president. I respected him when he hushed the "booers" and pledged his support for this new president. He is a wise man that knows we are in serious trouble on a number of fronts and I believed him when he said that he will work with soon to be President Obama in any way that he can to help this country. So I am choosing to support this "new man." A man some call our first 21st century leader, in the hope that all of those young people that I saw in Grant Park did not shed those tears in vain.

# Who's a Woman, Who's a Man?

It is a wondrous time to be alive. Medical and scientific advancements, strides in social and professional equality have reshaped how we think about things, opened up possibilities we never could have foretold. Could my grandmother have imagined an African-American man becoming the president of the United States? This was the woman, when I told her that I was embarking on a career in Marketing, replied by saying "will they pay you to go grocery shopping?"

So many things in previous generations that we accepted, were cast in stone, have broken out of the past constraints and frankly, are a bit confusing to me.

Who would have thought that the definition of who is a woman and who is a man could ever/would ever come into question? Have you seen or read any of the hype about the man who became pregnant and gave birth and is now pregnant again?

Pretty confusing, no?

Barbara Walters did an interview with "him" and "his wife" last Friday. I don't know about you but in my mind nothing is more mainstream than the subjects covered in Barbara Walter's interviews! So, what to make of all this? The nagging question naturally arises; what is it that makes one a woman or a man? I'm no doctor or scientist but apparently we have progressed medically and scientifically enough to bring this question into play.

This man who was a woman had surgeries and took/takes drugs to help him maintain his manhood, but he left his female reproductive mechanisms intact. What identifies a gender more definitely than your reproductive organs? I make no judgment on his actions; I'm just curious and a bit perplexed about how you consider yourself a man when you intentionally leave the most female defining of all body functions intact?

I saw the couple with their beautiful baby girl on Good Morning America this morning. They both insisted that they are just an ordinary family and would like the hoopla to stop. Yet he has written a book, granted interviews with a bazillion media outlets and had the birth filmed as a documentary scheduled to air this week. How can the hoopla stop when they are the ones exploiting the situation?

I am a true believer in personal freedoms so if he chooses to alter his sex and have the procedures and take the drugs to make it happen, that's his choice but don't try to convince me that there is anything ordinary about any of this. And don't complain about all of the media attention when you are opening the door and inviting them in.

As I stated at the beginning of this piece, I do believe that it is a wondrous time to be alive, but looking the word wondrous up in Webster's I discovered that among the dictionary's list of synonyms to the word wondrous is the word rattling.

# We Need a Little Thanksgiving

The market's down one day then the market's up the next. Prices in general for everything from necessities like food and clothing to the almost sinful indulgences like Milk Duds in the movie theatre are absolutely obscene but, on the other hand, gasoline prices are still dropping. The splendid colors of fall have given way to the icy-freeze of winter, yet that first snowfall made me want to flop in the backyard and horizontal jumping jack my first snow angel of the winter. There is always a silver lining if you just look for it.

So we are approaching Thanksgiving, one of my most favorite holidays. But, already there are Christmas decorations in the stores and Christmas Carols in the air. I realize that we are a nation of "instant gratification" and that everything has to be right now but when did Thanksgiving and Christmas turn into one holiday? It doesn't serve either day well and we are all the losers for it. The significance of the parts is minimized by the whole.

We find ourselves in a period of historical significance. Two wars being fought, with thousands of lives already lost, financial crisis threatening to drag us into a prolonged recession, a forever presidential campaign of negativity and ill will; excuse me while I alter the lyric from the musical Mame "We need a little Thanksgiving right this very minute." So, let's not give this holiday short shrift this year. I know that it is tempting to speed right through it headlong into Christmas. But let's not.

We need Thanksgiving more than ever!

My grandmother, who I quote very often in this column (it's amazing how much smarter she gets the older I get!) told me to wake up every morning and take one minute before rising from bed to count my blessings. It starts the day off on solid footing and helps to keep you grounded in what's real for the entire day.

And we all have things to count as our blessings. The market is going crazy but were you planning on cashing out? If not, wait and see. If you are an Indiana Republican and lost the Presidency take heart you retained the Governorship! Rosie fans can rejoice that she will be back on the air, while those that are not fans have lots of other programming options. Our current President is being more than gracious to our President-elect who is being more than gracious to his former rivals (Republican and Democrat alike), there seems to be no end in sight to the construction closures at I65/94 but the rest of the summer road construction is over and Michigan State is going to a Bowl game which makes my household very contented!

So my Thanksgiving wish for you all is that you follow Grandma Rose's advice and take the time to count your blessings this Thanksgiving Day and every day.
Happy Thanksgiving to you all

# Telephone Madness

I'm furious and I'm naming names! Over a month ago I responded to Comcast's offer to save me money. We were using Verizon for telephone and Comcast for internet and cable TV. I would garner significant savings from "bundling" and using Comcast for all three. I would retain our phone number and I would even get an upgrade in our high speed internet. The service date was set and all was right with the world.

The service guy came on Friday as scheduled but the order was wrong and he couldn't do his thing that day. I was told to call on Monday to set up a new service date.

On that Sunday our phones went dead.

Here's the abbreviated version of what transpired over the next 5 weeks without phone service...yes, I said 5 weeks. (Thank God I had a cell phone!)

The problem: Comcast had cancelled our phone service with Verizon but no service was performed to reactivate it. Result: I lost my phone service and phone number. (Apparently once your number is released into cyberspace, you cannot retrieve it)

Now those of you who have had problems like this know that every call you make to one of these companies takes forever just to talk to a real person let alone the person who can help you...oh wait, what am I thinking? No one can help you!

I made a flurry of such calls trying to get my phone working. I finally asked to speak to the person of last resort, you know the guy who tries to get their customers to stick with them instead of bolting to another company. I was promised that he would call me back within 3 hours and of course he did not!

Then and there I decided to screw the savings with Comcast and go back to Verizon.

Another rash of long, long, long calls and I was told a service guy would have to come out but that Indiana was the worst state in the country for Verizon service. Lay-offs, retirements and with the economy as it is; they were not replacing those leaving so it would take two weeks to get my phone operational.

O.K. Alright. So November 26th would be my "T" day. Yeah, the telephone would finally work.

At 4:00 p.m. on the 26th when the phones still didn't work, I finally reached a person at Verizon who assured me that they would be working by 6:00 p.m. At 5:45 I received a recorded message telling me that I would not be getting service that day but on December 5th instead.

You do not want to know what I did upon hearing that recording!

Then, miracle of miracles, Saturday I got a call saying the phones would be working that afternoon. I hesitantly picked up the receiver and oh my gosh...a dial tone after 5 weeks a real dial tone and I was content once more.

That is until this morning when I picked up the phone and guess what...no phone service!

# A Climate of Corruption

Do we live in some kind of new climate of corruption? My Husband (being from Michigan) often tells people that our marriage is a democracy. When we vote, since I'm from Chicago, I always win 2 to 1. It usually gets a laugh, but no one from Chicago is laughing now. I know you've heard the quotes from the transcript in the Federal indictment of Gov. Rod. Forget the moral and legal implications for a moment. Didn't you want to yell at him "you idiot, shut up!"

From all reports, he knew the feds were watching (and listening) and yet he still continued his very blatant very illegal power brokering. But is this some new climate of corruption we're living in today?

The fact is it represents business as usual in politics. Power plays have a long history in American politics and in Chicago specifically. Some of us are old enough to remember the "real Mayor Daley" and his backroom kingmaker prowess. But he certainly didn't start it. What of all we've heard of Papa Joe Kennedy, ruthless businessman, ambitious father, pretty much buying the nomination for his son John?

The fact is dirty politics in America has a tradition going all the way back to Thomas Jefferson. Yes, the Thomas Jefferson who so beautifully scribed the Declaration of Independence; the Thomas Jefferson who, with the other founding fathers, crafted this nation's political future by setting down a constitution which has held up to the test of time for lo these two and a half centuries. Yes, that same Thomas Jefferson mercilessly ambushed his dear friend John Adams in the press to assure his own ambition to replace him in the Presidency.

But this Gov Rod, so blatant, so sleazy...so stupid. He knew he was already being investigated!

I find it interesting that just the day before he was arrested, Gov Rod jokingly compared his situation to the Nixon tapes. I too make that comparison in regard to how I feel about all of this.

We know that there is and always has been dirty politics. We know that there has been deal making since time and memorial. But when I sat mesmerized in front of the T.V all those years ago soaking in the extent of our then President's involvement with the whole Watergate fiasco I felt very much as I feel now. I was stunned and to make it worse I felt that it was being pushed into my face. These powerful men elected to serve the people using their power and influence to only serve themselves.

So is the current climate of corruption really anything new? Or has the old "absolute power corrupting absolutely" just always been in our political make-up, part of our national DNA? Who knows, but with this new age of investigative reporting and technological advances one would think that someone who was able to get himself elected to a governorship would be smart enough to simply keep his mouth shut!

# Christmas

I wasn't going to write a Christmas column. It seemed somehow inappropriate. But then something happened.

Do you believe in Divine Intervention? You know those moments or occurrences that seem to come out of nowhere but end up being really important? They make one believe that there must be a Higher Source, something, some wonderful thing that provides inspiration, ideas, creativity...if not a Higher Source, from where would they be coming?

I happened to be driving yesterday thinking about this column and all at once I was struck with the absolute splendor of what was around me. I had grumbled at having to go out in this frigid, icy weather. I had a glut of obligations that just couldn't wait so out in it I was (and none too happy about it). As I was driving my mind wandered and all at once I truly saw what was around me. Ice was coating the branches forming a magical arch of sunlit dazzle surrounding me.

Everything seemed to sparkle about me, one spectacular visage after another; a "prismed" fantasy reflecting all the beauty that can be seen, even in the discomfort of the temperature, if only we take the time to notice. Whether Divine Intervention or just an excuse to write how I feel about Christmas...here goes with my take on it.

I love Christmas. That might seem like a strange statement coming from "a nice Jewish girl." But it is true nonetheless. Actually, I should have started by stating that I don't understand how anyone can not love Christmas. Even those of us not celebrating the religious aspect of the holiday can certainly appreciate the spirit of it. Peace on earth, good will towards man...don't we all want that? At the foundation of all three of the great religions of the world is a very simple principle, the golden rule. Forget the religious fanatics in all religions;

strip away the institutionalization of faith by the religious hierarchy, look past the frills and presents and obligations that this holiday has come to represent and see the simplicity of the message.

Some of my fondest childhood memories are of singing in the school choir those timeless, beautiful Christmas carols. My children hold dear their memories of their godmother (who was born a Moslem) having us over to decorate her Christmas tree. How's that for a mixing of faiths? But to me that is what Christmas symbolizes. Not only tolerating but relishing our differences and being able to rejoice in them.

There is nothing new about what I am saying. So why don't we get it? Why do we allow "forces that be" to taint such a pure sentiment?

Whether you believe that the savior has already been on earth or are still awaiting the arrival, we all have the power to save our own goodness, our own humanity, our own compassion from being lost in the crass, materialism that this season in some regards has come to represent. The message is simple; the concept universal.

So, I wish you all a very Merry Christmas.

# Historic 2008

What a year! "They" are talking about 2008 as one of those years with which historians are going to have a field day! In some respects I have to agree. Those of my generation and older have seen the unimaginable happen.

Institutions that were not only important to us but seemingly ingrained into our national fiber are now in turmoil and facing possible ruin. Could we have ever imagined General Motors, Ford and Chrysler facing bankruptcy? Could we have foreseen those "so much smarter than us guys" heading up banks, hedge-funds, major brokerage houses and even state governments being exposed as not only criminals but really stupid to boot? Now, I personally wouldn't have had much sympathy for any of them. Let them rot in jail or wallow in self-pity while being shunned by any right thinking person. The problem is that they have brought the national economy right down with them. But they are not totally to blame. We have become a "super-sized" nation. Forget the obscene sizing of junk food that is promoted to us as a better deal. We bought into the "McMansion" mentality where we had to have the house that was bigger than we needed and which we certainly could not afford; we wanted to believe that we had made it. We wanted desperately to prove that we could indeed afford that house on the hill and that BMW in the three car garage that only the rich people had in our childhood. And, like the rats in the Pied Piper, we were led unknowingly toward the precipice of financial demise.

Another monumental change is where we average folk get our information. Our nightly news shows have become big business catering to ratings and slanting stories toward the ideologies the networks have adopted. Newspapers are becoming obsolete. Our children don't have the attention spans to actually sit and read a newspaper. Instead they surf the blogs where anyone can print anything and pretend it is factual "news." I fear that we are becoming at best under informed and at worst a totally misinformed populace.

However, given all of that, the biggest news of 2008 will undoubtedly be the election of Barack Obama. His victory is the story. Whether you voted for Mr. Obama or not his election was truly historic. It was not only a triumph for Black America it was a triumph for all America. I fear that many will be disappointed for he is after all just a man, a man that has to maneuver the political process, a man facing enormous problems. Common sense tells us that he cannot "turn things around" quickly and of course only time will tell if his policies will produce the positive outcomes we are all hoping for. But, his election in and of itself is a magnificent statement of the "American Possibilities." And perhaps, just perhaps, having a sense, an experience of previously unimaginable possibilities makes 2008 an historic year indeed.

# 2009

# What Kind of Protection Was That?

When President Bush deftly leaned to the left (and how often does that happen!) to avoid being struck in the face with a shoe hurled by a reporter at a press conference in Iraq, and then had to maneuver again as the second shoe flew at him, my first thought was "where is his Secret Service detail?" O.K., I can see where the first shoe was a shock but this man had time to take off his other shoe, wind up and pitch it at George W and no one jumped in front of the President, no one crowded around him with weapons drawn staring down, with eyes of steel, anyone even thinking about making a move on our Commander in Chief, no one even yelled "stop that man..."What kind of protection was that?

When Mary Cheney spoke at the Forum I had my own little encounter with our Secret Service. I received a call from a freelance journalist about a week before her program asking what credentials he would need to interview Ms. Cheney at our usual pre-forum press op. I had no idea. I called the Secret Service Agent in charge of Ms. Cheney's security with the question. I was told that they didn't have enough guys to "be everywhere" so I would have to take care of screening the reporters myself.

I should screen the reporters? What in the world do I know about security screening other than the fact that I too dutifully take off my shoes in the airport!

The press would be within two feet of the Vice President's daughter in a secluded room behind the stage and they were leaving the security screening to me? What kind of protection was that?

O.K. here's another one. The Friday before the Presidential election I went into Chicago and had a manicure. As I walked into the shop there were two "men in black" at the bottom of the staircase I had to ascend. I walked by. They said hello. I said hello and I went up to the nail salon. To my surprise, there getting her nails done was Michelle Obama. First, let me say that television does nothing for this woman's looks. She's really quite lovely, very tall and thin. Anyway, I was astounded that the Secret Service guys didn't even ask my name before letting me up the stairs. For all they knew I had a semi-automatic in my very large purse and was set on blowing the next first lady's head off. Wouldn't you think that they would have a list of all those having appointments that day and check to see if I was on it? Not only did they not ask me for identification they didn't even ask my name. Just a smile and a hello and on up I went. What kind of protection was that?

I am the first to concede that we live in a dangerous world with lots of crazies running around and our public officials need protection, but it seems to me that our tax dollars are being wasted when an average gal like me has to ask, "What kind of protection was that?"

# Where Has This President Been?

Today is Monday the day I usually submit my column for the week. I had a few points to polish, but I felt comfortable that the column would be ready by end of day. Then I saw President Bush's final press conference this morning and I felt compelled to start all over again.

Where has this President been for eight years?

This man today was, dare I say it, eloquent! Relaxed, bold and confident, no flub-ups, few evasions, he was passionate, reflective, even at times expressing a bit of regret. A truly rounded personality stood before the microphone this morning. In the past I have often felt that a caricature of the man was what we saw at his press conferences...not this morning.

I don't know what others will be writing about it. My guess is that detractors will take issue at his statement that even in briefing sessions on the wars in Iraq and Afghanistan he had fun. Out of context it sounds horrible, deplorable but in context, he was speaking to the emotional toll of the office. While minimizing the "woe is me" presidents of the past, dismissing the "loneliest job in the world" proponents as whining, he was advising the next president to have people around him who not only are the best at what they do but can at times, when needed, lighten the mood a bit...and don't we all need that?

I am sure his staunch conservative base bristled at his marveling at the historic nature of Mr. Obama's election, his statement that he felt fortunate to "have a front row seat" for this period of our history and his glowing assessment of the Obama family. But they will be buoyed by his passionate response to the question of the government's slow reaction to the Katrina catastrophe. He countered strongly, with impassioned indignation that 30,000 people were air-lifted from their roof tops and taken to safety shortly after the hurricane hit; 30,000 people who felt the immediate response of his administration.

I have written in past columns of the graciousness this President has shown to the next President and today he went even further. He was reminded by a reporter of his campaign promise eight years ago pledging to unify not divide. He answered with heartfelt emotion and regret that the climate of partisanship and the vehemence of the rhetoric we have all heard from Capitol Hill, persisted under his watch. He went on to say that he never personalized or attacked members of either house of Congress, and to my best recollection that is true. Then, he ended his answer by asking for civility and respect to be afforded the next president.

I am not a supporter of the majority of his policies. I have felt frustration and anger at some of his stances, and only time will tell how his presidency will be regarded by future generations; but having seen the press conference this morning, in my mind he is going out in style.

# Israeli/Palestinian Conflict

I'm going to be doing something a little bit differently for the next few columns. I find that I am in a unique position to write about the Israeli/Palestinian conflict. I have had an extended personal journey through the splendor and the struggles that make up modern day Israel. My first trip there was as a tourist in 1995 and I have traveled there in various capacities 30 times since. During war and in so-called peace I have witnessed the glory and the pain of this spiritual, magical place.

I have had discussions with dozens of Knesset Members, Government Ministers and the highest ranking Military Personnel in Israel. I have had the privilege to be briefed on the various issues of the day by the past 5 Prime Ministers. I also have a very compelling personal reason to be concerned about this area of the world. My son, Rory, established dual citizenship and served in the Israeli Army for three years. He was trained as an anti-terrorism expert and currently provides security for the U.S. Ambassador to Switzerland.

I begin this series of articles with a story.

Several years ago, I was honored to attend an 80th birthday party for Simon Peres. I was fascinated to hear him tell this heretofore untold, true story.

After the Ben Gurion government was established, it was clear to all that the day might come when Israel, poor in population and resources would not be able to withstand the vast, surrounding Arab population with all their money and oil as well as the arms they had stockpiled. Peres, then Deputy Minister of Defense decided that a weapon was needed to insure the survival of Israel. The idea seemed wild. Who would give Israel the knowledge and resources for such a weapon? Ben Gurion asked Peres if he had a plan. His response was a simple yes. Without any details discussed. Without prolonged briefing, a nod by Ben Gurion gave Peres the go ahead to pursue the matter. There were no allocations required, no votes of the Knesset. It was indeed a very different time. At this same time the French were also battling the Arabs who were supporting the rebels in Algeria so Peres began establishing relationships with members of the French Government. Since they had a common foe he was successful in forging several unofficial alliances. So persuasive a diplomat, so charming a man was Peres, he convinced the recently ousted French Prime Ministers to pre-date an order, risking tremendous personal consequences, giving Israel the knowledge and supplies needed for production of an atomic bomb. To this day Israel has never "officially" acknowledged having nuclear capabilities, but if Israel chose to, she could completely destroy all of her Arab neighbors.

The underlying basis for the conflict between Israel and her Arab neighbors is very simple. Israel wants to be left alone; her Arab neighbors want her destroyed.

In 1948 when the Israeli state was established the Palestinian state was also established. The Palestinians refused to accept that "two-state solution."

# The Two State Solution (2)

Did you hear President Obama speaking at the State Department about the Israeli/Palestinian conflict? He again stressed the need for a "two state solution." In fact, his first call as President was to Palestinian Authority President, Mahmoud Abbas. And 60 Minutes ran a story on the "two state solution" this past Sunday. The concept is getting a lot of air time, but somewhere the reality seems to be missing.

Here's the deal. The Israeli's are often accused of not wanting the Palestinians to have their own state, but since 1947 every time a "two state solution" has been proposed Israel has agreed and the Palestinians have opposed it. The Palestinian leadership doesn't want it and here's why.

Statistics show that within 10 years there will be more Arabs than Jews living in Israel.

The Palestinian leadership certainly knows this. Yasser Arafat might have been a lot of things but he was not stupid. He was perhaps the all-time master of political stalling. He didn't want a separate Palestinian state; he wanted the State of Israel and was willing to wait for it. This is why he would talk, agree to anything that kept Israel thinking that peace was possible then call for the violence to increase when backed against the wall. Jab and faint, jab and faint, classic boxing strategy for tiring out your opponent. And it worked, so Hamas has now adopted a similar strategy. They were in no hurry under Arafat and they are in no hurry under Hamas. They know if they are able to stall long enough the numbers will deliver to them what they have sought for so long. If a majority of residents voting in the Democratic elections of Israel are Arab, they will take the reins of power in the Israeli government. There will be no more Israel.

One other misconception is that the media keeps equating the fanatical Muslims with the fanatical Ultra-Orthodox Jews. They neglect to point out that the Orthodox Jews do not run Israel while the fanatical Moslems do have control. In its report, 60 minutes seemed to imply that the Jewish settlers have the power to block the Israeli government from clearing the settlements, but just look at recent history. The government made a painful decision to clear the Sinai and return it to Egypt and a peace accord has existed between the two countries since then. Three years ago Israel cleared the settlers of Gaza and ceded rule to the Palestinians but instead of peace, thousands of Palestinian rockets have attacked and are still attacking civilian Israeli populations.

The biggest problem hindering a negotiated peace is that no one has control over the religious fanatics of Hamas and they are determined "to destroy all Jews." So all of Obama's good intentions, talking to President Abbas, mean nothing when the fanatics have the real power, whereas the Israeli government has shown its commitment to a "two states solution" by executing its power over the settlers and actually moving them out.

# A Very Personal Look At The Disengagement of Gaza (3)

No Israeli wanted to oust other Israelis from their homes and worse yet give that land that they toiled so hard to cultivate to their arch enemies. But to ensure the future of the state of Israel it was necessary and survey results show that more and more Israelis recognize that fact.

Three years ago, I sat stunned, as I watched Israeli soldiers and Israeli "settlers" struggling with the horrific position in which they found themselves. Every major T.V. network was covering the story and yet the world didn't seem to understand the significance of what was happening.

I have written and spoken of the necessity of this action if Israel is ever going to have an opportunity to live in peace alongside her neighbors. But to see these beautiful children (for most of the soldiers in the Israeli army are under the age of 25) and settlers alike shedding tears as families were being dragged from their homes, as S.W.A.T. teams evacuate synagogues and community centers, was heart wrenching.

The decision to commence this action was political; I feel a politically logical, necessary decision. The fact is that if there is not a separate Palestinian state within 10 years, there will be more Arabs than Jews in Israel. Being a Democracy, the non-Jews, as the majority could/would then rule Israel through legal elections.

A lesser known fact is that 80% of the Israeli National Budget is spent on defense...80%. Just try to imagine what it would do to our economy, our way of life if 80% of our national budget had to be spent on defense. Israel simply cannot afford to keep defending the 9,000 settlers in Gaza.

And finally, clearing the Sinai of Jewish settlers so many years ago resulted in a peace accord with Egypt that

lasts until this day. The hope was that peace with the Palestinians would also result from this action.
These are indisputable political and economic reasons necessitating the disengagement decision.

So, there I sat and watched as these children, following orders on one side, being forcibly evicted from their homes on the other; cried together, prayed together, perhaps neither side fully understanding the decisions of "the powers that be." Neither the political rationale nor the economic reasons for that action were foremost in my mind as the images on T.V. broke my heart. The emotional aspect of the decision seemed all that mattered.

I watched intently for a glimpse of my son, an Israeli soldier, hoping not to see him yet surveying the faces on the screen, desperate to catch sight of him. For months he and his fellow soldiers had strategy sessions, therapy sessions and various types of counseling to prepare them for this operation. But can one ever be prepared for such a thing? How could I have ever imagined that participating in such a situation would ever be my son's fate?

# The Israeli/Palestinian Conflict (4)

This will be my fourth and final column on the very complex, very emotional issue of the Israeli/Palestinian conflict. The resolution of this conflict is not only of utmost importance to the Jewish world but to the Christian world as well.

Let me tell you a story. Drew and I have friends who are Israeli Arabs. They are from Bethlehem but now reside in Jerusalem. They went home to Bethlehem for Easter. Bethlehem is in the territories that were given over to the Palestinians by the Israelis in one of the failed peace accords and is currently marshaled by Palestinian police. Our friend's family gathering was outside on the lawn. The children were playing; joyful laughing and jubilant giggles filled the air as their parents looked on reveling in their children's pure delight. All at once three Palestinian policemen arrived spraying machine gun fire in the air. The petrified group was told that only Moslem holidays could be celebrated and they had to disband or be shot.

Just because Israel is a "Jewish state" does not mean that Christians don't have a stake in attaining peace in Israel.

There are no guaranties that Israel will survive. Don't forget it is only 60 years old, not even a blip in historic terms. It is an experiment that will have to be proven viable. But in spite of the thousands of enemy rockets bombarding its borders every year, Israel still seeks a peaceful two state solution.

I don't know what will happen but I think that Jerusalem, home to some of the most sacred locations in all three of the world's great religions may hold the key.

It was mid-day in July and I was standing in the plaza in front of the Wailing Wall in the Old City of Jerusalem.

The sun sat high in a clear sky and the plaza was filled with people. All at once I heard singing. A procession of celebrants came into the plaza. A Bar Mitzvah boy sat high on his father's shoulders surrounded by his family and friends singing their joy as they came to celebrate in prayer at the Western Wall one of the holiest places in the Jewish faith. At that very moment the Moslem noon call to prayer rang out over the plaza from the Al-Aqsa Mosque directly above us. This Mosque is on the Temple Mount believed to be at the site where Muhammad ascended to heaven. And at that exact moment the bells from the Church of the Holy Sepulchre with glorious tones, majestically chimed. This church marks the spot where Jesus was crucified. In this holy city, at the vortex of the three religions, the voices of the Jews, the holy tones of the Muezzin and the bells of Christianity all pealed, all called, all rang out as one in a cacophony of tones. And at once it seemed not like a jumble of discordant tones but rather a symphony of blended song, of united sound glorifying faith. Not Jewish, not Christian, not Moslem; just faith.

And therein resides the hope, the dream, the very promise of peace.

# Flying, a "Bad Trip"

I used to love to fly. Everything about it was a miracle. I remember (yes, I am not too old to remember!) the night of my Junior Prom going to the outskirts of O'Hare Airport and laying on the hood of my date's car, in our formal attire, watching the planes make their magical ascent into that mysterious, awe inspiring expanse called space.

Back then arriving at the airport itself was one of the best parts of any trip. The people scurried, not frantically but rather excitedly, gaily discussing their plans with their companions. All seemed young and alive embarking on a great adventure and the excitement was contagious. We were all thrilled to be there. And once on the plane we were treated as appreciated guests; offered magazines, newspapers or playing cards. Even the food, though barely eatable, added to the experience. Imagine actually eating a meal thousands of feet above the earth!

Now, fast forward to last week. I went to visit my daughter in the Boston area. What follows are a few of the things that transpired at Chicago's O'Hare Airport.

I arrived very early for my flight out. I regret to say, as I looked around, I saw no smiles; no thrilled anticipation was visible on any of my fellow travelers' faces. Alas, things had changed!

I tried to use one of those "check-in machines" but it kept telling me that I didn't have a seat assignment when I had the e-ticket in my hand indicating my seat as 12B. I finally found someone to ask and was told to check it out at the gate. After, I kid you not, 45 minutes in the security line; I finally went to the gate. The woman behind the counter looked me straight in the eye and said, "Yes, you had a seat, now you don't." So, I was officially on stand-by.

Before boarding, the same rather rude young woman announced several times that the plane was full and requested that carry-on baggage be checked, if at all possible. Repeatedly she announced that the plane was full and told us not to put our coats in the overhead bins so carry-on bags could be stored. I was getting worried that I would not have a seat. As they began to board the plane, she called my name and assigned me, my old friend, seat 12B.

Once on the plane imagine my shock when I looked around and saw that it was a half empty flight! How did they not know that? Why all the announcements about the plane being full? And then I had just gotten settled in 12B when a very nice older gentleman leaned in from the aisle and said, "I think you are in my seat." Sure enough we both had boarding passes indicating seat 12B.

Doesn't exactly instill confidence does it?

I really shouldn't complain. After all, I did get there and back safely. But it does make you wonder why the struggling airline industry seems so shocked to be in trouble.

# Politics and the Movies

I am in my glory. What a great year it has been for two of my favorite pastimes: Politics and the Movies. I can't remember ever watching an Oscar show and truly not caring who the winners were because there were so many really good movies and great performances this season. And who could not have been swept up in the history making season of campaigning our presidential election afforded us.

But what about what's happening now? I'm having trouble keeping this all straight. We have a Wall Street bailout. We have a Bank bailout. We have an Auto Industry bailout. We have a Freddie and Fannie bailout. And, now we have the "Bad Mortgage" bailout with a few added extras on the side. Have I forgotten any?

I don't know about you, but I am really feeling overwhelmed. I'm tempted to just stop – have a total financial meltdown...Oh wait, we are already in a total financial meltdown!

I don't want to hear any more about it. I don't want to continue to try to understand it. I just want it fixed!

My initial instinct is avoidance.

This all leads me to my favorite method of avoidance...the movies. And how fortuitous is it that the Oscars were Sunday night; total, glorious escapism. Actually, it is quite interesting that the two top stories of last week were the Oscars and the Economy. Hmmmmm. The Oscars/the Economy, the Oscars/the Economy; it leads me to wonder does art imitate life or life imitate art? At the moment I think life should be doing the imitating.

Did you see the movie Dave? If not you should rent it. Kevin Kline, just an ordinary guy, happens to be the current President's identical double and finds himself in the presidency when the real Prez is incapacitated...O.K. let's give Hollywood a bit of artistic leeway. Dave is overwhelmed, bullied by his maniacal Chief of Staff, and wants to do good. Twists and turns, political infighting, a deal that if he can find the money in the budget he can fund one of his very worthy projects. Dave comes up with an idea so unheard of in Washington, so far thinking, so astonishing that no one in power has ever conceived of before...he calls his local, truly non-partisan accountant, Murray (I think that was his name) to figure out the budget. With no political agendas, no biases of any kind, Murray logically, practically slashes and cuts the National Budget into a balanced, working document...a lean, mean governmental spending machine!

Why haven't any of our Presidents called in a "Murray?" We should organize a "draft Murray movement" to get someone in there who is not affiliated, connected, or influenced by partisanship, you know a real plastic pocket protector, bean counter to cut, cut, cut. No one should come out happy in this process if Murray does his job correctly.

Ah, politics and the movies. If only politics were like the movies and the people could write the script.

# A Storm in Washington

In the age-old literary tradition of using Mother Nature as an analogy for our political climate, Washington D.C. is in the midst of a major winter storm. My first thought when hearing of the barrage of snow our capital is enduring this first week of March was "I hope it won't affect the cherry blossoms!"

In 1912 the mayor of Tokyo made a gift to our nation of 3,000 cherry trees which are resplendent every spring in full, colorful bloom throughout the Capitol. Several years ago I was lucky enough to be in Washington when all were at the height of their glorious color. Upon turning most every street corner I was engulfed in visual splendor and aromatic delight. On the national news this morning all I saw was tree after tree burdened with Mother Nature's frosty fury.

In this same first week of March, Rush Limbaugh et al and President Obama et al have taken off their "mittens" and are facing each other barehanded, at great risk of frostbite, in what appears to be the makings of a protracted battle over which party is spitting in the eye of the Constitution, which party represents the people of the United States' interests, which party has the answers to all of the woes plaguing our country.

While the outdoor temperatures in D.C. are not heating up, the political rhetoric certainly is.
This whirlwind of icy fallout has not only the streets of D.C. snarled with traffic, but the roads to political harmony as well. If you can divorce your thoughts from the grave problems facing us all for just a moment, and think about this in just "the business of politics" terms, it is very interesting. We have a remarkable system of governance. We are witnessing our two party system in all of its gory glory. This is a government of heated, sometimes seemingly endless, debate. And, that debate is escalating at quite a fast pace. My fear is that the two factions will end up shattering the wise political concept

of "make no permanent friends and no permanent enemies in politics."

I have no doubt that both sides truly believe that they know what is best for our nation, but they do no service to the American people by making permanent enemies of the opposite party.
I love Washington D.C. in the spring with its stately, majestic architecture. At every turn, its stature, the city itself exudes power and dignity, distinction and stability. There is true beauty to be found even in the simplicity of its cherry trees.

So I hope that the promise of spring and the blooming of those glorious trees will not be dampened by this brutal storm. I hope this is just the last flexing of Mother Nature's muscles before she yields her power to the onset of spring and the rebirth of the cherry blossoms and some political civility.

# Legislation Morality

The drug war that is going on just south of our border in Mexico has been getting quite a bit of press lately. Apparently, there are warring drug cartels vying for the very lucrative United States illegal drug market. Being the C.E.O. of a Marketing Consulting firm for the past 28 years, I can tell you that marketing has always been a cut-throat business, but this is taking the meaning to a whole new level! Close to 10,000 people have been murdered in the past year alone but unfortunately the bad guys are not only killing off their rivals, they are also targeting law enforcement and public officials who have the nerve to stand up to them.

With our financial institutions totally tanking, jobs being lost and families being put out into the street in record numbers, perhaps you are like me in thinking; "we have our own problems to be worrying about."

But what if a solution to Mexico's' problems could also go a long way in helping with ours?

President Obama invokes the name of President Roosevelt quite often, citing Roosevelt's handling of the Great Depression as an example of possible solutions to our problems. One of the first policy changes President Roosevelt enacted upon taking office gets much less attention than his jobs programs and the like. He repealed Prohibition. A new source of money streamed into the U.S. Economy from "re-legalizing" liquor. It was regulated and taxed and equally important, the era of violence that resulted from the prohibition completely stopped.

I haven't seen any studies showing that alcoholism dramatically rose due to the repeal of Prohibition. In fact, I have seen no studies that consumption rose at all. All that happened was that "booze became bona fide business." The bad boys now had to contend with taxation and the true sharks of humanity, competitive businessmen. Practically overnight the business of the booze battles were no longer fought in the streets and back alleys but in the boardrooms. The results were astounding. There was a major reduction in the cases of alcohol related violence that had plagued our country all during the prohibition era and, perhaps equally important, a substantial influx of tax revenues for the U.S. Government.

If we stop trying to legislate morality we could drastically reduce our prison population. A huge percentage of inmates across the country are drug related offenders. This could save millions of dollars a year spent on supporting these people (they have better health care in the slammer than my insurance provides!)

We could tax the living daylights out of this now legal industry, just like we do the tobacco industry. We could put "FDA type standards" on the product minimizing injury and death from "bad stuff." Add it all up; our nation and local governments would garner a ton of money annually in the process.

The prohibition of drugs hasn't worked. We enacted laws, spend tons of money on law enforcement and incarceration; we even created a "Drug Tsar" and none of it puts a dent in the problem!

The fact is anyone who wants drugs can get drugs. Why not make it legal?

# The Line Item Veto

Oh my goodness, it is time once again to be discussing that old campaign pet promise, the Line Item Veto. How many presidential candidates have vowed to get this elusive presidential power enacted? How many have cited the necessity of it if "pork" is really to be eliminated from every bill sent to the President's desk for signature?

To understand its significance and why congress has never and probably will never give this power to the President, we have to examine the role of our "Congress People." Those elected to both Houses of Congress are done so to represent their states on the national level. This includes relaying their constituent's feelings on matters of national security, public policy issues etc. They are also there to allocate "national funding." Here is where it has gotten so out of hand. It is my understanding; the projects within various states that are funded out of the national budget are supposed to be only those that impact on or are of benefit to the nation. All other programs of significance to the individual state alone are to be funded out of the state and local budgets.

I don't need to tell you that this is far from the reality of what actually gets funded by the Houses of Congress.

In the debates when one candidate accuses another of, let's say, not supporting a bill to properly equip our soldiers, it's probably because there was so much other, totally unrelated stuff tacked onto the bill that it was just "unsupportable." (If they would adopt my suggestions for overhauling the Presidential Campaigning Process laid out in a previous column this point would become moot.) And both parties do it all the time in their campaign literature.

In one of this past year's senatorial races, I saw an ad for Dick Durbin where the whole thrust of it was that he has the power to get money from the government for Illinois projects. What happened to his job description of supporting only projects that benefit the entire country? Effective "Pork Barreling" has become so blatant it is even the entire thrust of political campaigning!

So, to be re-elected a candidate has to prove that he/she has provided millions of dollars to their state from the national coffers. If a president were to have line item veto, he/she could eliminate the individual "add-ons" to any bill that crossed the presidential desk. Oh, wait a minute, our senators and congressmen couldn't have that. My gosh, how would they explain to their state why funds have dried up from the national coffers?

I wonder how and when our elected officials started "tacking on" other issues to important bills. Perhaps the solution is to limit each bill to only one initiative. Wow, now there's a thought, funding one project at a time on its merits alone. What an astounding idea.

# Yesterday

Picture a beautiful spring day; tooling along the back roads of a bit of the country still left untouched by developers. The windows are down; great tunes are playing on the radio (vintage Beatles) fabulous sunglasses UV protecting my eyes and the wind blowing through my hair.

Ahhh, spring in the country; what could be better? A time of rebirth, a rekindling of the spirit; I breathed in deeply and relished the sweet air. Is there anything better than the first great spring day and the time to enjoy it?

But wait. Amid all of the spring green I caught a glimpse of something red...flashing red in the rearview mirror. I pulled over and watched a tall, lanky County Patrolman approach my car. Rod Steiger In the Heat of the Night sunglasses perched on his nose, and a quite comical, if not effective, swagger with thumbs hooked into his holster belt ala Barney Fife; I had to harness a grin as he walked close enough for me to see that he looked to be no more than 11 years old! Can someone please tell me when I managed to become so much older than every athlete I watch, every bank teller with whom I deal, and now every policeman pulling me over!

His first words to me were "Do you know what the speed limit is on this road, Ma'am?"
Ma'am? Ma'am? When did I grow old enough to be a Ma'am?

"Do you know how fast you were going Ma'am?"
There was that "you are old by definition" word again.

"Do you know I've been following you for two miles, Ma'am?"

Why did he continue to assault me with that word which I somehow always associate with my grandmother?

Hadn't anyone ever told him that the term Ma'am was only to be used for doddering old women? Surely he could see that seated in the car in front of him was a hot babe, not a Ma'am.

Still unable to speak I looked around me. Not one car had I seen the entire drive on that country road – not a house in sight amid the bordering corn fields – not a person – not a dog – not even a scarecrow was in sight; didn't he have some other, more effective use of his time? O.K. I was speeding. I deserved the ticket even if I was endangering no one, but there he was again, at my car door, still calling me Ma'am!

"Let's slow down Ma'am." Were the last words he spoke to me.

I smiled, nodded and took the ticket. He waited until I had pulled from the side of the road before he again began to follow me.

I turned and his car continued on past, out of sight and I was free from him and the dreaded Ma'am designation. With smile broadening, I turned the CD back on, upped the volume and hit the gas just as Paul began to sing about Yesterday.

# A New Vocabulary

Several weeks ago while flipping back and forth between T.V. political pundits talking to their guests about the economy; I realized that we are all now being indoctrinated with a whole new economic vocabulary. Once the thought firmly planted in my brain, I became acutely sensitive to "new words" popping up not only on T.V. but in the print media as well.

We are being bombarded daily with the term toxic asset. Now there's an oxymoron for you. You can't get much more positive than the word asset or more negative than the word toxic. It's kind of like what we're being told about our economy as a whole; what was considered being in the black is now deemed to be in the red etc. And the villains are the bankstas, taking the hip-hop term gangsta and applying it to bankers.

Since we have these toxic assets that the "bankstas" created, we need somewhere to put them. So, to quote Thomas Friedman, noted editorialist for the New York Times and best-selling author, our government will establish a new agency: Crappy-Mae.

And poor President Obama. He has to deal with these same "bankstas" while trying to convince the American people that the spike in investor ponzi schemes, or "ponzimonium," as it is called, will be severely punished. And he must sell his plans for the government to commit huge sums of the people's money to solving the economic problems plaguing the nation. Obama must do all of this while keeping his "conservadems," fiscal conservatives within the Democratic Party, happy so they'll help pass his initiatives.

While on the home front all of us are facing severe belt-tightening economics of our own. Many are opting to take a staycation instead of that trip to the Bahamas because staying at home is the only vacation we can afford. Likewise, young men are finding funding for

traditional dating and the growing popularity of"
bromances," (we used to call this boy's night out!)
becoming increasingly expensive.

Working moms are firing their nannies and "mannies"
(male childcare providers) opting for the less expensive
day-care service.

But we are a nation of innovation and creativity. We rise
to the challenges and economic obstacles that are
thrown our way. There are those who are able to stick
to a tight budget and still manage to dress stylishly.
They are now called "Recessionistas." While being cash-
strapped yet still ever style conscious, the
"Recessionistas" are joining ranks with the "frugalistas"
in creating a new science: "Chic-onomics."

For a person who has always loved language and has
the utmost respect for the written word, I'm finding all
of this a bit hard to swallow. In my pondering of all of
this, I just couldn't come up with a word to accurately
describe how I feel regarding this new economic jargon
of ours. And then I heard it. The perfect word, needing
no explanation at all, summed up my thoughts on the
matter; we are being buried in "econoporn."

# The Sherpas of Our World

The term Sherpa is used to refer to local people who are employed as guides for mountaineering expeditions in the Himalayas, particularly Mt. Everest. They are highly regarded as experts in their local terrain. They are also the guys that do the heavy lifting!

As I write this the G-20 meeting has concluded and the President has participated in a NATO summit, a European summit and a stop in Turkey as well. For several days we have all heard others' opinions about what would/could/was accomplished, pre-visit insights into what would be discussed, speculation that France's President Sarkozy might actually bolt as he had threatened and the hope that Germany's Chancellor Merkel wouldn't shrink back when meeting the President fearful of the same "shoulder rub greeting" she had received from then President Bush in the not too distant past.

But is there really any "wiggle-room" for world leaders at these kinds of meetings? Their staffs have been working nearly round the clock for weeks on the particulars of what will be discussed; areas their respective bosses want discussion, areas that are off limits to pursue, etc. These political "sherpas" are the real unsung heroes of what some regard as merely photo-op meetings. Governmental public service often gets a bad rap. We only hear about the greedy, sleazy few who at best embarrass themselves and at worst damage our national interests. The truth is these men and women work tirelessly, behind the scenes to make our country, and yes, even our world a better place.

And they are not alone. Our country abounds with public servants and volunteers, our own local Sherpas, working oft times quietly, sometimes behind the scenes; men and women wishing only to make a difference.

Our economy is now paying the price for our obsession with the definition of success being dependent on how much money we make. Remarkably, and arguably because of this, we seem to be rediscovering the benefits of public service and volunteerism. Many public and private high schools require hours spent on community service projects, indeed many colleges and universities hold this as a prerequisite for consideration of admission. The term "giving back" is heard more and more. Wouldn't it be great if the generation of "what's in it for me" might just be giving way to "what can I do for you?"

For those doubters, those unable to see any "upside" to volunteerism, I have some advice. I heard in a national news segment on the unemployment rate and how to get a job, volunteering at a not-for-profit organization is highly recommended. It could be the proverbial "win-win situation" for those looking for work. Obtaining skills and experience makes one a more attractive possible employee and equally important, volunteering builds self-confidence and a sense of self-worth by being a part of making a difference.

So, when we look back on this problem-ridden period in our history, I hope we take the time to think of all the Sherpas that did the heavy lifting and guided us through it.

# Why Ford?

I was raised in a General Motors family. Every car we owned was made by G.M. I remember what a big deal it was when the auto makers "introduced" their new models every year. Chevrolets didn't look like Pontiacs, Buicks didn't look like Oldsmobiles and nothing looked like a Cadillac! Had anyone during those years mentioned the possibility that G.M. could be facing bankruptcy would have been instantly carted off to the loony bin.

Like so many others, I feel what is happening now to "my car company" is unbelievable. And the impact on our country in general and to Michigan in specific is unimaginable should it fail. How could this happen?

How did this happen?

Perhaps the better question is why didn't it happen to Ford?

Last year the CEO's of the "big three" American auto makers went to Capitol Hill to ask for money. When Congress offered short-term loans with strings attached, G.M. and Chrysler were forced to accept the terms but Ford was in a position to decline the offer and leave the table.

How was it that Ford was in a position so different from the other two?

In researching this question I found what I think is the answer and his name is Alan Mulally.

Mulally was hired by Boeing right out of college and worked his way up through the years. When passed over twice for the CEO position at Boeing, in 2006, Mulally took the CEO spot at Ford. He inherited a financially strapped company facing massive losses and declining market share. He hit the ground running by implementing stringent cost-saving measures. He suspended stockholder dividends and sold Jaguar, Land Rover and Astin Martin preferring to concentrate strictly on Ford. Volvo is currently on Ford's auction block as well. He worked with the Unions to modify their contracts and established partnerships with suppliers and dealers stabilizing Ford's financial position.

He has committed all Ford products to high fuel efficiency standards and pledges to make every Ford the best or equal to the best in every automotive category in which Ford competes. He has even been known to call new customers purchasing a Ford Fusion Hybrid over a Toyota Prius to thank them.

So, is Mulally really the reason Ford hasn't had to accept the governments strictly controlled "handout?" Some experts say it's simply a matter of timing. Ford hit its financial crisis back before the financial markets tanked. They were able to secure a credit line before the lines dried up, thus enabling the company to more readily weather this current financial storm.

So, is the answer talent or timing?

We won't know for sure until the business historians, sometime in the future, take a good look at all of this. Perhaps we will never know. But, whether through declaring bankruptcy or some other means of restructuring, I hope that G.M. makes it through all of this. It's not just my fond memories at stake here.

# What Has Happened to Baseball?

It's Baseball Season again. Mine was a sports fan family. Growing up, I knew and could discuss every baseball team with some semblance of confidence; I knew the players on them because they all came up through the team's system and most stayed on one team for their entire career. Then the anti-American (as far as I'm concerned) dreaded concept of "expansion" took over and sports became big business. Someone should check the definition of sports. Oh, wait a minute, actually I did! Webster's has it defined as "that which amuses: diversion; pastime; merriment; outdoor game or recreation esp. of athletic nature..." Nowhere is there a mention of profits or bottom lines or corporate images and concerns. Nope, just not there in the definition; none the less that seems to be the prevailing definition of our time. We now have baseball team owners throwing huge sums of money at players in the hope of buying a great team. Have they not learned that throwing money at a problem rarely works...oh wait again isn't that actually the example our government is setting? But I do digress.

As a result of all of this, instead of truly having a home town team, players are traded before we can even learn to correctly spell their names and teams move from city to city, state to state; and there are so many more teams and why in the name of the Sport's God are the American League teams playing the National League teams during the regular season before they make it to the World Series? Isn't that the point of the World Series, to pit the first place team of each league against each other to determine the best team in baseball for the season? How is a girl to keep up?

And if all that hasn't ruined the game enough, we now have these "baseball stars" whose egos are larger than their batting averages, are in the news more for the latest indiscretion in their life than any great play they made and who are more worried about the terms of their multi-million dollar contracts than the millions of fans that actually pay for their salary. I watch in amazement when a sportscaster seems totally overwhelmed by the fact that a young man he has interviewed is such a "nice kid." They all used to be nice kids! O.K. maybe not all. There were always the "bad-boys" of baseball but they were few and far between. When did nice kids become the exception instead of the rule? When did they become self-declared "stars?"

Am I ranting? Trust me I could go on and on but I think I owe you all an apology already for my venting. I don't know what has gotten into me. Maybe it's my age or the times in which we live or simply something in "the stars."

# The "Greening" Effect

I was flying home from a visit with my daughter earlier this month and was thumbing through the in-flight magazine. When I flipped to page 47, there to my surprise was an article beginning with "...Chicago has been reborn as the leader of America's Urban "green" movement." If I were starring in a "B" movie, my jaw would have dropped. Chicago?

O.K. it had my attention and I hope I have yours. It sounds good but what does being an urban "green" leader really mean? Green is such a generic term and it has rapidly begun to be much overused. Nonetheless, there are some pretty amazing facts about our "green," big city neighbor to the West. Once the home of fabled gangsters, legendary rough and tumble politics and Midwest middleclass industry, Chicago is now arguably the "greenest" big city in our country...and that is no accident.

Since 1989 Mayor Daley has methodically and consistently "greened" the third largest city in the U.S. For a place known for being blue-collared in spite of its magnificent turn-of-the–century architecture and ultra-modern skyscrapers, back in 2000 before one heard too much about it, Daley made a public commitment to make Chicago the most environmentally friendly city in the nation. The 11 story City Hall building became a test project for the benefits of green roofs. Don't forget at that time the term "climate change" was not even on the radar.

20,000 prairie-style plants were cultivated on the building's rooftop. And what a success it has proven to be. Air quality has improved and significant energy has been conserved. Because of that success, in the past 5 years, the rest of the city has jumped on board the "green" bandwagon. Now there are more than 4,000,000 sq. ft. of green roofing either completed or underway in Chicago...more than any other U.S. city and thus the basis of the title.

And the city of Chicago hasn't stopped there. Daley has issued a "green office challenge" calling on office building managers and tenants to compete to save energy costs, and there is the Urban Heat Island Initiative designed to mitigate the absorption of heat by concrete and asphalt surfaces in dense urban areas and the Chicago Climate Action Plan laying out a framework for reducing greenhouse gas emissions. Wow!

So, last week was Earth Week the concept of which was formulated to heighten our awareness of environmental issues and solutions; and it appears to have really worked. The word "green" has become the new "word de jour" and is being tossed around like crazy. It seems from advertising to media coverage to dinner conversation, "green" is in. All of the attention it is garnering is a good thing from a personal standpoint, for our country, for our planet; but I fear that with its overuse, the major saturation of its usage, we are running the risk of the term "green" becoming as meaningless as the terms "diet" or "lite" on food products.

# Red State/Blue State

With the party-jumping of Senator Arlen Specter last week, we were all besieged (albeit briefly) once again by the political pundits analyzing and hypothesizing about the "bigger political ramifications" of his actions. Like a big, hairy grizzly abruptly awakened after lying dormant during hibernation, the pundits were able to gloriously rise from their "non-election cycle" sleep, emit a roar of satisfaction as they dusted off their red state/blue state maps in their minds; secretly relishing the one or two days this story would fly allowing them to keep their claws sharpened, at the ready, for the next election season...any opportunity to hone their personally perceived political prowess being greatly appreciated.

I happened upon an interview of our own Senator Evan Bayh regarding the Specter decision and was reminded once again of how fortunate we are to have the two Senators that we have representing us.

Every few months there is yet another political scandal making the front pages of the newspapers. Governors, Senators, Congressmen, yes even Presidents have disgraced their offices and deceived not only the public but their friends and loved ones as well. Fortunately, here in Indiana we are represented in the Senate by two outstanding servants of the people.

Correctly or incorrectly Indiana is now considered a "swing state" by the media, neither wholly red nor wholly blue; appropriately we have one Republican and one Democrat representing us in the Senate.

Senator Richard Lugar is one of the most highly respected members of Congress by both sides of the aisle, serving Indiana as Senator since 1978. Time Magazine selected him as one of the ten best Senators in the U.S.

Senator Evan Bayh, in his relatively brief tenure, has also distinguished himself as a man of principles. It is said that he was on the short list of candidates considered for the Vice Presidency by Barack Obama.

While both men usually vote along their own party lines, each has had the courage and personal integrity to oppose party positions when they disagreed or when they felt it was in the best interest of Indiana and/or the country to do so. They are both known to work with the opposition and both promote ongoing, active dialogue on every issue with members of the opposing party.

If only the rest of our representatives would follow the lead of these two men. Communicating and working with those not within their party to reach agreements to serve the greater good, maintaining personal standards that our young people can look up to and admire, and ignoring the red/blue labels with which the media insists on sticking states.

Most of the electorate is in the middle politically. While there are extreme right and extreme left factions in both parties, the majority (often silent) tend to be in the center ideologically.

Instead of rising from their election coverage hibernation and dusting off the red state/blue state explanation of our country's make-up, perhaps the pundits would better serve the American people by taking a page out of Indiana's Senatorial representation.

# Simply Siblings

Do you think there's anything to the whole "sibling rivalry" thing? Hearing the national news this morning got me thinking about it. It was reported that Dom DiMaggio died at the age of 92. No not that baseball legend DiMaggio the other one...his brother, a pretty darn good baseball player himself.

While most of us with siblings don't have to contend with the superstar status of a sibling in Joe DiMaggio's league (forgive the pun) we do however have our own "axes to bear" when it comes to sibling interaction.

Having two older brothers myself, believe me I could write a book on the subject! But how does one deal with a sib that simply outshines anything you accomplish? We have had many examples of "brothers gone amok" in my lifetime. Can we forget presidential brother Billy Carter and his Billy Beer or baby boy Clinton and his bad music and drug use embarrassments? Not easy being the little brother of the most powerful man in the world. Well, in Dom's world it must have felt like his brother Joe was just as powerful. Had he not been Joe's brother, Dom probably would have gotten much more "ink" in the press and thus more fame and glory from the public.

Dom DiMaggio played his entire career for the Boston Red Sox, ironically the arch enemies of his brother's New York Yankees. His career batting average (encompassing a 13 year career) was .298 with 1680 hits and 618 runs batted in. He was selected to the All-Star team 7 of those 13 years of playing. And he was acknowledged as a much better defensive player than Joe. By anyone's standards Dom DiMaggio was a great ball player. All this having taken place a bit before my time, I asked around. A few people remembered Dom, but only as Joe DiMaggio's brother who also played ball.

Brothers! Those of you with sisters forgive me, but since I have none I cannot comment...but brothers, that I know a bit about! And I'll bet that you all have a story or two about growing up with your sibs.

Well here is your chance to share. Please send me (to the e-mail address below) a story or two that has "stuck with you" all of these years. Funny, touching, even mean; let me hear what it was like for you to contend with a brother or sister. If there is a good response from you, perhaps we'll take a closer look at this subject.

Now, the end to Joe and Dom's story. On and off the field Joe was simply magic even marrying every teenaged boy's dream come true in a woman, the incomparable Marilyn Monroe. We all know how that tragic story ended. Dom, on the other hand, is survived by his lifelong mate...acknowledged by all who knew them as the perfect, happy couple. So I guess it fair to ask, which brother was truly more successful in the game of life?

# Another Glass Ceiling Broken

I admit to knowing very little about horse racing. While I have gone to events at the track through the years, I never quite got what was so enjoyable about a few moments of excitement surrounded by seemingly eons of boredom between the races. Most of my pleasure on those occasions came from reveling in the beauty of those magnificent animals.

I think most of us are aware of "the Triple Crown." I would also think that most non-horseracing aficionados, like me, take more of an interest in the famed Kentucky Derby than the other two races, though personally it was the great mint juleps served at the annual Kentucky Derby party we used to attend that was the draw for me. But, apparently Rachel Alexandra winning the Preakness this weekend, is creating quite a stir in horse racing circles.

This weekend there was a lot more to the Preakness story than merely which horse won. Rachel Alexandra, not surprisingly by her name, is a beautiful filly. The exclusive, stallion dominated, winners of the Preakness in the past have now been forced to move over, the girls are now in the race too! Not only did she win, but she came within two tenths of a second of breaking the record.

With all that is happening in our world these days, perhaps this seems like a rather frivolous issue with which to be concerned. But, when I read that her own breeder/managing partner, Dolphus Morrison stated "...stallions should race against stallions. Stallions are the future of racing and shouldn't be messed up by a really good filly" it struck a personal cord.

Excuse me? Dolphus is a doofus! Does this man not live in the 21st century? This statement blatantly, and quite succinctly points out the tremendous hurdles that women (and fillies apparently) still face within their chosen professions.

Having been the first female in a management position within a department back in the late '70's, Mr. Morrison's statement really makes my "mane stand on end." I suffered through my boss's insistence on my having a typewriter in my office, even though I had a secretary to do my typing, because "it was less intimidating for the guys." I couldn't believe what I was hearing then and quite frankly it is even more inconceivable to me now.

So, why shouldn't fillies race with the "big boys?" How in the world is their participation affecting the future of racing in a negative way? Much like her human counterparts, Rachel Alexandra's training, fortitude and obvious heart, makes her imminently qualified to compete in and, might I add, to win the famed Preakness.

One can argue that the plight of working women striving for equality in the workforce, in our society, in our world, is one of the ultimate horse races. Gender equality at every level, in every "race" should simply be a given.

C'mon all you stubborn stallions out there, it's time to give we fillies a break!

# Money and Meetings

What in the world are the billionaires up to? Last Thursday reports started leaking out that some of the wealthiest people in the world had met in New York City. Invited by the two richest men on the planet; Bill Gates and Warren Buffet, the likes of Oprah Winfrey, Ted Turner and Michael Bloomberg, convened for five hours at the President's residence of Rockefeller University which is located on the campus of the Manhattan Medical School.

Mega-rich people having a five hour clandestine meeting at a Medical school; hmmmm, makes one wonder. The conspiracy theorists have got to be in hoggy heaven over this bit of news.

And once found out, these usually publicity hungry barons of business had their spokespersons all insist that "it was 100% about philanthropy and was never meant to be a secret." Not meant to be secret? They all spend tons of money on P.R. firms to make sure that their philanthropy is not only promoted but splashed throughout any and all media outlets possible. If they didn't want it to be secret, we would have all heard about it from the get go. It begs the question; what were they up to?

O.k. I'm sure you have heard that this is what happened in New York last week. But did you know that at almost the exact same time 30 of Latin America's biggest businessmen accompanied by their sons and nephews, also met, convening in Mexico City for a three-day "gabfest" hosted by Carlos "Slim" Helu? To be honest, I must admit that I have never heard of Senor Helu, even though he is Latin America's richest man; but I've got to say I like this guy already...who doesn't like a man called "Slim?"

Anyway, according to one participant, Slim footed the bill for the whole event, which included a trip in private planes to the Mexican coastal resort town of Ixtapa. And what was the reported purpose of this high power meeting? Well, a source insisting on remaining anonymous stated that it was "an encounter between fathers and sons so that these business leaders could get to know each other."

Let's recap here for a minute. Gates and Buffet with their billionaire's club, powwow secretly for five hours in New York while at the same time, Slim, down in Mexico City, shells out hundreds of thousands of pesos so the rich guys of Latin America can have a kumbaya moment?

Billionaires in Manhattan/Billionaires in Mexico City...meetings with no press access, with only after-the-fact confirmation that they even met; how cool is this? I sense a mega-blockbuster hit in the making for next summers' movie viewers. I see Tom Hanks as Bill gates, Oprah can play herself, and how great would Benicio del Toro be as Slim? Under Ron Howard's masterful direction, big money, secret meetings all amid an atmosphere of global financial doom, wars, pandemic viruses; oh wait. There is one nagging problem. How would it end?

So, I'm back to asking, what in the world are the billionaires really up to?

# People of Courage

I met a most remarkable woman, young of years, old in wisdom. Tiny of build; she takes on the world with experience, insight and knowledge. An ever-questioning soul, she stands fearless amid a world of suppression and terror.

Irshad Manji as a young child was ousted with her family from her homeland of Uganda when Idi Amin took power and declared Uganda to be a "Black Nation" expelling all non-black residents. Irshad's entire Muslim community was among those forced into exile.

And so Irshad found herself living in a multi-racial, multi-cultural community in British Columbia. Her family, oppressive father, compliant yet loving mother, and two sisters were forced to start a new life. Nonetheless, her father insisted on holding firm to the strict Moslem disciplines of the past. So, she attended a Medrassa (a traditional Moslem school) in which the study of Koran was to be the essence of all education. There, in that stifling, oppressive, male-dominated environment, the Irshad Manji of today emerged.

Not yet a teenager, she dared to question.

"Why couldn't a woman lead prayers?" Hearing of her impertinence (how could she actually ask such a question) her father chased her around the house brandishing a knife and threatening to cut off her ear. She sought refuge on the roof of their building where the vastness of the sky and the mysteries of the stars inspired her to seek her own answers to all of the troubling questions in her mind. Several years later, with both ears still intact and many important questions never answered in school, she was finally expelled from the Medrassa and she began her journey of self-education, a journey in which she sought to understand her religion and one which she hoped would give her reason to remain in the Moslem faith. The public library became her private school.

It is this struggle to discover the truth of her religion, what the Koran actually says rather than blindly following the dictates of the fanatics who have established themselves as the champions of Islam, which is the basis of her amazing book, "The Trouble with Islam." A fast read, part history, part culture study, part philosophy, the book is written displaying a wonderful sense of humor. Irshad takes the very complex issues of the difference between the Islam of the Koran and the Islam of the Imams and Ayatollahs of today, making simple sense for her reader to follow and learn. While all religions have their fanatics, it is only within the Moslem faith that the fanatics are the "ruling power." Amid Fatwas calling for her death, she beckons to the huge silent majority of moderate, non-Arab Moslems to rise up and take back their religion.
Perhaps the lesson to be learned from Irshad Manji isn't really about the Moslem faith. Perhaps it is a call to us all to face the "enemies" in our own lives. With fortitude and strength we can become our own people of courage within our own lives.

# Hugo Chavez—His Own Worst Enemy?

Could anyone look more like or act more like the stereotypical Latin American fascist dictator than Hugo Chavez of Venezuela? His inflammatory rhetoric, self-aggrandizing gangsteresque personal style and tactless (to put it kindly) approaches to "Western Nations;" all seem to lend credence to the opinion that he is simply crazy and must be watched because you know crazy people have been known to do crazy things! It's as if he can't help himself. He simply has to make trouble when "playing with the big boys."

I heard Dr. Greg Wilpert speak a few weeks back. He is a Fulbright Scholar, has written several books on Venezuela, lives in Caracas and is considered, in some circles, to be an expert on its modern history. As I listened to Dr. Walpert's speech I was shocked and amazed. According to Dr. Walpert, the mainstream western media is guilty of a campaign of "disinformation" in its characterization of Chavez and his accomplishments in Venezuela.

It prompted me to ask, "Who is this other Hugo Chavez?"

According to Dr. Walpert (and much to my surprise) the following accomplishments can be accredited to Chavez:

Chavez promised to clean-up the political system. To that end a new constitution was passed in 1999 and Chavez supporters swept the ensuing election. Since then 14 elections have taken place certified by international observers as being legal and fair.

49 new laws were passed. A sweeping land reform program was initiated weakening the "elitist's stronghold" on ownership and empowering the lower and middle classes. He financed numerous progressive ecological community development projects and doubled the previous investment in the educational system which

tripled the number of literacy courses available to everyone. His reforms also reduced unemployment by 5%. All of this gave Chavez tremendous populist support and equally tremendous power.

During this time the price of oil was on the rise (1/4 of U.S. imported oil comes from Venezuela) providing vast sums of money for his reform programs including:

Hiring Cuban doctors to provide medical care to remote villages and less populated urban areas while at the same time opening up private hospitals in the larger cities to all Venezuelans not just the rich. This significantly lowered the infant mortality rate.

Instituting participatory democracy by establishing community councils wherein anyone can vote to bring a measure before their National Assembly for consideration.

He nationalized currency rates, utilities, and telecommunications while instituting price control for food.

He has accomplished all this and more for the Venezuelan citizens...and the people loved him for it. The term benevolent dictator comes to mind.

It sounds pretty good for the majority of his people, but it makes one wonder, why is the obnoxious tough guy act "out in public" necessary? Perhaps his oil wealth emboldened him. The problem now is the price of oil has plummeted and he has had to renege on some of his promises and his popularity is faltering because of it...perhaps he would be better served as would his people if he would roll back the tough guy rhetoric and play nice for a change.

# He Who Shall Not Be Named

On Friday Mahmoud Ahmadinejad was declared the winner in the presidential election held in Iran; big surprise. Today (Monday) the news is filled with vivid, in some cases difficult to watch because of the violence, images of the demonstrations taking place in that land so very far away (anyone else out there having flashbacks to the 1968 Democratic convention in Chicago?).
Here are some of the disturbing facts that have so many Iranians angry and fed up enough to risk life and limb to demonstrate in the streets.

The vote was done by paper ballot. Estimates are that 30-40 million people voted, an 85% turn out that "I'm a dinner jacket" (thanks to Whoopie Goldberg for that pronunciation of Ahmadinejad) is using to assert his mandate. However, it was only a couple of hours after the polls closed that the victory was announced. I don't know about you, but I have to question their ability to accurately count 30-40 million hand written ballots in only a couple of hours.

In Addition, the Iranian Government shuttered coverage of the election by newspapers. They shut down websites and television bureaus. Text messaging was silenced and e-mailing curtailed. And finally, as we are now seeing, critics are being thrown into prison.

Because Mr. Dinner Jacket is such a high profile ignoramus, much of the media attention in the past has been focused on him. Of course I am sure he is thrilled about this but there is a back story. There is a man behind the curtain that yields the true power. His title is Supreme Leader. Whoa! Major title there! And much like the villainous Man Who Shall Not Be Named in the Harry Potter series, the Ayatollah Ali Khamene seems to be the lurking menace in the shadows.

He is much more "out there" domestically yielding absolute power. Anyone thinking that the Iranian president runs the show only needs to know that it is Khamene who decides on who can run for the presidency.

Many think that this man is very politically savvy. He did not publicly endorse any candidate for president. But knowing that Mr. Dinner Jacket has a great deal of support among his people it was a no-brainer for him to declare Ahmadinejad the winner in such a timely manner. What he didn't anticipate was the degree of unrest and the numbers of people willing to voice it in the streets. So now, as any seasoned political leader would do, he has called for an investigation.

Thus we are witnessing the largest political unrest in Iran since the revolution which ousted the Shah. No doubt Ahmadinejad will be confirmed as president and he will make sure to cement his position as the face of Iran to the world. But much like the villain in Harry Potter, the Iranian "He Who Shall Not Be Named" has been exposed to the world as the real, somewhat elusive phantom of power in Iran.

# My Passion Theory and Young People Today

It began with a glance, a mere fleeting look, but there was something, something more to it. Then less tentative looks, one to the other; neither quite sure of the other's intention. And the occasional nod, smile; she tossed an errant strand of hair from her face coyly, he rolled his shirt sleeve up just enough for her to see the taut muscle flex as he played with his keys in apparent absentminded thought. Stolen, steamy glances finally heralded the mutual, sensual connection they had made. He came to her in the soft candle light, his hand gently caressing her shoulder. Shards of feeling bolted through her at his touch as if branding her skin red hot with desire for more...

I have a theory about passion.

There is no denying the fantastic, all-encompassing emotion of "first-time passion." Nothing compares to that delicious build-up, the totally absorbing anticipation of the unknown leading up to that first encounter with a new mate. Sadly, many of my contemporaries yearn for that passion which they feel they have lost. They say that the passion has died because of the fights, the kids, the struggles, the day-to-day mundane realities of marriage.

O.K, there is a magnificent splendor to that first-time passion. Though married for 34 years, I'm not too old yet to remember! But I contend that true love...long lasting, committed love can be even more passionate.

I am no Pollyanna. Believe me I have had my share of family problems that have oft times created very challenging, strenuous moments in my marriage. But there is something so strong, so empowering about coming through all of that. Something about surviving the difficulties that leads to such a wonderful place that every once in a while because of the pain and tears, the fights and struggles, the shared moments of merely comfortable contentment there comes other moments, sexy, sensual, intense moments that could never have been if not for the years you've shared, if not for the pain you've endured together, if not for the comfort of truly knowing that this person has seen you at your very worst and loves you still. There does come intensely satisfying, yes, wildly passionate moments.

So, what does this have to do with the young people today?

I had a conversation with a middle school principal several years ago and she informed me that there was a nation-wide study conducted indicating that 60% of America's sixth graders have had sex. 60%! Whether or not you use the "Clinton definition of sex" it is a staggering statistic. By eighth grade the vast majority of those same middle school students had had 4-6 different partners.

I fear that because sex has become such a routine thing for our young people, no more than merely another after-school activity, they will never know the amazing potential of "the act." With raging adolescent hormones so easily satisfied, they may become numbed to the emotion, never truly feeling the intense meaning of it all, a meaning they couldn't possibly understand with such casual acquiescence to their every desire without the maturity required to understand it. I fear they will not only be unable to recognize true passion when they are mature enough, but perhaps they may not even be able to experience it.

I hope I'm wrong.

# We Get It

We have lived through a week where it seems like everyone in America has been on a feeding frenzy of celebrity death. T.V. specials, news shows, cyberspace inundation, tabloid lunacy and even dinner conversations all seemed to be about one thing, Death.

So who died?

Ed, everyone's favorite side-kick, the proverbial king of "second-bananaship," Farrah, who embodied every man's dream of the ideal woman (so I'm told) who is all at once the girl next door and curvaceous sex-kitten wrapped up in one woman, and the world lost Michael; troubled, tainted, but oh so talented. Celebrities all, but is celebrity enough to warrant such massive media coverage?

I consider myself a caring person. I truly do feel for the families and friends of these famous people, but I have to wonder, why are these stories so big?

Do you know when Jonas Salk died? Do you remember where you were when you heard the news of his death? Did you even hear the news of his death? He died June 23, 1995; 14 years almost to the day of Michael Jackson's death; yet this man who developed the vaccine for the dreaded disease, Polio, passed away relatively unnoticed. This man saved millions, perhaps billions, of people (mostly children) from the paralyzing effects of that heinous disease. This was a man who refused to patent his vaccine having no desire to profit personally from it but merely wishing to see the vaccine disseminated as widely as possible. Now there is an oddity for you; a man not wanting to profit from a discovery! Jonas Salk was a true humanitarian, dedicating himself to preventing human misery. Yet, I don't recall hearing any national or international voices of bereavement. My guess would be that it was reported on the news the night of June 23, 1995 though I don't remember it. Do You?

So, why the huge hoopla about these deaths?

I'm sure that the technological advancements in communication have a lot to do with it but I think there is a more interesting possibility. We are living through a very complicated time in our history. We don't "get" the economic difficulties, we don't "get" global warming, we don't "get" the healthcare system crisis, we don't "get" the two wars we're fighting; I could go on and on. Our world is so confusing. Can anyone say they truly understand it all?

So, now we have the deaths of the famous and we are all at once united in understanding. For each and every one of us understands the loss, the pain death brings. Death is the universal unifier, indiscriminate, unpredictable, inevitable and always so very sad. Yes, death touches all of us. We get it. This is one thing in our crazy world that we all understand.

So, feeding frenzy or not, warranted or not; all of the hype, all of the buzz might, just might, make us feel a bit more connected in this disjointed world of ours. For death is something "we all get."

# Oh Sarah...

When first selected by John McCain as his Vice-presidential choice I, like many, had never heard of Sarah Palin. This little known Governor from Alaska, burst into the oft times glaring lights of rough and tumble national politics. Justly or unjustly she was skewered by most of the media while at the same time energizing McCain's campaign with her "back home," obviously sincerely felt conservative convictions. With her almost inexplicable star quality, she generated a level of excitement within the conservative base I had never seen before in Republican politics.

Those of you who read my article about her selection at the time may remember that I was less than enamored with McCain's pick. Then, through the subsequent weeks of the campaign, I think she exposed just how unprepared for the job she truly was. Yet, at the same time she garnered unquestionable support from huge crowds of people who related to her message.

I have no doubt that she is a bright, capable woman. But I feel she failed to grasp that being an outsider, a maverick (as she repeated ad nausea) didn't mean that she didn't have to do her homework. Her job as vice presidential candidate required a firm grasp of the pressing issues of the day. Being a "simple woman"(as she also characterized herself) while attractive to some of us who are fed up with the slick sleaze of politics, didn't mean that she could "simply" ignore the details of our complex world and its problems. Catch phrases and self-deprecating jokes couldn't mask her basic lack of the thorough understanding needed to speak to the complicated national and international issues.

After the election I, like many others, thought that she would return to Alaska, do her job as Governor and "study-up" solidifying her place as a force to be reckoned with in four and/or eight years. I felt that she really had a chance to be just what the Republican Party needed to revitalize its future. Instead of biding her time preparing for future national office runs, she chose to remain in the national public eye making what ended up being bad choices for public appearances and reaping a ton of bad press from them. And now she has chosen to resign from her Governorship as well.

Few of us will ever know the toll a national campaign exacts or the pain of constant media scrutiny. Couple all of that with the agony of the alleged back-stabbing by her own party and the personal attacks she has endured; one has to wonder how the woman is still standing. And now we have her announcement this past weekend of her resignation. In a rambling obviously off the cuff statement she gave her reasons for resigning. Put simply, it just seems like quitting to me.

As time unfolds we will find out what the future holds for Sarah Palin. But for now, while I am not quite old enough to be her mother, I have this maternal urge to give her a big hug, pat her on the back and sympathetically whisper "Oh, Sarah, what have you done!"

# Exit Strategy

I don't remember when first I heard the term Exit Strategy. I am sure that it was used in a military context. I do remember seeing an interview with Thomas Friedman shortly after we had decided to go to war in Iraq wherein he expressed several concerns about the military path upon which we had embarked. He, as most of us, supported going in to find and/or destroy the Iraqi stores of weapons of mass destruction. But, he also expressed grave concerns about our apparent lack of an exit strategy. His was the only voice I can recall expressing that concern. At the time I remember thinking, "surely there was such a strategy; we were just not privy to it." I don't need to tell you how wrong I was! Now, it seems that Friedman's concerns of the past pertain to more than just military exit strategies.

Wikipedia, in part, defines "exit strategy" as the means of escaping one's current (typically unfavorable) situation.

I think that President Obama needed a better exit strategy for the way he handled the first part of this massive economic recovery undertaking.

Let me explain. We were sobered by the two presidential candidates telling us in one of the debates that we would be feeling the effects of this recession for a good ten years. And after elected, President Obama's economic message was consistent and somber. We believed the President when he spoke gravely of the need for the stimulus package; we were, after all, in really bad economic shape. He had done his job of convincing us, and rightly so, that we had to be in this for the long haul and that it was likely to get worse before it got better.

But, then, seemingly unexpectedly, the first positive economic signs flared. The markets took an upswing.

But instead of staying the rhetoric course, so to speak, President Obama changed his "slant." He seemed to adopt a new strategy. Upon hearing of a few positive indicators he began tempering his solemn rhetoric and stressing the positive. He spoke of seeing signs that the measures we were taking were working, pointing out that indicators looked good. We all felt a little better. We were even hearing that the economy would be turning around more quickly than anticipated.

Our "good feelings" were short lived, dampened when we only saw joblessness increasing, cities and states facing bankruptcy and our retirement dreams turned into financial nightmares.

Instead of jumping at the opportunity to show progress, President Obama's strategy should have been to keep reminding us that recovery would be a long, very long, drawn out process. We were resigned to accept that message.

No one expected President Obama to perform miracles. His eagerness to jump at the first signs of hope is understandable, but I think veering from his initial strategy, giving into the temptation of showing us all, that he is indeed the man for the job, may have damaged him in the long run.

# Title Fight: Martha Stewart vs Goldman Sachs

I have never been a "crafty" type of person. I confess that Martha Stewart kinda gives me the willies. With all of her doodads, glue guns and fabric scraps that she turns into centerpieces or dinner guest gifts or my favorite, the oh so special picture frame kinda makes me laugh. But I did feel for the woman when she was carted off to prison.

While I am not a lawyer or an economist, I don't claim to understand the finite details of business and industry; I am a tax payer and as such am appalled at what I just heard on the news. Reports of the earnings of Goldman Sachs have been leaked (officially due to be released later today) showing huge profits. I have to believe with the revelation today that the officials at Goldman Sachs made and are still making millions of dollars while taking obscene amounts of money from the government...from us, has to have Martha, in the quiet of her own home, screaming at the walls, "and I had to go to prison!"

Martha, like many of us, inexperienced in the nitty-gritty of investing, got caught in an insider trading snafu. She listened to her financial advisors and her lawyers and ended up in the slammer. She winds up in jail teaching other inmates to knit while the big boys, the experts at Goldman Sachs, having done their part in creating the financial mess we are in, get to walk away with mega-bucks and perhaps even more distressing, their freedom.

Does this seem fair to you? What are those of us who work hard, play by the rules and just want a good life to think of all of this?

I believe in meting out punishment for criminal acts. I believe in the rule of law. I'm not saying that Martha shouldn't have gone to jail. I am just having difficulty with the seemingly injustice of having these Goldman Sachs officials free to enjoy their loot.

So Goldman Sachs will release its earnings for the quarter this morning giving us a pretty picture, a profitable picture of where the firm stands today. It is anticipated to show millions in profit, massive earnings and bonuses having been and will continue to be paid. They gladly took Federal monies. A bailout was accepted. And we the people have subsidized it all. We paid so they could keep up their privileged lifestyle.

Yes, they will release a very rosy picture of their operations today but, I have to ask, "What is wrong with this picture?" Am I the only one feeling that we have been duped?

So, the "crafty" title has been usurped along with plenty of our money. In my opinion, the reigning queen of "the crafty" Martha Stewart must yield her title to the unmistakable new champions. All hail Goldman Sachs, the Kings of "the crafty."

# Fire Them All!

Enough already! It seems that our elected leaders in both houses of congress have absolutely, totally, inarguably lost any sense of what they were elected to accomplish; let alone what they promised they would do. I don't know about you but I am really fed up with the bickering, the slandering, the fabricating, the misrepresenting, the political positioning and on and on, coming out of Washington from both sides of the aisle. This is a non-partisan, equal opportunity rant...

I say: Fire Them All!

We supposedly have a one man one vote system, so let's put it into practice. I've been mulling over an idea whereby we can eliminate the endless, nonproductive, party motivated actions and inaction of the current Congress. Here's how it could work.

1. Only one issue of national importance at a time can be brought for a vote. Let's really eliminate "pork."

2. Detailed explanatory information would be provided in advance of a vote for voter's consideration.
(and here's the kicker!)

3. Via internet, every American Citizen, of voting age, may cast his/her own one vote per issue; thus negating the need for a Congress as we know it.

O.K. I know what you're thinking, cause I'm thinking it too; too many pitfalls, glitches, hacking, software sabotage possibilities for this to work...not yet anyway, but I know my kids can figure it all out at a later date.

So, in the meantime, how about some new election rules and reforms?

Those elected to both the Senate and the House of Representatives should have a limit of one term consisting of 5 years. If they can't get their agenda on the table in 5 years they shouldn't be there. This will eliminate the common practice now permeating the Capitol of making decisions during the last ¾ of their term solely on whether or not it will get them re-elected.

Their benefits, perks and pensions will be the same as we lowly non-government peons. It will be like a regular job, a real person's job where benefits are provided while you work there. They are stopped once you leave office. Just think of the millions of dollars in savings to our country this would provide.

And, to borrow from my own recipe for Presidential election reform, candidates may not talk about their opponent during their bid for office. Let the news media dredge up the dirt (which they are eminently qualified to do). So, candidates may only speak publicly of their own competency, communicating their own plans and programs and ideas of how they would govern.
And, for pity sake, our elected officials have to use at least a smidgeon of common sense in their decision making.

Governance is serious business. We have too many important, urgent issues facing our country to allow our representatives to waste our time and our money on partisan pettiness. We need them to get it together. Maybe the only way to get the message through their "thick-headedness" is to fire them all.

# Hillary Help!

Did you see the interview last week with Secretary of State Hillary Clinton? I have to say she is really making me proud. Not only has she taken her presidential election defeat graciously and with dignity, but she has flawlessly, jumped into her new role as chief international diplomat and key advisor and team-player to the President on foreign affairs.

Don't you wonder if, behind closed doors, he is asking her about this healthcare thing? I'll bet she is overjoyed not to have to be down slinging mud in the healthcare reform fiasco taking place in Congress. Let's not forget that she had her own go at this contentious, difficult problem herself back in 1994. In fact, many are now comparing that battle to this one saying that this is doomed to fail to reach enactment no matter what form it takes, "just like in '94."

Not that it would make a difference but, if I were Hillary, here's what I would suggest to President Obama.

First, Mr. President, stop allowing this bill to be referred to as "Obama's healthcare bill"...it's Nancy Pelosi's bill. Then, Sir, it's time for you to take charge of the process instead of trying to explain it. You have the chance to rise to the status of a statesman not merely a politician and, at the risk of jeopardizing the support of the left faction of your party (after all they are more concerned about re-election than about making any truly meaningful changes) you need to take this legislation back as your own. With all due respect Sir, you must "draw some lines in the sand" making the following abundantly clear:

If it doesn't verifiably cut spiraling costs you will veto it.

If there are not strong consumer protections, including insurance company oversight, you will veto it.

If consumers cannot keep their current coverage and their own choice of doctors, you will veto it.

The President needs to be the catalyst of change that we all hoped he would be. He needs to resist the "pull of the power" and take the party politics out of the game. If risking reelection for his fellow Democrats and himself is what it takes, then he needs to assume the risk.

I wish that behind the closed door of the Oval Office, the hugely politically savvy Hillary who has taken her own beating due to this issue, would suggest that by getting even a partial plan passed, if it is a good plan; he would not be jeopardizing reelection, he would be helping to secure his legacy as not only the first black man to be elected as President but the first statesman we have seen in office for a long time.

# The Woodstock Generation

Forty years ago I was working my summer cashiering job at Muntz Cartridge City, an establishment offering the very latest in music technology...the 8 track tape! Now, those of you who do not know what an 8-track tape or 8-track tape player was, are simply too young and need not read any further!

That August of 1969, I had heard rumblings about a music/love fest that was going to happen in N.Y. I had received what I thought was inside information, seeing as though I was in the music biz and all (me and about a million other teens). I heard rumors of great bands to be heard and even greater times to be had. But, it never occurred to me to try to get there. Truth be told, I didn't give it any thought at all until after-the-fact when that weekend was seemingly the only topic of conversation for months and then years. Imagine my chagrin when the recordings from the "happening" were released and then horror of horrors, the movie came out and I was mortified to realize that I had missed the bragging rights for my whole life by not going to the seminal event of my generation.

Through the years I have been astounded by all of the people of my age that say they attended. There is of course no way of checking, no attendance was taken and it is so very cool to be able to say that you were there. I mean really...they all were there? But I fear that my cynical nature is showing. And what a pity it is too. For you see back then I was not cynical. I truly believed that the masses congregated that weekend at that farm to promote peace, love, and of course music. I believed that LSD was taken to expand one's mind not to get high. I believed that we could change the world.

Don't get me wrong, my generation has been instrumental in many of life's changes since, not the least of which is that now we have music festivals all of the time. Every summer. Everywhere. Of course they are mostly organized to promote the promoter's pocket books not the ideals of this generation, but hey, we are after all a capitalistic society. Seems like "if you put on a rock concert they will come" is the motto of our current time. With their port-a-potties and their medical tents and their space assignments, something is off kilter. When the pond on site is an added attraction instead of a necessity, something of the spirit of Woodstock has been lost!

And now 40 years later, that festival is not only still remembered but has achieved legendary status. This 40th anniversary is upon us and I can't help but reflect on all that has changed. Looking back at that somewhat naive teenage girl behind that counter, I think my biggest regret is not that I wasn't there but that my idealism and that of an entire generation has, justified or not, morphed into cynicism.

# Socialism, A Dirty Word?

I hear the cries. I hear the yelling. I hear the name calling, the predictions of horrific consequences, the panic in voices raised proclaiming that our cherished Democratic form of government is teetering on the brink of being smashed into shards of scattered dreams. The fear is that the pieces of the dream of American Democracy will then be haphazardly glued back together into a misshapen, grotesque form of Socialism. If healthcare reform ends up taking the shape it is reputed to be taking, the dreaded Socialism will be the result. Of course there is yet to be a final healthcare plan proposed, but when did common sense prevail when screaming and ranting can overshadow intelligent debate and fact finding!

Amongst the name calling I particularly take offence at both political parties throwing the label of Nazi around as if bantering about a bad choice of necktie, so callously minimizing the true horror of that designation. I am a believer in personal expression and creativity, but labeling healthcare reform proponents, with whom you disagree, Nazis...?

I am nonetheless intrigued by a discussion I heard this past weekend on T.V. The overwhelming fear, through red-faced anger, was expressed that this attempt at reforming the healthcare system will result in the US adopting Socialism instead of Democracy as its form of government. First off, Socialism is not a political system. It is an economic system and as such should be compared to our Capitalistic system rather than our Democratic system. But technicalities aside, if one looks at many of our current governmental services, laws and provisions, Socialism already exists in our government and our lives.

For those "Uber Capitalistic Americans" who think that we are not a Socialistic society already let's take a closer look. Our Estate Tax laws were established basically out of fear that powerful wealthy families would become the ruling aristocracy and take control of our nation. So, the Astors (John Jacob being the first recorded millionaire in our country) and the other so called robber-barons were, and still are, required to pay a specific tax...an estate tax, upon death, established to more equally distribute the wealth in our country. But, hey, why should only the super-rich pay...enter income taxes that all of we working Americans have to pay. Tax the rich to pay for the services needed by the poor...sounds a bit, dare I say, Socialistic to me!

What about our Welfare System and Social Security? "Social " Security...hello! And lastly (because I am running out of room) we have Medicare and Medicaid; tax payer funded, government run ie. Socialistic.

My point, I guess, is that in and of itself, Socialism isn't a dirty word. I think that forms of it have served our country pretty well through the years.

Perhaps it's time for our Legislators and influential politicos to tone down the rhetoric and really debate the options. Enough with semantics. We have serious problems and should expect that serious consideration be given to them.

# Presidential Vacations, the Boy and the Dog

I was poised, pen in hand so to speak (that sounds better than I was staring at the blank computer screen) ready to write about some grumblings being heard around Washington which focus on the President taking a vacation at this critical time in the Healthcare debate. I was trying to find the words to describe/define the intangible usefulness of taking a moment to do nothing. Everything seemed trite ...the need for recharging, and that old standby, the benefit of clearing one's mind to more acutely focus on a problem or situation. But, the usual lingo just wasn't doing it for me.

As oft happens, something began nagging at me. Something I had written last week after the sweep of storms passed our way. And then I remembered...

I sat working outdoors in a plaza. Storms had thundered through all night, downing limbs and wreaking havoc on power lines but now in the early morning a newly risen sun shone and the smells were fresh and cleansed. A young man, barely in his teens by appearance, entered the plaza. I didn't want to stare but became transfixed no matter how hard I tried not to. He was accompanied by his seeing-eye-dog, a beautiful yellow lab who worked diligently, effortlessly, guiding his master through the trees, the shrubs and the benches. The dog obviously took his job very seriously and he did it with such aplomb. They approached an open space and the master took the harness from the dog's shoulders hardly still restraining the dog by a leash. And, as if on cue, I watched the "working dog" turn into a pup romping and playing. Everything about him changed, his very carriage loosened and his step brightened. No more boss and employee, rather now a boy with his dog in the park blossomed forth in front of me. The affection was obvious. Harness off even though still leashed, the pup exuded freedom.

Have I mentioned that the plaza happens to be on the grounds of a federal prison in downtown Chicago? Built right in the Loop, this modern windowless structure looms, getting some sunlight in its interior from narrow rectangular slits of glass geometrically placed in the yellowish concrete slab building. I was amused at the irony of the dog being given his freedom here in the plaza of a house of incarceration.

I wonder if the President feels incarcerated by his monumental challenges, and even on vacation while not technically still yoked with the harness of the Whitehouse he is still nonetheless tethered by the leash of Governance. Vacation? Naw, simply a looser leash.

I hadn't intended to write a column about this but rather keep it as a page of remembrance in my personal journal, a private wonderment but as I watched the master, while sightless, being able to see so clearly his dog, his friend. It seemed an experience to share.

# What a Strange Week

Last week was a very strange week. Hanging over all of the other occurrences was a unseasonable weather pattern making our usually steamy late August weather seem more like late October. Of course my very wise grandmother used to comment that she didn't understand why anyone living here complains about the weather; after all no one moves to this part of the country for the climate. Nonetheless the dank, rainy, bone-chilling weather seemed the perfect backdrop for a week filled with the bizarre.

Did you see the Bears game Sunday night? Do we of the long-time Bears fan persuasion hope to dream of actually having a real Quarterback? Not being around when Syd Luckman played, I have never experienced a Bears team with a "dyed in the wool" Quarterback. Don't get me wrong, I loved McMahan. What football fan wouldn't love a guy that had no fear, would do anything it took, risking life and limb, to help his team win! But in all honesty we all know that he wasn't what one would call a great Quarterback. So, now we have Jay Cutler, looking good on Sunday Night Football...

We also lost Teddy Kennedy last week. I don't quite know where to start on this one. By anyone's estimation he was an extremely effective Senator, authoring and securing passage of more legislation then anyone in recent memory. But I personally could never quite get over that whole Chappaquiddick mess. The best case scenario, Teddy was a really bad guy! But the nation, once again, proved true to its ever forgiving nature and allowed him to live an extraordinarily effective life of public service. I was amazed at the stories of his personal attention to his constituency and the comments made by his Republican rivals regarding his practicality and willingness to compromise, understanding that a good "part" of something is better than nothing at all.

Which brings me to healthcare and President Obama's declining numbers. I heard a very interesting statistic; 40% of Obama voters in 2008 were 50 years old or older. And it is that almost half of his constituency that Obama is scaring into non-support by keeping us all in limbo. Don't you think it is time to take a page out of Teddy's playbook on this healthcare fiasco? Obama has tossed up a Hail Mary waiting for someone else to make the play when he needs to thread the needle with a precision spiral pass. Put forth your plan, in detail, Mr. President, for the people and their representatives to see.

Yes it was a strange week. I can't in good faith actually think the Bears will go to the Super bowl this year any more then I think Democrats and Republicans will put partisan pursuits aside and reform a system vital to all of the American people.

If I have learned one thing throughout the years, it is that Chicago sports' teams and national politicians, if at all possible, will disappoint you.

# The Good War

"Iraq is a bad war, Afghanistan is the good war" seemed to be the campaign message during the election season. Republicans and Democrats alike tried to distance themselves from the disastrous and very unpopular Iraqi war while at the same time, not wanting to appear soft on terror, introduced us to the good war. And now we come to find out, maybe it isn't such a good war after all.

What in the world is a good war? Lately, I have been hearing that term again as a description of our involvement in Afghanistan. I don't know about you, but this seems like Déjà vu, Vietnam all over again. Look, we cannot win a war through P.R. and righteous indignation. We cannot count on societies and cultures' half way around the world to castoff thousands of years of traditions, customs and eons of hatred just because we say that we know best and try to make nice. Ah, c'mon. It ain't gonna work.

And quite unbelievable, we are hearing of interrogation techniques coming under fire once again, the appointment of special prosecutors being looked into, ethics panels perhaps being established etc. etc. etc. Do we torture, don't we torture? Should we torture, shouldn't we torture; call me crazy but here is how I see it.

War is hell. It is supposed to be so horrific that no one wants to engage in it. War is supposed to be the end all, be all, deterrent to government sanctioned abhorrent national behavior. War is not supposed to be "politically correct." To the contrary, it must be totally politically incorrect to be an actual deterrent. The sad but unavoidable fact is that any kind of war creates collateral damage, the military's polite way of saying that innocents will be harmed or killed. That is why every other option for avoiding war should be pursued.

But if there are indeed no other options, if in fact our nation must enter into an armed conflict (and I mean must!) then for goodness sake enter to win. And, I can't believe I, of all people, am going to say this (being the biggest Dove I knew in college...an era dominated by doves!) but we should let it be known that if someone attacks us on U.S. soil; we will blow them off the face of the earth. It's like in the Godfather, you attack the U.S. you die, your family dies, your friends die, your country dies.

Seems to me with that kind of incentive, perhaps fewer "innocents" would be willing to harbor and provide aid to the fanatics of this world who threaten not only Americans but anyone who believes differently than they do.

I am all for being a kinder, gentler nation. I am all for respecting human rights and dignity. But when it comes to war...and let me reiterate, it should only come to war as a very last resort, I believe there is no good war; there is only winning the war.

# Truthers?

Eight years ago I sat in horror watching the events of 9/11/01 unfold before me on the TV screen. Thoughts jumbling, emotions swirling...are my children safe? I was able to relax a bit when realizing that my son was at Purdue and my daughter was living and going to school in the South of France. I felt instant relief that they were not in or near a big city. When the second tower was struck I grabbed the phone and cancelled my meetings for the day knowing that I could not move from the set. Like most, I imagine, I was stunned and had trouble fathoming what I was seeing before me.

Are you familiar with the term "Truthers?" I have to admit until I happened to stumble upon a National Geographic show about their theories a couple of weeks ago, I had never heard of them. And then last week Van Jones, Obama's "Energy Czar" had to resign because, among other things, he had signed some document supporting the Truther's claim that our government was somehow involved in the attacks of 9/11.

What in the world is a Truther and can what they insist actually be true?

A Truther believes one of two things; either our Government knew about the plot to bring down the targets on 9/11 and did nothing to prevent it, or that the government was actually behind the plot.

And why would the U.S. do this? They feel the attacks were carried out to enable the launch of the wars in Afghanistan and Iraq and/or the attacks created justification for our government to curtail civil liberties.

I don't know. Call me naive, but I'm having a bit of trouble with these explanations of why our government would have a hand in the most horrific tragedy in our own country's history.

But, it is not just a few "Conspiracy Theorists." Apparently, survey results show that 36% of Americans agree that the U.S. had something to do with the 9/11 tragedy...36%!

Having known nothing about all of this, the National Geographic program was amazingly interesting and Indiana has a big time connection. Purdue University conducted a 2 year engineering experiment to determine exactly what happened to the World Trade Center and Pentagon on September 11, 2001. With limited space I can't detail the Truther's contentions about what really happened and why the 9/11 Commission's findings were wrong, but the goal of the Purdue project was to prove or disprove the 9/11 Commission's conclusion of how the towers came down.

So, Purdue engineers went to work and their results were documented with a state of the art simulation of the events. They found the 9/11 Commission's report consistent with all of their findings.

Not surprisingly, the Truthers are still not convinced.

Perhaps we will never know all of the details of what really happened eight years ago, but I choose to go with the scientific evidence and leave the Truthers to their own truth.

# Unlikely Power

So, President Obama made the rounds on the Sunday talk shows, but what fascinated me were the constant references to Olympia Snowe. Her name just keeps popping up whenever the odds of passing a healthcare bill are discussed. Until the healthcare debate, did anyone outside of Washington or Maine ever hear of this woman? Snowe, known to be a moderate Republican, is to whom the Prez is looking for that oh so important "bi-partisan" label to be attached to a healthcare bill. In addition, her approval could not only help swing the much needed moderate Republican vote but the Democratic centrist Senators as well. Who would have thought that this little known female Senator from Maine would be in a position of such power?

It got me thinking of other women who wielded unlikely power.

Jenny Jerome Churchill, American born mother of Winston, single-handedly got her husband, Randolph, elected to Parliament. Even though she herself did not believe that women should have the right to vote, with her astute political savvy and limitless energy she waged multiple successful campaigns for hubby while he was hunting and fishing with boys! Upon Randolph's death, she easily segued into being son Winston's experienced political advisor, grooming him to take his place in the world arena...her success is, as they say, history.

And here in the Unites States, we never would have had, some argue, our country's best President, Franklin Delano Roosevelt had it not been for his wife Eleanor. Stricken with polio, he all but gave up on politics choosing rather to retreat to a quiet life. Eleanor, who up until this time had been virtually invisible, began her own campaign to keep her husband in the public eye even though he himself was nowhere to be seen. It was her speeches and high profile on Franklin's behalf that eventually led to his becoming President of the United States.

In Jeffery Toobin's award-winning book, The Nine, we get a glimpse of yet another woman wielding unlikely power. Supreme Court Justice Sandra Day O'Connor was appointed by Ronald Reagan who assumed her to be in line ideologically with his conservative stances. And, he was right in his assumption except in one area, "Women's Rights." Somehow the topic never came up in her vetting process. An unlikely beneficiary of the "don't ask don't tell" policy in this instance, Justice O'Connor, constituted the "swing vote" on every issue facing the Court dealing with women's rights. It was said of her tenure that all one had to do was get O'Connor's opinion and one had the opinion to be handed down by the Court.

So, perhaps Senator Snowe, who has now become nationally known for her ability to influence the outcome of close votes, has taken a page from the book of these and so many other power-wielding women who have come before her. Perhaps she is someone the Republican hierarchy should take a good look at when the Presidential election craziness begins again.

## Iran and Dancing With the Stars

Oh my, my, my; what are we to make of what was revealed last week about a secret nuclear facility buried deep within Iran? I find it interesting that this information was released just after "Ama Dinner Jacket's" speech at the U.N. The release of this information prompted the U.S, Great Britain and France to stand united in asking for "severe sanctions" to be imposed against Iran. It was good to see France standing with the U.S. for a change; but, where were Russia and China? France is nice; they make good bread and great cheese but without the support of Russia and China, sanctions, severe or not, won't work.

And, what oh what are we to make of the new Dancing with the Stars Season featuring none other than former congressman Tom "the Hammer" DeLay?

It started me thinking about the similarities of these two seemingly unrelated occurrences. Bear with me here while I explain.

On the one hand we witnessed a political dance; on the other a celebrity dance. Both will be judged.

In both instances partnerships are paramount to success. In both we have proven, seasoned pro's having to deal with oft times outlandish amateurs. Then, there is the ever so important poise vs. style vs. execution factors. And, finally, we have choreography and conditioning.

With this analogy in mind, here's how I see the judge's scoring.

The U.S. needs China and Russia as partners for the choreography and execution of severe sanctions to be successful. Much like "the Hammer" needed the talents and support of his professional partner or it would have been even more embarrassing for him (and the viewers) than it was.

Deduct a few points from the U.S. for lacking adequate partner cooperation.

Points must also be taken away from Ama Dinner Jacket for poise, style and execution. Ranting, Holocaust denying and launching two missile deployment tests most certainly alienated the judges not to mention public opinion.

Which brings us to choreography. The U.S. appears to be using a progressive choreography, each step being predicated on the execution of the previous one, while Iran just seems to be improvising. Points must be deducted from both sides.

As for conditioning, the U.S initiated high level negotiations with allies, tried to calm inflammatory talk from other world leaders, and began gently maneuvering across the dance floor of international relations. Positive points scored here.

Ama Dinner Jacket, with loss of support at home (ie the unexpected election protests), no support from the Arab Moslem nations who are Sunni and have no love for the Shi'a majority of Iran, seems to be standing alone, "partner-less" and pretty much winging it. Oooh, big loss of points!

Results of the first round: The U.S. exhibited promise. DeLay looked stiff and silly while Ama Dinner Jacket looked relaxed but spouted silly.

The scary part is DeLay's negative effect is only to his own dignity. Iran's negative effect could mean the future of our world.

# Dreams; Roller Derby, Olympics and Obama

Drew Barrymore was everywhere on T.V. and in the Print Media over the weekend promoting her new film Whip It. If you have lived under a rock for two decades, she was that adorable little friend of E.T. whose real life saga included addiction, divorcing her parents and all sorts of other wild behavior. She then grew up, went on to become an accomplished actor and movie producer who now has achieved a self-proclaimed dream, that of directing a movie. All of this has been documented "ad nauseam" for the world to see through the unflattering eye of the Tabloids.

After one of the countless interviews with Ms Barrymore about the movie, which is a "slice of life" tale following the struggles and triumphs of female Roller Derby participants, a Chicago newsman informed us of a Chicago connection to the spectacle of Roller Derby. Did you know that Roller Derby was "invented" in Chicago and the inventor's hope, actually his dream, was it would one day become an Olympic sport?

Which brings us to another story also occupying the spotlight of media news coverage; Chicago's bid to host those very same Olympics. Amid what has become common place political nonsense from both parties was the debate as to whether or not the President should have left the country to make the plea on behalf of his home town. Both he and Mrs. Obama expressed their dream of an Olympic Games to be held in Chicago.

Dreams...hmmm. Barrymore dreamed of directing a Roller Derby movie, the dream of Roller Derby becoming an Olympic event and the Obama's dream of Chicago having the spotlight of international media attention shine on it by hosting the Olympics; pretty interesting this dream stuff.

I personally didn't care if our neighbor to the west hosted the Olympics or not. I heard that every Olympic host city made money and then, subsequently, I heard that every Olympic host city lost money. Like most political processes, proponents professed a boom, opponents professed doom.

My friends and family living in the city were dead set against it. The years of construction impacting on traveling about and the prospect of the financial liability to Chicago citizens weighed very heavily on their minds. And of course the crowds it would have drawn; I had several people ask if they could come stay with us for the duration of the games!

Here in Northwest Indiana, most thought it would be great. We would be close enough to reap many benefits without having all of the inconveniences and financial obligations.

But alas, much like Roller Derby becoming an Olympic event, the Olympics in Chicago just wasn't meant to be. But the dream of Chicago hosting an Olympics was good; wasn't it Mr. and Mrs. Obama? But, was it worth using up some more political capital to personally make the pitch?

The Olympics in Chicago...dream or nightmare?

# Should We Care About Letterman?

I doubt that most of us care if David Letterman had affairs or not. Unlike the arguments of some that political figures should be held to a higher moral standard (yea right!) and that the "character issue" is not only relevant but paramount in deciding on a political candidate, Dave is, after all, a mere T.V. celebrity, a comedian whose only impact on people's lives is whether or not he can get you to stay up past 10:30 P.M. and if he can then make you laugh enough to convince you that you made the right decision to forego an extra hour of sleep. But really, are his personal life and or misdeeds any of our business?

It's not the affairs; let him work that out with his wife, but the question of sexual harassment that bothers me.

Early in my professional career I worked for the Midwest Stock Exchange. This was long before anyone had even heard the term "sexual harassment." The trading floor of the Exchange, that bastion of power and ego, was at that time for men only...literally. There were no women allowed on the floor at all, ever; except, once a month when I had to breach the testosterone barrier and venture in amongst the boys in the "Old Boy's Club" to end all "Old Boy's Clubs."

At 23 years of age, I was literally sick the night before I knew I had to enter that trading floor. My job entailed keeping the stock signage up to date, so once a month I had to go onto the trading floor, with my trusty X-acto Blade in hand, to remove the obsolete signage and replace it with the current offerings. The placement of the signage required that I either bend over or get down on my knees to accomplish my task.

I think you get the picture.

Whichever way I chose to do this part of my job, I was subjected to the most crass, sexually blatant, totally offensive comments you can imagine. More than once I found myself holding up the blade as a deterrent when a hand patted my bottom, and worse, to peals of laughter from "the boys."

I knew I had no recourse. There were no harassment policies, no one to complain to who didn't think it was really funny. As soon as a new job opportunity came along, I left.

But now, lo these many years later, we do have workplace protection. And, for good or bad, the evolution of our litigious society and greed, harassment suits have become as common as dirt!

So, back to Dave's behavior; to date, none of the women with whom he, admittedly, had affairs have filed any harassment suits against him. None have said that he used his position of power to force any actions. None have charged workplace abuses. I have to admit to being torn on this one; but, if the women aren't complaining, should we care?

# The Nobel Peace Prize

So, President Obama received the Nobel Peace Prize to much outrage, applause and comedian attention. "Did he deserve it or not" was being thrashed about both cable and network TV. He even voiced his own misgivings about meriting the award. Some suggested that it was given "for things to come." Some said it was given for his restoration of "hope for the future." Some argued that "the prize is nothing but a sham if it is given to a man currently waging two wars." And there are always those citing the "liberal cabal flexing its muscles in Obama worship."

I have been lucky enough to have met a former Nobel Peace Prize recipient, the author, international humanitarian and Holocaust survivor; Elie Wiesel. And I think we all know about the amazing life of famed Mother Teresa, another prize recipient. The brave martyr for peace, Anwar Sadat of Egypt, had his life taken because he dared hope for peace with Israel, also received the prize. But, then so did Yasser Arafat, architect of the most deadly period in Israeli/Palestinian relations.

What gives? From looking at the recipients in just this partial list, it seems like "peace" is, at best, in the eyes of the beholder!

Makes you wonder; what are the actual criteria for prize consideration? What are these Nobel Prizes all about?

By all accounts, Alfred Nobel was a highly principled man who had a passion for scientific experimentation, literature and the wellbeing of his world and fellow man. His invention of dynamite, while well-intentioned, resulted in the undesired reality of death and destruction

Upon the death of his brother Ludvig, a French reporter, in the obituary confused the two brothers writing about the still very much alive Alfred and describing him as "the merchant of death." This malevolent title greatly affected Alfred to the point where on November 27, 1895 he rewrote his last will and testament giving the largest share of his fortune to a series of prizes, the Nobel Prizes.

One part, the Peace Prize, was dedicated to "the person who shall have done the most or the best work for fraternity between nations, for the abolition or reduction of standing armies and for the holding and promotion of peace congresses."

There you have the real deal, the actual wording of what would merit the prize...you decide if you think the President deserved it or not.

I have a different idea for this year's prize. What if they hadn't awarded it at all?

The U.S. is engaged in two wars; N. Korea, Pakistan, India, Russia, Israel, China; volatile nations, all with nukes. Iran threatening...the perpetration of horrific violence throughout the world goes on and on.

What a statement it would have been if the committee had said, "Enough, there is no one in this violent world that is doing enough to bring peace. We choose not to award the Peace Prize to anyone this year."

# Change

I might have previously alluded to the fact that I think we Americans give a lot of lip service to the concept of change. Oh yes, we do like change. We even elected a president on the premise of change. Unfortunately, what we don't like; what we actually fear, is CHANGE.

Did I mention that I am on vacation? We left bright and early, on a driving trip...I haven't embarked on a driving vacation in years but with the multitude of changes, all negative, to air travel, it seemed like a great idea to once again take to the roads.

Driving east toward Niagara Falls (I am embarrassed to admit, I had never before seen the Falls) the concept of the two types of change came to me. As we drove amid the awesome splendor of burnt orange giving way to vibrant red; tawny tan yielding to spectacular gold; leaves shimmering in the morning light, those seemingly unrealistic landscape paintings of the fall colors all at once were rendered totally accurate in my mind.

And I thought, now this is a change we can all embrace, all relish, all rely on and in which we can all take comfort.

Once at Niagara, my breath was indeed taken away by the magnificence of nature's fury and the splendor of the falls. Doing all of the touristy things offered I learned of the changes to the topography, through eons of time, that it took to manifest this beauty, the spectacle of splendor cascading before me. Now, that is what I call a magnificent example of change!

We next arrived at Saratoga Springs and were instantly thrown back in time to the late nineteenth century when the pace of living was slower and the wealthy of the time came to this place to luxuriate in the calming mineral baths only to then be whipped into a frenzy at the nearby race track. This seemed a place where change, capitalized or otherwise, just didn't occur.

And as the week passed and we drove through upstate New York, the rain and wind blew. And it continued to blow until all of those golden, red and orange leaves eddied to the ground, to change, change once again, this time to a sickly brown heralding the inevitable decay; never more to shimmer in the sunlight. On the drive home I marveled still at the CHANGE the wind and rain had accomplished. All of the barren branches bordering the roadway stood lifeless and old where just the week before the magnificent colors shimmered with life and had totally captivated me.

So, I guess this all adds up to the oxymoron that change is a constant. It eases us into a comfortable progression of the inevitable. But, CHANGE isn't comfortable. It can be stark and disquieting. Oftentimes it is scary, unsettling and yet isn't it nonetheless necessary?

# One Year Later

This week marks an anniversary; our President's election was one year ago. I remember so vividly, as I'm sure you do, the hope generated by his victory. Even former President George W. Bush said that the election of President Obama was a remarkable day in our country's history.

So where are we a year later? From my perspective while President Obama has shown that he cannot walk on water, he is nonetheless a pretty good swimmer.

I wrote about change last week. And it is change that we all expected from this administration. But change, just for change sake, is not the answer. I think that, unlike the critics that say our President is expecting too much, doing too much too soon; I think he isn't going far enough. We live in a new world; a fast and furious world. The game has changed whether we like it or not and we have to get back in it if we are to have a chance of winning it.

Here are 5 things I think we should do. (I have more but am limited in space!)

Since government is only getting bigger and taxes are the only income our government has, radical change should occur. We need to adopt either a flat tax, or a value added tax.

Anyone receiving public assistance of any kind should be required to be randomly drug tested. In many jobs drug testing is a requirement for employment. Even my son was randomly tested to be on the LaPorte football team. Why shouldn't it be required for public assistance? We, you and I, are the people working to support all of the various forms of public assistance; why should our hard earned money go to those who, by choice, take drugs? It's simple. If you choose to take drugs, you get no government money, none! By the way, I would include alcohol in this requirement as well.

Marijuana should be legalized and taxed to the hilt. This will provide additional income and eliminate a big part of the violence caused by gang/turf wars.

To address the rest of the street violence, we should pull out of Afghanistan and Iraq and have our young men and women in The Service patrol our own streets helping to deal with our own urban problems instead of those in countries half way around the world.

Finally, our young people, right out of high school should be required to participate in one year of national service. Whether it be in the military or other government approved community service organizations, it should be a requirement for all. I have seen first-hand the discipline, the focus and the maturity that Israeli young adults derive from their national service requirement.

One year later, looking back with nostalgia, I still think there is great promise for this land. Call me "a cock-eyed" optimist but I still say "yes we can."

# Noise

Last week I was patiently awaiting my turn at the bank drive thru when a tremendous rumbling disrupted my daydreaming. I was momentarily startled to realize that my car was shaking. I actually felt the vibration of the bass before I heard the music – oh wait – I really can't call what I heard music because the bass tone volume was so elevated I could not discern a melody of any kind. I did however hear quite clearly the beat.

As I sat for what felt like forever (which in reality was about four minutes) I noticed that there was a baby seat in that boom box pretending to be a vehicle behind me and to my horror, a baby sat in it. All I could think of was "what is that noise doing to that baby's tiny little ears?"

The baby being subjected to that level of noise got me thinking about the countless teenagers I have passed on the street or shopping in a store with those ear-bud things connecting them to their IPods or whatever, blaring so loudly that it seemed too loud even for me standing several feet away. If I am annoyed by the volume at a distance, can you imagine the damage it is doing to their ears?

So, I decided to do some checking. Noise-induced hearing loss (NIHL) is an increasingly prevalent disorder that results from exposure to high-intensity sound, especially over a long period of time.

According to a position statement released by the American Academy of Audiology, "The average, otherwise healthy, person will have essentially normal hearing at least up to age 60 if his or her ears are not exposed to high noise levels."

Aha, did you get that? There is the rub...no exposure to high noise levels. I'm no expert but what I was hearing coming from that car made the term high noise level sound like a whisper.

So what is the outlook for that baby's ability to hear in the future? Well, NIHL can already be identified in the adolescent and young adult population as well. The Hearing Alliance of America reports that 15 percent of college graduates have a level of hearing loss equal to or greater than their parents. And, remember, this study is based on the pre-IPod generation.

This does not bode well for that little baby.

We will have to wait for the studies and the research before we know the real extent of the damage all of this loud noise is doing to our young people. I don't see the trend ending anytime soon so I guess my only hope for that precious child is that research finds a cure for noise-induced hearing loss...or wait. I have a novel idea. What if that young mother stops for a moment to think about the welfare of her child and simply turns down the volume?

# Going Rogue...

She's back! The political pundits are once again in a feeding frenzy. The release later this week of Sarah Palin's autobiography has them almost giddy with the prospect of days, maybe weeks, of fresh fodder. Due to the timing of her media blitz, this column is being written before several of Ms. Palin's interviews, but here is my take on it all so far.

We are being subjected to a national "gaper's delay." Like a train wreck, try as we might to avoid the nastiness of a disaster, we are nonetheless drawn to it. The fact is, there are people who are just a force of nature. Some of us love them while some of us hate them; but few of us are indifferent.

Apparently (I have not read the book) she is blaming a lot of people for a lot of things. I wonder if the American people want to look back. I would advise (if asked) that she fess up. Say she was not prepared for the "whole package" of being on a national ticket and move on with her agenda. Agree with her or not, I think that would be refreshing and "rogue" to just say "oops, but I'll do better." The American people are very forgiving. I think it would serve her well. Then, David Brooks' cryptic response to her book, "she's a joke," and others like it would be neutralized.

The one thing that I am sure of is that Sarah Palin is no joke. Much like the opening line from Richard III, she recognizes that "this is the hour of our discontent" and she is taking advantage of it. In a recent poll only 34% of Americans said that they would re-elect their representatives to congress. People are afraid. Unemployment, 2 wars, street violence, health concerns; all contribute to a climate that fueled Ms. Palin's message. She is no dummy. The self-proclaimed rogue, the renegade, the maverick; she fired up her supporters vowing to stir things up, throw out the conventional and make a better, more honest government.

Sounds good, no? Well, for a person who told Oprah that "she is just not into all of the drama," she has organized this dramatic, sensational media tour including interviews by Miss O herself and the Goddess of interviewing, Barbara Walters; Good Morning America, 20/20 just to name a few. Not into drama?

Let's get real. Sarah Palin is putting her toe in the water and making mega bucks doing it. She will travel around in her Palin mobile taking the temperature of the country. Whether she will run in 2012, will hinge on what she experiences around the country. But what will be equally interesting and telling for her political future will be how many republican governors in 2010 facing reelection will want her coming out in support of them.

Is she a God-sent or pariah? Only time will tell, but one thing I do know for sure, to play on Nixon's famous quote, "the press will have Sarah Palin to kick around for a good while to come."

# Independent's Thanksgiving

I was going to write about Thanksgiving but got side-tracked. I sat listening to yet another rehashing of the significance of the two gubernatorial races won by Republicans earlier this month in New England and I couldn't resist commenting on it. Republicans are on the attack heralding these two state races as an indication that the people have lost their fascination with Obama and the Democrats are doomed to fail. While the Democrats are pointing to the fact that these were isolated state races and bear no reflection on the solid commitment of Obama supporters to the Democratic Party.

To both sides I say Bull @#$% or in honor of the season Turkey @#$%. (Let me apologize in advance for implying such language...my emotions got the better of me)

I know I have said it before but I think it bears repeating; I am no political strategist. I tend not to pay much attention to the credibility of the "possible omens" better known as political polls. I do think, to coin an old phrase, "it ain't over till it's over!" The wild card, as in the past, remains the Independents. As the number of Americans that consider themselves politically independent grows so to the concern by some that our two party system as we have known it is rapidly becoming obsolete.

The notion being expressed by both parties that because Obama garnered the Independent vote in the presidential race it automatically signaled an increase in those supporting the entire Democratic Agenda (oh wait, do they actually have a united agenda?) Or that because two Republican Governors were elected out East indicated a surge in the popularity of the Republican Party and a vote of confidence in its leaders (Ahh, who are its leaders again?) I think the Politicos should check their dictionaries.

News flash...Independents label themselves as Independents because (duh) they are Independent. Is it just me or do you agree it is not a very complicated concept?

Look, with both parties catering to the extremists within and the fact that the majority of Americans classify themselves as centrists, is it any wonder that so many have given up the concept of straight ticket voting? What a unique idea: every candidate should be evaluated on his/her own merits. No more being told how to vote but rather exercising one's own right to vote for the best candidate for the job.

It is certainly not as easy as toeing the party line. It takes resolve to read position papers and listen to interviews and public statements. But I think it is our government at its best.

So to come full circle back to Thanksgiving, this year as I reflect about what I am grateful for in my life, in addition to family and friends and good health, I think I'm going to throw in all of the Independents out there that are giving the politicos such headaches. Yeah.

# Season of Miracles

There is a place, a place in the Negev Desert in Israel where the hand of God is in full view. The expanse of the desert when first I saw it so astounded me, I could take not a step, utter a word nor move a muscle. What stretched out before me was both horrifying and magnificent at the same time. We made our way slowly, for one can't rush in the heat, steps mired down by the dry muck of sand. For in this place, time has left a mark, a mystical, magical mark on the landscape. In this arid, desolate place, a place of quiet where not a man-produced sound can be heard, what one can hear is the sound of God. The wind, unobstructed by tree or structure hums and roars and sings as it swirls the sands of time into a frenzy. It whips the sand in giant eddies humming the particles in the rhapsody of lifetimes, of centuries, of eons in this place. And the swirling continues, has continued from the beginning until this day. This day when I stand here above the twisting gorge the winds have carved out of the sand. Carved and polished thorough the years, deeper, deeper, they are now millennia deep and they are smooth, ever so smooth. The emery of the sand has left a flawless glasslike facade on the walls of these sand gorges compressed and hardened and then polished to a high shine. This age hardened ribbon of valley threading through the desert hills inspires the soul, makes one humble.

And then at sun-down, at that moment when calm descends on the earth and the quietude of existence draws nigh; when the toiling and talking and temptations of the day ease slowly away; I stand on the brink of that precipice, on the edge of eternity itself. Then all at once a shard of moonlight streaks down from above. A powerful beacon from God illuminates his majesty and I stand watching, staring, gaping as the flash picks up velocity and brilliance then ricochets off of the reflective walls below me speeding through the twists and turns, exploding the path, shooting light. And all at once as if this holy laser show was produced just for me to see, hope and joy, inspiration and awe at the splendor of all that we don't know and have yet to understand fills me. On past me the sparkling shard of silver streaks and then up, back on up into the sky above; back to the heavens.

I stand stunned.

In reflection upon that moment it is as if Earth had received a most precious gift sent down from God. And I watched Earth respond in gratitude by heightening the glow and sending it back up to the heavens.

There is a place, a place in the Negev Desert in Israel where the hand of God is in full view.

# Something Has Changed

I have a confession to make. When I heard the first news broadcast of what would come to be described as "the Tiger Woods story" I sloughed it off. One maybe two days of shelf life was what I would have predicted. How in the world could I have been sooooo far off the mark? We are now in week two of the seemingly non-ending soap opera and interest seems to be diminishing not in the least. With two wars, an embittered health care debate raging, jobless numbers continuing to rise, the deficit skyrocketing with no end in sight and a national economy in the crapper; one of the Sunday "political round table shows" ending with their customary opinion piece chose Tiger to be the topic. Tiger?

The man plays golf!

Now, before all of you golf nuts out there get on my case let me say that I come from a golfing family. My mom was a good golfer. My dad was a really good golfer and my two brothers were/are excellent golfers. If you do the math, that adds up to four people, and if you know anything about golf you know that it is played in foursomes. So, by the time I was of age to play, our family foursome was filled. But, before you think that I was neglected or felt left out, let me tell you that I wouldn't have competed with my older brothers on that turf in a million years. Rather, I picked my arenas of sibling competition very carefully with a vigilant eye to contests I actually had a chance of winning. But I do digress. My point is that like many of you who really do not play the game, we are aware of those who play it exceptionally well.

Actually it was a golfer, the great Arnie Palmer who first made his ability in a sport become the basis for a multi-million dollar enterprise...yep the likes of Michael Jordan and the Manning brothers and all of the other over-paid, over-valued sport celebrities have ol' Arnie to thank for paving the way to their fortunes.

But something has changed. The country loved Arnie. He was a friend making those commercial pitches. There was no drama. That was no controversy and I don't think I ever heard anyone moaning about the fact that he was making a lot of money.

So I ask, has the collective nature of our country changed? I think so. We have become obsessed and greedy and we look to others, or our government to solve our problems. And we create celebrities out of pro-athletes or fine actors or no-talent sensationalists who are elevated to celebrity status simply because they are celebrities! And in tough time these people seem to have it all, do it all. We are envious. And oh how we seem to relish the big fall when it comes because it makes us feel better about our own lives.

What has happened to us? Tiger Woods is a man who plays golf!

# Common Sense

While watching and listening to various media outlets analyzing and speculating and proselytizing on the issues of the day, it occurred to me that many of the perplexing questions can be answered by invoking the sage wisdom of my grandmother. One of the rules of life for that great lady was, "use common sense;" so simple, yet so ignored by so many.

Here goes...

Deductions, Dependent's and Loopholes, Oh MY!
I think we should throw out the personal income tax system. I apologize to the CPA's and tax attorneys out there but they are the only one's benefiting from the current jumble of bureaucracy, regulations and indiscernible rules. How is it acceptable that we all have to adhere to a taxing system that 95% of us can't understand? Establish a flat tax. Everyone, everyone, everyone pays a minute percentage of their income...no loopholes. No tax shelters. Everyone pays and if the rich complain, remind them of the huge savings they are accruing by not having to pay the exorbitant fees of their tax attorneys!

Oh, My Aching Head!

The healthcare fiasco is giving me a headache...actually it has evolved into a real pain in the butt! I say scrap it all. That's right; to really have an effective healthcare delivery system we have to start from scratch. Everyone would be covered by a basic, essentials only, government managed provider. Private insurance companies would offer varying levels of additional services for additional personal cost. Basic needs are provided while those that can afford the extras have the option to buy them; one from column "A," two from column "B." Eliminate all the "pork." Start with only basic care that all can agree on as, dare I say it, the public option and let those that can afford more buy more. The ugly truth is, in life, those that have more money can afford more/better things. As long as the basic healthcare needs of all are met, I think we have done our civic/humanitarian duty.

How Dumb Can Smart People Be?

Did Tiger learn nothing from Eliot Spitzer or Bill Clinton? Of course I could fill the whole column with the names of other powerful, successful, reputed to be really smart men who had not the common sense of a warthog. And let me officially apologize to the warthogs of the world for putting them in such supremely stupid company. In the early days of the fledgling feminist movement decades ago when Cosmopolitan first hit the newsstands, an interview with founder Ms H G Brown explained the "cardinal rule of cheating." (Let's just put the whole moral issue aside.) She cautioned, "never, never, never, have an affair with someone who doesn't have as much to lose as you do." Oh, Tiger! How could you think that your choice of paramours would keep it to themselves? So, in addition to asking for forgiveness for cheating you should also ask forgiveness for being so monumentally stupid.

Don't you agree; we could use a bit more common sense adhered to in the New Year to come!

# Secret Santa's

I love Christmas. That might seem like a strange statement coming from "a nice Jewish girl." But it is true nonetheless. Actually, I should have started by stating that I don't understand how anyone cannot love Christmas. Even those of us not celebrating the religious aspect of the holiday can certainly appreciate the spirit of it. Peace on earth, good will towards man...don't we all want that? At the foundation of all three of the great religions of the world is a very simple principle, the golden rule. Forget the religious fanatics in all religions; strip away the institutionalization of faith by the religious hierarchy, look past the frills and presents and obligations that this holiday has come to represent and see the simplicity of the message.

Don't you just love when your faith in human nature is restored? And how great is it when it happens at this time of year? I was watching a Sunday morning news show this past weekend and saw a wonderful segment. There is a group of CEO's from all across the country who wish to remain anonymous, choosing to call themselves "Secret Santa's." They are spreading the joy of this season in a magnificent way. They have personally contributed over $300,000 to a fund and are going to thrift stores, soup kitchens, bus terminals etc. in various cities across the country and handing out money. Yes, you heard me correctly (well, read me correctly). They are anonymously giving away money to the needy in amounts ranging from $100.00 to $400.00 a pop. From the map that was briefly displayed on the screen, it seemed that they are heavily concentrating on smaller cities rather than the large metropolises of our land but that detail remained unexplained. Perhaps those are the areas in which they live...but we will never know for sure...oooh, a Christmas secret; how fun is that?"

Can you imagine? CEO's actually giving money away and not taking any credit for it? Unlike many generous

Hollywood, television and big business types who are indeed donating money but insist on having the cameras rolling as they do so to get the bump in popularity it affords them; these CEO's insist on remaining unnamed.

It would be so nice to think that this group of Secret Santa's consists of the investment firms and large bank CEO's who are awarding themselves those huge Christmas bonuses this year. Maybe they are using those millions of dollars that they are giving themselves to ease the plight of the needy...Ah, I don't think so. If it were them, they would make sure that their P.R people got front page placements extolling their generosity!

No this is a group of individuals who, in my mind, exemplify what this time of year should be all about. We should be expressing our gratitude for our good fortune in any way we can by helping those around us who have not been as fortunate as we have.

So, I say Bravo Secret Santa's!

# Twelve Stories of 2009

(To be sung to the Twelve Days of Christmas)

It's the end of the year so it's time to look on back
T'was the year of two thousand and nine

At the start of the year we watched history unfold
Barack's inauguration
T'was the year of two thousand and nine

Then Michelle's fashion sense hit the newsstands
everyday
Michelle the fashionista
Barack's inauguration
T'was the year of two thousand and nine

For the Senate a loss when an elder statesman died
Kennedy has died
Michelle the fashionista
Barack's inauguration
T'was the year of two thousand and nine

Then the Madoff investors got stabbed in the back
Bernie's sleazy life
Kennedy has died
Michelle the fashionista
Barack's inauguration
T'was the year of two thousand and nine

Another loss was felt like a jolt around the world
The king of pop OD'd
Bernie's sleazy life
Kennedy has died
Michelle the fashionista
Barack's inauguration
T'was the year of two thousand and nine

Then Captain Scully saved the day and a hero was born.
Scully is a hero
The king of pop OD'd
Bernie's sleazy life

Kennedy has died
Michelle the fashionista
Barack's inauguration
T'was the year of two thousand and nine

The Supreme Court welcomed Ms Sotomayor
She is a justice
Scully is a hero
The king of pop OD'd
Bernie's sleazy life
Kennedy has died
Michelle the fashionista
Barack's inauguration
T'was the year of two thousand and nine

Ex-Gov Blago's escapades well they really took the cake
Foolish foolish Blago
She is a Justice
Hero Captain Scully
The king of pop OD'd
Bernie's sleazy life
Kennedy has died
Michelle the fashionista
Barack's inauguration
T'was the year of two thousand and nine

The Twilight Vampires took the world by storm
Passing vampire fancy
Foolish foolish Blago
She is a Justice
Hero Captain Scully
The king of pop OD'd
Bernie's sleazy life
Kennedy has died
Michelle the fashionista
Barack's inauguration
T'was the year of two thousand and nine

To day-time TV watchers Oprah brought a tear
Oprah's last season
Vampire passing fancy

Foolish foolish Blago
She is a Justice
Hero Captain Scully
The king of pop OD'd
Bernie's sleazy life
Kennedy has died
Michelle the fashionista
Barack's inauguration
T'was the year of two thousand and nine

There were billions given out to keep our land a float
Average Joe is drowning
Oprah's last season
Vampire passing fancy
Foolish foolish Blago
She is a Justice
Hero Captain Scully
The king of pop OD'd
Bernie's sleazy life
Kennedy has died
Michelle the fashionista
Barack's inauguration
T'was the year of two thousand and nine

Tiger got caught for the life that he was leadin'
Now his wife's in Sweden
Average Joe a drowning
Oprah's last season
Vampire passing fancy
Foolish foolish Blago
She is a Justice
Hero Captain Scully
The king of pop OD'd
Bernie's sleazy life
Kennedy has died
Michelle the fashionista
Barack's inauguration
T'was the year of two thousand and nine.
Happy New Year to all.

# Connecting the Dots

I sat with my three year old Grandson over the holidays and he watched ever so intently as I showed him how you draw a line from A to B to C, and so on, until the shape of a bunny emerged eliciting giggles from him.

We live in an extremely complicated and very dangerous world. That is the reality. To think that every attack, every danger, every act perpetrated by the deranged can be averted is simply fantasy. Terrible acts occur...and will keep occurring as long as sick people live among us. Those that value their warped ideals over human life do exist in this world and while most of them can be contained or detected in time, there will be those that are not thwarted.

In the '80's when the words terrorist act were not in our daily vocabulary or even in our collective consciousness, I had an interesting discussion with a friend who was a former Secret Service Agent. He totally stunned me when he said that President Kennedy first acknowledged that anyone willing to die could take out any target. How ironic and prophetic that statement was.

There is no foolproof method to prevent a terrorist act nor will there ever be. Are we expecting too much? Since the Christmas Day debacle there has been discussion, lots of hand-wringing and the predictable political ranting. Machines that will make us all into unwilling centerfold models for all in the airport to see (without the airbrushing) are being touted as the solution...I ask, solution to what? With technology improving at a dizzying pace will these "catch-up measures" really keep us safer?

I guess the good news to this story is that Al Qaeda is still using airplanes as their mode of destructive acts and that the would-be bomber was so poorly trained that all he succeeded in doing was to light up his genitals.

The most disturbing element of all is that our "Department of Homeland Security," in my mind, has shown itself to be totally ineffectual. The bazillions of dollars we have spent establishing yet another Governmental Department, with the charge of coordinating all of our information gathering sources, has been flushed down the toilet.

For pity sakes; the guy's own father warned us he was a threat.

We are into the eighth year of the learning curve on attacks using airplanes. Will someone please tell me how we can still not have a coordinated information system in place for identifying and tracking potential terrorists?

I am told that a search similar to Google's system is all that is needed. Come on. Hire the Google folks for a special project...wait, better yet, appeal to their humanitarian instincts and get them to do it for free.

Eight years ago the 9/11 commission reported the embarrassing and staggeringly stupid failure on the part of our government to "connect the dots." Eight years later it is obvious that the amazingly difficult art of connecting the dots still eludes us.

Oh, and at three years old my grandson was able to create a perfect square by connecting the dots!

# Politics and the Movies (2)

Movie lovers are in "hoggie heaven" this time of year. The studios, indie producers and any movie mogul wannabe with a film, wait until one month before Oscar nominations are announced to release their films. The industry believes that the memory of great performances or wonderful films having been seen before this time are fleeting and the Academy voters wouldn't/couldn't remember earlier released contenders.

So, right in the middle of our national healthcare debate, our staggering economic woes, one failed terrorist attack another fatally successful and the two wars still raging with no end in sight; we all can go and escape. Well, at least that was my hope.

I wanted to see what a half a trillion dollars looked like on the movie screen so I went to see "Avatar." It was a stunningly beautiful film but now all I am hearing is how "politically incorrect" it is. By painting Big Corporation America as monumentally greedy and casting aspersions on rogue, power abusing military personnel; the film is being trashed for being anti-American. The fact is Big Corporate America has proven itself to be obscenely greedy, ie. Bail-out bonuses, etc. And, military personnel have abused their power, remember Abu Ghraib?

Then, I went to see the star-studded "Nine." Amidst mostly unfavorable reviews and disappointing comments from my friends, I found it to be a really fascinating exploration of the creative process and how one man worked his way out of a "block."

But instead of simply enjoying it, I find myself, here again, putting it into a current political context.

Creativity is a solitary process. Pen in hand, alone in a room; the writer conjures up a world unto itself. All is possible. Ideas can come true. But, having that creation succeed becomes a very complicated, labor intensive

147

reality. No matter how good the script, if the actors are bad or the lighting horrendous or the set designs outrageous (I could go on) the entire film is in jeopardy of failing.

I found that instead of being able to simply enjoy the memory of "Nine," I was thinking of our President's current situation in its context. As wonderfully creative, idealistic, hopeful, a president or a writer may be; the reality is that others always impact on the fate of his/her personal vision. Unless that vision is clearly mapped out and strategies are delineated in detail, he/she runs the risk of a disaster at the box office...or in getting an agenda accomplished.

One last movie/politics quandary that has come to my mind as of late...remember the movie The Mouse That Roared? It was a film about a small country wanting foreign aid so they declare a war on the U.S.

Hmmm.

Could it be that Yemen, with no oil, no water and pretty much not a lot of anything else, grasps the advantages of harboring and facilitating al Qaeda? After all, we might be prompted to win their hearts and minds by building schools, infrastructure etc.

Oscar season, political?

# 2010

# "W" and "Bubba"

I'm sure that we all watched in horror as the devastation unfolded before us. Haiti was laid to waste by earthquake. Plagued by a totally unresponsive government in the best of circumstances, the citizens of Haiti who survived had nowhere to turn, no one to look to, no one in charge as their world lay crumbled all about them. While there are still life-threatening shortages and more human misery than anyone should be asked to bear, the world and the U.S. in particular have once again restored my faith in human nature. Taking charge of the relief efforts, organizing make-shift medical facilities; this is our country at its best and for one, I am very proud. At times of horrific adversity, the U.S. responds and responds well. Amidst our own national problems (some would say crises) the American people are opening their hearts and pocketbooks to help.

I was interested to see and hear from our two most recent presidents over the weekend. They have joined together to spearhead various U.S. efforts in Haiti.

I have to say that it was a bit shocking to see the two men, one Republican, one Democrat, who presided over our country during some of the most divisive, nasty, polarizing presidential terms in recent history; sitting side by side, in complete accord, promoting a humane, common purpose.

And they were not only more than civil in the various interviews, they were downright friendly! But the biggest shocker to me was when asked how they had gotten together in this effort to aid the Haitians, "W' stated that he had often spoken to "Bubba" during his presidency to ask advice or talk over a situation and they had indeed become friends.

Wow...makes one think.

While I am certainly not equating our political climate with the disaster in Haiti, I can't help but ask why "W" and "Bubba" don't use their "friendship" to help this country? Isn't it time to really stop the cat fights and do what's right for the American people? Why can't they agree to exert their own considerable political power within their parties to work on the people's business instead of their own party's business in the same way they are uniting in the efforts for Haiti?

Here are two, two term presidents. I have to believe that most of the powers that be in their respective parties will indeed still take their call.

I say to them, "Make the calls!"

Both had their reputations tarnished while president. I have to believe that neither man wanted the overriding "rep" that he ended up with when he left office.

But just think. If in addition to exhibiting humanitarian bipartisanship in their endeavors on behalf of the Haitian people, they could agree to flex their political muscle to curb at least a bit of the vicious partisanship in Washington; I think it would go a long way in enhancing their respective legacies.

Who'd a thought..."W" and "Bubba" statesmen?

# The Small Life

Most of us lead a small life, but small and meaningless do not always equate. The vast majority of us do lead meaningful lives, but often we fail to recognize that fact. We are so easily caught up in the grand scheme of things we miss the fact that our lives are valuable; valuable to our family, valuable to our friends and valuable to the enigma that is mankind.

I have often written of "major" national or international concerns and /or "huge" seemingly insurmountable problems without mention or even thought to the constant, unshakable, unwavering "power of a small life."

We get blinded by the radiance of the brightest star. We might even envy its popularity that it is instantly recognizable but we fail to see that without all of the other stars it would just be a speck in a black sky. It is the combination, the comparison, the differing sparkle, the unique alignments that together make the constellations that delight and inspire us when we take the time to look up and see them. We need to look up.

Millions of dollars have been donated to assist in Haiti. We see the big boats, we hear of the vast commitments of money and assistance, but do we take the time to think that all of that vastness, all of the large efforts really come down to the one person caring enough to give. They give of themselves on the ground in Haiti or they give of themselves in any way they can. It is the small life that touches the soul and makes things just a little bit better.

All too often we lose sight of that. I am as guilty as the next person. We get so wrapped up in the vast expanse of the sky we fail to recognize the splendor of one lone star. We see the North Star shining above; to me the most recognizable star and fail to wonder at the plethora of teeny tiny sparklers that in unison make the glory of the night sky.

There was a telethon over the past weekend. The phones were manned by dozens of high profile "celebrities." Millions of dollars were raised for the relief effort in Haiti. No one can argue that all of their efforts were for a truly worthy cause. But it does make me wonder. So many of us are willing to jump on board when there is a big, publicized need. We are attracted to those brightest of stars.

And that is fine. They deserve credit for helping in the way that they can. But there are so many other small stars that we don't know, wouldn't recognize, who deserve our thankful wonderment as well.

They are the ones that teach us that we all can be a star in the night sky no matter how small our lives may seem. You don't have to be the North Star to make the night sky shine...tonight, just look up and you'll see.

# It Dirties Us All

Most of us living in Northwest Indiana watch the network television broadcasts coming from Chicago stations. As a result we have been bombarded with Illinois primary contenders for what seems like forever.

Politicians, almost to a man (or woman) in vaulted rhetoric and with unanimous conviction claim that taking the campaigning high road is the path they will follow; the right path for servants of the people. We all know how that story ends! They inevitably fall into the same old, same old hate mongering and mud-slinging modus operandi.

Unwittingly, I have actually been paying attention. I've noticed that they do start out on their "clean campaigning path." Yes, they begin by introducing themselves, oft times surrounded by their perfect, all American looking family; but, as soon as the polling numbers start coming in, those not faring so well start the sleaze ball rolling. The negative ads aimed at tainting the reputation-ah wait, I mean destroying the lives of their opponents in the hope of increasing their own chance for victory, keep popping up in that promised clean campaign. Once the smear card is played by the underdog the mudslinging war of words begins. As the day of decision approaches the down and dirty get down and dirtier.

What is it about political nature or perhaps human nature in general that compels one to totally disregard their own integrity in the hope of slandering that of someone else?

Is all fair in love, war...and politics?

At one time war had rules. It was actually pretty civilized, if killing can ever be characterized to be civilized. Opposing forces faced each other in formation and on signal the battle commenced. But, once it became clear that an advantage was to be had by noncompliance with the rules, all hell broke loose.

Unlike war, history shows us that politics was never played by the rules...what rules? Our own revered forefather Thomas Jefferson methodically ripped at the reputation of his good friend John Adams in his quest for the presidency.

And now with the advent of media technology the mudslinging and the smears are right up in our faces and dirty us all.

In one of my columns appearing in this paper more than a year ago I set forth my own rules for political elections. I think one of them bears repeating so here goes:

Those running for any office should be banned from saying anything about their opponents. They can only speak to their own accomplishments, vision and plans for governing. Believe me the Press would fill in the sleaze gap; we're really good at that! I for one just want to hear from the candidates what they are proposing with their candidacy.

So, what do you think? It's quite a unique concept, no? Just imagine, elections actually being decided on the merits of the candidates' proposed policies, vision for the future and experience.

# Just When You Think...

Maybe it's the weather. Maybe it's all of the financial negativity bombarding us from the media. I don't know but I just feel...well, pretty down. If you feel that way too, here is a story that might help.

I happened upon a conversation between two 11th graders talking about our national economic situation. What struck me was they seemed to genuinely care. They wanted to understand and know what to do in the future to insure that they would not be in the same situation as their parents.

I was shocked. They were really interested, concerned, having a conversation about the economy. 11th graders...OMG!

Then, shortly after my shocking eavesdropping experience, I was able to participate in a fascinating program for eighth graders. It was called The Reality Store. It was a program run by volunteers from civic and service organizations in Chesterton.

Each participating eighth grade student was given a profession based on a survey of their interests, their grades and their ambitions. They were then assigned a salary for that profession, the dollar amount based on national norms.

They then spent half a day at the high school. The gym was set up with the volunteers manning tables, each representing a monthly expense category. There was a housing table where they had to decide to rent or buy. If they chose to buy they went to the mortgage table. There was an insurance table, a utilities table, a food table where there were three optional plans available, a clothing table again where functional, trendy and haute couture were options. After each decision on spending was made by the student, that amount was deducted from their monthly take home pay. By the time they arrived at my table, all of their essential monthly costs were deducted. I was the investing for retirement person offering a monthly deduction to be put into a 401k plan.

I sat waiting for the kids to make it around the huge circle of expenses chipping away at their monthly take home pay....just like we all weave our way through the paying of our monthly bills. So, there I sat expecting them to be totally disinterested in what I had to say. Eighth graders interested in retirement savings? What, was I nuts?

Well, guess what? Most of them seemed to really get it. I was shocked at how many of those eighth graders expressed interest in planning for the future. They wanted to fully understand how a 401k plan worked. Many took some time working through just how much they thought they would be able to afford to save.

Just when I thought there to be no hope for our future I receive a one/two punch of young people fiscal responsibility! Hmmmm, just when you think...

# One-Upsmanship

By the time this column runs you'll probably be filled to the gills with "bye-bye Bayh." Surprisingly, I had already written the words for this week before the Senator's announcement...

I think that life lessons learned early prove to be the most valuable. Here are two such lessons I learned in early adulthood that I think could be of benefit to our members of Congress.

Pick Your Battles

My children attended a co-op pre-school. This meant that several parents were in attendance in their classroom every day to help out. We were scheduled in rotation which translated into my being there approximately one day every two months. Truth be known, it was actually really fun.

The school was located in the basement of a church in Chicago's Lincoln Park neighborhood where street parking was non-existent. As a result, one of the parents' jobs was to stand outside to take the children being dropped off for school from the car into the classroom.

One morning I was on "curbside duty" when Jonathan's mom pulled up. As I opened the car door I realized that Jonathan was still in his pajamas. They happened to be adorable astronaut footies, but that's beside the point. Looking to his mom, before I could get a word out, she simply stated, "Some battles are just not worth fighting."

I suggest that each member of Congress occasionally let one of the other idiots wear his astronaut P.J.'s on the hill!

If All Else Fails...Use a One-upsmanship

Prolonged, heated battles will destroy a relationship. There is no magic to that statement, no mystery, no depth of thought or hard earned understanding. It is simply true. When first wed, my husband and I realized that some issues simply cannot be resolved by two logical yet stubborn people insisting that each of them is right. Most relationship disputes don't have a definite right answer but rather they revolve around the adamant feeling of each party of their own "rightness" on the issue. So we devised "one upsmanships."

We allocated an initial 5 to each of us with the rules being that if a seemingly irresolvable issue was truly important for one of us "to win" we could use one of our one upsmanships and be the uncontested, indisputable victor; no more discussion, no more bickering. Once this system was put in place, we soon realized that we were ever so much more willing to compromise. An instant victor card was so valuable it became clear early on that it was not to be "played lightly" just in case something more important for its usage came along. I won't say that it stopped our fighting but it did make us put compromising to the forefront.

Bayh's decision not to run again just punctuates Congress's need to focus on accomplishment instead of political power, compromise instead of combat.

So, I suggest instituting a congressional "one upsmanship" program before those of us in the middle of the political spectrum have no one left representing us.

# Mother Nature

Mother Nature gave a good wallop to Washington D.C. earlier in the month with a winter storm never seen before in D.C. written history. Then shortly after in nothing less than extreme mean spiritedness, she withheld snow from the Winter Olympics' site of Vancouver. Man, that Mother Nature sure is a cranky ol' broad.

But maybe instead of simply being grouchy because she can, she is actually trying to tell us all something.

Never one to be overshadowed, perhaps the storms constantly raging in Washington got her dander up. The sea squalls of the Senate, the hurricanes of the House; the ever increasing nastiness of gale force winds gusting out of Washington over the entire country; what an affront to her power. Don't they know that she and she alone has the ability to destroy by natural disaster? Who do those in Washington think they are? So she showed them just how powerless they really are in the face of true might. She dumped a record number of inches on D.C. which brought the whole town to a standstill. Yep, the city was brought to its proverbial knees, ground to a staggering halt, nothing, nada was getting done. Were we in the rest of the country tearing our hair out, bemoaning the tragedy of losing our great knights of democracy? Were we keening for the paralyzing effect shutting down our government had on all of us? Ah, no. Did the rest of us even notice that our government was not functioning? Oh, what am I saying? It hasn't been functioning for quite some time now.

Then in another show of power Mother Nature withholds snow from the winter Olympics! Why on earth would she go and do that? Could it be that she is just fed up with the stupidity of the Olympic Site Selection Committee? This International Committee in all of its wisdom selected Vancouver for the site of these Olympics...these Winter Olympics; winter being the optimum word, with all of the fabulous skiing events, events obviously dependent on great snow conditions.

Did no one on the committee simply Google "Vancouver weather" to discover that at this time of year their average temperature is 44 degrees?

I have to confess that I have not watched very many of the events. Nonetheless, I have come away with a pervasive feeling about the games from which all of us, especially our representatives on Capitol Hill should take a lesson.

Those kids, those athletes took what was handed them and did their job. They approached every event with their whole heart. When conditions are tough you can still do your best. Not everyone can earn the Gold but Bronze isn't so bad. You can lose and still compete again or retire with dignity knowing you did your best. You don't have to win gold to have accomplished something wonderful.

Perhaps all of us should take a lesson from those kids on skates and skis. And maybe that is exactly what the sly Mother Nature had in mind all along.

# The Census

There is Divine Intervention. I have been reminded of this on many occasions and it happened again this morning. I heard a discussion of the billions of dollars needed to take the upcoming census and I realized that I know very little about what it is and what exactly the Constitution demands. Then, this morning I was watching the end all be all commentary on our political process, a West Wing rerun, and the skies opened, the seas parted and a glorious sun instantly appeared. C.J. Craig (the Presidential Press Secretary on West Wing) admitted that she knew very little about the census and asked for a basic primer of what, when and how...all things census in five minutes.

Tell me that some Power that Be didn't intercede on my behalf!

We all know that every ten years the census counts how many people live in the United States. What I didn't know is that's all the Constitution says about the census.

Article 1 Section 2 of the Constitution actually gives us only one sentence on the census. This section basically deals with the requirements for election to the House of Representatives and taxing authority, both to be based on state population. Then the one sentence of note for our purposes is, "the actual enumeration shall be made within three years after the first meeting of the Congress of the United States and within every subsequent term of ten years."

That's it. That's all the guidance our founding fathers gave us. So every ten years we have to get a count of how many people live in every state.

Through the years more than just numbers of people were collected by the census. It has become our best data source for national numbers. The questions differ from census to census. Congress is given the charge of determining what other data should be collected.

Back in the beginning, a house to house count was made. Now we are mailed the census form to fill out and return. I've been told that if not returned, another form will be mailed and if that one is not returned, home visits may occur. Thousands of temporary jobs will be established to take this year's census; thus the discussion of the costs involved.

That is what first drew me to the issue, the billions of dollars to be spent on the census, but then an even more interesting discussion caught my attention. How do we deal with the illegal's residing in all of our fifty states? Since they are illegal, should they be counted? Are they entitled to representation if they are here illegally? The language used in the article seems based on numbers alone. No mention of citizenship appears, but like so much in the Constitution it is open to interpretation...after all, the Supreme Court needs something to do!

I certainly have no answers. All I really know is that it is very important to our community, our State and the Nation for the census to be filled out and submitted. The information gathered will impact on us all for at least the next ten years...then we can revisit it all over again.

# The American Soap Opera

I heard our current state of politics being described as the great "American Soap Opera." Then, the next day, in a pre-Oscars interview, the entire Academy Award's process and hype was defined as the "soap opera to out soap any soap opera." Hearing those two separate yet similar descriptions of two seemingly diverse subjects, well let's just say that my curiosity was heightened. Apparently I am not the only one who finds amazing correlation between movies and governance.

I am no more an expert on Soap Operas than I am on politics. I watched one once for a semester in college. There was a TV in the laundry room of my dorm when All My Children began its 41 year run (yes, I am that old) lo those many years ago with me as a once a week viewer as I did laundry. Then my class schedule changed for second semester, my laundry time moved to evening and my soap watching ended.

So what was meant by the analogy of Politics and Academy Awards to soap opera? And which of the two is truly the Great American Soap Opera?

In support of Politics, I have to once again cite my college soap experience. I only watched the daily show once a week and yet I never felt like I had missed a thing. I was able to pick up the story line as if I had seen all of the shows. Much like the health care debate, one can take a break from the heated discussions playing out in the media and weeks later tune in and know exactly where each party stands.

While the political soap opera is all about Republicans and Democrats, the movie industry soap opera was about a woman vs. the old boy's director club and the ex- spouses vying for the same prize. You had Mr. "King of the World," maker of the most expensive movie ever which garnered more gross revenue than ever before competing against his ex-wife, Ms. Indie filmmaker working with no budget, making a film no one went to see, but was critically acclaimed.

So which saga is the most "soap opera-esque?" Much like the academy awards themselves where you don't get a vote (unlike politics where you do but most choose not to exercise that right) I am going to proclaim the victor in this competition.

Here goes. In both arenas the media fuels the competition. They set up the climate for animosity and then sit back and let the participants try to destroy each other. In the case of the political climate it has worked...but in the academy award drama the participants wouldn't play. We kept hearing about the whole husband vs. ex-wife tension and the female director vs. male director tension and the big budget vs. small indie film tension...but wait. Katherine Bigelow had nothing but good things to say about her ex and likewise James Cameron nearly gushed over his delight that his ex had made a great film and was in the running. Oh this was not good for a run in the Great American Soap Opera category. Why weren't they belittling each other? Where was the animosity? Where the vehemence?

The envelope please...

Gosh, Hollywood, I gotta say you lose this one. Politics has you beat hands down!

Yep the winner is; Politics, the Great American Soap Opera.

# Planned Obsolescence

I don't know how to write a blog. I don't twitter or tweet or even whistle for that matter. I am many years past the actuarial midpoint of my life and I am forced to admit that this once very "with it" individual has become one of those...you know, older women.

I find that the longer I live the fewer answers I have and the more questions plague me. Like, why is 50 degrees warmer in March than it is in September? And why do most of us have an old refrigerator in the basement or garage that works just fine when we have already had three service calls on the new one in the kitchen? And why, just when I think I have mastered some form of technology, I find that it (and perhaps me) has become totally obsolete and for my intents and purposes useless.

The phrase "planned obsolescence" comes to mind. When the saying "it will last a lifetime" really meant it, a lifetime was about 20 years less than it is today. And companies seemed back then to take pride in the fact that you didn't need to replace their product every few years. Now, I think it is a strategic plan to have products fail (just after the factory warrantee expires) to insure that new sales will continue to rise.

I look around me at the totally technically savvy young people and I'm beginning to think that maybe we humans were meant to have a planned obsolescence. Were we designed to fail before all hell broke loose and due to our advances in medical technology our elder years are now fated to be spent in the garage or basement with that old refrigerator; the motor, while still working, cast aside for a new "improved" model?

While this might sound a bit depressing, I choose to see it as the, if not natural at least inevitable, progression of things. The risk taking, throw all caution to the wind, mentality of youth is what drives progress, what has made our country and the world keep improving. I remember when opportunities came along earlier in our marriage and Drew and I used to say "let's go for it. We can always start over!" And we did go for it and although a few times we indeed had to start over, the times we succeeded by taking a risk were not only monetarily beneficial they were simply amazing. And now that we are no longer willing to start all over again, it is the turn of the young to follow in our footsteps.

So, I am approaching my planned obsolescence with genuine hope for the future. I might not be able to blog or tweet but I can still make a mark. I am still running albeit in my "garage location" having been replaced in the kitchen by a newer model. Yet I can look around me and wonder; wonder at the great strides our young people are making and will be making in the future.

And I can wonder at the mystery of why 50 degrees is so much warmer in March than it is in September.

# The Battle Over Healthcare

When out and about, many people have approached me and asked why I haven't weighed in on the Healthcare reform debate. I have been able to successfully dodge that question and change the topic of those conversations. Now, with the vote yesterday (Sunday) in the House, slim victory that it was for the Democrats, I guess I should try to express my take on it.

There is just so much in this Bill; did you get a look at the volume of paper it contains? Both sides have ample fodder to speak the truth... ah, or at least their perceived truth as to what it will or will not do for and to the American people. Both sides have their economic facts supporting their stance, both sides read and interpret the numbers provided by non-partisan entities to their own advantage and both sides have sent their cheerleaders out rallying their supporters and trying to get the American people to get on board their own particular healthcare ship needing as many "Maties" as they can muster for the tumultuous seas ahead through which they will have to navigate.

What? Did you think that it was over? Well, think again. It has only just started and my guess is that it is really going to get bloody now.

I choose to ignore all of that. I think those ships will be floundering in the uncharted waters of healthcare reform until the people get a good handle on "what's in it for me." Don't get me wrong, I think that most Americans in a perfect world would love everyone covered, equal access to the best care possible and all of that at reasonable rates. Of course we all would want that. Unfortunately, that just ain't gonna happen so each of us will be waiting to see if we are either better off or, at the very least, maintaining the status quo in our own rough seas of managing our health.

I don't pretend to have any answers to the very serious questions both sides of the aisle are raising about the other side. But there is one given upon which everyone agrees. Our current system of healthcare delivery is non-sustainable.

Democrats got the votes needed by defining this bill as just a first step, with refinements and "tweaking" to come. Republicans see it as totally unacceptable and needing to be ripped up entirely. Unfortunately, both sides have already dug in their heels, loaded the broadside cannons and dropped anchor for an all-out battle on the healthcare sea to the death. And why not? Our Senators and Congresspersons all know that no matter what physical injuries they incur in this battle, they have great insurance coverage to take care of any medical services required for their full recovery. My question is, how many of us will be able to say the same thing about our coverage once this battle is over?

# If the Cliché Fits...

Do you get what you pay for? I wasn't always sure but after trying to redeem those "free airplane miles" I think it is all too true. It seems like a great deal. I should have remembered that if something sounds too good to be true, it is.

We wanted to take my mother and her significant other on vacation to celebrate their respective "80th and 90th Birthdays." The plan was to cash in the miles we all had instead of paying for the flights; after all, a penny saved is a penny earned.

I had miles good on any airline. Everyone else had American Airline miles.
Since American flies to Cancun, I assumed there would be no problem getting us all on the same flights. I should have remembered that to assume makes an ass out of u and me!

I called American. The only flights available departed in the wee hours of the morning, had a stop and a plane change. Yuck! But, with no choice, I booked their seats.

I then called for my "any airline miles" and asked for those flights. I was told my free miles for those flights would cost me well over $300.00 in fees. You could have knocked me over with a feather. But, before I had time to gulp he said that he could do much better for me. Fearing that there was something rotten in Denmark, I listened carefully. There was indeed a method to his madness. I could take a different flight leaving at a better time and flying directly to Cancun; no stops, no plane changes, no fees. Who'd a thought! Delighted, I asked if there were three other seats on that flight. And there were... but he was unable to change the others' tickets. If at first you don't succeed and remembering that you catch more flies with honey than with vinegar I used all of my charms to get him to make the change in their reservations...to no avail.

I called American back.

As sure as shootin', American could not put my husband, et al on the better flights even though there were indeed seats available! There seemed to be neither rhyme nor reason to this dilemma. Thinking it must be me and that there were certainly bats in my belfry, I asked for an explanation. After all, they were American Airlines and there were seat available on these American Airline flights.

I was then treated to a lengthy explanation of how certain seats were reserved for certain free mile plans and all of the American Airline free seats on those flights were already taken.

There was nothing left to do except cut my losses and run...and fly separately! Having persevered through thick and thin, I have to give the devil his due, for we had a trip to remember all the days of our lives.

Ahhh...I guess All's well that ends well.

# Personal Freedom

Personal freedom used to be a pretty simple concept. But, like so many things in our world today, what was once simple has almost inexplicably become very complex. I thought that personal freedom meant that one could do pretty much as one pleased as long as their action didn't hurt anyone else. I can't say when nor can I say why but that simple definition has changed.

Have you ever used a tanning bed? I have to confess that I have not but I also confess to having a long standing fear that they are just not good for you. And I am not alone. The evidence is building; the studies indicating that our insatiable need to look good is once again interfering with our ability to stay in good health. A Food and Drug Administration advisory panel is meeting to consider increasing restrictions on tanning beds. As many as 1 out of 4 melanomas (the most serious and oft times fatal form of skin cancer) in young women can be attributed to their use.

Don't get me wrong, I like a great tan as much as the next gal. In my teen years I was that girl at the beach with a mixture of baby oil and iodine slathered over every inch of exposed skin to get the darkest tan possible! But sadly, that was so long ago skin cancer was barely found in anyone's vocabulary...actually it was the time when the word cancer if ever spoken at all was cautiously whispered with eyes darting around the room to see if anyone heard.

So, now it appears that we have yet another topic for the proponents of personal freedom to include on their list of endangered species. Should our government be in the business of regulating, legislating and/or outlawing actions taken "against oneself "in the best interest of the individual choosing to participate in that behavior?"

While tanning beds are not being banned...yet, it does appear that they are going down the already paved tobacco road. Tobacco, being found to be a cancer causing factor, is regulated; taxed and vast sums of money are being spent educating the public to its dangers. Educating is a good thing, but what is government's role if after being educated the individual chooses to continue the behavior?

Personal freedom. What is it? Are we running the risk of making the term obsolete by our government trying to decide for us what is in our own best interests? If the information is out there, children are being taught the risks and parents, hopefully, are doing their job; if an individual still chooses to opt for a behavior that harms no one else except himself; do we have the right to take away that choice?

It's a sticky question with amazingly far reaching ramification. I wish I had an answer. I wish someone had a clear cut definition of personal freedom. I wish tanning beds weren't so bad for us so we could all walk the streets with that healthy, fit, radiance that comes from a deep golden tan.

# Diplomatic Immunity

Have you heard about the Qatari diplomat's fiasco on board a plane last week? To recap for those unaware of the incident, a diplomat from Qatar went into an airplane restroom and lit up a cigarette. When questioned through the closed door about the smoke emerging, he quipped something to the effect of, "I'm lighting my shoes on fire."

There are just so many things wrong with this scenario I hardly know where to begin and given my limited space, probably won't be able to cover them all, but here goes.

First; what an idiot! Who thinks they can smoke in a plane's lav and not get caught?

Second; who'd be dumb enough to "joke" about lighting anything on fire in a plane let alone his shoes with the obvious reference to the attempted shoe bombing which resulted in all of us having to walk through airport security in our bare feet – just a side bar, in Zurich they give you those little paper booties to wear as you walk through the scanners! I'm just saying...

And to add insult to injury, he was on official embassy business to meet with a confessed terrorist in prison, so he had to be even more familiar than most with the sensitive nature of anything terrorism related.

The good news is that there were indeed Sky Marshals onboard the plane and they were immediate in their actions to secure the situation. There is some comfort in knowing that. What is not comforting is the information that we are now hearing about this jackass being protected from any charges by his Diplomatic Immunity.

Fighter jets were scrambled. The President was briefed. Tens of thousands of dollars (which our government does not have) had to be spent. The plane had to land. The other passengers, at best, had to waste time and perhaps lose money by the delays and at worst had the most frightening experience of their lives. I mean with the world the way it is and all that we hear in our 24 hour news cycles, can you imagine what it felt like being caught on a plane with a possible terrorist and smoke coming out of the john?

So, how will this play out? He gets Diplomatic Immunity absolving him of any ramifications other than being sent back to Qatar.

Diplomatic Immunity? Every T.V. crime show and a bazillion movies have used the Diplomatic Immunity story line as either the plot or subplot of their dramas. We know these diplomats can do pretty much anything that they want with relatively little consequence but, how about having him pay for the mayhem?

I have been briefed on the importance of Qatar to our Middle East policies. Apparently it is a "staging area" for our troops in both our Iraq and Afghanistan wars so we don't want to disrupt our relationship with that country. But honestly, shouldn't someone have to pay for his monumental stupidity?

I think we should find a way to make this idiot pay.

# Risk

Have you ever played the game of Risk? It's a board game that hit the peak of its popularity in the late 60's early 70's. It was a particular favorite among college kids, who after conquering their "munchies" turned their attention to conquering the world. To this day it is a really fun and very interesting game. Players need to develop strategies, both political and military. They must have an accurate sense of not only their own strengths and weaknesses but those of their opponents. The goal is to amass armies and take control of countries and geographic areas. A huge factor in winning oft times is knowing your opponents and forging strategic alliances. The color coded little blocks indicating troop size are piled up on the game board map and hours later a King or Queen of the world declares victory.

I have to confess that while I was usually one of the last remaining players as the game drew to an end, I very rarely won. See, I was naive enough to believe the other players when they struck alliances, pacts and treaties. Silly me thinking they would indeed abide by them. Ah but that was, let's just say, a while back when I was young and not quite as cynical as I find myself to be these days.

Risk is a compelling game with its backroom negotiations, conflict oriented mindsets and power-seeking ambitions; this game...oh wait, is that a description of the game of Risk or the game being played at this point in our own geopolitical history?

When the recent Nuclear Security Summit concluded with various smiling and hand shaking photo ops acknowledging apparent accomplishment, it made me wonder if there really isn't some lesson to be learned from the game of Risk. Let's, just for the sake of argument, switch out those little colored blocks on the Risk board map indicating manpower strength for quantities of Nukes possessed by any given country and let's also ignore the fact that the truly worrisome players at this point in history were not even among those attending the summit at all...well, now things get really interesting and evermore dangerous.

There are currently loud voices railing against players on the world stage for saying one thing in public and quite another in private. Ahhh, news flash. That is not only how the game of Risk is won but it is how world politics work. Right or wrong that is the way it is. Given that, the unanswerable question becomes, "how do we really know who to trust?" Beats me!

But, there are a couple of things I do know. I learned from playing that game all of those nights ago that one must be wary of relying too heavily on the word of others for those who are friends today may one day prove not to be, and an absolute given is that the players will continually change.

I also know that this whole nuclear security issue is not some part of a board game being played. This is our lives.

# I Know It When I See It

I love dogs. We had family dogs during my entire childhood. Drew and I owned dogs throughout most of our marriage up until three years ago when our Black Lab Spike, at the age of 14, had to be put down. I now have two grandpuppies, Radar, the best Yellow Lab of all time and Bob, the most wonderful Sheppard Mix on Earth. Anyone disagreeing can meet me at dawn accompanied by their Seconds.

I do miss Spike's unrestrained demonstrations of joy greeting me every time I enter the house. I miss having a living thing to talk to so I don't feel like I am crazy talking aloud when no other Humans are in the house. And I miss his sixth sense; always instinctively knowing when I needed a little extra snuggling. Contrary to what you may now think, I am not one of those "dog crazy people." I didn't put Spike into doggy therapy when we moved...to ease his transition. I didn't purchase a doggy grave site with headstone for his canine remains, and I don't light a memorial candle on the anniversary of his death.

But, the thought of dog fighting, which is outlawed (just ask Michael Vick) repulses me. And the thought of individuals making a profit off of videotaping and photographing dog fighting is equally repulsive. Up until a recent Supreme Court ruling the selling of dog fight videos and pictures was illegal...but no more.

Does this seem right? Don't get me wrong, I am a firm believer in the First Amendment cited in the Justices' decision. I uphold the right to free speech. I truly believe the test of a free democracy is not only allowing someone to speak words that boil your blood but also being willing to fight to uphold his right to speak those abhorrent words.

But, I have a hard time translating the right to use words into the right to produce vicious torture for monetary gains and self-satisfying purposes.

When the Supremes heard and ruled making an exception to the First Amendment in the famed pornography case in 1982, Justice Potter Stewart commented, something to the effect that, I don't know how to define hard core pornography but "I know it when I see it." The videos and pictures in question in this case, well let's just say, you would know it if you saw them.

This whole First Amendment, Freedom of Speech thing is tricky but, alas, the Justices didn't ask for my opinion. So, with only one dissenting vote, they ruled in favor of allowing these videos and pictures to be protected by the First Amendment.

At least we still have the safeguards against hard-core pornography; or do we. It is being speculated that with this decision, pornographers will be lining up to challenge that decision as well. Makes one wonder, do these Justices still "know it when they see it?"

# Supreme Court Architecture

Many years ago before children, before my fascination with politics, before I realized the true importance of our Supreme Court Justices, Drew and I were invited to attend an intimate reception for the then newly appointed Supreme Court Justice, John Paul Stevens.

The reception was held atop the stately Conrad Hilton Hotel on South Michigan Avenue which in the same design wisdom as those making the decision to land a UFO atop Chicago's Soldier's Field, had placed a new, boxlike, addition atop the hotel. Don't get me wrong, I've heard the "new Soldier's Field" is a much needed improvement and those party rooms atop the Hilton have likewise proven to be great space maximizing the spectacular views of the lake; but couldn't both of those objectives have been accomplished with designs that complimented the original architecture?

Anyway, I went to the reception not really knowing what to expect. Drew was busy talking to several other attorneys and I caught a glimpse of a lone man sitting by himself on one of the couches looking as lost in the setting as I was feeling. As I approached I noticed the very "not in" bow tie about his neck and his rather nerdy posture and general appearance.

I sat. We talked for many minutes, to be honest, I don't remember about what, and then to my total surprise and embarrassment, our host introduced my outcast companion to the group as ...you guessed it, the honoree, the new Justice of the Supreme Court, John Paul Stevens.

Justice Stevens has since distinguished himself on the bench. He is now heralded as a champion for liberal positions. We seem to have forgotten that he was a Republican, appointed by a Republican President. Apparently, as the court changes so do the definitions for the Justices' labels.

So, now skip ahead all these years. President Obama has just, this morning, announced his replacement for Justice Stevens, Elena Kagan, former Law Professor and current Solicitor General (the U.S. attorney representing the nation in cases brought before the Supreme Court). Elena Kagan is reputed, by those who know her and have worked with her; to be brilliant, dedicated and brings a conciliatory presence to the table, preferring to listen to all points of view and easing conflicts between our two parties. I heard it said that "she's just plain likable!"

So, my "friend from long ago" will retire and a new Justice will take his place. I hope that the confirmation process will not sink to the base level of partisan politics to which the electoral process has sunk. And, perhaps, instead of being a box or a UFO stuck atop the Supreme Court, Elana Kagan, if confirmed, will not only change and update but blend in with and add to the distinct architecture of the Court creating a new stronger, functional edifice; the type of edifice our founding fathers intended the Supreme Court to be.

# Israel's Peculiar Position

I was watching Morning Joe one morning and as happens (seemingly more and more) a mike was left hot when it was supposed to be turned off and Joe Scarborough made a very interesting comment. They had been discussing Iran in regard to the Nuke talks that were being held and thinking to be talking only to his cohorts sitting around the table, but in reality broadcasting across the country, he said something to the effect that "well, not to worry, Israel will take care of it."

In many discussions I have had with friends and those I have heard in the media. This line of thought seems to be pretty common among Americans. The feeling seems to be that if all else fails and things really get out of hand, Israel will just take 'em out.

Recently, I was sent an article written by Eric Hoffer for the L.A. Times on 5/26/68, 42 years ago almost to the day, summing up Israel's peculiar position then...and now.

"The Jews are a peculiar people: things permitted to other nations are forbidden to the Jews. Other nations drive out thousands, even millions of people and there is no refugee problem. Russia did it, Poland and Czechoslovakia did it, Turkey threw out a million Greeks, and Algeria a million Frenchman. Indonesia threw out heaven knows how many Chinese-and no one says a word about refugees. But in the case of Israel the displaced Arabs have become eternal refugees.

Other nations when victorious on the battlefield dictate peace terms. But when Israel is victorious it must sue for peace. Everyone expects the Jews to be the only real Christians in this world.

Other nations when they are defeated survive and recover but should Israel be defeated it would be destroyed. Had Nasser triumphed last June he would have wiped Israel off the map, and no one would have lifted a finger...

No commitment to the Jews by any government, including our own, is worth the paper it is written on. There is a cry of outrage all over the world when people die in Vietnam or when Negroes are executed in Rhodesia. But when Hitler slaughtered Jews no one remonstrated with him.

The Swedes, who are ready to break off diplomatic relations with America because of what we do in Vietnam, did not let out a peep when Hitler was slaughtering Jews. They sent Hitler choice iron ore, and ball bearings, and serviced his troop trains to Norway.

The Jews are alone in the world. If Israel survives, it will be solely because of Jewish efforts, and Jewish resources. Yet at this moment Israel is our only reliable and unconditional ally. We can rely more on Israel than Israel can rely on us. And one has only to imagine what would have happened last summer had the Arabs and their Russian backers won the war to realize how vital the survival of Israel is to America and the West in general..."

Written in 1968 and still all too true.

# Who Can You Trust

I don't know about you but the recent "recalls" announced by the FDA really have me shaking my head in despair. Apparently, some of the most trusted names in medicine for children have proven to be, well let's just say, totally untrustworthy. The FDA states that McNeil Consumer Healthcare (a subsidiary of Johnson and Johnson) has recalled infant and children's liquid products due to "manufacturing deficiencies which may affect quality, purity, or potency."

Quality, purity and potency; will someone please tell me what else is important in medication, especially medication intended for use by children?

So, what specifically is wrong with these products? Well, they may not meet required quality standards, or they may contain a higher concentration of active ingredients than specified or they may contain active ingredients that didn't meet internal testing requirements and finally, they may contain tiny particles.

Let me see if I have this straight; unmet standards, too much medication, released to the public even though their own internal standards were not met and the kicker, in my opinion, unidentified tiny particles. Excuse me; they may include tiny particles... of what?

Oh, phew, what a relief. I thought it was going to be really bad.

This recall affects certain liquid infant's and children's products, products like Tylenol, Motrin, Zyrtec and Benadryl. Is there a mom or dad out there reading this that doesn't/didn't have Children's Tylenol in the medicine cabinet? Come on, these are our kids we're talking about. Hey, McNeil Consumer Healthcare/Johnson & Johnson, where is your quality control? Where is your production oversight?

Who can you trust?

Growing up Johnson & Johnson was a name known for quality and dependability. From Baby Oil to Band-aids, Listerine to Visine; I would venture to say that all of us have at least one of their products in our homes right now. These are products that our parents used and they are products that we never even thought to question as far as quality or safety.

And it is not just this case. I am talking about all products, whether medication or automobiles (lest we forget Toyota) that dramatically impact on our health and safety. We assume these products have met all standards, and then some, before being released to the consumer.

Maybe I am totally naïve, but I thought there were some things that one could still believe in. I know we are in a much different world than that of my childhood, but I still want to believe that there are companies out there that really do care more about their customer than their profit.

So, what do we do about it? We now have to research and prod and poke into the companies who make every product we purchase. We have to read Consumer Reports and search the internet and solicit opinions from anyone who will voice them about any given product before we make an informed purchase decision.

To be honest, I don't want to have to work so hard at being a consumer. Can't anyone just tell me...Who can you trust?

# It's a Gusher!

Remember those oh so dramatic scenes in old movies when the lead characters, teetering on the brink of financial rack and ruin, get the phone call in the middle of the night? They were being beckoned to come to their oil rig where their loyal employees have been working for nothing, and that is exactly what they had struck so far...nothing, in an attempt to find oil? And then, lo and behold, the ground is rumbling as our main characters approach. The heretofore lifeless oil rig comes to life and suddenly oil bursts forth from the ground scattering wood from the rigging and dousing our hero and heroine in a slew of black, thick goop. They dance jubilantly about, sloshing in the muck and reveling in their good fortune. They dance, they hug and they dance some more, broad smiles erupting on their oil blackened faces.

Flash forward to our current gusher, spewing we don't even know how many barrels of oil a day into the Gulf of Mexico, and you have not the jubilation of the films from our past, but British Petroleum's (and the Gulf coast's) worst nightmare.

I keep hearing that the Government is not doing enough fast enough. Ironically, some of the loudest voices are coming from those whom also scream that Government is too large and too invasive. Some are calling for Washington to "take over" from BP and solve the problem. But you see there seem to be multiple problems at play here ranging from rampant governmental incompetence, flagrant (if not illegal then certainly unethical) lobbying effort, to corporate negligence and greed; not to mention the ecological devastation. Even if Washington had the means, manpower and expertise; is it in our government's purview to immediately step into a private company's mess and fix it? Now, before anyone screams bailouts...I'm just raising the question...

What is the true role of Government?

Several years ago I became aware of a scientist named Dr. Steven Chu. At the time I was hugely impressed with his credentials and accomplishments and last year when the President appointed him to be the Secretary of Energy; I thought it to be a great pick. I even began a file on Dr. Chu and hoped to write an article about him at some later date. Well, this article is not about him but he has become a player in the Gulf Spill debacle that is playing out in the media for most of us and in the shattered lives of those living in the affected areas.

Dr Chu has been charged with assembling the brightest minds in the world to look at this situation and make suggestions on how to solve it. Interestingly, his own immediate personal suggestion to use Gamma Rays to much more accurately determine the extent of the leakage and pinpoint the affected areas of the pipe line has proven invaluable.

So, as of now, nothing has worked to block the spillage. I am no Steven Chu and I certainly hope his band of the best and brightest can help; but I have a suggestion. BP should call MacGyver. While just a T.V. character not an old movie oilman, there was never a problem he couldn't solve with his trusty duct tape.

# Ah, Spring

This is my annual spring column. One Spring I wrote about my run in with the law as I was driving wrapped in the splendor of the season, windows opened wide, listening to old Beatles, songs. One Spring I wrote of my encounter with a beautiful pigeon while "hiding from my office responsibilities" in the park.

This year, again, I find myself in a familiar setting where not too long ago I wrote of an amazing young man and his seeing-eye-dog. I'm sitting in one of the few areas of Chicago's Loop where one can perch on actual benches instead of the massive stone blocks installed in front of buildings to keep car bombers from crashing into the structures after 9/11.

Not very well versed in flower species, suffice it to say I am surrounded by blooms of brilliant yellow, deep magenta and creamy white; dew, last night's all too perfect gift, glistening on fragile petals in the early morning sunshine.

To those of you who have written to me that your favorite columns of mine are those in which I am expressing my anger or frustration with something going on in our country or in the world...well, sorry; that's not going to happen today so you can stop reading right now!

Today I am marveling at the ever so slight wind blowing the trees, relishing in watching the birds preening their feathers before me and, believe it or not, even enjoying the screeching and clanking of the El trains above and the siren of an ambulance as it passes by. Today I am wonderfully melancholy, thoughts of long since remembered joy and adventure keep popping into my head. Today I haven't a thought of deficits, oil spills, dysfunctional legislators or calling the plumber about that on again off again bathroom leak. No, today I am carefree, even if only for the briefest of moments; I feel, as it should be with spring, reborn.

O.K. confession time; all of this pastoral bliss is not just about the glory of the season...nope, there's more to it. I have a new grandson; born just days ago. So tell me, how can I rant and rave or snarl at what all of a sudden seems so meaningless in the shadow of a beautiful new life?

Every once in a while the former teacher in me surfaces as it is doing right now. I am assigning all of you some homework. Please take or make some time to be outside, doing nothing except observing, relishing in the beauty of all that surrounds us. And take another moment to marvel at the miracle of your children and/or your grandchildren. Please, do this for me...and for yourself!

# The Devil's in the Music

I am really mad. I don't mean peeved or ticked off, I'm talking irate. I have written before about my battle with several telephone companies...well through no fault of my own, that saga continues.

I, like I'm sure so many of you, am totally baffled by the bombardment of advertising proclaiming huge savings, upgraded features and the benefits of something called bundling, touted by every phone service company in existence.

To all of them I say: "You are the Devil!"

These Devils prey on the innocent, the meek and the "please hold and a service representative will be with you shortly" weary among us. Shortly? By whose definition is holding for over twenty minutes listening to that God-awful music, considered shortly?

Simply put, telephone companies have morphed into evil incarnate.

I am of an age where I remember my home phone number being Hillcrest 6-2119. Yes, for those of you younger than I, our exchanges were words back then in the Stone Age, not numbers. I remember when "Ma Bell" had her monopoly and choices were nonexistent. One thing that I don't remember is ever having difficulty with phone service unless a storm knocked out the power lines and Ma Bell always came to our rescue in what seemed to me a timely manner.

But, progress must have its way and we now have choice, lots of choice; but who can make good choices when all of the fine print prohibits us from comparing apples to apples?

Intrigued by the allure of lower rates, I did my due diligence to the best of my ability. Much to my surprise, my very own company seemed to have a package that would reduce my bill and provide all of the services that I wanted. So, in an attempt to reduce my monthly payment, I called the Devil with which I currently have service to change my calling plan. After the mandatory waiting period on hold which was longer than that required to purchase a hand gun, I spoke with a very nice woman who assured me that there would be no problem.

No problem? Imagine my surprise upon returning home from work yesterday to find that I have no phone service at all. Yep, the phones are dead. No dial tones, no buzzing, no crumby "on-hold" music, no nothing...nada.

As I type I am once again on hold, waiting to speak to a representative. Of course with no home phone service I am using my cell. It is going on twelve minutes of holding now and I think I have figured out the secret of their peculiar music selection. I am beginning to feel rather numb. It is as if hypnotized, my thoughts seem a bit foggy. I see an imaginary pendant swinging before my eyes; is this hypnotic drone they call music the Devil's calculated attempt to wear us down before convincing us that they will provide good service and not dead dial tones?

Fie, I say! What a fiendish ploy; for I now know the Devil most certainly lurks in the music!

# They Are Only Human

I remember a time when Alan Greenspan was considered almost a God. If he was to appear before Congress, breathes were held, fingernails bitten awaiting his edict from on high regarding interest rates. On radio and television his name was spoken in reverential tones for he knew, knew so much more than we. He was so much smarter and understood all of the complexities we mere mortals just couldn't comprehend. Presidents from both parties relied on his expertise to navigate the financial waters so they could tend to other problems worthy of presidential attention.

I have heard many suggesting that our financial meltdown should be laid directly at his feet but, back then, he was an American Hero.

Not so long ago the only reason most people cared about professional golf was summed up in one word, Tiger. Even those not at all interested in golf were interested in Tiger. He was perfect. No one on the circuit could touch him in athletic ability, star appeal, fan loyalty and epitomizing the classic American Dream. When he swung that driver and flashed that million dollar smile in satisfaction, we all somehow felt satisfied too.

Hours of television coverage and thousands of print media words have documented his fall from grace; but back then, he was an American Hero.

In the all-American sport of baseball the umpire is the God on the field. Though usually a bit over-weight, balding or graying and padded to resemble the Pillsbury Dough Boy; the umpire is the arbiter of baseball diamond justice. He is the master of the baseball universe. We expect them to be perfect. But with the recently mistaken call heard round the baseball world which deprived a young pitcher of his dream of a no hit game; the umpire too came plummeting from his idealized perch of perfection.

And our current President had that American hero status. If only for a fleeting moment, our country seemed to relish in a new found feeling of pride and hope for the future, all because of this one man. And now, in what seems to be a never ending cascade of crises, the President is being barraged by the angry voices being raised, not only from the expected political opponents but by the disillusioned as well.

Some say that there are no heroes anymore. But I wonder if there ever were any? If the heroes of the past were measured by today's standards and scrutinized by today's 24/7 news cycles having every move they make sent round the world from someone's IPhone pix and every word they uttered recorded for posterity, could those heroes of long ago have passed anyone's hero test today?

Don't get me wrong. I think that we need heroes in the sense that to strive towards the betterment of all we need to have positive examples and role-models. But, should a requirement be that they are perfect? Perhaps what we should be remembering when they fall is that heroes, no matter how high we elevate them, are after all merely human.

# Half Empty or Half Full?

So, is the "world news glass" half empty or half full?

The Economy has lost none of its catastrophic impact on so many lives. And, to add insult to injury, uncountable American lives and incomes threaten to be devastated by the now infamous BP spill. Ironically, the best analogy of the devastation is the old ripple effect. Throw a stone into a body of water and see how that action impacts the previously calm water. Well throw millions, if not billions, of gallons of oil into the Gulf and the destructive ripples spread throughout the country and even beyond our borders. We see the multitudes of volunteers from all over the country assisting in whatever way they can in the clean-up effort and wonder if any of it will be enough.

On a lighter note, there is the World Cup Tournament. Truth be known, I had never even heard of the World Cup growing up. But, I remember when the worldwide popularity of the sport of soccer began to seep into my consciousness. We were traveling in Europe during a World Cup Tournament and much to my amazement, walking down most every street in most every city we visited, chairs had been set up in lecture hall fashion facing television sets that had been moved outdoors so passersby could take a few minutes to sit and catch-up on how their favorite team was doing. It amazed and delighted me. These businesses and residences actually set all of this up just for strangers passing by.

By now there probably isn't much talk about another sporting event; that record breaking Wimbledon match. You know the longest one in tournament history? With bodies worn out, flesh on toes worn off and nerves worn so much more than merely thin, these two young men battled through the pain, through the exhaustion, long past anyone's expectations of their endurance and thus worked their way into every sports enthusiast's heart.

But the big story, in my mind, was about a supremely capable and highly decorated commander of our forces in Afghanistan and his utter stupidity in the handling of an interview with a reporter from, of all publications, Rolling Stone Magazine. I'm sure you have read and heard more than you probably wanted to about this matter, but what struck me was "the non-political party" response from both sides of the aisle and both sides of Main Street. It somehow gave me hope that there are circumstances in which we can come together as Americans and not stand apart as Democrats or Republicans.

I think the most heartening thread running through these seemingly divergent events is the human nature factor. Strangers helping their neighbors in crises, appreciating the will and the guts of athletes, reveling in the joy of sharing a favorite sport; and yes even coming together in a non-partisan manner when simple patriotism calls for it.

Today I choose to see the glass as half full.

# Where to Find the Answers?

There was a bird, having been caught off guard by an automatic sprinkling system, preening its wet feathers before me. Several feet away sat a man enjoying what I assumed to be his first cigarette of the day. I watched somewhat amazed as the bird all at once seemed drawn to the waft of tobacco smoke emanating from the man's exhalation. The bird drew closer and closer appearing almost mesmerized by the scent.

How very odd. I would have thought that the bird would have been repelled by the odor but instead it edged ever closer toward the man creating the pollution. Huh, made me wonder...do birds have a sense of smell?

So, to the internet I went.

After asking "can birds smell" of the geniuses at bing.com imagine my surprise to see that 18,300,000 references were listed. 18,300,000! Suffice it to say my task became a bit more daunting.

I have long worried about the value of the internet as a research tool. We have a whole generation relying on what they read on the internet assuming it to be fact when in reality anything anyone puts out into cyberspace can pop up in a search.

I'm told that the internet is a huge time saver but a brief perusal of the first page of references from my search gave me totally divergent answers. Rather than saving time, I found I was spending time on figuring out how many of the references giving the same answer would be required to satisfy my quest for the truth.

Unlike a good reference library where authoritative looking tomes line the walls and one never thinks of questioning the validity of the texts, using the internet is a much trickier matter. I could employ the old journalistic, Woodward and Bernstein, standard of three collaborating sources to determine the truth but I had already found several references ranging from "birds do have nostrils called nares but they are used for quite different purposes," to "some birds do and some birds don't" to "birds have a great sense of smell;" all with at least my requisite three collaborating references and all sounding equally authoritative.

With the quantity of possible sites to read, the point can be made that not having to go to the library truly saved me very little time at all...if any. And, truth be known, I missed the time spent walking to the library and around the reference shelves.

I find that, what has come to be regarded as the dirty word, "downtime," is to me an essential respite from the hectic hurry that has become our modern-day lives. Call me old fashion but perhaps all of the stress related illnesses and complaints we hear so much about could be somewhat curbed by a periodic, simple stroll through the library.

Alas, I have yet to definitively solve the mystery of the olfactory capabilities of our feathered friends but what I can definitively say is I plan a jaunt to the library soon to enjoy the walk and find the answer to my query the old fashioned way.

# Spy Swapping

The thick mist of the approaching dawn obscures sight
making, instead of recognizable shapes and structures,
an eerie almost supernatural looking landscape. There is
a chill in the early morning air as shards of sunlight
creep into view from the East. Focus begins to clear and
the sight of a bridge looms before us. At either end of
the bridge, parked perpendicular to the massive
structure, sit two identical black sedans, tinted windows
closed tightly. As if on cue from some invisible stage
manager lurking in the wings, the passenger doors open
and one lone man emerges from each vehicle. As they
make their way slowly toward each other on that bridge,
breathes are held, fleeting backward glances in what
appears to be fright at the prospect of being shot in the
back, alters not their ever increasingly hurried steps. No
smiles are exchanged as they pass each other exactly at
the midpoint of the expanse. They dramatically make
eye contact for the briefest of moments and continue
their escape from imprisonment to freedom.

Such an iconic representation of our Cold War years
where spy exchanges between the Soviets and the U.S.,
while not happening routinely, happened often enough
to be a part of our national
consciousness.

To my memory, there hasn't been a spy swap meriting
either dramatic re-creation, or much international press
since the Cold War ended in December 1991. You might
be wondering how I know precisely when the Cold War
ended. It's because we have an International Spy
Museum in Washington D.C.! Did you know there was
such a Museum? Curious, don't you think that a museum
was created documenting a profession whose sole
objective is not to be documented, seen or even
acknowledged?

Anyway, now we have this cabal of Russian spies in the
U.S. apparently being watched by the FBI for some time.

But instead of the cloak and dagger, subterranean, stay below the radar activities of the past, we find a modern day Mata Hari with videos saturating the web and even a few soft porn photos in cyberspace thrown in for good measure. She was "the spy who came in from the cold" apparently to find some clothes.

These Russians were not very good spies. They had trouble concealing their motives, whereabouts and activities. I think, like society in general, the spy game is suffering from technology mania. With competition for who can have the most "friends" on Facebook, to tweeting about grocery shopping, we are obsessed with putting ourselves "out there." But shouldn't someone have told this 21st century batch of spies that the very definition of a spy is; "one participating in clandestine activities?"

And where was the dramatic swap on a bridge? Instead, two planes landed and simply switched passengers.

How unsatisfying to those of us who respond to, yes even relish in the dramatic.

Alas, not only the spy game but Spy Swaps as well just aren't what they used to be.

# So, What Will it Take?

I saw a most interesting video clip the other day. It was a compilation of sound bites from our past eight presidents. All the way back to Nixon, every president has addressed the "pressing need" for the U.S. to reduce our dependence on foreign oil...back to Nixon! And their rhetoric, reasons and reprimands from Obama on back, were as if all had been written by the same speech writers. Yes, these eight men, so different in political philosophy and style, possessing divergent oratory prowess and yet the message was perfectly clear. We must reduce our dependence on foreign oil.

This was not and is not a Democratic or a Republican thing. This was not and is not some kind of jockeying or pandering for political favor. Eight presidents have called for something to be done in passionate, authoritative, yes even emotional terms and yet we have done nothing.

But it is not just foreign oil dependency that disturbed these national leaders. No, it is much more than that. If we do not reduce our own total oil consumption, forget where it comes from; we, our children and our grandchildren are in very serious trouble.

Like most of you I've watched, mourned and fumed at all of the devastating ramifications of the BP oil spill as it continued to gush and gush. Because of this tragedy, once again, the topic of oil is being bandied about the talk show circuit. But, what I am hearing is the old debate: yes or no to continued offshore deep water drilling, to drill or not to drill in protected forestry lands and the influence of the oil companies on our regulatory agencies and our legislators. What I am not hearing is a serious discussion of the American people taking some responsibility, acting in our own interests to attack the problem.

For starters, what if we could get foreign oil at a reduced rate?

If we joined with China and the other, let's say five largest oil consumers purchasing from OPEC, we could demand that they reduce their price for oil down to say...$10.00 a barrel. Why shouldn't we finally take some control in this situation? Impossible you say? Well, if we stand firm, who else will they sell to? But let's say OPEC refuses. I guess we would then be forced to do what we should have been doing all along; some good old American belt tightening. Oh, and there is a really great additional fringe benefit to this scenario. If we don't pay their exorbitant prices and their money supply is cut off, no more funneling funds from OPEC members to worldwide terrorist organizations. Hey, pretty good perk!

But seriously, now that it appears the latest attempt at capping the leak is working, are we once again going to put the whole oil dependency thing on the back burner or do we have the guts to really do something? I don't know what the answers are. I just know that eight presidencies is a long time to be struggling with a very definable problem. So, what will it take?

# Beating a Dead Horse

I hate to beat a dead horse but I can't resist a small "I told you so." Within this column I have expressed my concern about what pops up in electronic communication. How does one know if any of it is factual and/or valid? The old saying "you can't believe what you read" seems so much more relevant today than ever before.

Enter this past week's brouhaha involving Shirley Sherrod. Here's this woman literally crucified within hours over an edited, intentionally misleading electronic communication to which the government and the media responded without doing their due diligence in substantiating its validity. Even I know, and I am a total techno doofus, that every eleven year old out there can edit video in the comfort of their own bedroom and zap it out into etherland. While I do not consider my neighbor's eleven year old daughter to be a threat because she has this technical capability, I do recognize and yes fear the consequences of hate-mongers and fanatics using this capability to promote their own contemptible agendas.

Don't get me wrong. I am not condemning the legitimacy of electronic communication. I am firmly committed to the principal of freedom of speech but I do worry about anyone reading their favorite blogs etc. and blindly taking everything posted as fact.

Now, just today we have a variation on the theme...the electronic leak of secret military documents dating from 2004 to January of this year. From what I have been able to glean, there is not much in them that some or most people didn't already know or suspect. War is messy and dangerous. Allies one day could possibly become enemies the next. Bad things inevitably happen under the cloak of war. Hello! War is supposed to be hell; that is why we should avoid it at all costs!

The real problem with this "electronic leak" in my view is not so much the information contained in the documents as the ease by which anyone can get a hold of any piece of information and send their "spin" about it to the far corners of the world in a matter of seconds.

With modern technology being so efficient in distributing information, instead of "leaks" we should call them "floods!"

But could something good come of these two modern age communication incidents? Wouldn't it be something if they serve as a catalyst to raise an old fashion debate about two pressing issues facing our nation? Perhaps they can spur us to honestly and intelligently discuss the logic of keeping our military in harm's way half way around the world at a cost that is bankrupting our country; and maybe we can have the frank discussion about racism in this country that is so long over-due.

Beating a dead horse? Perhaps the horse isn't quite dead yet!

# Our Consumption Mentality

So, there is this town in California outside of Los Angles where the City Council figured out a way to totally rig the system and allocate obscene salaries for themselves. While close enough to the uber-rich, jet setting, star studded Los Angeles elite to be darkened by their shadow, Bell, California is a small, middle to lower middle-class town struggling to keep afloat. I don't think I exaggerate using the word obscene when the City Manager of this small town makes $800,000.00 a year— yes, $800,000.00; he makes more than the President of the United States. The Chief of Police makes $450,000.00. And then to add insult to injury they announced massive budget cuts to support their own greed. Apparently, this hoodwinking of their electorate has been going on for seven years and would have continued unchallenged if not for an investigative reporter from the L.A. Times.

I cite this case as just another example of the "me first" greed that seems to have become our national character. From Wall Street to Main Street, we are suffering from a rampant personal consumption mentality and to me the prognosis for recovery is not good. When did the American dream become defined as having more and bigger than everyone you know? When did we allow shopping to become a daily ritual for our teens and pre-teens instead of as few outings as possible to buy the necessities? And how do we combat the constant brainwashing from advertising hammering into our heads that we should have, are entitled to have, the shiniest, the biggest, the best of everything and, by the way, two of everything is better than one.

This pervasive consumption mentality has been building for decades and has finally reached crisis proportions. So, what do we do now?

Perhaps it is human nature to want the other guy to bear the brunt of hard times. I can't tell you how many e-mails I get from people agreeing that we need to do something about our economy but at the same time they are furious if their benefits and services might be cut. The cries for change are deafening...as long as it's everyone else that has to change.

But hey, I'm right there with ya! I don't want my lifestyle to change. But we are at a truly pivotal point in our economic history. It is past time for all of us to take a good look at our own lives as well as how our government functions and come to some decisions.

Over three decades ago, I heard the phrase zero-based budgeting for the first time. Briefly it means you throw out every line item of your budget and start from scratch. Then, you cannot allocate any money for anything without at least an equal amount of income coming in.

Hmmm, zero-based budgeting...

I think it's time for us all to go cold turkey on the greed, steel ourselves for sacrifices across the board and insist on implementing zero-based budgeting in our homes as well as in our government.

# The Dreaded "D" Word

Have you been hearing the dreaded "draft" word being bantered around as much as I have? It has been popping up in political roundtable discussions with rationalizations for its usefulness ranging from the quite creative to the essential in importance.

Supporters have put forth many explanations for why it would be a good thing to mandate service by our young people. The latest being it would eliminate the commonly acknowledged apathy about the war in Afghanistan on the part of the majority of Americans. Is this noticeably national apathy the President's best ally in continuing the fight?

The point can certainly be argued but, the supporters of a draft firmly believe that if everyone's son or daughter were required to put their lives in harm's way fighting a war with fuzzy objectives and no sense of an end game strategy, the people would rebel to such an extent that we would have to get out. They feel strong evidence for their case can be presented by looking at our not so distant past...Vietnam. The position contends that by ending the draft, President Nixon allowed the Vietnam War to extend well past when the public would have demanded it stopped.

To me that argument falls into the "maybe so; maybe not" category.

My argument in favor of a "draft-like" program for 18 year-olds or whenever our children graduate from high school has nothing to do with "to be in a war or not to be in a war." I would make the case on altogether different considerations.

I think we expect way too much of many eighteen year olds. Most don't have a clue about life beyond their front door and yet we expect them to decide on a career, pick a major if they go to college, and feel that somehow they are inadequate or stupid if they don't have "it" all figured out. A two year commitment to either military service or sanctioned public service (volunteering in a day-care center, nursing home, animal shelter etc.) would provide a multitude of benefits to our young people.

They would see, experience, first-hand what life is like outside the classroom bubble. They would have to learn to deal with people, problem solve and maneuver through real-life challenges. They would acquire the self-fulfilling sense that only comes from serving and helping others and they would be getting valuable work experience for when they are ready to make those career decisions either after their two years of service are up or after they graduate from College.

Most kids go off to college having never left home before. No wonder so many of them have trouble handling the freedom and so many don't graduate. By putting in 2 years of service, by the time they are ready to go to college...they are ready to go to college.

The D word need not be dreaded. To me it stands for helping our children gain much needed Direction.

# Back To Our Roots

Apparently the people of California aren't too happy about their "Governator" having a cameo role in the Expendables, a film released this past weekend. Some argue that with their state finances in worse shape than even our national economy and the whole gay marriage question roiling in the California courts; it is appalling that Arnold would take the time away from these pressing matters to shoot a movie.

To them I say... for Pete's sake. You were the ones who elected an actor to be your Governor. And, if you know anything about human nature you would know that most of us, at some time or another, return to our roots.

I'm here to tell ya, I think that's a good thing.

Example: If you have children or grandchildren I think I am safe in saying that there are times when even the best children make you want to pull your hair out...am I right? We do our best as role models, we try to instill the values that our parents instilled in us and yet in most every child's life there comes a time when, as if by some alien force, they become possessed by the Rogue Rebellion Rash that seems to run roughshod over their heretofore sensible, reliable former selves. I'm not too old, yet; I do remember my own rash of rebellion in the sixties!

But there is hope. Yes there is. For so many of the wildest kids I knew back then are now the staunchest Republican voices around!

All kidding aside, it seems to me that there is a natural progression of maturing that includes these rebellious "glitches." In order to reach maturity, I think, one has to strike out and that striking out takes many shapes and forms before we settle into, or back into, what is at our core, back to our roots

If we take this observation one step further and apply it to our national identity, well, don't you think it is time for our nation to get back to our roots?

We've had a couple of decades of "me first" and a greed induced coma-like numbness in regard to our fellows, but it is time to get back to the basics of our national nature. We Americans work hard. We Americans play hard. We Americans take more pride in our accomplishments than ourselves. We Americans look out for our neighbors, we love our country and we want a good life for our children.

Yes, I do think it is good to get back to ones' roots.

So, Californians, you should be thrilled that it was the acting roots to which Arnold went back...otherwise you might have seen your aging Governor clad in one of those "muscle-man," glorified g-strings instead of on the big screen!

## When You Don't Care, See What Happens

We've all heard the stories, the almost urban myth-esque theory that once you don't care about something somehow miraculously you get it. How many couples have we heard of who after desperately trying to conceive either settle on adoption or simply give up trying and BOOM; next thing you know they are pregnant. And, what about the desperate single (we all know one of these people) who wants so badly to find that special someone? Once pushed to the brink of despair finally they decide to let it go, move on with their "single life" and finally come to terms with and actually begin to enjoy their life...then BOOM; they find true love.

O.K. you get the point; but, what if our politicians, who seemingly only care about getting re-elected, suddenly stopped caring and just did what they believed to be best for their state and their country? Ya know what? I think that would get them re-elected!

Case in point; New Jersey's Governor Chris Christie. Man, have you heard what this guy is doing? He must be committing political hari-kari by alienating everyone. He has cut, cut, cut his state budget, leaving basically no one unscathed. When he said at the beginning of his term in office that he didn't care if he was re-elected, he sure must have meant it. In spite of the yelling by the power brokers, disgruntled unions and the cries from civil service employees in his state, Christie has dramatically reduced spending. Who'd a thought he could hold to his campaign promise...he is balancing the New Jersey State Budget without increasing taxes.

It begs the question (to be answered later) "but at what cost politically has he done all of this?" Everyone seems very angry.

Personally, I'm having trouble understanding all of the rancor.

Look, to make any kind of a dent in our humongous deficits, whether state or federal, all of us have to pay one way or another. Either we suck it up and take the cuts in services and entitlements necessary or we pay higher taxes. As unpleasant a thought as that is, it is not difficult to understand.

Chris Christie understands it. He also understands that making the necessary cuts to avoid increasing taxes might just cost him his governorship when his term is up. Yet he has the courage of his convictions and doesn't care...isn't thinking about a next term. He is doing his best to fulfill his campaign promises that put him into this term in office.

And guess what? In spite of or maybe because of the fact that he doesn't care about re-election and even with all of the yelling and screaming by his constituents; he still has over a 50% approval rating. If the election were held today, he would win.

Looks like not caring about getting re-elected might just be the key to getting re-elected! Perhaps the President, Congress and other Governors in our nation should take note.

# North Korea's Kim Jong Il

Who would have thought that a little crazy man from North Korea could single-handedly redefine the job description of "Former President of the United States?" Kim Jong Il, North Korea's bizarre little leader might be diminutive in stature but he is unquestionably humungous in ego.

Kim Jong Il, born February 16, 1941 is the de facto leader of the Democratic People's Republic of Korea (most commonly known as North Korea); the official leader of the country is still his long-deceased father Kim Il-sung, the founder of North Korea.

Hold it! Does this not seem strange that a man who has been dead for decades is still the official leader of the country? So, if Kim Jong Il is not the leader of North Korea what is he?

Well, he is the Chairman of the National Defense Commission, General Secretary of the Workers' Party of Korea, the ruling party since 1948; and the Supreme Commander of the Korean People's Army, the fourth largest standing army in the world. And let us not forget he claims to have an arsenal of weapons of mass destruction including but not limited to nukes.

In April 2009, the North Korean constitution was amended and now implicitly refers to him as the "Supreme Leader." He is also referred to as the "Dear Leader," "our Father," "the General", and "Generalissimo." Now those are some pretty spectacular titles!

Last week the "Dear Leader" made international news once again, insisting that a former President of the United States personally come to North Korea for some photo ops...oh and by the way, effectuate the release of a U.S. citizen being held. Replicating the mission of Bill Clinton to attain the release from Kim Jong Il of two journalists last year, former President Jimmy Carter successfully negotiated the release of Aijalon Gomes, an American prisoner held in North Korea since January. Gomes had been teaching English in South Korea and was sentenced to eight years of labor in a North Korean prison after entering the country illegally.

So, what's up with all of this?

Practically neglected by the international press, dismissed by many as a whacky little man, the Dear Leader seems to have found a way to garner, in his mind, an internationally covered voice. Whether smart politics or simply yet another egomaniacal exercise in flexing his international muscle; he has once again captured that all important news cycle sound byte and those oh so envied photos of him standing with a former President of the United States. One wonders if the pictures are hung on his office wall!

I am making light of all of this; but given his oft time bizarre behavior, the size of his army and the facts regarding North Korea's ability to possibly wage a war of mass destruction, this little guy is someone to be taken seriously...but he makes it so darn hard to do so!

# Google Doodles

My Father was a telephone doodler. Ninety-nine percent of his day he exhibited absolutely no desire to pursue, nor talent in, any of the creative arts. I never saw him put pen to paper to write a non-business word. A paint brush was never clasped in his hand. I can't even recall a novel ever gracing his bedside table. Yet as soon as he put a telephone to his ear, a miraculous transformation occurred. He became quite a masterful doodler.

Always in ink, his creations were very geometric, symmetrical and quite elaborate. If there wasn't a scratch pad near the phone, any old receipt, torn open envelope, or most any paper "thing" lying around became fair game, instantly being transformed into a canvas for his pen and imagination. My favorite was the discarded newspaper. I remember turning the paper around clockwise following his intricate patterns as they traveled winding and weaving around the boarders of the newsprint.

My father passed away more than twenty-five years ago and finally his creative outlet of choice is getting its just due. The doodle has been elevated. It has risen from the obscurity of being regarded as mere scribbling (if regarded at all) and has become an art form thanks to, of all things, the internet.

Have you heard of "Google Doodles? "

I hadn't until a short time ago, but apparently an awful lot of people have. Google changes its homepage logo art every twenty-four hours and those constantly changing images have come to be known as Google Doodles.

For those of you that don't know, I have been a Marketing Consultant for over 30 years. Changing an established company logo daily...well let's just say it makes me shiver at the mere thought of it. Logos are sacrosanct. They represent your image, your brand. No one deviates from the decided upon logo in anyway...it is image building's rule number one.

Ah, well, maybe not anyone except Google.

Not only do they break the rule, they have a staff of four full-time artists whose only job is creating the Google Doodles. They even post different doodles for different countries.

So what do these doodlers do?

They take the Google Logo and create theme oriented variations. These variations acknowledge holidays, historic events, current events; most anything really. There are only two subjects they won't touch...politics or anything that can be construed as a commercial.

These doodles are so popular; there is even a newly established "Doodle for Google Kid's Competition." The winners receive college scholarships, and judging by some of the entries I have seen, those four full-time Google Doodle staffers better watch their backs!

I hadn't thought about my Dad's doodling in perhaps decades. I wish I had saved some of them. I can only imagine what he would have thought of his seemingly mindless patterned creations becoming a twenty-first century art form. I would love to have seen his face.

# McCain the Maverick

Now that John McCain has denounced his Maverick Mantle, declaring in his bid for yet another term in the Senate that he is not a maverick, what oh what shall we do to fill the lack of "Maverickness" in the political world? Well, actually John McCain took care of that for us some 26 Years ago when he provided the seed for the growth of his own heir to the maverick throne.

I first caught a glimpse of the young Meghan McCain during her father's campaign for the presidency prettily smiling for the cameras at his side. I was unaware that she had quite a following at the time for her blog "McCain Blogette" which chronicled her adventures on the campaign trail. But now she has emerged, well more like exploded, on the Republican political landscape as some would say the new face of the young, moderate Republican. Others have called her a disgrace to the Republican Party.

As a weekly Contributing Editor to the Dailybeast website and author of a recently released book (interestingly titled "Dirty Sexy Politics") Meghan McCain is not only ruffling Republican Party feathers but those of the old rooster at her own family dinner table as well.

But this is nothing new. After the election she rankled the hard-line Republicans by going on national television with some very uncomplimentary statements about Sarah Palin, Rush Limbaugh and a multitude of other very popular republican voices.

Young Meghan has chosen not to be a younger female version of her father but rather take on those of his views with which she disagrees; actively pursuing what some feel is much needed change if Republicans want to be relevant to younger voters.

She has been making the talk show circuit promoting her book. In a recent interview when asked about her father's reaction to all the hype regarding her views, she said they had a "come to Jesus" moment agreeing to disagree about many things; not the least of which is the don't ask/don't tell issue plaguing our military and the rights of gay Americans in general. She went on to state that she wants to work within the Republican Party. It needs to change with the times and confront what she feels is a disconnect with the younger generation. When asked how she could call herself a Republican, she stated that she didn't feel there to be a conflict between her views and the basic Republican philosophy of smaller government and lower taxes.

Apparently, the Republican Party is not happy with Ms. McCain's outspokenness. She detailed being subjected to harassment and vehemence at Republican rallies. But in spite of all of that, much like her father of old, she is sticking to her guns and continues to speak out on "hot button" items with which she disagrees with the party line.

For those of us that would love to see a rejuvenated Republican platform, perhaps it is time for the Grand Old Party to sit up and take notice of the new maverick in the McCain household.

# Mid-term Primaries

What is happening in the Republican Primaries across the country is nothing short of "a God-sent" for pundits, political satirists, comedians and Main Street pontificators at the local diner; I myself admit being among them. I'm hearing them all laughing (if Democrats) at the "Tea-Party" candidates' victories, espousing with certainty that the GOP is once again shooting itself in the foot and bemoaning (if Republicans) the fact that these fringe candidates have no chance of beating the Democrats in November and thus are costing their own party seats that could cement a takeover of the House and possibly the Senate.

The old guard, the past spin doctors of the Republican message; the likes of Carl Rove, are talking up a storm denouncing these" fringe groups," indicating them to be nothing more than a bit of a glitch in the steam roller that his party will become on election day 2010, flattening the democrats and once again regaining the oh so coveted majority in Congress.

I think the GOP is being rather slow on the uptake with this movement. Hey, party big shots! Time for you to figure out that these self-named Tea Party members would rather fight and lose this November with one of their own than win with one of yours. What does that say about party unity?

And you Democrats out there, you can't afford to be smug, gloating that this is a Republican problem that will only benefit the Democratic Party...very short sighted!

Historically, one issue campaigns can be very effective in swaying an election. If the Tea Party can hone its one issue message, if they can steadily create an image of fiscal responsibility and not fringe lunacy; both parties will find themselves in trouble.

So how will this all play out in November? I haven't a clue.

Perhaps the more interesting question is how will this impact the Presidential election in 2012?

If history truly is an effective indicator of the future then here is one likely scenario.

President Obama is now perceived as very far to the left. So, the mid-term elections are making the natural correction, the historical correction of veering way to the right.

Again, based on past voting history, by primary time in 2012 the country will be once again looking for a candidate from the GOP that can straddle that "leaning to the right," middle of the road fence with aplomb. So, who fits that description?

A good guess would be Mitt Romney. He looks Presidential, an asset never to be underestimated. As a Republican Governor he ran, arguably, the most liberal state in the Union and he has a ton of money. But, will he be the ultimate winner of the tug of war over the direction of the Republican Party and can he win the whole shebang?

I don't know! There are so many variables between now and November 2012, but how fun is it for those pundits and comedians and yes even for we Main Street diner debaters to have such juicy political junk to digest in the meantime.

# Tricks and Gimmicks

I've seen several interviews with Rob Reiner recently. You know Rob Reiner; son of Carl, T.V. comedy writer (The Smother's Brothers Show), Meathead on All in the Family, award winning movie director, and now; philosopher. I say that because at the end of one of the interviews when asked what his philosophy was for making such good, memorable films he answered, "...Honesty. It doesn't take tricks and gimmicks to make it work."

I love that statement.

What if we all lived by that simple concept? No tricks. No gimmicks. I venture to say that we would not be in the mess personally, domestically and internationally which many of us find ourselves today, if everyone practiced that "new golden rule."

You remember the Golden Rule? Great concept; so great in fact it is said to be the basis for all of the great religions of the world. Peel back the tricks and the gimmicks, the smoke and the mirrors of religion and you find the simplicity of how human beings could/should live together in harmony.

Don't adhere to it and ...well we find ourselves in this whole "Mosque at Ground Zero" mess. Though not garnering headlines anymore, apparently ABC will be running several specials this week examining the "American Islamophobia" gaining attention in the world. Talk about a situation bringing out the worst in people; what is this all about? They own the land. They live in a country founded on the principle of religious freedom. They have the right to build on that site.

But is that "right" really the basis for the controversy? I have recently heard of Donald Trump's attempt to, in his words, "solve the dispute." He has offered to purchase the site from the developer currently holding title to it at

25% above the price he paid for it. While citing altruistic motives..."people are going crazy over this...it would create such good will for the Islamic Center and for the developer if they moved the location," he also admits that it makes smart investment sense, a win win situation for all concerned. He wants to "take the vitriol out of the situation" by giving the developer a healthy profit (more than enough to purchase an alternative site) procuring a valuable piece of Manhattan for himself, and quelling the tide of hate festering in the streets not only in New York but across the country; the Donald is painting himself as the arbiter of sanity in being able to divorce himself from the emotion and look at this from a business standpoint. But alas, the developer is asking several times more for the property than what the Donald is offering.

Tricks and Gimmicks?

It is not about one's right to build on one's own property; it's not even about the still raw emotions of Americans regarding 9/11.

No Sirree Bob.

It appears to be about using this emotion filled situation to procure the largest profit possible.

Wouldn't it be a grand world if everyone lived by Meathead's simple statement? It shouldn't take tricks and gimmicks to succeed.

# Frankenfish

It was very late. My bedroom was pitch dark. Though four windows flanked the two exterior corners of the room nary a sliver of moonlight nor starlight was to been seen. I couldn't sleep; couldn't move; could barely breathe. I was very young. I can't remember my exact age but I do remember watching the movie Frankenstein on T.V. that evening with my brothers and cousin. I heard a noise downstairs. I curled into a ball. Was it my parents returning from their night out? Or was it the monster of the movie, huge and ugly and...scary? And, I also remember having the viewing of that classic horror film alter my nightly routine of restful sleep for weeks to come.

Lo these many years later, enter Frankenfish.

Like many of you, I really enjoy salmon. It's healthy, easy to prepare and tastes really good. When first I heard the term Frankenfish a subtle chill rose up my spine triggering memories of that terror filled night so long ago. But then I was fascinated to find that the, to my mind ill advised, moniker was referring to my beloved salmon. It seems we are now scientifically advanced enough to take the growth hormone from larger, meatier species of salmon and inject them into the smaller species creating this new "monster salmon." They are bigger, fatter, reach maturity much faster and proponents say they are completely safe. Opponents say...well does genetically engineered fish seem right to you?

The FDA is close to approving the sale of these genetically engineered salmon. That means that we will be seeing them in stores soon thereafter. The inevitability of this made me think about other "scientifically engineered" food. There is nothing new here. Scientists have been altering the food we eat for decades. Processed foods, for example, are engineered for longer shelf life, greater durability, and let's not forget that all important "yummier looking factor."

But salmon? Salmon has such a natural, healthy connotation. When you eat it you feel like you are doing something good for your body. Will we still be able to pat ourselves on the back for making the healthy choice of salmon for dinner? In this case is bigger better? Are we taking new and improved too far?

Maybe I am just getting cynical in my old age but just that term "genetically engineered" gives me the heebie-jeebies. I think there is enough to worry about in this world of ours without messing with my salmon. I don't want my children and grandchildren to find out years from now that all of this genetic tampering results in negative health issues.

There's an old express that I personally think applies here. "If it ain't broke, don't fix it."

But the truth is I don't know if this is good or bad for us. But I do know two things for sure:
I really like salmon. I really don't like Frankenstein.

# Know Your Horse

Have you seen the movie Secretariat? It is old fashioned and hokey. There is no violence, no sex (actually I don't remember even a kiss on the lips) there are no special effects, no computer generated avatars, nothing blows up and we all already know how it ends; yet...I loved it!

Other than attending an annual Kentucky Derby party, I really know very little about the world of horse racing; but I do remember vividly Secretariat's Triple Crown win.

I had a good friend who was a true horsewoman and Secretariat was her passion. At the time of the horse's Triple Crown victory we worked together at the Midwest Stock Exchange. When entering her office, one's eyes couldn't help but be drawn to a large picture of that magnificent animal prominently displayed on her wall.

My guess is that if you asked any American over the age of fifty to name a great race horse the overwhelming answer would be Secretariat. I think that most of them, whether race enthusiasts or not were caught up in Secretariat's race for the Triple Crown chronicled in this movie.

I confess that I tend to analyze movies from the perspective of extrapolating meaning to our lives today and thus since seeing the movie that is exactly what I have been doing.

This is a story of drive and guts. It is a tale of trusting your instincts and intuition. It is a story of having the courage to risk everything for what you believe.

Mostly it is a story of "knowing your horse."

Bear with me while I "extrapolate!"

I am so sick and tired of the ads for the mid-term elections. In various states across the country it seems that the down and dirty of the final stretch of campaigning has gotten farther down and ever so much dirtier. I have heard of a Nazi re-enactor running. We've all seen and heard of the whole teen-aged witchcraft saga and the homophobic "foot-in-mouth" speech of one candidate has pundits talking while scratching their heads.

The country's anger has given rise to many first time candidates. They have never been vetted. They haven't the experience in campaigning. Some say this is a good thing but good or not it has, in my opinion, resulted in floods of fodder for their opponents to exploit.

I heard one pundit say that the theme this campaign season is to focus on the shortcomings of the candidates and not on the issues. I ask you, when has a campaign season not been run that way?

I think we as voters need to take a lesson from that hokey movie and the story of Secretariat. We should trust our instincts and intuition. We need to have the drive to dig into the candidates' stands on the vital issues and we must muster the guts to seek out answers.

And the moral is; "know your horse" before placing the bet!

# O.J. Revisited

I was very surprised to see the ad promoting the appearance of Mark Fuhrman on Oprah last week. This is, after all, her final season and being touted as the best ever. Isn't Fuhrman and the whole O.J. trial thing rather old news? Remember Mark Fuhrman? He's the detective that committed perjury; was totally disgraced and some even credit him with significantly contributing to the Jury's innocent verdict. So, why after all of these years would Oprah have him as a guest?

Perhaps giving into a bit of morbid fascination, I found myself wanting to see what he was going to say about those horrific circumstances that resulted in what some regard as the most famous trial of the twentieth century. Remember how most everyone was talking about the murders and then the subsequent trial? You couldn't get away from it.

Talk about a reality T.V. show! Who knew we were all seeing a new television genre unfold?

In 1995, I hosted a dinner party in my home for F. Lee Bailey, one of O. J.'s famous "dream team" of attorneys. To set the time-frame, this was about a year after the trial had ended and O.J. was a free man.

F. was annoyingly egotistical, at times anti-social and downright rude. Surprisingly, he was also extremely, even brutally, candid about the trial and those that participated in it, including himself. He had harsh criticism of the prosecution explaining that they had wrapped their whole case around DNA evidence and then failed to sufficiently explain it to the jury. You have to remember that this was long before all of the crime scene dramas wherein we now expect DNA to be used for definitive proof. Back then, DNA was an abstract, and in many minds, an unproven bit of evidence.

F. was no more forgiving of the defense team. In fact he made the statement that "every lawyer working on that trial could have, perhaps should have been disbarred!" (Ironically, in 1996, F. was indeed disbarred and sent to jail while O.J. at the time, was a free man!)

But his harshest criticism was leveled at Judge Ito. Relatively inexperienced and unprepared for the spectacle, F. credited Judge Ito's lack of control and Judicial incompetence with creating the circus which unfolded before all of us watching. He said that if Judge Ito had only allowed pertinent evidence into the trial it would have lasted no more than two weeks. The Judge totally lost control as the two sides of the table fueled each other's fires resulting in a spiraling of theatrics and a plethora of what should have been inadmissible testimony.

I found it amazingly interesting that most of what F. had said that evening long ago was very similar to what Fuhrman said to Oprah.

In hind sight, I think there is a truly important result of that trial. All these years later and gauging by the large viewing audience Oprah garnered for this show (myself included) it is a significant though most unflattering commentary on our modern-day society.

More than just creating reality T.V., this case made the heinous crime of murder acceptable entertainment.

# Pelosi vs. the CIA

Almost two years ago-remember when we had a huge brouhaha erupting on Capitol Hill over whether or not the CIA briefed Congress on some secret ops mission? Leon Penetta, who had recently been appointed to head the CIA, went to the hill, admitted that this program had existed for many years but insisted that he just found out about it. Next thing you know, Nancy Pelosi began a tirade accusing the CIA of never briefing her on the operation and of consistently lying to Congress.

Well. Duh. If you were in charge of maintaining our national security by executing covert operations around the world, would you trust the vital details of those operations to the leak-prone, oft time irresponsible members of Congress?

It reminded me of that great scene in A Few Good Men when Jack Nicholson, on the stand, gets bullied into exposing his duplicity. Ole Jack snarls "You want me on that wall...you need me on that wall....You want the truth? You can't handle the truth!" That kinda sounds like something Pineta should have said to Pelosi.

Well, the sticky wicket was that there is a law instructing that Congress be briefed on such things. Of course there is also a law that says one cannot drive over 55 miles an hour on four lane highways in some parts of our area but I can tell you, if you are driving 55 on one such highway, even the huge Mack trucks will be passing you by as if you are doing 20!

But, back then; this was the lead story of every major news outlet for several days.

So, why take this stroll down memory lane? The truth is I wanted to write about the upcoming elections. I think them to be very important but alas I can't seem to get away from the campaign ads. They're dirty and loud and quite frankly, in most cases, focus on the inane. To me there is nothing even remotely interesting or informative about the majority of these ads with which we are being bombarded. To the contrary, I think they are hindering the campaigning process.

Thus, I found I was without a topic for my column this week which led me to refer to the notes I keep on subjects of interest. I happened across the above tidbit from almost two years past. It once again drew my attention.

That story of infighting between the CIA and Congress dominated the headlines at the time. You could not pick up a newspaper, turn on a news broadcast or listen to a talk radio show without hearing something about the incident.

Then Wall Street received its bailout; the healthcare reform battles raged, the BP oil disaster devastated the Gulf and a myriad of other important headlines were penned upon which we focused instead.

And now "enter the mid-term campaign ad shenanigans" capturing our headlines.

With less than two years passing and oh so many more fantastic headlines created, I find I can't even remember how that whole brouhaha between Pelosi and the CIA ended. I hope these ridiculous campaign ads will be as easily forgotten.

# A New Election Recipe

Now that the mid-term elections are over it is obvious to me that the current process of selecting our representatives both in Washington and locally is sinking into an ever deepening abyss.

We need a new recipe for elections.

O.K. Here is part of my solution. Let's call it "Wendy's Simple yet Satisfying Election Creation, Part 2." (E-mail me if you missed part 1 which ran before the 2008 Presidential campaign.)

1. Campaigns are limited to three months: if a candidate can't effectively communicate his/her stances, opinions, game plans in three months, they should not be running for office. (Ingredients: qualified, articulate candidates)
2. No candidate or campaign is allowed to say anything about an opponent. Let the media do the hatchet jobs. Rather the candidate can only define his/her vision, describing the various relevant situations and explaining how they will deal with them. Position papers on all of the vital issues of the day must be posted and let the public take some responsibility for reading them. (Ingredients: voter responsibility with a pinch of journalistic integrity)
3. No money can be accepted by any candidate. Media outlets must provide "service announcements" anyway, so let them be position statements by the candidates and debates between the candidates...remember they can only talk about what they will do, no attacking their opponent. (Ingredients: responsible media)
4. Finally, average out the millions that all of those PAC's, Corporations and Washington Insiders have donated to political campaigns for the past 5 elections and make them give it annually to pay down the national debt until it is eliminated. (Ingredients: Corporate/Special Interest Group's responsibility with a dash of humility)

So, what do you think? I've been told that I am naïve and it could never work. But why not? We have been adding too much sugar to the mix for years and it is time for us all to go on a "campaign diet."

And while we're at it, I think it is time to reexamine the purpose of our representation on the Hill.

Representative government came about in large part because the populace couldn't get to Washington to cast their own votes on issues of importance for the nation. But now technology has advanced to the point where everyone need not attend a session of Congress to cast their vote, they can e-mail it. The role of Congress would then be to create legislation on issues of importance to put before the nation and let us all vote on them.

One item, one citizen, one vote.

This would totally eliminate "pork pile ons." If the proposed single item legislation is something of importance to the nation, we will vote for it.

O.K. I admit this might need a bit of fine tuning before we settle on the correct ingredients; but, when a recipe is creating unsatisfactory results you either change it or toss it. As much as I am tempted to say "toss 'em all out" I think we need to look at some changes that could make our whole legislative process a bit more appetizing.

# Optimism

It's hard to be an optimist. I don't need to recount the day to day, moment by moment worry that most feel about this current point in history in which we find ourselves. There is uncertainty. We are confronted by incivility slapping us in the face at what seems like every turn...I ask, how many "other cheeks to turn" do we have? There is no greater example of what I'm talking about than the recent election campaigns.

But, the elections are over; campaigns put to bed. The Republican resurgence happened as anticipated, however, polls are showing that the Republican Party has only a 23% approval rating and judging from the election results that of the Democratic Party can't be any higher. I don't think the vast majority of people voted for either the Republican Party or the Democratic Party. I think they voted their frustration with a government that just isn't working.

Are you as worried as I am about all of this and what it means for the future of our children? Will Washington ever be able to work effectively without a fundamental restart? Has our two party system run its course...and our country into the ground?

So many questions; so few answers.

Just when I think my optimism to be buried forever something happens to remind me that there is still hope. Isn't it funny how life has a way surprising us?

I had a most uplifting evening.

I was flattered and quite excited about being asked to judge a speech contest at La Lumiere School here in LaPorte County. While I had never before judged a speech contest, I was anticipating if nothing else, an interesting evening.

Having never been to the La Lumiere campus, I was struck by how much like a summer camp the school seemed. And also, like a summer camp, I saw an abundance of smiling teens roaming in small groups excitedly chattering away. Their obvious delight, the joy on their brisk October afternoon reddened faces warmed my heart. Call me sentimental, call me naïve, but just seeing them lifted my spirits.

The students I had the chance to talk with before and listen to at the competition were bright, engaged and wow, wow, wow, so obviously optimistic. I was all at once reminded of how wonderfully energizing that feeling really is...optimism. To have hope; to have the expectation of a bright limitless future, thinking that anything can and will be accomplished...well let's just say someone should bottle that feeling so we grown-ups could all get our hands on it!

I have raised two solid, responsible children. They are now two young adults in whom I have every confidence. While at times I am tempted to say, "This is all too much!" and leave it to the younger folks like my children to sort out; and then something happens, like visiting La Lumiere and all at once I remember. I remember that feeling of hope and excitement. I am all at once optimistic once more.

# Veteran's Day 2010

We observed Veteran's Day last week. I was invited to attend the Valparaiso Kiwanis Club luncheon commemorating and acknowledging the service to our country provided by our military in past wars and those serving today.

The keynote speaker was a WWII veteran and a good friend of mine, Ray Cohen. With all of the fiction, non-fiction and history texts I've read; the movies I've seen and the conversations I've been a party to about that war; I was silly enough to think that I knew pretty much all there was to know about our second world war. But I was so wrong.

Ray was part of a selective program which took our best and brightest (many of whom achieved fame and fortune in civilian life later) and had them learning and training in their various fields of expertise for entry into the service as officers. Well, not only in life but especially in war, often the best laid plans go awry. After the D-Day invasion, the program was discontinued due to the urgent need for more infantry. These highly educated, specifically trained "brainiacs" found themselves literally in the trenches having been deployed as Privates into the infantry.

As I sat listening to my friend's story, I was filled with such pride in his generation's achievements and in our young people today - serving their country now; their service and sacrifice truly exemplified by the way with which Ray handled his particular war experiences.

I couldn't help but reflect on my own son's decision to place himself upon the field of battle in a very different location and a very different conflict but resulting in equally horrific experiences that have now turned into everlasting memories.

I sat on that sun filled Veteran's Day wondering what would happen if the mothers of "war appropriate aged children" were the ones with the power to decide whether or not a country actually went to war. What then do you think the prospect of war would be?

At our table sat several other WWII Vets and as the meal progressed each of them told tales of their own experiences, not only the terrors of war but things they had seen, military programs and procedures of which I had never heard.

No matter where they served. No matter what their rank or length of service; and no matter if they received physical injuries or not; I believe that no one comes home from war uninjured.

How foolish it is to think that any of us, not having been there, are truly knowledgeable about the events of any war.

With our busy lives we tend to forget to be grateful for our freedom and grateful for the amazing sacrifices required by our service personnel and their families to ensure that freedom. How unfortunate for it to be necessary but how good it is to have such a day to make sure we remember.

# North Korea

I had written what I think was a very cute Thanksgiving column ready to be sent in yesterday. But, as happens on occasion, I felt compelled to shelve it. So, what pre-empted my annual turkey day thoughts? Nothing less than a real threat of, to quote a Russian official, "catastrophic events escalating in Korea."

I must confess to knowing very little about either North or South Korea. I was but two years old when our own war involvement ended there in the early 50's. I have however, done some due diligence on Kim Jung Il, the head honcho of North Korea, for a column I wrote several months ago. He is a very strange little man who has been methodically positioning his son, Kim Jong Un to take over the reins of the country.

Somewhat bizarre reports, including the wearing of high heels and religiously watching Desperate Housewives, have been circulated. And it is reported that he is obsessed with being taken seriously. While not much is known about the heir apparent, there is ample reason for concern.

Late last night, North Korea delivered what seems to be the very calculated second of a one-two punch series aimed at positioning itself in a run for the title of "top tier international contender."

First there was the invitation made to a U.S. scientist. He visited North Korea and as expected, announced to all who would listen that North Korea has a new uranium enrichment facility. This broadcasted to the world their impending capability of producing nuclear weapons. Apparently our officials were already aware of the facility but weren't giving North Korea its due as an international powerhouse; thus the visit of a non-politico to ensure the media coverage to which they felt entitled. After all, he couldn't keep what he saw there a secret!

Effective right jab.

And now we learn that President Obama was awakened early this morning with the news that North Korea has reportedly dropped more than 200 shells on Yeonpyeong, a disputed Island controlled by the South. Their justification being that South Korea refused to halt military exercises in the area. So the South responded with its own artillery blasts leaving the residents of the small island in the crossfire.

Solid left hook.

While not a knock out combination, these two political moves certainly have the international community taking notice. I think that Kim Jung Il is formally throwing Kim Jong Un's hat into the ring and announcing to the world that they are to be taken seriously.

Having made what I hope to be their point, perhaps now would be a good time for our President to call on China to weigh in and defuse what is looking like an escalating conflict. It is certainly not in China's interest to have a full scaled war break out on its border.

So, calm is being cautioned. The call for diplomacy is being heard round the world. One can only hope that this turns out to be a sparring match and not a no-holds-barred title battle.

# WikiLeaks

The wind was howling. A fine mist blurred vision. It was dusk and the dim sunset was blotted out even further by ominous looking clouds blowing in bone-chilling gusts. Two trench-coated figures, with collars turned up, came into view.

Shoulder to shoulder they stood looking, not at each other but out across the roiling sea in front of them. From our vantage point we could not see if they even spoke. In fact, if not for their close proximity, they appeared to be totally unaware of each other's presence. But just that scene alerted us to the fact that some serious, secret information was being exchanged.

How many of these cinematic exchanges of vital, sensitive, national information have we been a party to on the big screen throughout the years? For as long as I can remember; this is the way most of us assumed ominous secrets, you know the Deep Throat kinda stuff made famous by Woodward and Bernstein, were divulged.

Fast forward to 2010 and enter the internet...and WikiLeaks!

WikiLeaks released, to the public, 250,000 U.S. State Department Diplomatic Cables over the Thanksgiving holiday. These were meant to be private communications exchanged between individuals. Now, for all to see, they make many of our Foreign Service employees and many of our Allies' Diplomats look like the biggest turkeys of the holiday!

Man oh man some of this stuff is embarrassing. Makes one think about what we all put in our communications sent into cyberspace everyday. I don't know about you, but I would be mortified if some of my e-mails were put out into the public...and who in the world cares about my e-mails? Common, people talk behind other peoples' backs; but these communications...they are another story.

There is the embarrassing name calling. There are the unflattering descriptions of both friends and foes. But there are also telegrams signed off on by our Secretary of State, devastating stuff about the Iranian nuclear program including the Saudi Ambassador saying his King urged us to "cut the head off of the snake" and apparent proof of Pakistan's nuclear stockpile vulnerability to rogue Islamists.

At the very least these leaks will create tension and distrust between our diplomats and our friends around the world. At worst, our enemies could use some of this information to severely damage our country.

This is no joke. This is scary stuff.

One of the reasons given for the release of these communications is that the more information the public has the better off they are. But, I for one don't totally agree. Timothy Garton Ash a journalist for Britan's "Guardian" summed up the dilemma as I see it.

"There is a public interest in understanding how the world works and what is done in our name. There is also a public interest in the confidential conduct of foreign policy. These two public interests conflict."

In this case, I would have preferred this information to be revealed to the public the old fashioned way; by historians, many years down the road, doing their due diligence and uncovering these documents. Then their release wouldn't have the potentially devastating effect that this leak, at this time, might prove to facilitate.

# "W" Is Back

Many years ago I had a delightful, capable young woman named Pat working for me. She was a devout Catholic and explained to me one day the reason she seemed never to worry. She said that whenever she was troubled she would stand at the window in her kitchen while doing the dishes and say "Hail Mary's." She would instantly find peace knowing that she had done all that she could and the rest was in God's hands. I was amazed and a bit jealous. I would love to have that kind of faith where I could just give it all up into God's hands and not have to worry.

In listening to one of the many interviews George W. Bush has been giving touting his book "Decision Points," the memory of that conversation with Pat came to mind.

While Bubba continued in his very public life, campaigning, advocating, speech-making and Jimmy seemed set on diminishing his already less than accomplishment-filled presidential legacy most every time he opened his mouth; "W" has been virtually silent since leaving office. Now he's talking. From early in the morning till well past his reputed 10:00 p.m. bedtime; he is hitting the airwaves, fielding questions from interviewers.

In one such interview he described the helicopter flight after the inauguration of President Obama in this way. "We had given our all and we were heading home." To paraphrase his next comment, he and Laura were starting their "afterlife in the promised land." To another question he answered that he was proud of what he saw in the mirror and that he never second guessed his decisions. He never compromised his principles for political gains. Much like my secretary Pat, he did what he "knew was right" and then left the rest in God's hands.

That's what "W" said and I believe him.

241

Whether you agree with his presidential decisions and accomplishments or not, what you saw was what you got. I don't think he was sneaky or by any means a master of guile. He was all right out there. Sam Donaldson (also born and raised in West Texas) commented that a West Texan when confronted by a rattler doesn't convene a panel; he doesn't take a poll to determine how he should react. He shoots the sucker and then eats it right off the spit from over the open fire.

What spoke to me loud and clear in the interview was that "W" was content in the knowledge that he had done what he thought was right and the rest was out of his control...in God's hands.

So, he has broken his silence. I for one am glad to see that self-assured (opponents might say misguided) spirit still intact.

While there were many of his decisions with which I totally disagreed, I never once thought that he wasn't doing what he genuinely felt was best for this country.

Whatever else "W" is; he is a true believer...and lest one forget when disparaging his Presidency; we elected him twice.

# The Song of America

I was driving home from work on December 7th. You know December 7th "the day that will live in infamy?" That date, the day Japan bombed Pearl Harbor, was arguably the most important date in our geopolitical history. The attack set into motion a series of events destined to culminate in our nation becoming the lone super-power in the world.

I was listening to the radio and, unannounced; Whitney Houston's rendition of the Star Spangled Banner began. A brief moment of surprise at that song being played on the station I was listening to was quickly replaced by a reactive chill heralding the familiar swell of patriotism which I often feel when hearing our National Anthem beautifully sung.

Our National Anthem is a nightmare of a song to sing really well. It takes extraordinary vocal range and almost total vocal control. If sung with proper phrasing, one needs the lung capacity of an Olympic athlete! Through the years many failed attempts have been made to change our anthem to an easier song to sing for just these reasons.

But, Whitney nailed it!

When she sang it at the Super Bowl so many years ago, she was our country's singer. Movies, Grammies, sold out concerts; she seemed to have it all. Then, like so many, she plummeted from the top of the world into the depths of her own created personal Hell. For years the tabloids had a field day detailing her self-destruction.

As soon as she hit the final note of the Star Spangled Banner, alone in my car; I found my thoughts wondering to our own nation's falling from the pinnacle. The U.S.A used to be on top in every measurable category. We seemed unstoppable.

We rocked!

But like Whitney, we now find ourselves in a seemingly never ending, self-actuating downward spiral. We have the memory of the greatness that was and yearn for that feeling of perfect pitch, breadth of range and melodic confidence to be with us once again.

And like the song, our country, our democracy is extremely difficult to do well. There are variant interpretations of how it should be accomplished, which components to stress at any given time and which to minimize. Through the years both the song and our country have been stylized to conform to popular trends.

Some might say that the mid-term elections were similar in intent to Whitney's family arranging an intervention; a stark wake-up call in the hope that we can curb the descent and once again rise to our former greatness.

If so, we face a time of hard choices. Do we give in and just find an easier song? Do we make the harder choice and hone our craft, rebuild our lung capacity and once again soar to the high notes of democracy that when sung well have the ability to lift us all to that longed for and certainly not forgotten pinnacle?

These are serious choices to make in the coming months and years, but I think none of us want to see America's song diminished by our own lack of discipline and resolve.

# Just Let Babs Sing

I am not an Oprah fan but I am a huge Barbra Streisand fan; that voice, her movies... So when I heard that She would be on Her show I had to watch.

Let me just say; BIG MISTAKE!

Don't get me wrong. I loved the clips from Babs' movies and performances (all of her friends reportedly call Ms Streisand Babs) but the actual interview just cemented my long held thought that people really should stick to what they know and do well.

I grew up with Barbra. I remember the way we were; me and Barbra. I would come home from school and sequester myself in my room and play my album of Funny Girl over and over. I sang everyone's part along with the record. I imagined myself as Fanny Brice. I imagined myself as Barbra playing Fanny Brice. That show and Barbra had a profound effect on my formative years.

In the stroll down memory lane portion of Oprah's tribute I was once again transported back to my room with that old record player indulging in dreaming the impossible dream...whoops wrong Broadway show!

But then Oprah, as she has a tendency to do (and the reason why I really don't like watching) started asking these questions designed to draw out some profound insight or universal truth from basically just an entertainer; albeit a great entertainer but just an entertainer none the less. And Babs responded by giving Oprah this "what are you asking me that for" stare and muttered a basically non-answering answer.

I still think that Babs is wonderful. As she has aged (and so have her vocal cords) she has adopted more stylized renditions of the songs that made her famous. She did sing The Way We Were and I was yet again moved.

But, Oprah, pleeeeese. I don't want to hear about an entertainer's politics or their never before revealed secret to this or that having nothing to do with the reality of any non-celebrity's life. I for one just want to hear the voice sing.

Barbra Streisand became a household name at age 21 appearing in her Broadway smash Funny Girl. In her almost five decades since she has amassed 2 Oscars, 11 Golden Globes, 8 Grammies and an Emmy. She was the first woman to write, direct, produce and star in a movie...Yentl was nominated for multiple Oscars. There is no taking away the greatness of this woman's career.

But why should we feel that just because someone is great at something they innately have the ability to reveal all of life's truths that we mere mortals couldn't possibly discover on our own?

I know that there are many out there who will mourn Oprah's departure from network T.V. after this season; but never fear. Now, instead of just her own show as a vehicle to glean the cosmic truths of the universe from her guests, Ms O will have her own entire network at her command to do so.

Honestly Oprah, all I wanted was to hear Babs sing!

# Twelve Stories of 2010

(To be sung to the Twelve Days of Christmas)

It's the end of the year so it's time to look on back
T'was the year of two thousand and ten

Promises made seem in the distant past
War wages on
T'was the year of two thousand and ten

Dems got slammed in the mid-term vote
Tea Party Rocked
War wages on
T'was the year of two thousand and ten

The Gulf found itself in an oily tragedy
The Brits slicked the Gulf
Tea Party Rocked
War wages on
T'was the year of two thousand and ten

A new word was added in everyday use
What's a Wikileak?
The Brits slicked the Gulf
Tea Party Rocked
War wages on
T'was the year of two thousand and ten

Golf lovers mourn the declawing of their star
Tiger's lost his roar
What's a Wikileak?
The Brits slicked the Gulf
Tea Party Rocked
War wages on
T'was the year of two thousand and ten

Cheers round the world for the rescue of the year
Chile miners saved
Tiger's lost his roar
What's a Wikileak?
The Brits slicked the Gulf

Tea Party Rocked
War wages on
T'was the year of two thousand and ten

The gal from Alaska refused to sob and sulk
Palin's everywhere
Chile miners saved
Tiger's lost his roar
What's a Wikileak?
The Brits slicked the Gulf
Tea Party Rocked
War wages on
T'was the year of two thousand and ten

Those in the service can finally stop their lyin'
Do ask, do tell
Palin's everywhere
Chile miners saved
Tiger's lost his roar
What's a Wikileak?
The Brits slicked the Gulf
Tea Party Rocked
War wages on
T'was the year of two thousand and ten

The Justice system took one squarely on the chin
Blago's still a joke
Do ask, do tell
Palin's everywhere
Chile miners saved
Tiger's lost his roar
What's a Wikileak?
The Brits slicked the Gulf
Tea Party Rocked
War wages on
T'was the year of two thousand and ten

Bizarre hit the stage in a dress all made of meat
Gaga is a Lady?
Blago's still a joke
Do ask, do tell

Palin's everywhere
Chile miners saved
Tiger's lost his roar
What's a Wikileak?
The Brits slicked the Gulf
Tea Party Rocked
War wages on
T'was the year of two thousand and ten

Congress has addressed the increasing national debt
The Loony's added trillions
Gaga is a Lady?
Blago's still a joke
Do ask, do tell
Palin's everywhere
Chile miners saved
Tiger's lost his roar
What's a Wikileak?
The Brits slicked the Gulf
Tea Party Rocked
War wages on
T'was the year of two thousand and ten

Happy New Year to all.

# Healthcare Reform-Too Much to Chew

I am one of those people we heard so much about when the administration was making (some might say unmaking) its case for the healthcare reform package. I have a "pre-existing condition" which, though not life threatening and totally controllable with proper meds, kept me from having any choice at all for health insurance. There was one company which agreed to cover me so I was stuck paying exorbitant prices for what amounted to catastrophic care coverage. I was stuck. What could I do?

So when I heard one of the positive points being lauded as being a part of this new healthcare bill was making insurance available to those with the dreaded pre-existing condition, I was thrilled. This convoluted, lengthy plan which I most definitely didn't understand could actually do something for me.

My joy was tempered and then totally tromped upon when I began receiving quotes for coverage.

While insurance companies must offer coverage, the healthcare bill doesn't prohibit carriers from charging whatever they want. I would have never believed that my current coverage was actually the best deal around!

I admit to only focusing on this one point of the bill, but what about the rest of it? What is this legislation that was passed?

Bob Woodward was on one of the weekend political roundtables. He is a man who has been granted unprecedented access to Presidents of both parties while writing their biographies. This is a man who really knows those "in the know" on Capitol Hill. Woodward made an amazing statement. He said that he knew someone who had "actually" read the bill...all 2,000 plus pages! His emphasis on the fact that he knew just one someone who had read the bill struck me. Does that mean that those who voted for or against it hadn't even read it?

When in school we were all obligated, at the very least, to read the materials required for passing a course. Yet here was a man who is invited well into the very inner circles of both Republicans and Democrats saying that it is a rarity that someone has actually read the bill. No wonder, even though passing, the bill is still a controversial subject; even being touted as one of the first things on the Republican's agenda to address in the new Congress.

So what in the world were they doing on Capitol Hill? This debate waged for months...years and they couldn't take the time to actually read what they were supporting or condemning?

If this one element of the bill affecting me makes me ask, what is the point of having the ability to get insurance if you don't have the ability to afford the prices; what else in the bill is ill-advised and impractical to implement?

Over 2,000 pages which few decision makers even bothered to read, affecting all of us gets passed; don't we need to ask, was too much bitten off that couldn't be chewed let alone digested?

And we deserve the answer.

# 2011

# Airport Security

Just in the *midst of* the recent holiday travel pandemonium, with snow storms pummeling and wind storms thundering, yet another airport had to shut down due to a possible bomb detected in some piece of luggage. The travelers frustrated and delayed by this latest potential terrorist attack were those trying to fly into or out of the airport in Newark.

For those not familiar with east coast travel, Newark is one of the alternative airports servicing the New York City Metropolitan Area. A lengthy delay there causes lengthy delays in most other airports around the country. It's the whole domino effect thing.

While I do not question the need for action in such a case; after all not only my children but millions of other mother's children traveled this holiday season, what I do question is the methods and resulting circumstances in use by our security agencies.

Of course we want all travel to be safe...and we want our government to insure that safety. But I have seen for myself a much more efficient, more logical and more time saving system at work for bomb threats in public places.

Currently in every U.S. airport, we hear a continuously looped recorded message cautioning us not to leave bags unattended. A reasonable assumption is that unattended baggage could contain explosive devices. Thus, when one such bag is left unattended in a U.S. airport, safety precautions demand that the terminal and perhaps even the entire airport be "shut down" until the threat can be assessed and appropriate measures taken before resuming normal airport operations.

Many years ago, in the Israeli airport, long before 9/11 when Israel seemed to be the only country dealing with terrorist plots; I observed a remarkable event. I was waiting for a flight when several H.A.S.M.A.T.-like suited individuals ran past us and approached a bag that had apparently been abandoned on the terminal floor. They cleared a space of approximately 50 feet around the bag, set up a tent like structure surrounding the bag and immediately, safely, blew it up.

Yep, just blew the sucker up.

In Israel if you leave a bag unattended or if there is any suspicion of dangerous materials in one of your bags it will be unceremoniously, safely blown up.

Now, back to my story; the "bomb boys" gathered up the debris having been completely contained in the tent and within 10 minutes, it appeared as if nothing had happened. No delays. No panic. No problem.

Can someone please tell me why we have to shut down entire airports impacting on travel around the country when the Israelis have been handling this stuff with ease for decades?

Doesn't anyone at TSA have access to solutions already in place to handle this stuff? It seems a no brainer to me to at least check with Israel. After all, they have been dealing with their security issues since their inception and have never had a successful attack at either their airport or on one of their planes.

C'mon TSA guys...we deserve better!

# Chicago Politics

Maybe it's the cynic in me or maybe I'm just a life-long, fascinated spectator of Chicago politics; but the upcoming Mayoral election has not only caught my imagination, it has stimulated it.

Come back with me if you will to the time of "the real Mayor Daley," legendary king maker, consummate behind the scenes political deal maker, the man behind the men in Democratic politics for decades. Ah, that was the time.

All at once I find myself in a somewhat dreamy state, mind wandering, not quite awake yet certainly not asleep. Thinking, thinking of the way it used to work in Chicago...

Ahhhhh. A young, bold, newly elected Senator endorsed by a media mogul for what to most seems like an impossible run for the presidency, approaches Mayor Daley. Is it Ritchie or the real one? I can't tell. Alas, such is the way with daydreams...but, anyway Chicago's Mayor is approached.

"What will it take?" the young Senator asks.

"All will be revealed" is the answer from the Mayor.

Wham, bang, the Senator is elected President and wants his best friend to be his Chief of Staff. The friend remains undecided. He has always wanted to be Mayor of Chicago but as long as Daley is in the picture, that seems impossible.

So, to Daley the President goes once again. Most Chiefs of Staff last for only 2 years. If Daley will decide not to run for re-election, the timing would be perfect for the friend to make his run for Mayor. Daley has grown weary of the job and with a terminally ill wife... Daley agrees.

Fast forward two years. The friend resigns from his Chief of Staff post and throws his hat into the mayoral race...but wait. The politically powerful black community of Chicago wants a viable black candidate. Several enter the race but only two are left with whom the friend must contend. Oh and what's this? The one with the best chance of defeating the friend, already a Congressman from Illinois, all at once drops out of the mayoral race. Did Daley make a call? Could the President have whetted the Congressman's whistle with some congressional carrot to pave the way for his friend's election?

In my dazed daydream, even in that diminished state I can see that something just isn't adding up. Daley is the one doing most of the heavy lifting here. When does he get something for all of his assistance?

Wow, just like that it comes to me. Another Daley brother, a very qualified political animal enters the picture. And would you believe...yes the President appoints him to replace the friend as the very important Chief of Staff.

Isn't it just amazingly ironic how all of this played out? One would think that it had all been planned in advance.

I startle myself back to full wide awake. That wild and crazy imagination of mine; what outlandish scenarios the mind can conjure up if left to its own devices?

# When Should We Act?

So many things in life come down to a balancing act. When do you know something should be done? How do you know what/how much action should be taken? I've never seen the T.V. show "What Would You Do?" I have seen the promo's for it. The premise is that you see something happening in public that is just not right. Do you say something? Do you do something?

When should we get involved?

We have all been watching and hearing about the Congresswoman from Arizona as she struggles to heal from that horrific attack. We have seen the spooky, fear inducing mug shot of the alleged shooter. We have also heard first-hand accounts of just how very disturbed this individual is. Multiple accounts of a plethora of anti-social behavior have been documented. All of these warning signals seem to have been ignored, never reported and intervention in an attempt to preclude the devastation that this young man allegedly perpetrated never took place.

When do we intercede?

I just became aware of the story of a public school teacher receiving all kinds of flak resulting from her actions regarding a bully in her classroom. Apparently this little boy's bullying was known to the administration. Staff had to intercede multiple times on the playground. It had gotten so extreme within her classroom, this teacher had private conversations with her students asking what their experiences were with this child. Their replies were so disturbing, everything from hitting and kicking to threatening to bring a gun to school to kill them; the teacher reported all of this to parents and various members of the administration.

Did I mention that the child is only seven years old? Seven and he is threatening to bring a gun to school and kill people.

When no supportive action was taken, the teacher went to the police to inquire about the legality of getting a restraining order against this student.

Guess who is in trouble in this scenario? You got it...the teacher. She has been suspended.

I can't help but wonder if ten or fifteen years from now we will all be looking at this child's mug shot, while a shiver inches its way up our collective spines, wondering how could someone not have seen the signs? Couldn't someone have done something to prevent this? And perhaps we'll even ask ourselves how did we as a society let this kid fall through the moral decency cracks?

I for one applaud this teacher. We need professionals who deal with children to have the guts to see potential dangers and expose them. Unfortunately those that do are also exposing themselves to a whole smattering of personal consequences. Man, what does that say about our society?

What does it take for us to acknowledge that today's bully could very likely become tomorrow's murderer?

Those willing to step in and try to do something should not be subjected to personal attacks and work place recriminations.

When is the right time to step in and do something?

# Yellow Lights and the State of the Union

So, I was driving to my office this morning thinking about the President's State of the Union Speech last week. Though I do have a tendency to be a bit "lead footed" I was going the speed limit. The traffic light ahead turned yellow at that precise moment when a quick decision needs to be made. Do I slam on the brakes throwing my purse and many loose files that I all at once regretted not putting into a briefcase, flying toward the windshield or do I continue on through?

I had learned in Driver's Ed, more years ago than I choose to remember, that a yellow light's purpose was so traffic could clear the intersection before the light turned red. I also remembered that if you didn't have to accelerate to get through while still yellow, you were within the legal rules of the road.

Did you see the State of the Union? Have you heard some of the assessment and interpretation of it? I did and I have and it makes me wonder; has there ever been a State of the Union delivered where anyone thought it was great? We have always had challenges...political "speak" for problems. The good old days had plenty of not so good stuff happening. But, every year our President whether Democrat or Republican is charged with enlightening us all as to the "State of the Union."

I think that any citizen, who cares to know, already has their own opinion on the state that our nation is in and there is really nothing a President can say that will change that fact.

In so many ways I think that our country is smack dab in the middle of the yellow light dilemma. Should we break hard, throwing all that is comfortably nestled on the passenger seat into the dash knowing that we might shatter the safety and security of our old stand by windshield?

Should we accelerate risking the consequences of retribution from external forces?

Should we rely on our current momentum hoping that it will be enough to get us through before the light turns red leaving us vulnerable to being side-swiped by cross street traffic having earned the right of way and proceeding no matter what we decide?

I think these are the choices our representatives have in trying to steer us on the right course. The problem is that there are no clear answers. Any one of the choices could prove to work out or not. It is up to our leaders in Washington to work together to ensure that we as a nation do not get side-swiped by other countries, we don't break too hard risking the shattering the safety of our windshield but rather smartly, jointly gauge the speed and conditions to navigate through on the yellow.

By the way I did not accelerate and I cleared the intersection before the light turned red. I hope our country can do the same.

# The Wild Mustangs

There's a common saying out west among horse people, "The outside of a horse is good for the inside of a man." I believe that.

While certainly not a horsewoman, I do love horses. I find them to be majestic, elegant creatures serving not only the pleasure riders of our time but as a reminder to us all of their invaluable role in shaping this county's past.

While racehorses have that spectacular musculature and almost melodic grace as they run the track, there is something close to legend when thinking of the headstrong, oft times prairie ragged wild Mustang.

Do you remember the movie the Misfits? It was written by the American literary star Arthur Miller for his wife Marilyn Monroe; an effort to convince her adoring public that she was indeed a serious actor. It was the last film in which Marilyn and her co-star the fabulous Clark Gable appeared before their deaths.

The gist of the story centers on the wrangling of wild mustangs. A distraught Marilyn can't rationalize the capture of these wildly free animals much to Clark's chagrin.

While today we don't have Marilyn on one side of the issue and Clark on the other, there is a fight being waged over the rounding up of wild mustangs for permanent penning or adoption. It's an interesting issue that brings many fundamentally American values into play.

There are approximately 33,000 wild mustangs roaming 26 million acres in 10 Western states specifically designated for their habitation. The powers that be have determined that the other wildlife trying to co-exist on that acreage is being killed off...too little food supply for all. So, much to the dismay of animal rights groups, 12,000 mustangs are being herded by helicopters and penned or given out for adoption to relieve the glut on the natural resources. Proponents say it is necessary to maintain the natural balance of the area. Opponents say it is inhumane and regrettably it "takes the wild out of the west."

Is this really anything that can be of interest here in the Midwest? Ah, yes! According to a CNN report, it will cost an estimated 60-70 million dollars, of our tax dollars, to keep these 12,000 mustangs in long term holding pens. 60-70 million dollars! Is it that important to maintain what some consider a proper balance of animal life on very well defined parcels of land?

We are not talking about culling any species into extinction.

I understand that for some this is an emotional issue...for me it is pure economics. My take on this is we can't afford to house these animals. Let them continue in the tradition of their ancestors. Let them roam free. I'm sorry for the other species that are finding it hard to forage, really I am, but I gotta think we have better uses for 60-70 million dollars than to house wild horses.

# Term Limits

Until our representatives have the burden of continuous reelection taken away, I fear that any real progress on the daunting problems facing our nation has little chance of succeeding. Oh there might be the token concession to common sense ala dems actually sitting next to reps at the State of the Union but honestly do they really think that we cannot see the difference between tokenism and actual progress? There needs to be truly non-partisan cuts, major cuts, and significant cuts to programs that we have come to believe to be sacrosanct.

We are a humane people. Our collective heart breaks when confronted by those truly in need. But the reality is that the only income our government receives comes from our taxes and so in lieu of staggering rate increases we must all call for cuts in spending...and not only to those programs that don't affect us personally. We must all be willing to see equitable cuts in those programs which we ourselves have come to expect.

But, in order to be reelected our representatives cannot dare to get out the scalpel and make the necessary amputations. Politics is their profession. They have become dependent on the constant task of assessing trends and polls, strategically analyzing the benefits of any given vote they may cast and honing the image they project to please the majority of their constituents in the hope of insuring their reelection. Can you spell job security? And of course making the other guys out as villains is how elections have been won in the past. God forbid a compromise is reached, a good bill gets passed and the other party gets credit for it!

Our leaders are so concerned with how many seats their party occupies in congress and who has control that they seem not to see that the government has lost control. They need to recognize that our economic state is a war we should be fighting with the same vigor and resources we have given to Iraq and Afghanistan. We are fighting for the health and wellbeing of our nation. We are fighting for the future of our children. Our representatives need to recognize that in war, as unfortunate as it is, there is loss of life and limb. While we may all mourn that loss, it is necessary to come out of this battle victorious.

The really big issues confronting us, our very way of life in this country; this stuff is just too big for one party to deal with alone. Since we seem to have lost the ability to make most any non-partisan progress due to the pressures of re-election and party power; read my lips...term limits. Actually listen to my screams...Term Limits! If we take the pressures of reelection out of the congressional mix and increase the length of one term of service, I personally think great progress could be made.

# The Oscars and Drama

Those of you who have been reading this column from the beginning (and I truly thank you for that!) know I am equally addicted to both the movies and politics. Not incongruous passions; I often find myself unintentionally focusing on the amazing similarities between the two disciplines. While there have been many points in time which have fed my addictions quite satisfactorily, what is happening now is a political/movie junkie's dream.

Talk about drama; all I can say about this place in time is; I am in my glory.

The fiery occurrences in the Middle East ignited by the whole upheaval in Egypt seem to be heralding, at the very least, governmental changes in many countries. Tens of thousands of people are taking to the streets daily in several countries expressing their desire for so many of the freedoms we here take for granted. The story line is a Hollywood favorite. What audience doesn't cheer for the underdog? Talk about drama! Will a unique "Middle Eastern form of democracy" be created or will the powers that prevail simply usher in yet another type of oppression?

Right here in our own country the truly dramatic blaze of emotion coming out of Wisconsin has the entire country watching. Will/should the public sector workers (and only a select group of those) be singled out to bear what they are describing as the disproportionate brunt of the Wisconsin financial dilemma? Will this spark the debate on the viability of unions in the future? Wow, the plot surely is thickening.

And, there is almost white heat being generated by this year's Oscar races. An excellent year for movies, the buzz started early and has only intensified as the date of unveiling approaches. Not always the case, this year I have actually seen most of the contenders in the major categories so I feel particularly qualified to have strong opinions. But, will my choices for the winners prevail?

In all that is happening this week I think there is one common denominator that keeps us enthralled...anticipation. The expression "the anticipation is killing me" is so not accurate. The anticipation is fueling my excitement.

At the movies don't you just love to watch a good story unfold especially when you haven't a single clue as to the outcome? Geopolitically, what a rush to think that what was inconceivable just a few years ago might actually come to pass...really, democracy in the Muslim Middle East! And isn't it time we have the discussion about, not only the role of unions in the public sector but about all of the variables contributing our current financial woes?

I have written my own script for how I think these situations should play out. No doubt you have your own storylines as well. The Oscars will be decided on Sunday. Unfortunately, the other situations will not be resolved with a tidy vote by the Academy. No one will be announcing in those dramas, "And the winner is..." anytime soon.

# The Angel in the Red Dress

He was a large bear of a man. As so often the case, the imposing physique masked a gentle soul. With my children on the floor at his feet, he sat in a chair that always seemed a bit too small for his massive frame. He would tell stories; wondrous stories of his past.

He told of growing up in Vienna. On weekends he would dance in the park reveling in the music of the modern composer Strauss. Waltzes were played from an open air gazebo while girls in full satin skirts were twirled around by their morning-suited beaux. He told of stowing away on a tanker with no papers, no money; coming to his future in America. He told of losing his two brothers to war.

But the story loved most by our family was "the Angel in the Red Dress." After Richard stowed away to America, he wound up in Chicago working as a night watchman in a laundry. It provided him with a room in the back and his days free so he could attend school. The owner of the laundry kept asking him to come to dinner at his home but Richard kept refusing. One night, in a dream, he accepted the invitation and found himself in his boss' living room. There was a knock at the door. When opened there stood a beautiful angel wearing a red dress. Richard woke knowing that this angel had been sent to him.

When asked to dinner again, Richard accepted. Sitting in the living room, sure enough, there was a knock at the door. There stood a lovely young woman named Gerda...wearing a red dress.

Gerda came to this country from Berlin, Germany in 1940 just before the rest of her family fell victim to the NAZI's. She became an accountant and established her own private practice. She and Richard married and led a life of contribution to community and society. She was an avid reader, a philanthropist and astute follower of

269

politics, often sending letters to the Mayor and the Chicago Tribune.

They had no children. With no siblings, nieces or nephews thanks to the war, my children were blessed to receive that love, that gentle guidance, that inexplicable and oh so valuable gift of unconditional love from these two truly wonderful people.

Richard passed away many years ago and Gerda joined him just this past week.

Most every American has an equally interesting story of how their family came to this country. What is somewhat unique to the Jewish immigration stories is that there are those now saying the Holocaust never happened, that it is all a lie. As inconceivable as that is, the numbers of Holocaust deniers is steadily growing. We have lost most of the eye-witnesses to the horrors of that time but we cannot afford to lose the stories as well.

I have told this story in memory of a very special woman who has died. Please tell your stories, whenever you can, so the truth about what happened in World War II will not die as well.

# Reflection on the Snow of 2011

Now that we are past the worst of winter, shall we reflect on our near record-breaking snow falls? Living in the snow-globe that was continuously shaken for what seemed to be the entire winter was so spectacular to look at, it makes one almost forget the nightmares it produced when trying to maneuver around in it.

Out our back windows instead of the half brick wall surrounding our patio, I saw only a mid-window high expanse of snow; the drifting so deep as to eliminate the entire patio up well past that wall. I told myself that if only I could open the door I would once again fall into an old family tradition...and I do mean fall. You see every big snow while my children were growing up, I made a snow angel outside our breakfast room window.

I would don my one-piece ski suit, heavy boots, ear-muffs, hat, scarf, gloves and flop backwards with no thought of injury or discomfort; wanting only to be one with the snow and winter sun.

But, alas, the one piece ski suit has long since been given away. There are no children to laugh and make fabulous fun of their mom acting like such a "silly-goose," and even if I still had the snow suit and the kids were still living at home; I'm simply too old. No sir. No more flopping back into a heap of snow for me.

What are you nuts? I could hurt myself! And once down, I would probably die of exposure from the length of time it would take me to figure out how on earth to get up!

When did I have to begin to think about the best way to get up from the ground? I never thought about it before. I was sitting on the ground with kids or doing some activity one minute and then all at once I was standing. Never gave it a thought. I wanted up and voila, I was up. Now, if I have to get down on the floor for some reason it takes genuine thought to get up. I need a plan, a strategy...grab onto this counter or that chair for support in my rising.

When oh when did that happen?

I've heard a lot of moaning about the snow this year. I also continue to hear a lot about how good things used to be and how much we miss the way things were. I confess to doing a bit of it myself. Not that I would want to, but I really would like to know that should I choose to; I could indeed still pop right up from making the perfect snow angel in the back yard.

Certainly much has changed, but much about the good old days still exists. So, with spring around the corner, let's have no more complaining about the way things used to be. No, let us all rejoice in one constant: there will be inconvenient, pain-in-the-neck to drive around in but oh so gloriously beautiful snow in Northwest Indiana during winter.

# Time to Increase the Choir

Is it just me or do the events of our very recent past have you wondering "what's up with that?" We've seen devastating manmade disasters. We've experienced horrific natural disasters. We are reeling from our own personal financial disaster and to top it off we have the Charlie Sheen train wreck!

Due to our advancing techno savvy, we are able to see and experience all of the frightening details of these events. If you are one of the millions of U.S. citizens who indulge in the "electronic mastery of communication" available to us, you are not only aware of what is happening minute to minute; you are right in the thick of it. The horror can now be instantly thrown in our faces.

Could it be that we are in the midst of some cosmic wake-up call? Or perhaps the likes of all of these horrific events have been periodically occurring since the beginning of time and we just didn't have the technical advancements to be so instantly aware of them.

The devastation to the Gulf Coast caused by the BP oil spill and the subsequent ripple effect slamming numerous industries across our country is still having an impact on us. The financial crisis fueled by not only corporate greed but by our own greed as well, led to a recession from which we are all still reeling. And now we have this apocalyptic earthquake/tsunami killing tens of thousands and causing a potential meltdown of a nuclear power plant. One can only imagine the ensuing tragic effects should that happen.

I don't know about you but that little "do-do-do-do" eerie science fiction, "Twilight Zone," theme song is playing in my head. Have we finally followed Rod Serling into that other dimension he invited us to enter in decades past on T.V.?

So, is there anything we can do?

How 'bout self-examination; it couldn't hurt. Periodically looking at our lives and thinking about how we can do better...could that be what all of this is about? Could it be that we are being deluged by a large cosmic bucket of ice water in an attempt to awaken us and we just keep on ignoring it?

So, if we have been drenched and awakened, what now? Natural disasters are truly out of our hands but for the manmade devastation, aren't there things to be done?

There is an old expression "you're preaching to the choir." I think that applies here. So many of us truly want to do better, think of and do for others, try to aid in making this a better world for all but we are the only ones listening to and connecting with those "preaching to our choir." I think that if our children are going to have a country, a world that we can be proud to pass on to them, we better start making some changes now. I don't know exactly how to begin but one thing I do know; it's time to increase our choir!

# Lincoln and Forgiveness

What is going on in this world? The cascade of one horrific problem after another seems never ending. I think that whether you are an Obama supporter or not; you have to feel really sorry for the guy. Talk about having to multi-task! I would hate to see the length of his to do list!

He must feel as I do with my own list that just when you have everything "triaged" in descending order of importance, something out of the blue happens and there goes your list. A new number one item has usurped the first spot and caused all of the neatly prioritized items below to be shuffled and reorganized. Just imagine, if you can, what the President's to do list looks like. And then think about the minute to minute reshuffling he has to do...who in their right mind would want that job!

I recently heard a very interesting story about President Lincoln. He too had a tremendous amount of problems on his plate. Can you imagine his to-do list? Save the Union. Command the country's forces in a devastating civil war. End slavery. Deal with a truly loony wife!

Anyway, back then people actually kept journals and not just the ladies that lunch, Oprah Book Club types; I mean most everyone. And they wrote letters detailing the goings on in their time in history. These written accounts are the basis for many of our historical texts.

The two people most involved with Lincoln's day to day life and activities were his secretary and his body guard. Fortunately for all of us, both of these men kept very detailed journals of the activities in which the President participated.

Lincoln was, of course, noted for his writing prowess and for a great sense of humor. In one of the accounts found within the journal of his Secretary, John Nicolay, was this event.

In the midst of the war a man came to Lincoln's office demanding to see the President. Just as a sidebar, this was not uncommon back then. Anyone off the street could get a meeting with the President if he was available.

Anyway, this man shows up asking to see him. Lincoln was in a meeting so Nicolay told him it might be quite a while. The man responded that he would wait because "I elected this President and I want to speak with him."

After quite a lengthy time several men emerged from the office and Nicolay went in to see if the President could meet the man.

Lincoln asked Nicolay what this man wanted. His secretary answered that he didn't know but the man said that "He got you elected." Lincoln answered with a smile "In that case, we better let him in."

The man entered boldly and Lincoln extended his hand saying "I understand that you got me elected." As they shook hands the man answered "Yes Sir, I did." To which Lincoln responded "I forgive you!"

I wonder if President Obama forgives us for electing him.

# Libya-the Ultimate Video Game?

Do you find taking in all of the news of what's happening in Libya to be as exhausting and overwhelming as I do? It's all so complicated that I am having trouble focusing on any of it. But, I heard one story today that I can't get out of my mind because I found it to be so disturbing in a way completely unintended by the journalist.

I watched a report from Libya by a journalist accompanying the rebel forces as they approached Gaddafi's home town with the intention of then going on into Tripoli. Here was a man on the ground with the rebels. When asked to describe the make-up and current numbers of the rebel forces; his answer stunned me.

He said that there are perhaps thousands of rebels in the fight with more, after picking up weapons along the roadside as they go, joining up every day. He went on to describe why there is no way to know the numbers because most of the rebels are just getting into their cars and driving to "the front," participating in the battle for a time and then driving home to go to work the next day. The flow in and out of battle has been consistent. These untrained, undisciplined, haphazard warriors make it virtually impossible to put an accurate number on the "rebel force."

The inability to get a count, which was the crux of the report, was not what troubled me.

Believe me, I appreciate and sympathize with those who have suffered decades of tyranny at the hands of Gaddafi and I applaud their struggle for freedom. But what is disturbing is that all of this lifelong frustration that has been building up for generations is now being released by the rebels in real time, in real, deadly battle; not by professionally trained combat troops who have undergone both military and psychological training to equip them for war but by "weekend warriors" jumping into and out of the fight using real weapons - not only killing and maiming but risking being killed or maimed as well.

What will the future effects be on these participants in this ultimate of video games being played out not with battling avatars but real people?

I don't claim to understand war. I am not by any means an historian on the topic, but I do have a son who fought in war in the Middle East and I know the extensive military and psychological training he received beforehand and the support that is available to him now. Yet, with all of that preparation I still see, I feel as his mother, the effects on him of participating in war.

I can only imagine these rebels, experiencing in real time, real life the adrenaline rush of combat without the preparation to deal with it. I have only to look at a teenager's face in a video arcade as he frantically pushes that firing button and the subsequent elation when he has indeed destroyed his enemy; and once experiencing that feeling, unchecked he wants to do it again and again.

No one can know what all of this is doing to the mind sets of those young men fighting, but I gotta say I for one am concerned.

# A Valid Comparison?

A slew of laudatory messages flooded into the celebrity news media outlets upon the recent death of Elizabeth Taylor. It seemed as if no one missed the opportunity to weigh in on her life, character and public persona. A few, who claimed to know her well, even gave us what they considered a glimpse of the "real Liz."

But I think I already knew everything I had to know about the woman.

No one, in my lifetime, could play the tortured beauty like Elizabeth Taylor; or even an over-weight tortured bitch à la her Oscar winning performance in "Who's Afraid of Virginia Wolfe," for that matter.

She had IT; that indefinable quality that made her bigger than life not only in close-ups on a huge screen but at all times. She lived bigger; a recipient of the opulent "Studio System" promotion. She loved bigger; nine marriages after all. She received bigger; who could forget the 69 karat diamond Richard Burton gave her? And she struggled bigger with drugs and near fatal illnesses.

She gave us everything we desired from a true movie star.

The tributes detailed her life from child star extraordinaire to arguably the most famous movie star ever and finally to humanitarian with her very controversial stand on AIDS when it was certainly not popular to even mention it.

I got to thinking about the "timeline" of her life...Child star, to mega star, to humanitarian star and it struck me that our own country has been on sort of the same trajectory as the arc of her life.

When I mentioned this to Drew he kinda scoffed and said that it seemed that the comparison was a pretty big stretch; but I think I can make the case.

The U.S. began as a "child star" of nations exemplifying potential, the founding concepts appealing to all those seeking freedoms and a better life. While there were certainly missteps, along the way, we matured as a nation; our star shone ever brighter.

We weathered dissention from within and battled wars both on our own soil and abroad. Some might say we reached the pinnacle of national success and emerged as the world's only super star...ah sorry, super power.

And now many are saying that we must clarify and redefine our role on the world stage.

Our President and others are stressing that our actions against Libya were humanitarian in nature. I am not saying they were not. But, we are at a really crucial point in our history. As a member of the "world movie cast" and the most powerful star in the film, we can be perceived as and even become the bully on the set quite easily.

While I don't think that Liz lived an exemplary life by any standard; she did have her moments and perhaps now is our moment to focus on only intervening in the rest of the world's affairs with humanitarian efforts when we can and concentrate our sizable talents on our own domestic performance.

# Cyber Security

I attended a seminar that scared the bejeebers out of me. I thought it was going to be about understanding and preventing "cyber threats." Silly me; what I learned was there is no way to prevent them. As soon as a security system is developed, it is cracked...hackers are really smart.

The first computer virus was discovered 30 years ago this year. Newbies at the hacking game basically held the information they had stolen for ransom. But today's hackers have truly come a long way, baby.

It is estimated that 50,000 computers a day are hacked... that's 50,000 a day! And then there are the internet scams. In 2009 there were 140 billion "fake e-mails" sent out, 140 BILLION with a B! And we're not just talking about you and me average Joe computer user becoming victims. The Pentagon averages being hacked four times a month by intruders they cannot track. Heaven only knows how many hackers a month they are able to track!

I went into the seminar thinking that there was a pretty select group of these cyber gurus around. After all, you had to be pretty techno savvy to figure this stuff out, right? But guess what; you, me or any Joe Blow can buy "Hacking for Dummies" at the local book store. There are "Hacking" magazines available. There are even hacker conventions, right there out in the open.

What is up with that?

20,000 viruses, worms and Trojan horses are sent out every day. If you are like me, a bit of definition is required. A worm is a program or piece of code that is loaded onto your computer without your knowledge and runs against your wishes. Just as worms tunnel through dirt and soil, computer worms tunnel through your computer's memory and hard drive. Viruses are like worms but they are self-replicating and thus can transmit themselves across networks bypassing security systems.

Trojan horses are software programs that masquerade as regular programs, such as games, disk utilities, and even antivirus applications. These programs are designed to do malicious things to your computer. They write over certain parts of your hard drive, corrupting your data.

Then there are Botnots or ZombieBots which string all of the power of different hard ware together forming a huge capacity hacking machine. Rootkits are being planted which are designed to conceal that a computer system has been compromised. And Key Loggers look like a typical thumb drive but when inserted log every key stroke made without the user being aware of it.

Do I have your head spinning yet?

Makes me wonder how banks, the government and everyone you buy anything from continue to promote "on-line" this or that touting the fact it is totally safe and secure!

Leaving the seminar I was really mad at the pervasive viciousness of it all. Now I am just sad because it is such a waste. Think what these creative, obviously very industrious hackers could do for humanity if they chose to help the world instead of sabotaging it!

# Does Our Freedom Threaten Our Future?

Decades ago, well before 9/11, when a deliberate terrorist attack on innocent American civilians was unthinkable; I attended a briefing by the Prime Minister of Israel. He was asked, "Why should the rest of the world care about what happens in Israel?" He answered that what happens in Israel is an indicator of what will eventually happen in the rest of the world. At the time, terrorist attacks, while being a reality for Israelis, were not even in the consciousness of most Americans. Unfortunately, his words seem very prophetic now that so many nations have fallen prey to such terrorist attacks.

That statement has stuck with me all these years and surfaced again in my mind after reading two recent articles. One was written by President Reagan's former Communications Director, Pat Buchannan, the other by Former Prime Minister of England Tony Blair. In short, they write about the huge influx of Muslims into the United States and Europe and how that is affecting the "make-up, the fiber of these countries." The Heads of State of many of the European countries have expressed concern, not about the large numbers of Muslims immigrating or even the increased birth rate demographic by their Muslim population, rather it is the desire of the Arab Muslims not to assimilate and become citizens of the respective country they inhabit. They don't want to nor do they have any intention of becoming French, British, Swiss or German. The articles suggest that host nations are being unfairly taken advantage of by those who want Western benefits but not Western values. Within Mr. Blair's article he quotes this sentiment from speeches given in the recent past by the leaders of these European countries.

So, how does this relate to that answer given so long ago by the Prime Minister of Israel? Currently Israel has approximately 6 million people, but more than 1 million of those are Muslim Israelis – they are Israeli citizens working, living and practicing their faith there. Statistics show that within 10 years there could very well be more Arabs than Jews living in Israel. If that happens, an Arab Muslim government will be established and there will be no more Israel. Israel is a Democracy and as such would have to abide by a democratic election. Many might cry that the U.S simply wouldn't let that happen but think about it. What could we do if an Arab government is duly elected and declares that Israel no longer exists, replaced by an Arab Theocracy?

I subscribe whole heartedly to "the melting pot of America" characterization of this country. I firmly believe that one of our true greatness factors is the weaving of strengths from all over the world into the American fabric. But, my ancestors and I'll bet yours as well, wanted to be American. They wanted to be part of the greatness of this country.

While Europe and the U.S., at present, are not facing the statistical realities that the Israelis are; we are beginning to struggle with the larger question of how we preserve our freedoms when it is those very freedoms that might threaten our future.

# A Budget Draft

If you or I sat down with a handful of other adults who year after year balance our own personal budgets, making the hard decisions to keep our families solvent; we could hammer out a balanced budget for this country...I'm sure of it. So why are our elected officials unable to do likewise? Aren't you getting tired of the foul smells coming out of the Congressional kitchen? With every one of our representatives insisting on leaving in their particular favorite ingredients, what results is a reeking concoction not the least bit pleasing and certainly not healthful. But this obsession with brewing a potion for reelection, at the expense of the financial wellbeing of the American people, has been going on for so long; does anyone have an idea how to stop it? There are just too many cooks in the kitchen...too many fingers in the pie...O.K. enough with the cooking analogies! But, I do have an idea.

First, deal with the items in the budget upon which compromise can be reached and cast them in stone.

Second, for the remaining line items, I say look to professional sports. Like the drafting process in sports, I think there should be a Budget Draft.

Here's how it works. One Democratic Squad Leader and one Republican Squad Leader pick their squads from their own given party. Each squad should have an equal number of...let's say five team members. These established team players are there to advise their Squad Leader as to the strategy to employ in the draft when their turn in the selection rotation comes up. And because the President is after all the "Squad Leader-in-Chief" he has a place in the rotation as well.

The three squads then take turns, alternately selecting a line item of the budget upon which compromise was not reached. The squad using their "pick" for an item can then craft it to their specifications. No discussion. No bickering. Once the choice is made, the legislation will be just as the drafting party dictates.

Great thought must be given to not only your own squad's order of line item selection, but to gauging how important any given line item is to the opposing squads as well. You don't want another squad picking an item you want before you get around to it.

I think that the threat of no discussion and no recourse on items you failed to draft could very well make compromising in the beginning go a little smoother. Maybe all would come to realize that getting something of what you want is better than risking getting nothing of what you want.

And if a sports-like draft doesn't work, we can always go another route.

Outlandish wrestler, turned Governor, turned conspiracy theorist Jesse Ventura, a huge hulk of a man, famously locked the doors of the Minnesota legislature when budget discussions stalled. He then stood in front of the doors saying that anyone wanting to leave the room before the budget was hammered out had to go through him!

It's just a thought...

# Osama Bin Laden

Since the attack on September 11, 2001, Osama Bin Laden has been #1 on the FBI's "most wanted list." For all of these years this clandestine killer sporadically poked his head out of obscurity releasing tapes created to roil his followers into frenzies of hate and prompting acts of terror and murder.

Over the past several years, with our own huge domestic problems, this heinous human being seemed to have not only slipped out our physical grasp on several occasions but from our national collective consciousness as well. I don't know about you, but I can't even remember the last time his name was mentioned. Fortunately for us and the peace-loving world, he did not slip from the consciousness of our Presidents, beginning with George W. Bush, then Barack Obama and the entire United States security community. Countless unnamed, unheralded public servants did their jobs well to insure the success of this precise, well executed and ultimately victorious operation.

Our war on terror has affected so many lives here in the states and abroad. We have made so many sacrifices on behalf of righting an almost inconceivably terrible wrong. For a decade we have been at war. And now we as a nation have come to the point where most of our citizens want us out of the wars we are waging; the efforts are just too costly in human life and money.

Perhaps this 40 minute operation, executed with precision and purpose will confirm to our leaders the manner in which our war efforts should be conducted in the future. Only time will tell.

But, this operation has dramatically shown, not only our enemies but our citizenry as well, the amazing expertise we have and what we as a nation can do with it. Perhaps this successful operation will help us focus on the America that rises to the task, perseveres no matter the length of time and gets the job done instead of focusing on petty differences and the nonsense spewing climate in our political landscape we are currently experiencing.

It seems to me that the assault of September eleventh began a downward spiral of spirit within our country. From the initial rallying surge of patriotism, when we seemed more united than I had ever seen in my lifetime, we lapsed into a mounting malaise as one domestic problem after another was foisted upon the backs of the American people and our elected officials sank into name calling and personal attacks. Perhaps this can be another, positive wake-up call to us all.

As days and weeks pass, no doubt more and more details will be revealed about this raid and the preparation leading up to it. By the time this column runs there may very well have been retaliation against the United States by Bin Laden followers. Make no mistake, the death of this one man, while self-satisfying and just, heralds not the end to this war. Yet, I have faith and optimism that the ideals of freedom and justice, the pursuit of humanity extended to all people will prevail in the end.

# Kleptocracy

"Kleptocracy, alternatively cleptocracy or kleptarchy, from Ancient Greek is a term applied to a government subject to control fraud that takes advantage of governmental corruption to extend the personal wealth and political power of government officials and the ruling class (collectively, kleptocrats), via the embezzlement of state funds at the expense of the wider population, sometimes without even the pretense of honest service. The term means "rule by thieves". Not an "official" form of government (such as democracy, republic, monarchy, theocracy) the term is a pejorative for governments perceived to have a particularly severe and systemic problem with the selfish misappropriation of public funds by those in power."

Have you ever heard this term? If you answered no, don't feel badly. In a very informal survey, I asked everyone with whom I spoke for a period of several days if they had heard it and not one answered yes. I hadn't heard it until recently and it made me wonder why that was. It is such a great word; has such a powerful sound to it. That strong "K" at the start followed by the staccato "toc" holding up the middle and finally the ever popular "racy" at the end...no pun intended! And unlike so many words in our collective vocabulary, it says so undeniably just what it means: the "Klepto's" are running the asylum!

Perhaps the reason it is not a term used often goes back to biblical texts...you know the whole, "let he who is without sin cast the first stone," or popular age-old adages such as all of that "pot calling the kettle black" stuff. Or could it be a smidgeon of fear that keeps one national leader from flinging the term at other national leaders? 'Cause let's face it, there so many examples of Kleptocrats running around and ruling within our world today, they could form their own fraternal order!

Hey, wait a minute. Actually that is not a bad idea. Let's see now. How would this work? I think the most abusive Kleptocrats should form their own exclusive club, you know a bloc of sorts whereby they actually can flaunt their "kleptocism" in front of the rest of the world. It would have to be a very exclusive club because these guys have got egos, wow, wow, weee, the size of oilfields!

Membership in this exclusive club would be restricted to those of similar backgrounds and resources, like a typical fraternity or sorority house membership. And the rest of the world, due to their own, albeit more minor examples of Kleptocracies, would be reluctant to criticize the group publically while at the same time privately envying the club members and secretly lamenting the fact that they were not blessed with the resources required for membership in the club themselves.

Yes, yes, yes, this could be really great. And I even have the perfect name for this elite group of "uber Kleptocrats." How does O.P.E.C. sound?

# Spring or Sting?

AHHH, spring is upon us...or is it?

I had the T.V. on while doing stuff around the house. It is, after all, finally feeling like spring. We all know that natural phenomenon, that inexplicable burst of energy brought on by the emergence of spring that prompts us to action. Is it finally seeing the yellow, red and white, oh so delicate, tulips popping out of the seemingly winter deadened earth? Or is it the sound of the mowers and trimmers competing with the joyous chirping of the strutting birds prancing on the lawn outside the open window? Whatever it is, it is good.

After months of blizzards, freezing rain and the teasing of a spring like day here and there, can we dare believe that spring 2011 is indeed upon us?

I was surveying the damage done by the "household chore lethargy" that this past, seemingly endless, winter caused within me, looking around the house making a mental agenda of spring cleaning tasks needing undertaking. It took some time of hearing bits and pieces from a report on the tube before I finally stopped what seemed like a personal bout with perpetual motion and focused on what was being reported.

There is a woman in Florida on trial for hiring an undercover agent to murder her husband – not exactly an unheard of crime. But what fascinated me is her defense strategy. She claims that it was all a hoax. Her husband, by her account, was actually the mastermind of the whole thing in an attempt to get on a reality show. Her attorneys went on to contend that the police were even in on it.

Wow, innocent by "make-believe!"

The meeting when she hired the "hit man" and the subsequent police interviews were captured on tape by the camera crew of the reality show "COPS" which she contends reinforced her belief that her role in this hoax would be featured on the show.

Guess what? Not only was she charged with the crime but can you believe, even worse, she came to learn that she would not be on the reality show!

It was all some kind of reality show sting by the police to get her to confess.

There is just so much wrong with this scenario. For sure it begs the question "what is real" not only on so called reality shows but in actual life. I don't know the nitty-gritty of this woman's case. It appears that the police did employ deceptive tactics (not illegal) in trying to obtain a confession from her...but, it just sounds so absurd!

We seem to be living in an age of photo-shopped images and entire campaigns of misinformation designed to keep us from the reality of the "true picture," convincing us that what we are seeing or hearing is indeed the real deal. How is one to know the truth? I don't envy those jurors.

Back in my little, spring loving, naïve world; I just hope that Mother Nature isn't concocting some sort of elaborate seasonal sting and that spring is really, really upon us at last.

# The New Newt?

The American people have proven time and time again that we are a forgiving nation. We like nothing better than to cheer for a soaring phoenix, rising from the ashes, proving that it can fly once more.

Did you see the interview with Newt Gingrich that's causing so much chatter? As I watched a composed, self-reflective, congenial man before me, keeping an almost eerie calm about him even when asked the personally tough questions, my thought was; who is this guy and who snatched the real Newt?

It is certainly not an uncommon phenomenon for a politician to recreate himself. It happens all of the time. One need only to look at the Labor supporting, very vocal Democrat turned beacon of the Republican lighthouse steering generations of hopeful G.O.P. candidates to the victorious shores of election, avoiding the rocks and currents of political destruction...you know of whom I speak...Ronald Reagan.

But, back to Newt. The Newt I saw last weekend was very different indeed from the one we've all seen of late. Newt had been catering to the far right; Trying to grab the mantle of "the Tea Party Crusading Candidate." But, now it appears, the realistic politician within him is pointing him in an altogether different direction. He even spoke of his need to be more controlled and acknowledged that the majority of the country views themselves as centrists leaning slightly to the right; so that seems to be what he is as well...for now.

There will never be a perfect candidate. All of them "waffle," all of them adapt to circumstances but is that a bad thing?

As House Majority Leader he began his tenure preaching the fire and brimstone of the Republican cause...lest we forget he ended his tenure in Republican purgatory for making so many concessions to then President Bill Clinton.

But wait, just days after the recent interview, the new congenial Newt has somewhat disappeared already. He's accusing the interviewer of "setting him up" and "ambushing him." He has even issued a formal apology to Paul Ryan and his followers for remarks he made during the interview pulling back from his new centrist leanings.

Does he even know who he is anymore?

So, does Newt have a real chance for the nomination? Beats me. Those of us who would like to see a truly viable Republican candidate seem divided in our speculations.

We should not forget that President Obama won, in large part, by roiling up the emotions of the 18-30 year old first time voters, promising a new way of doing business in Washington and almost infecting them with hope for the future...then he hit the brick wall of how things really work on the hill.

Those now disillusioned 18-30 year olds and the new first time voters in the upcoming election don't know Newt. To them he is new. If he can sell them on his conciliatory, controlled nature and firm stance a bit to the right of center, perhaps he does have a chance at the nomination.

Problem: does he have a conciliatory, controlled nature and firm stance on anything?

# The Storm of War

There is a new book out on the Second World War entitled The Storm of War. It was written by Andrew Roberts an award winning British historian and master story teller who combed through reams of NAZI transcripts documenting meetings and conversations within Hitler's inner circle. These documents have only recently been translated into English and released to the public.

While I have yet to read the book, I saw an interview with the author and found his theories, detailed in the book, to be amazingly intriguing. The most interesting to me is that Roberts contends if Hitler had not been a NAZI he would have won the war.

Roberts states, "Hitler's ideological imperatives overtook his military judgments."
I on the other hand would say, "The deranged, anti-Semitic lunatic let his twisted hatred run rough shod over any war time practicality he might have possessed."

If you'll recall (my recollection is from the history books but I know that many of my readers are survivors of this war) Hitler had a very successful alliance with Stalin. The Russians were living up to their end of the bargain. Germany was truly in a very good position to win the war in Europe.

But Hitler was so consumed by his ideological fervor, instead of biding his time and concentrating on winning the war, his maniacal obsession with eliminating the Jews in Russia as well as Europe, blinded him from seeing the practicality of maintaining his alliance with Stalin.

The book cites multiple meetings and conversations where Hitler's advisors pleaded with him to focus on the battles at hand, the strategies for victory on the battlefield; but, the Fuhrer's myopic focus on the minutia of the Jewish extermination protocols occupied his interest.

So, instead of being able to successfully supply his troops, he used his trains to transport Jews to their death. Instead of winning the war and then, from a position of supreme power, continuing the battle of eliminating the Jews; his troops were starving and freezing. Instead of focusing on the hard realities of the war and getting it won, he forced his army to fight on an additional front, facing a Russian frontline which was so large as to be deemed effectively unbreachable; all to quench his thirst for Jewish blood.

What was he thinking? Had he been patient he could have had it all; the domination of Europe which would then facilitate his goal of eliminating the "Jewish problem." After that, who knows...the world?

So, what can we learn from all of this? How 'bout having our politicians knock off their almost fanatical ideologies that have become more and more prevalent in U.S. political campaigns and concentrate instead on the bigger picture; the rights of all Americans to believe and think and speak freely, respect for those that disagree and to be willing to compromise for the betterment of the nation.

If Hitler had concentrated on the big picture instead of the minutia fueling his ideology of hate, today you all might be goose stepping and yelling "Sieg Heil" ... I of course would be dead.

# Women's Lib

I have always hated the term Women's Lib and the stereotypical portrait that evolved of the women leading and participating in it. While growing up in the midst of the sexual revolution, I just wasn't comfortable with the stereotyping. The labeling and prejudging of any group or ideal seems very dangerous to me...in the abstract. In reality I think we all do it to some extent.

Anyway, now decades later, I had assumed that the Women's Movement had made huge strides in leveling the playing field for women in the workplace. Apparently, I am very wrong about that.

I heard an interesting and eye-opening debate on the topic of the lasting, and even more disturbing, growing disparity in all aspects between men and women in the workplace. Statistics show the numbers of women in upper management, their pay level and prestige still fall short of their male counterparts. One male participant in the debate, when the discussion turned to female sexuality playing a role, stated the very nonpolitically correct opinion that women should use their sexuality as an asset to succeed. A lengthy discussion ensued about men's perception of women and the male vs. female psyche.

Do you remember that infamous movie scene where the beautiful Sharon Stone is being interrogated by a panel of detectives as a suspect in a murder investigation? She is seated facing the group of men. When asked a tough question the camera panned from her face to the now famous "up her skirt" shot as she spread her legs – cut to a shot of the men flustered and speechless. They then backed off of the question. I almost laughed out loud in the theater. I turned to my husband and whispered, "Are men really that stupid?" His reply was simple, "Yes."

Later, in discussions of the movie amongst our friends, opinions were unanimously drawn along male/female lines; the women thought it was absurd to believe that a quick peek would derail an investigation while the men held fast that it was not absurd at all.

And now 20 odd years later I am hearing a discussion about whether or not women should use their sexuality as an asset in the workplace.

I think workplaces are very complicated microcosms of our very complicated world. Every employee brings into it their own unique set of assets. Whether consciously or subconsciously everyone chooses which set of assets to use on any given assignment on any given day. Do I have to say that not only are men and women different ... every person is different! We need to try to ignore our predisposition to stereotype and assume and learn for ourselves what the mettle of the person standing in front of us really is.

There will always be workplace games. There are those that play really well and those of us that just manage to eke out a completed game. In life, as in sports, innate talent, acquired skill and just plain luck may vary but for heaven's sake, isn't it time to have men and women participate equally on, at least, the same playing field?

# The Great Race

I really didn't pay much attention to the Indy 500 this year. Truth be known, I just don't get watching cars, even if they are going hundreds of miles an hour, driving around in circles for hours. And the chance that there could be a really cool crash holds no appeal for me either ... my bad!

While car racing just doesn't do it for me, I do enjoy watching other types of races and I am not alone. Nary a month goes by without some news show reporting on an oftentimes bizarre competition somewhere in the country.

And now we have another race threatening to replace our own Indy as the granddaddy of all races; enter the Sleazebag Derby.

With the latest entry into the long history of idiotic, not to mention disgusting, behavior by some of our male politicians, this whole Weiner sexting debacle has him solidly in contention for the title. Following closely on the heels of John Edwards and Arnold Schwarzenegger, who were previously neck and neck in the obviously coveted Supreme Sleazebag Trophy race, and just when one of those letches seemed the inevitable winner; a dark horse competitor, Anthony Weiner, has added to the suspense making the competition a real nail biter.

What is with these men? How can seemingly really smart guys be so stupid? Let's just ignore the moral aspects of this seedy affair for the purposes of our discussion. Message to Weiner: never ever use technology you obviously don't understand.

I have often owned up to my own techno doofusness but even I know that once tweeted or posted the material is, in all likelihood, available to anyone wishing to find it. I don't know which indicates more idiocy; that he didn't know this or that he would risk his job and his reputation, not to mention his marriage, by sexting in the first place.

I believe that a politician's personal life should stay personal as long as what is done isn't against the law and it doesn't impact on the job he or she is doing. Hello Mr. Weiner; once posted, it isn't personal anymore. It is out there. It is public. And what in the world were you thinking when you got caught and then denied it? Have you learned nothing from the whole Bill Clinton, "I did not have sexual relations with that woman" scandal?

If you have to act stupidly, revving your engine to feel mighty or sexy, at least when caught confess, you moron. You know you are going to have to take responsibility for your actions at some point in time. Save yourself some small speck of self-respect and own up to it sooner rather than later.

Alas, this particular race has become every bit as boring to me as watching the Indy 500 so, c'mon you guys wise up. You're gonna get caught?

For Pete's sake: Gentlemen stop your engines!

# The Future Of Books

I love books. I have them in most every room in the house. From a très petite, antique, four volume set of French mysteries in my dining room, to the cookbooks in my kitchen and the various shaped and sized book shelves in most every other room; I feel happy surrounded by books.

So, when first I heard about these electronic reader thingamajigs, I thought that they seemed to be clever gismos but the unthinkable; the impossible result of their fad-like emergence would never put my beloved books in jeopardy.

Have you seen the commercial for one such device running on T.V. with a young man and woman discussing the advantages of reading with one of these electronic readers instead of reading a book? Well let me tell you, I was ready for the book reader to really let the device reader have it. I wanting to hear how there are no words to describe how a book feels in your hands. You can't duplicate the suspense as you slowly turn the page before you have even completed the final sentence of it, not wanting to miss one second before beginning the new page. And if the publisher has done the job right, you can feel the paper quality and register the fonts used and seek the insights into the soul of the text by studying the jacket cover design; all adding to the ambience of the content, adding to the enjoyment of the reader. But, the book reader in the commercial could only come up with the satisfaction derived from folding down a page to mark the spot. Say what?

I began writing my first novel in 1974. Religiously I took red ballpoint pen in hand and constructed sentences, oh so painstakingly, on yellow legal pads. Much like the olfactory offensive lucky socks of the professional athlete not wanting to tempt fate by washing them; it would never have occurred to me to place my thoughts, my words down in any other way.

Before long, word possessors became the rage for professional writers and then personal computers hit everyone's desk. Still I wrote long hand in my red ink on my yellow legal pads.

I was finally dragged kicking and screaming into the new world of easy cutting and pasting, the wonderful world of spell check and running word counts...what had I been so stubborn about? This creating on computer was great.

With those memories in mind, I straightened my back, took a deep breath and marched into the electronic reader infested present; I bought one!

So, here is my take. I like it. It is convenient. Downloading books takes very little time and prices are better than in the book store. It is easier to tote along than a book so the unexpected wait can turn into reading time very easily.

But, just as I still have my red pen and yellow legal paper drafts of old, there will always be a place in my heart and my home for books. Nothing can ever replace owning a real book.

# We All Need a Recess

 You may have noticed that I have been somewhat uncharacteristically silent on the whole debt ceiling debate. Every time either side starts spouting their talking points and using their buzz words all I can think of is "ho hum, been there heard that." Well, no more!

O.K. watch out cause here comes the spewing of incredulity accumulated in all that time I spent mute.

Have you seen the clip from a speech the President made last week where he used his children's discipline in doing their homework as a means by which to take a jab at the Congress? Let's give the man his due; it was a great analogy of the situation. What the @#%* are they thinking on Capitol Hill? When they've known for months about this decision that must be made why haven't they acted before the witching hour? Obama used his kid's homework for the framework of his poke, I just use common sense. In all of our lives, when decisions need to be made, we gather as many facts as possible and then make them. Even the hard decisions, some literally life or death; we make them.

I confess to being less than astute when it comes to high finance and the intricacies of our massive economic system but I have had experience in balancing budgets and debt, both professionally and personally. I'm sure we have all had to sacrifice and make some tough choices in our lives. Is it too much to ask of our representatives to do the same; to stay the course until an agreement is forged that will avert what everyone is saying could be a catastrophic financial disaster? After all, that is the job they were elected to do.

And the kicker ... Congress was going to take a two week recess for the 4th of July holiday right in the middle of this crisis.

Who gets two weeks off for the 4th? And those two weeks were in addition to the 45 days of recesses they have taken already this year! 45 days and the year is only half over. 45 days, that is a month and a half out of six that they have not been on the hill doing what we sent them there to do.

I don't know about you, but in my 35+ years in business I have never been given more than 2 weeks a year, total, for "recess!" I've heard the arguments about their need to get back home to hear from their constituents, but I am a constituent and I would rather my representatives stay in Washington and make some progress on our huge national problems than come back here with excuses and all of their political ideology spouting.

So, do they need all these recesses? It seems to me they get plenty of perks that we commoners only dream of. I think it is all of us who need a recess...a recess from representatives who seem unable to figure out what the real job they were elected to do really is.

# My Mom

In this space of five hundred words, give or take, I have often referenced my Grandmother's common sense and innate natural instincts. Yesterday, while working on my words for this week's column it struck me that I have not referenced any of the truly valuable, humane and sensible advice offered to me by my Mother.

My Mom passed away two weeks ago so in tribute and to rectify the gross omission on my part stated above; here's to you Mom.

My Mom lived 86 years in style and grace; a woman of intelligence, compassion and generosity. She was a most loving daughter, wife, mother, grandmother and great grandmother; a staunch and loyal friend. My Mom was in every sense "the epitome of the good woman." Born with the riches of a loving family, she was a golden child adored by parents and a close knit extended family. She had it all, brains, talent, beauty and the power that comes with being truly loved. From her early teen years when she and my Aunt Blossom appeared weekly on the radio as a "sister act" where she sang and played the straight man for Blossom's jokes, until her last days, she sang in clear pitch-perfect tones and to my mind she lived her life pitch-perfect as well.

As in all lives she endured pain and the uncertainties that are inevitable in our human existence but she always not only survived but thrived with her wonderful sense of humor and joie de vivre which seemed to infect all who knew her.

My Mom was a really good time!

She had room in her heart for all who came in contact with her. Even at the end of her life she was still finishing crossword puzzles daily...in ink!, playing bridge, attending current events lectures, the theater and reading her novels. She never stopped feeding her intellect and spirit.

She was my Mother, which between us meant my harshest critic when called for, my wise mentor, and adored loved one. Anything that is good within me was born and survives because of her nurturing and never-ending, unwavering love. If I am a good wife, mother, grandmother; it is because of her example.

I don't know of a mean spirited action or harsh word spoken by her with intent to harm or debase. She was kind and generous and in very many ways simple in the purest, positive sense of the word. She lived, she gave of herself, she loved and fittingly so, she was and always will be loved in return.

For those of you still lucky enough to have your mother in your life, please tell her how much she means to you; give her that "just because...hug" for believe me you will miss having the opportunity to do these things once she is gone.

Finally, I want to thank all of you who sent your condolences to me via the below e-mail address. Your very kind words, well wishes and prayers were and are truly appreciated. I love hearing from you all.

# A Tale of Two First Ladies

I was not even a teenager during the whole Camelot Presidency of John F. Kennedy. To be totally honest, I knew very little about what was going on in Washington and cared even less. I do remember bits and pieces of Jackie's notoriety. But, as the years passed and the media exposed more and more of the "IT Factor" that she definitely possessed, I followed her life with not much of an opinion one way or the other.

Imagine my surprise when I heard of her death and I realized that tears were streaking my cheeks. I was unexplainably truly moved. Where in the world did that reaction come from?

We lost another First Lady last week; Betty Ford and not one tear did I shed. I was, shall we say, less than emotional.

It got me thinking about my very different reaction to the passing of these two very different First Ladies. Hmmmm...

What had Jackie actually done as First Lady? She famously redecorated the White House. She, some say, elevated fashion designers from having only notoriety amongst the elite to true celebrity status. She and her young family brought vibrancy to the White House and the country after eight years of the certainly not so vibrant Eisenhower's.

Betty Ford, on the other hand, not only changed but shattered the unspoken, strenuously adhered to rules traditionally imposed upon political wives. She altered the role of First Lady and dramatically changed our society as well. She, for the first time, was a First Lady willing to expose her frailty. She spoke openly about her illnesses and even her addictions. I vividly remember thinking at the time ... "What, is she nuts?" She tirelessly championed causes and raised funds for and helped to build the now famous (or infamous) Betty Ford Clinic for the treatment of addiction.

Unfortunately, also because of her honesty, we now have all of these celebrity confessions (political and non) filling the airwaves and the glut of tell all autobiographies lining the book store shelves.

Perhaps her greatest accomplishment was that she forced the nation and the world to recognize that true addiction is an illness. How sad it is to find so many now misusing her efforts by creating "addictions de jour" as an excuse for bad behavior.

But, even though there have been some negatives resulting from her example, she was courageous and honest and she channeled her afflictions into positive actions. Whether we realized it or not she influenced our lives.

I just can't figure out why I shed tears at the death of one First Lady who arguable didn't do much, while hardly reacting to the death of the other who truly impacted our world.

Maybe it was Jackie's obvious discomfort with any media attention and quiet, mysterious demeanor that made her so much more appealing than the outspoken crusader that was Betty Ford.

Or perhaps it is simply that indescribable "IT Factor" once again proving to be indescribable.

# Still Blowin' In the Wind

In what seems like another life and a very different time I played the guitar and sang in coffee houses to earn spending money while in college. It was a time of Puff the Magic Dragon, Sgt. Peppers and a plethora of protest songs. We were high...on life, engaged in what we saw happening around us and truly hopeful, in the way that only youth can feel; thinking we could make a difference.

Some of my favorites to sing and some of the audience's favorites to hear were the tunes of Bob Dylan. For me the lyrics were provocative and as a side bar, perhaps equally important, his songs were not particularly difficult to play (important because I could only play well enough to accompany myself!).

I was driving home from my office last week and a local radio station played the Dylan classic, Blowin' in the Wind. I hadn't heard (or sang) that song in many, many years. As I listened I was struck by the relevance today of the lyrics written all those years ago. To me it is a song about human folly. The answers to so many of our problems are right in front of us and yet because of political gamesmanship, personal biases or just plain stupidity, they seem to be as elusive as the wind.

I just saw a news report about a man in Oslo who mowed down a multitude of children at a camp in order to shed light on his bigoted philosophies and ideals. We are still fighting wars that no one has the stomach for, forcing us all to witness the loss of life and limb of so many American soldiers. Our political leaders still jockey for position instead of compromising for the well-being of our nation.

Perhaps it is time for us all to revisit the hope and aspirations of that generation of young people past. Perhaps it is time to revisit the lyrics that made so much sense to us then:

How many roads most a man walk down
Before you call him a man?
How many seas must a white dove sail
Before she sleeps in the sand?
Yes, how many times must the cannon balls fly
Before they're forever banned?
The answer my friend is blowin' in the wind
The answer is blowin' in the wind.

Yes, how many years can a mountain exist
Before it's washed to the sea?
Yes, how many years can some people exist
Before they're allowed to be free?
Yes, how many times can a man turn his head
Pretending he just doesn't see?
The answer my friend is blowin' in the wind
The answer is blowin' in the wind.

Yes, how many times must a man look up
Before he can see the sky?
Yes, how many ears must one man have
Before he can hear people cry?
Yes, how many deaths will it take till he knows
That too many people have died?
The answer my friend is blowin' in the wind
The answer is blowin' in the wind.

The answers, it seems, are still Blowin' in the Wind.

# The Debt Ceiling

Look. Up in the sky. It's a bird. It's a plane...no, it's the Super Committee!

So, we now know the outcome of the Debt Ceiling fiasco...ah, sorry, debate, that we all have been subjected to for gee, I don't know, eons! There are just so many things wrong with what has transpired over the past couple of months; I hardly know where to begin. But the most disturbing is the fact that the really hard stuff has been tabled for future discussion and resolution (yeah right!) by a Super Committee to be appointed later.

Say what? Super what? It seems to me that we already have had 2 super committees addressing the issues. One was the Debt Commission appointed by the White House. After months of negotiations their suggestions were completely ignored. And the most recent was the "gang of 6" whose suggestions were also ignored.

Here were six legislators doing the unthinkable thing of actually sitting down together (Dems and Reps) and working out a compromise to the immediate Debt Ceiling crises. They were not appointed by anyone. They were our representatives; finally, six out of the whole batch, taking their jobs seriously and representing not only their own interests but those of the nation as well.

How can anyone think that yet another appointed committee, even if we anoint them as super, will be successful? While I haven't read what was passed today, it is my understanding that nothing this super committee comes up with will be binding...so, it will be back to more of the same lunacy we have come to expect from our legislators.

Did you know that most countries don't have a Debt Ceiling? Doesn't that beg the question, why do we? Congress has to appropriate all spending, why do we need a Debt Ceiling?  It is their job (or should be) not to appropriate more money than we have coming in. If we have over spent, it is congress's fault for passing the spending bills.

But, the National Debt Ceiling is not synonymous with our National Deficit. So, now that the debate over raising the Debt Ceiling has been kicked to the curb for the rest of the year, attention will be shifted to the deficit. And make no mistake, the deficit is not going to be any easier to address.

There seems to me to be a very simple idea which would begin curbing the deficit problem. We can start by making all legislation brought to the floor address only one specific topic … no add-ons, no nothing else and let our representatives vote on the items' merits and whether or not we can afford it.

Or we can do as The Sage of Omaha suggests:

"I could end the deficit in 5 minutes," Warren Buffett told Becky Quick of CNBC. "You just pass a law that says that anytime there is a deficit of more than 3% of GDP, all sitting members of Congress are ineligible for re-election."

I would add one more thing.  All of their life-long benefits would be cancelled as well!

# Generation Gap

An older gentleman was sitting on a park bench. It was one of those beautiful days; sun shining, light breeze rustling the lush foliage surrounding him. He inhaled deeply as he lifted his eyes from the newspaper he was reading and smiled at the sights and smells and sounds of the idyllic natural wonders engulfing him. Young families with buckled into stroller babies, giggling romping toddlers with smiles and laughs seemingly spontaneously erupting from their faces passed him by on their way to more good times.

A boy approached. He couldn't have been more than eleven or twelve. He had a modern gizmo in his hands. His head was bent, eyes fixed intently on the small screen. As his thumbs wildly pumped, whirs and beeps emanated from his rectangular gadget. His face alternated from grimace to gleeful beaming. With hands in constant motion he sat next to the man apparently not even noticing him, still so wrapped in the techno-wonderment of his satellite fueled cyber world.

Whether it was the bemused stare of the man burning into his face or the need to simply come up for air, the boy lifted his eyes to meet those of his bench mate.

They both smiled.

"Reading the paper, huh?" The boy queried.

"Yes, this is my time to catch up on what is happening in the world each day. But I never seem to have enough time to read all that I would want to."

Smiles were exchanged and they both went back to their mid-day distractions.

"You need one of these." The boy stated after a few moments. "All of the papers have websites now." He lifted his handheld gizmo for the man to see.

"I think not. I'll stick to the paper kind." The man replied with a smile.

The boy instantly slid closer to the man and thrust the gizmo in front of him so he could see the screen clearly.

The boy looked down at the newspaper the man had dropped to his lap and hit a few keys. In a matter of seconds the newspaper's homepage appeared on the small screen.

"See you can get the whole thing in seconds, scroll down the article headlines to see if you want to read them or you can search the archives for any articles you might have missed in the past. Then you can move on to another paper for their take on what's happening. Saves you scads of time. You could get all the news you want in probably half the time. Pretty cool, huh?"

The man smiled. He was so enjoying the enthusiasm and zeal of this boy.

"So, you don't read newspapers?" He asked the boy.

The boy looked incredulous.

"Uh, no." He said flatly with that DUH! intonation.

"If I did I sure wouldn't read them that way. Man, I just don't know how you managed growing up without the internet, and gaming systems and IPods! What in the world did you do?"

"Not much...we just invented them."

The man smiled as he lifted the newspaper to begin reading again.

# Do Your Homework—Be Specific

O.K. so we have the Republican field of Presidential hopefuls shifting a bit after this weekend's win in the Iowa Straw Poll by Bachmann and the withdrawal from the race by Pawlenty. I don't know about you but I am already tired of 2012 Presidential campaigning.

Is there anyone out there that feels the way that I do? Campaigning is so far removed from actual governing it is almost an exercise in futility to try to make a decision based on campaign platitudes and promises.

Candidates, both parties included, can and do say most anything to get elected. No matter how unrealistic, they can generically promise solutions to whatever ails us. They spout slogans, catchphrases and buzzwords; all in the hope of convincing the general public of their worthiness to lead this great nation. But as witnessed these past several years, the execution of those promises, the actual working out of the details is an all together different story.

I want to believe that they believe in what they say. I want to believe that their motivation is to be of service to the American people. I want to believe that they have some knowledge of how to get things done.

So, to all those who would be President, here are my suggestions as to structuring your campaign from the outset and then how to act after being elected.

My instincts say do your homework and know the problem issues, their causes and their possible remedies.

For Pete's sake, you have close to 2 years of campaigning; do some detailed homework. Then, craft concrete plans of action for the major issues before announcing your candidacy – if you stick to your solid, detailed message on each important issue there will be no doubt as to why/how you were elected once you are put into office.

The reality of the office will kick in when those pesky politicians from across the aisle plant their feet firmly in the righteousness of their positions. When they try to obstruct at every turn; you can remind them of your firm well defined, well communicated stance, which you brought before the American people...and won.

Isn't the clear cut voice of the people, evidenced by your win, the most powerful bargaining chip in negotiations with the other party?

"I was specific and I won! Get on the program." Then keep reminding the public why they voted for you. If the opposition fails to create a positive political environment of compromise and cohesion, all working for the greater good of the country, you make sure the public unequivocally knows about it.

Of course changes to your stated plans will inevitably have to be made in the true spirit of bipartisanship and the realities of actually holding the office as opposed to merely running for it. But, any changes that have to be made to your "campaigned on, specific policies" can be rationalized by acknowledging that there are some things one cannot possibly know until you actually are the President.

So, there you have it. I would just like to know what any given candidate would/could realistically do if elected. Is that too much to ask?

# The Cone Collar

Have you seen the car commercial with the adorable dog wearing one of those funky cone collar thingamajigs? I think it is a commercial for Volkswagen and it is really quite clever and good.

So, the dog is wearing his cone collar – you know those alarmingly uncomfortable looking contraptions designed to keep Spot from licking or nipping at either stitches he has had put in or irritating other sensitive areas due to allergies or injury or just 'cause he wants to "over-lick."

The pooch is waiting anxiously, with cone in place, for his car ride. One can almost sense his obvious anticipation; the wind blowing through his hair with eyes closed to everything except the pleasure of the drive as he sits with head hanging out of the open window.

His master (remember this is a car commercial) looks quizzically at the dog with the quite large contraption about his neck. There is a look on the man's face. He is perplexed as he realizes that the cone will cause a drag on the forward motion of the car.

Hmm. And then inspiration erupts spreading over the man's face and he brilliantly inverts the cone to make it aerodynamically advantageous rather than detrimental to optimum efficiency. Instead of a problem the cone has now become an asset facilitating additional speed for their afternoon drive.

Clever, effective, well executed.

It got me thinking. Our country needs a cone collar. Bear with me here. What if we view the dog as our troubled economy? He obviously has some kind of condition which calls for the dreaded cone collar. Our economy, likewise, has been through the ringer and is in need of precise healing attention.

The dog is being tended to, thus the cone. We seem to be having stitches put into our economy here and there to quell the "bleeding out" of the system. But the stitches are in constant jeopardy of being nipped out by political forces.

Voila! We need a cone collar to let the wounds, which have been stitched already, heal. This would allow more attention to be directed to areas still needing curative measures.

But there is one more aspect of the analogy that comes into play. Do we leave the cone as originally conceived and constructed, thus causing a bit of a drag on the afternoon ride, or do we invert it, cleverly keeping the principal of its use in tact but allowing it to now become a booster of the speed and precision possible?

Personally I say go for the innovation and invert the darn thing. There are ways of complimenting and updating and yes even improving the old tried and true without losing the intent and the purpose.

As the campaign season continues to unfold I'm hoping to hear some creative, workable solutions to some of our glaring problems. I am going to look for the folks that invert the cone collar.

# Cheney – His Side of the Story

I don't know Dick Cheney; never met him, never talked to him. But, I have met and spoken, quite extensively, with his daughter and a person, who worked with, spoke with him on a daily basis.

His memoirs, In My Time, will be released today and is already creating quite a stir. Just the fact that the book got published is unique. To my recollection, no other vice president has ever gotten a book deal unless he went on to become president. But then no other vice president had the imprint on both national and international policy than did Dick Cheney.

No one can argue with the fact that he was one of the most influential vice presidents this country has ever had.

Having heard excerpts of his book in advance of publication, my fascination with this hugely controversial political figure has been intensified. Lest we forget, he began his political life as a self-proclaimed liberal and evolved into the quintessential, arch conservative. While that evolutionary journey is not documented in the book (I would have enjoyed learning of his transformation from the horse's mouth) the book is full of other character defining details.

Based on what I have been told by those who know him, the book is a very accurate representation of the man himself. It is straight forward, non-apologetic and exudes a self confidence that is the foundation of his life.

In the book, he not only "goes after" his acknowledged political enemies, surprisingly many of whom are republicans, but seemingly anyone who didn't agree with him. No political bias here. He is a true non-partisan when it comes to subjecting those in disagreement, to his wrath.

I appreciate that he lays his side of the story out for all to see. Unlike so many political memoirs these days, it is unvarnished by an influential ghost writer. Having labored as a ghost writer on two separate books, I can tell you that we try very hard to put our "authors" in the very best light possible avoiding or at least minimizing any blow back upon publication. Trust me, there are ways to make anyone look and sound good.

Well, not here. I found no glossing over of the "sticky points." There was little doubt that he still firmly believes in his advice and his role in the execution of plans and strategies he created.

But, pretty intense blowback is already occurring. Some are contending that it was/is the wars, promoted by him, that have thrown our economy into a tail-spin and have diminished the U.S. in the estimation of the world. Many are angered at the lambasting of Colin Powell and Condoleezza Rice to mention only two of his targets. Even conservative columnist George Will is calling on Cheney to issue an apology. Good luck with that!

In the end, history will evaluate Dick Cheney's public life. But, I think, with this book, he is getting in there first. I think this book represents his last will and testimony. He is bequeathing to the world "his side of the story."

# A Hanging Offense

While listening to the pundits defending and attacking the unfortunate use of the word treason which presidential candidate Rick Perry rather cavalierly used regarding the prospect of the Fed Chair "printing new money" to help in our current financial difficulties; I began to think about the charge of treason.

The fact is I really didn't know what actually constitutes the charge. So, for those of you in the same boat, here is what our constitution says on the matter.

Article III, Section. 3:
"Treason against the United States shall consist only in levying War against them, or in adhering to their Enemies, giving them Aid and Comfort. No Person shall be convicted of Treason unless on the Testimony of two Witnesses to the same overt Act, or on Confession in open Court."

While we hear the term batted about a bit in the media from time to time, the actual legal accusation and trial of it is quite rare indeed. The two most famous cases in our history involved Aaron Burr being charged with it, but he was then acquitted. And John Brown who was found guilty of it and hanged.

The U.S. has only tried about 30 treason cases in the nation's history and many of those trials were brought by states not the federal government. I was surprised to learn that in most of those cases, when found guilty, the perpetrator was imprisoned not condemned to the commonly held thought that treason is a hanging offence.

In the United States we don't really seem to do treason very often or very well.

Do you remember the film Braveheart? It chronicled the Scottish patriot William Wallace's fight for freedom from

English tyranny. Even by our narrow definition of treason, Wallace was certainly guilty.

Now the English, at that time, really knew how to do treason. Once captured Wallace was hung, stretched, eviscerated and finally decapitated. Do you think that is what the Governor from Texas had in mind for Bernanke?

I think the use of the term was unfortunate and the media played it for way too long. I would prefer they draw attention to the plethora of other bizarre statements made by the man putting forth his beliefs and positions.

This is a man who just a couple of years ago suggested that Texas secede from the nation. He voiced the opinion that our senators be appointed to office instead of being voted into office but then also condemned the appointing of Justices to the Supreme Court. He has questioned the need for a Department of Education because "it has not educated one student." And, believe me I could go on and on expanding the list of questionable statements made by the man.

I don't know about you but I think that the proverbial "those that live in glass houses" thing should be taken more seriously by Rick Perry or he might be the one finding himself being charged with perpetuating a hanging offence.

# Thank You Misters President

Like so many others, I tuned into some of the coverage of the 9/11 tributes over the weekend. There has been so much written, so many stories and tales of heroism, I won't even try to recap the event. But what struck me, and I think many others as well, was the picture of our current President and our past President standing together, much like the country stood together in the immediate aftermath of that horrific day.

I think it is long past time for all of us to stand together again.

Now ten years into two wars, we have been inundated with both sides blaming the other for all of our country's woes. With all of the name calling, fingers of blame pointing, and political posturing we have come to expect from our politicians (and they never cease to meet those expectations!) I think we have lost sight of the truly monumental job our presidents have undertaken in the service of this country.

Past presidents are members of a very elite club indeed. No one can understand the job unless having held it and campaigning is so totally removed from actual governing. Can you imagine that first day on the job when the newly elected president receives his first briefings? I have to believe that even their wildest imaginings can't measure up to the reality of all that will be required of them.

My husband Drew likes to tell of how our children went from thinking that we, as parents, knew everything when they were young, to their teenage years when all of a sudden we knew nothing and understood even less. Then, somehow when they reached adulthood we miraculously became intelligent again!

That reminds me of a story I heard about JFK and Ike. While campaigning and then taking office, it was no secret that JFK thought that while a good, strategic general in his day, Ike had become just an old man whose time had ended. Then the Bay of Pigs pulled the United States into the closest we have ever come to a nuclear war. I think you can guess who JFK called once the mission failed and the danger passed. It was Ike to whom he turned to gain some insight into how he had failed the country and what his strategies should have been. From has-been to valued advisor, all of a sudden Ike was intelligent again!

They were from different parties, yet they were joined by the shared experience of being President of the United States of America.

There is a lesson to be learned from all of this. I think that if we are going to overcome the vehement partisanship that has crippled our representatives' ability to govern, a good first step would be for all of us to acknowledge the huge personal and professional sacrifices that our presidents, from both parties, have made and continue to make in their sincere service of this country. I think a good place to start toward a more unified nation, at this time of reflection, would be for all of us to say:

Thank You Misters President.

# Diamonds Are Forever?

There are hundreds of stories. The stories are of oppressed people, throughout history, running for not only their freedom but for their very lives. We have all heard the stories, seen the countless scenes in countless movies of the desperation in their eyes as they nervously sew a few shiny diamonds into the lining of a coat or hidden pouch within some other article of clothing. The stones represent their only hope, their only chance for survival.

We have all grown up understanding the time honored value of the sparkling gems. Unlike the value of gold, the euro, the dollar or the yen, a diamond's value rarely fluctuates...except to rise. They are considered rare enough to pass from generation to generation as heirlooms. They are smuggled and hoarded. They are the symbol of a young man's "rock solid affection" for his future wife. And they are, after all, a girl's best friend!

But, wait. What is this I hear? There has been a remarkable discovery. A planet...you heard me a whole planet that is made up of crystalline carbon or as we non-scientific sorts call it...DIAMOND!

Just when I was almost over the heart-wrenching demotion of poor Pluto from planet status, here comes a new planet, one consisting of diamond no less. And to further embarrass poor little Pluto, this new planet is about five times the size of the Earth! How is Pluto, a puny, no longer a planet, consisting of common stuff to compete with that?

My first thought was how great. Not only will this jump start a slew of NASA projects directed at "shooting for the diamond," but just think if we were to get there. A small miner's pick and a few taps from a hammer and voila, the solution to our economic problems. Of course a minor detail is that the planet is 4,000 light years away, which is about one eighth of the way toward the center of the Milky Way from Earth. But one can dream can't one?

Can you imagine; stepping foot on a diamond planet?

And then some other realities began to hit me. What if we were to reach the diamond planet? What if we had access to all of that diamond mass? What would happen when there was a glut of diamonds on the market?

Is there anything to replace the small size, big value diamond that can be sewn into those secret stashes? What would my grandmother's ring and all of the other grandmothers' rings out there be worth? Would they be reduced to purely sentimental value? And would there have to be another token in outstretched hand from bended knee proposer to compensate for the devaluation of the diamond ring?

On second thought, while it is still very cool to have discovered a planet made of diamond, I think we should just leave it there to "twinkle, twinkle in the sky."

Scientists estimate that the diamond planet could very well be around for billions of years. I hope that if we just leave it alone; diamonds will be forever.

# The Middle Eastern Script of Conflict

I was very pleased when Julianna Margulies won an Emmy last week for her role as "The Good Wife" in the CBS weekly drama. The show's backstory is set in a Chicago law firm and exposes sex scandals, law firm relationships and the piece-de-résistance, behind the scenes Chicago politics. It doesn't get much better than that.

The show's season premiered this week and I tuned in. Given the Palestinian statehood resolution debate at the United Nations and the continuing drama of the Israeli-Palestinian non-peace process peace process; I found the premise for the storyline of the show to be quite interesting.

The action took place at a fictional Chicago college campus. A Jewish student had been killed. The case was being investigated as a hate crime as pro Moslem and anti Moslem demonstrations erupted into more violence. Thus began the hour long drama.

Hidden agendas ran rampant within both the D.A.'s and the Defense teams' offices. There was lots of personal and professional history coming into play.

An influential Jewish group wrangled for position to out P.R. the pro Moslem P.R. being generated. A very well funded Moslem group started throwing its money around in a similar effort. Allegiances and motives were being questioned.

And, just as a side bar, how the firm romance sizzled! Past conflicts re-erupted. Schemes and plots were hinted at...but I do digress from my point. (E-mail me and we can chat about all of that!)

With all of the players vying for position, all of the impassioned rhetoric being spouted and each side firmly convinced that they had the just cause to defend and promote, not only did the victim become lost in all of it, but the young Moslem eventually accused of the murder was manipulated about by both sides of the courtroom. Emotions ran high as the two sides fueled each other's growing passions.

And then there was that moment.

The Good Wife (should she be renamed the good lawyer?) stopped and said to her assistant, "Maybe we are looking at this from the wrong perspective."

And poof! Everything began to fall into place eventually resolving itself with the true murderer being exposed.

Ah, television. If only those script writers could write us out of the Middle East morass and into a tidy, hour long, totally satisfying resolution.

To my mind, the show provided an analogy of the whole two state solution thing in the Middle East. I fear there is just too much history. There is too politicking and too much violence. There is too much emotion for peace to ever be achieved if we keep going at it in the same old way.

I have my own very strong ideas about the very complex Middle Eastern debate. Many hold equally strong ideas directly opposed to mine

As in The Good Wife, could it be that all sides are looking at the conflict from the wrong perspective?

If only someone could write one of "those moments" into the reality of the Middle Eastern script of conflict.

# Shakespeare and the New Movie
## Anonymous

It was a time when we fought for the right to wear pant suits to school changing the dress code which mandated skirts and only skirts. It was a time when we still feared disappointing our parents, our teachers, our spiritual leaders; when having earned a detention at school was an humiliation inspiring shame and dread rather than, like today, representing a badge of honor, an accomplishment respected and even envied by fellow students.

I sat, a bit nervous, in an A.P. class on the first day of my senior year of high school. It was a class on Shakespeare and, oh my God, it was being taught by the Chair of the English Department, the fear inducing, Dr. Guest. He was tall and big, aloof and rarely taught a class; and to further add to his mystique, he spoke with a British accent!

I hadn't read much Shakespeare and I certainly didn't understand what the big deal was about this author of old, but this class would take care of my college freshman English requirement so there I sat.

As Dr. Guest entered the classroom on that first day, there was an instant and complete silence; breathes were held and backs were straightened.

Speaking not a word to the class, he opened his obviously use worn, leather bound copy of the complete works of Shakespeare and began to read out loud the first lines of King Lear.

For an hour I sat listening, transported back in time by the dramatic, deep voice of Dr. Guest; enthralled by the words of the Bard. From that day forward I was eternally hooked on Shakespeare in specific and on the power of words in general. That class, those two men, one having written the words and one having read them so eloquently, changed my life. The trajectory of my adulthood was from that point forward guided by my love for the written word.

Have you seen the ads for the new movie Anonymous? The premise is that my good friend for all these years, Bill Shakespeare, did not write the immortal words of Lear and Macbeth, Romeo and Juliette, Hamlet and the Merchant of Venice.

This is certainly not a new proposition. For years questions have been asked, books have been written contending that good old Bill simply couldn't have written those, universally considered, masterpieces of literature. He was relatively low born. There are no definitive accounts of any education or tutoring. Through the years these speculations only added to Bill's mastery, the aura of his genius, the panache that made the story of his life every bit as engaging as the characters about whom he wrote.

I am anxious to see the movie but whatever slant it takes or interpretation it makes, to my mind really doesn't matter. I choose to look at the whole "did he or didn't he" thing much in the same way I look at religious faith.

Without definitive proof, I simply believe.

# Get Over It

We now have new census data this week indicating that income has gone down more post-recession than it did during the recession. Forgive me if I am a bit confused. I'm still trying to figure out how anyone can say that the recession is over, especially in light of these new figures, but that's another point altogether.

So, how are we dealing with this deepening non-recession recession? Well, we have the Democrats blaming the Republicans for our financial mess. Likewise, we have the Republicans blaming the Democrats for our financial mess.

And I thought that our elected officials couldn't agree on anything. They sure proved me wrong. They all agree that it is the other party's fault! Do they not realize that pointing the "it's all your fault" accusatory finger does nothing to solve the situation we are in now?

It reminds me of the grown man still blaming his adult failures on the fact that he had, in his mind, bad parents. They are responsible for all of his problems. I want to refer to that great scene from the movie Moonstruck where after Nicolas Cage professes his love, Cher, without missing a beat, whaps him in the face and screams "get over it!"

And, we the people aren't any better than that bitter, excuse making, adult child. Every none-politician is looking to Government to "just fix it and be quick about it," while every politician is looking to blame the other party to get re-elected.

WHAP... "Get over it!"

I say to all of the Americans unwilling to acknowledge their own culpability in this financial riptide and insist that government fix it with no personal ramifications for our own part in getting us into this mess; whap..."Get over it!"

I say to all of the politicians who can't think of any other way to get elected than to blame the other party; whap..."Get over it."

At some point in time that adult child has to say O.K. my folks did, or didn't do this or that but I am an adult now. It is up to me to make my own way.

Our government can't just fix it. A jobs program, I don't care who proposes it and what's in it, can't just magically fix it. We all have to stop looking to someone else to make it all better. It's like the sad single person thinking that if only they could find the right person they could be happy.

Someone else can't make you happy; you have to make yourself happy. The right person can support and comfort. The right person can listen and be a sounding board. The right person can be a partner in your quest for happiness but they cannot instantly make everything great, make all of your problems go away and make you happy any more than our government can simply and magically make our financial problems go away. We all have to do our part. It's time we stopped the blaming game.

Whap... "Get over it!"

# Just Another Week in Politics

Lots happening in the world of politics last week. In what seems to be the never ending race for the Republican nominee for president, we had the truly anticlimactic announcement from Chris Christie that he will not be throwing his hat into the race.

I, for one, was shocked; shocked I tell you!

I thought for sure that he was chomping at the bit to run...Oh wait a minute, isn't he the guy that has repeatedly said that he would not run? Isn't he the guy that asked a crowd of supporters in frustration "Do I have to be in a coma for you all to believe me? I am not going to run!"

Some of you might remember a column I wrote on the then newly elected Governor of New Jersey in which I speculated that a future president might be in the making and now he has exhibited why I think he would make a good president...someday. He was honest enough to say I am not ready. I have only been a Governor for a few years. I am not ready to be president. Wow, a guy who actually thinks he is not ready and is honest enough to say it. I still like this guy!

So, Christie is gone but not forgotten because he instantly turned right around and endorsed Mitt Romney. And we all know Mitt. He's the energizer bunny of the Republican field who keeps running and running and running!

Then, all of this quasi-drama led up to yet another Republican candidate's debate; this one dealing strictly with the economy. I liked the candidates seated at a table. I found it to be quite interesting that their placement was determined by how they are polling.

Romney, as front runner, sat at the center of the semi-circle. Ironically, if he doesn't adopt "center stances on issues" I don't think he has a chance of getting elected...but that is just my opinion. Anyway, then we had Herman Cain who came from apparently nowhere to surge up in the polls and secure a spot next to Mitt.

Who is this Herman Cain guy anyway? I saw Chuck Todd's interview with him recently and I have to say he has some impressive qualities. Calm demeanor, well spoken and much to everyone's surprise, has actually put out a tax reform plan...with a catchy moniker to boot: "999. "

He contends that his plan will flatten the federal taxes and actually result in lowering dollars owed for the majority of Americans. Hummmmm, sounds good. And, unlike those other Republican flashes in the pan, he is willing to be specific even though it means that he now has a huge bull's-eye on his back and will have to be defending his plan. I like a man with guts!

But, let's not get too excited about this Herman Cain guy. Odds are he is simply the republican "candidate du jour" much like Bachman, Trump and Christie were. But, then again, one never knows.

Maybe he's the guy that can pull the plug on that energizer bunny after all!

# The Devil You Know

Another bad guy has fallen. There is no disputing the fact that General Qaddafi was indeed a bad guy. Anyone who has followed Middle Eastern politics for the past several decades has, at times, been both appalled by his brutality and perplexed by his apparent lunacy.

The man was so weird that the world couldn't even decide on how to spell his name. In four different newspapers reporting on his death, I documented four different spellings of his name: Gaddafi, Kaddafi, Khaddafy and then the one I am choosing to use; Qaddafi.

In her new book, "No Higher Honor," Condi Rice details a very bizarre set of meetings she had in Libya with Qaddafi. (Take note that this is her spelling of his name thus the reason why I am using it ... if the former Secretary of State doesn't know the correct spelling, who does?)

She relates how he referred to her as an "African Princess" and wanted to meet with her in his tent. He also informed her that he had made a video tape for her. I don't know about you but I think in any language, any culture that's just creepy.

But all nonsense aside, with yet one more tyrant toppled in the region, what does this all mean? Does this really herald a new era of Democracy and freedom in these countries?

Perhaps a look into the past might sober some of the jubilation. Let us not forget what happened in Iran when the Shah was deposed. Educated, forward thinking activists toppled his reign. In a relatively short period of time fanatical Muslim extremists distorted and usurped the cause thus beginning a new era of repression and fear. Women allowed to be educated under the Shah's rule are now hiding in basements, swathed in black, if they want to read an "unacceptable book!"

But, let's get back to one of the current pages in ouster history. The jury is still out on the fate of the revolution in Egypt. Many are already disillusioned. They fear that religious fanatics will come to power and they will be forced to live in yet another oppressive state. Many say that the current rule by the Military is just "more of the same." Only time will tell.

Meanwhile, another bad guy has fallen. Qaddafi is dead. Thanks to modern technology we have even seen his capture and his corpse. And we have seen the riotous joy in the streets with hundreds firing their weapons into the air. (Just a side question here: where do all those bullets fall? Are people at risk of having vast quantities of small missiles splattering their brain matter after gaining momentum coming back down to earth?)

Anyway, I'm not saying that evil tyrants should be allowed to reign. Nor should we condone the brutality and abuses of power in the world. All I am saying is that sometimes the devil you don't know is every bit as evil as the one you do know.

# Steve Jobs: The Genius Among us

I waited to write anything about the passing of Steve Jobs because once the eulogizing was over, once the laudatory blathering from everyone who had ever been in a room with him had their five minutes of fame; I knew that a darker side of the man would emerge. Much like Jekyll and Hyde of literary fame, it seems that the genius among us always have a monster lurking within, popping out at will.

As is the case with most great (and not so great) people, a biography was authorized, written by Walter Isaacson and has now been released. In 1984 Jobs had a meeting with Isaacson who was then employed by Time Magazine. Jobs went to pitch the Mac to him, wanting ink in the magazine to help promote it. The two men forged a business relationship with Jobs approaching Isaacson whenever he had a new product to launch wanting a cover story about it in Time. It was in the mid eighties that Jobs asked Isaacson if he would write his biography. After agreeing, Isaacson really forgot about it for a couple of decades.

Fast forward to 2009, just after Jobs had his liver transplant, Isaacson met with Jobs and wife Laurene. During the meeting the couple basically said "Do the biography now."

Fascinating stuff abounds within its pages like the influence that the music of Bob Dylan and the Beatles had on Steve Jobs both professionally and personally.

But what fascinates me is how much like one other of Isaacson's biographies this one is at exposing the nature of genius. Isaacson wrote what some consider the definitive biography of Albert Einstein. Like Jobs, Einstein wasn't the smartest guy in his field. There were certainly others with "better minds" than either of these men. But what they had that defined their genius was the ability to see the world differently.

When asked why he didn't use focus groups to get ideas for new products, Jobs answered, "If Henry Ford had used focus groups; he would have tried to invent a faster horse."

It seems so simple. People of genius see things differently. But seeing things differently inevitably had an effect on other aspects of their lives. Both men seemed to "drink the Hyde potion" in dealing with others. We have heard of the badgering and intolerance, the perfectionism and the anger that defined the management style of Jobs. Likewise Einstein was noted for dysfunctional relationships.

Yet the core group of Jobs' employees, stayed with him for decades until his death. We have heard of the relationship problems he had with his wife and children and yet they were all there by his bedside when he died.

I think it begs the question; is bad behavior endemic to genius and if so should we excuse it? If they do see the world differently, should the genius among us be held to a different standard?

# Herman Cain and the Royal We

I saw a clip from Jimmy Kimmel's show Monday night. His guest was Herman Cain. Just as a reminder, Monday was the day when, flanked by that pillar of righteousness Gloria Albright, yet another woman made accusations of sexual misconduct against the former front runner in the Republican primary.

In spite of the story breaking that very day, Cain asserted his intention to move on from those allegations and stressed wanting to stay on track with his message. Being a better man than I, in light of the flurry of media coverage none of which was too flattering; he actually seemed to be having a great time. Wow, impressive. If I had been blasted in the media that day as he was, I would have found a very deep hole and buried myself in it...oh wait a minute. Isn't that exactly what his opponents are trying to do to him?

Anyway, much to his credit, he was able to be funny, relaxed, and effortlessly spouted all of the catchphrases and buzzwords that he so artfully delivers. And, lest we forget, he has that great personal narrative and we all know that the American voter traditionally loves a good story.

But that story is getting all mucked up with the media frenzy over these sexual misconduct accusations.

I have written several times about the stupidity of powerful men, especially those running for office, who don't think that their bad behavior will be exposed.

Now, before all of you Cain supporters out there jump all over me, let me say that I don't know if Cain falls into this category or not. The man might be, as he professes, innocent of misdeeds but there was something new in his delivery of his proclaimed innocence Monday night that really began to irk me.

He has begun referring to himself in the third person and using the "royal we."
Excuse me?

The "royal we" was used as a reference to the divine nature of royalty itself. A monarch never let his/her subjects forget that they were divinely anointed to rule and thus always referred to themselves as "we" indicating that their words and actions came as a joint edict directly from God.

And there was Herman Cain adopting it in reference to himself in the interview.

Who does that? I don't know about you but no one I know refers to themselves as "we."

Even though Cain has a great personal narrative that obviously resonates with a lot of people; this whole "we stuff" just smells of arrogance.

And if these sexual misconduct allegations stick and another type of arrogance, one of a more heinous nature, is exposed, well it does not bode well for Herman Cain's future in politics.

But, not to worry. He is after all quite funny and articulate, can carry a tune and while it is not the kind of publicity he might have hoped for; he is getting a lot of attention.

"We" think the man has a great future in television!

# Kids Love Their Coaches

It was 1999. Our daughter had graduated from LaPorte High School and was looking forward to attending Indiana University. I had taken her on trips to view several universities while her father, once the decision was made, was the one to "get oriented" with her at IU! I ask that you think back to that time in that university's history...it was still the era of Bobby Knight.

So, the two of them are on campus after hearing about all of the programs and opportunities available to our daughter and Drew comes up with the idea that it would be great to get basketball tickets for the IU/Michigan State game. For those of you who do not read my column regularly, my husband Drew is a Michigan State alum and...let's see how shall I put this...a Spartan crazy person! Anyway, he and our daughter went to the box office.

When Drew innocently asked for tickets for the MSU game the reply he received was "Which year?" Not quite getting the message he replied "Well, this year." and the clerk began to laugh. There were no tickets available for any basketball game until the year following our daughter's graduation from the school! He was however, informed that he could have all the seats he wanted for any football game!

My guess is that a similar experience would be had by incoming freshman dad's requesting football tickets for Penn State's Nittany Lions. While the sports in question might be reversed, the situations are precisely parallel. Joe Paterno is to college football what Bobby Knight was to college basketball; one of those few coaches who, just the mere mention of his name, attracted the finest talent to their programs and the most loyalty from their fans.

But, oh my, my, my; what a sleazy, despicable mess this whole Penn State scandal has turned out to be...and the beloved Joe (say it ain't so Joe) Paterno is in the middle of it all.

Bobby's outrageous actions eventually led to his dismissal by Indiana. Joe has been dismissed by Penn State for egregious inaction.

Apparently, Joe did all that he was required to do legally when charges of sexual abuses allegedly performed by one of his coaches were brought to his attention; but morally...he fumbled the ball.

I remember the phone call from my daughter the night that Bobby got the axe. She was watching the crowd of students from her dorm window forming below in protest. Eventually there were hundreds out there on the lawn showing their support for "their coach" Bobby Knight; loving him no matter what he had done.

And there were the Penn State students, in the hundreds, protesting the firing of Joe Paterno; showing their support no matter what he hadn't done.

Whether it be slapping the face of a player or slapping us all in the face by inaction, the evidence seems to indicate that no matter what they do or don't do, what they have or have not done, our kids still love their coaches.

# Thanksgiving 2011

I have had a stuffed up head, clogged ears and the resulting cough for what seems like forever. A virtual plethora of over the counter allergy, decongestant and antihistamine self-proclaimed miracle drugs, line my medicine cabinet but afford no relief. I'll bet someone you know is complaining about similar symptoms. I'm told it's going around but my question is can't it go around somewhere else?

I personally think we have screwed up the environment so much; all of this excess mucus is the result!

But it is not just internal mucus about which so many of us are talking. We have news cycles spewing "super disgrace" sputum, spattering different politicians, celebrities and sport's figures every day. Don't get me wrong. I am not saying they don't deserve some of it but this trend of bombarding us with detail after detail (some true some not) has turned into a disgusting story all of its own.

And our nation still suffers from the terrible debilitating drain of our economic decline.

Oh yes my friends I could go on. There seems to be a never ending supply of gunky stuff we would all like to spit up and flush. It is very easy to dwell on problems. Yes, that's easy and we don't seem to hesitate to waste our time doing just that.

More than two decades ago, my Grandmother lay dying in the hospital after falling and breaking her back at age 88. I sat by her bedside thinking back on so many wonderful moments we shared.

I sat looking at her...really looking at her. She seemed so serene so very beautiful. But all at once I realized that she had always seemed that way to me. She never seemed ruffled. She never seemed riled; in fact, I couldn't remember her ever raising her voice in anger.

There I sat thinking about this when a conversation we had came back to me.

She had told me this simple truth; life can be very hard but hard isn't all bad nor is it all there is. She told me that it is so easy to dwell on the hardships and the pain and the disappointments that we all suffer in life but you can't give in to that. You can't allow despair to run rough shod over all of the good.

When I asked her what I could do to not become victim to all that I feared, her answer was beautifully simple.

We all can find an abundance of wonderful things in our lives for which we should feel truly grateful. If you take one moment when you first get up in the morning...even before you get out of bed and think about those things, think about the good in your life. It makes all of the difference. Just count your blessings every day...simple as that.

Every year at Thanksgiving her words come back to me. We have a whole National Holiday devoted to giving thanks but how many of us truly do?

So this Thanksgiving instead of wishing you a happy day (though I do hope it will be joyful for you and your families) I relay my Grandmother's advice. Not only on Thanksgiving Day but every day...count your blessings

# What Can One Person Do?

When I finally pushed myself away from our Thanksgiving dinner table last week I felt like I was the stuffed bird. I'll bet you know exactly what I'm talking about. Thanksgiving is one of those holidays where we give ourselves permission to over-eat to the point of bursting at the seams. How great is that; a whole day to indulge to our hearts content...food glorious food!

Oh, wait a minute, one day to indulge? Is that all we're entitled to? Silly me. How could I forget that we have evolved into a culture of overindulgence in most every aspect of our lives? Overindulgence has become the new norm. We are a people who want it all and want it now. Unfortunately, our need for indulging is beginning to take its toll; physically, economically, politically and every other "cally" known to man!

It's easy to throw our hands up in frustrations lamenting the fact that there is nothing one person can do to make things better, to make things change. We might feel hopeless and helpless and we then commiserate with our fellows by eating yet another piece of the leftover pumpkin pie!

To that I say "physician heal thyself!"

We can change. We can make a difference, each and every one of us. But we have to begin at home. We have to look to ourselves and our children first. We can start by looking at a major health problem facing our nation...obesity.

The CDC statistics are staggering. 1/3 of adults in our country are obese; 17% of 2 to 19 years olds are obese as well. Here in LaPorte County 28% of our populace is obese...28% of you and me and our neighbors are obese. Is that number as disturbing to you as it is to me?

So, what can we do?

In a world where congressional lobbyists have pressured Congress into declaring pizza to be a vegetable, we cannot look to our government to fix this mess. We will have to take charge of our own lives, our school meal programs and our children's eating habits. It won't be easy but it is something that can be done. We, you and I can make a difference. But we have to act. No one is going to do it for us.

I saw an interview with T.V.'s Dr. Oz and his wife and they have set up an organization loosely based on the concept of the Peace Corp called Healthcorps. It basically has recent graduates going into schools and communities to educate our youth on a variety of health issues. While kids will tune us old folks out, the response to their peers on these issues has already yielded results.

With so many problems in our world, addressing one at a time, addressing the alarming rise of obesity in our country, in our homes is a place to start. It is something that we can do as individuals. No one will do it for us or for our kids. We can all help. Please go to healthcorps.com to learn more about what can be done; not only for your own healthful future but for the healthful future of our children.

# Bye-Bye Cain; Hello Newt

So, yet another shooting star of the Republican primary race has become a flaming, descending meteor. Oh Herman, Herman, Herman; what were you thinking when you decided to run? Did you not know that past bad behavior would be exposed? Did you not think that humor which plays on the golf course or at a cocktail party would be scrutinized and criticized on the campaign trail? And how could you imagine that quoting lyrics from the "Pokemon" movie would garner anything but ridicule from not only serious political analysts but yield fodder for the late night comics as well (brief confession here, I have no idea what/who Pokemon is nor did I know that it/he had a movie!).

There are some lambasting you for quoting movie dialogue in past speeches as well. I cannot say boo about that for I do it all of the time, of course I am not running for the Presidency.

But, Pokemon in your announcement of withdrawal from the race?

Who, pray tell, is giving you campaign advice and where has your common sense gone? I want to think that this reference was an attempt at humor, a subtle proclamation that you are still the same funny guy, unscathed by all the bad press and plummeting poll numbers; still uniquely Herman Cain and arguably very personable. But, I gotta tell ya, you could not have come off less Presidential if you had intentionally tried. Ah, you didn't intentionally try did you?

O.K. so, Cain, (following Bachmann, Perry, Trump, et al) is out. I feel like we the people are the sandwich makers in a Deli line yelling...NEXT, who's next?

Newt! Yes Newt is now the candidate du jour. He is soaring in the polls. He has everyone on the tube talking about him, all of the columnists writing about him. He is boasting and strutting and exuding confidence...of course this is nothing new. He has always had no qualms when it came to blathering 'bout his brilliance even when his polling numbers were in the low single digits.

So, is he a new Newt or the same old, same old Newt?

For what seems like decades...oh wait it is decades; Newt has been described as erratic, undisciplined, grandiose, caustic, and lots more. He's even been accused of being the architect of the current state of destructive partisanship which holds us all victim. You see the old Newt was not content with merely beating an opponent; he had to destroy them, pulverize them, demonize them. The result, instead of healthy honest debate on differing opinions and approaches, we now have candidates from both parties not only wallowing in the mud themselves but pulling us all down in there with them.

Has Newt changed? Will Newt, new or old, prevail? My guess is, in that deli line, Mr. Romney's number will end up being the final one called.

(I have written about all of these candidates in columns past. Should you wish to read those columns please go to wendylevenfeld.com under the "Columns" heading and do a search for their names. The columns will pop up.)

# The Answer to Our Problems

Have you heard the news? We've been given an answer to "what is wrong with our world?" A Saudi Arabian, American-educated, retired professor, has published his finding from a study he conducted pointing to the culpable culprit, the evil enabler, the villainous vermin responsible for oh so, so, so many of our woes. What horrific, monstrous practice can be at the middle of all that is wrong with our world? Well ... ah ... before the big reveal, let me just take a moment to go into the study itself.

It is based on "unstructured direct interview methodology" conducted in two unnamed Arabian Gulf countries and one unnamed Northern African country. In other words, there were no set questions and no apparent pre-determined parameters. It is my understanding that this method of unstructured direct interviewing is primarily used in reputable studies to obtain a profile of the respondents. The answers given are used to determine the respondent's suitability for "rounding out" the cross section requirements of the actual study...a true cross section of the population being the optimum result.

But, strangely enough, unanimous answers were received to all of the questions asked in this study ... unanimous answers to all of the questions asked! Makes one wonder about the randomness of the people questioned doesn't it? I don't know about you, but I find that when people of like minds gather they tend to agree!

O.K. enough about the methodology, onto the findings; so, what is at the center of what ails our world? Is the suspense killing you yet?

Drum roll please ... the evil is: women having the right to drive an automobile.

Excuse me?

Oh yes, all of the people he asked were not only against women driving but felt that it was the reason behind all of their societies' woes, citing many examples of what does happen where it is allowed and what could happen if Saudi Arabia were to allow it.

The study results state that women driving leads to adultery, divorce, rape, illegitimate children, homosexuality and much, much more.

Oh My! Oh My! How can civilized nations allow such a thing? That despicable, depraved, practice of allowing women drivers; that is definitely what is responsible for all of the problems of the world. Why has no one thought of it before? It is so very obvious...right in front of our faces the whole time!

I would personally like to thank our retired professor for his selfless efforts to aid in mankind's struggles by bringing this important research to light.

But, it was not for me that he released his results. His desired audience was his home country. He warned the Saudi royal family, which is leaning toward allowing women to drive, to "tread carefully and slowly when it comes to women's rights because one thing might lead to another, until homosexuals start demanding and getting rights."

What a true visionary this man is!

# Twelve Stories of 2011

(To be sung to the Twelve Days of Christmas)

It's the end of the year so it's time to look on back
T'was the year of two thousand e-lev-en

The Monarchy's future seems safe and secure
Will married Kate
T'was the year of two thousand e-lev-en

North Korea morns the death of Kim Jong Il
Bizarre tyrant dies
Will married Kate
T'was the year of two thousand e-lev-en

Our economy has stalled taking Europe down with it
E U's in peril
Bizarre tyrant dies
Will married Kate
T'was the year of two thousand e-lev-en

At last we can all make a sigh of relief
Obama got Osama!
E U's in peril
Bizarre tyrant dies
Will married Kate
T'was the year of two thousand e-lev-en

More silly men think they never will be caught
Weiner showed his weiner
Obama got Osama!
E U's in peril
Bizarre tyrant dies
Will married Kate
T'was the year of two thousand e-lev-en

Cheers round the world for another tyrant gone
Qaddafi dies at last
Weiner showed his weiner
Obama got Osama!
E U's in peril

Bizarre tyrant dies
Will married Kate
T'was the year of two thousand e-lev-en

Lots of people tee'd off by upper one percent
Protests in the streets
Qaddafi dies at last
Weiner showed his weiner
Obama got Osama!
E U's in peril
Bizarre tyrant dies
Will married Kate
T'was the year of two thousand e-lev-en

Optimism for what is called the Arab Spring
But, who's in power now?
Protests in the streets
Qaddafi dies at last
Weiner showed his weiner
Obama got Osama!
E U's in peril
Bizarre tyrant dies
Will married Kate
T'was the year of two thousand e-lev-en

The Justice system finally came down very hard
Blago's off to jail
But, who's in power now?
Protests in the streets
Qaddafi dies at last
Weiner showed his weiner
Obama got Osama!
E U's in peril
Bizarre tyrant dies
Will married Kate
T'was the year of two thousand e-lev-en

Earthquake, tsunami and even a nuke leak
Japan's triple whammie
Blago's off to jail
But, who's in power now?

Protests in the streets
Qaddafi dies at last
Weiner showed his weiner
Obama got Osama!
E U's in peril
Bizarre tyrant dies
Will married Kate
T'was the year of two thousand e-lev-en

Our government is grid-locked and can't seem to act
Congress should be fired
Japan's triple whammie
Blago's off to jail
But, who's in power now?
Protests in the streets
Qaddafi dies at last
Weiner showed his weiner
Obama got Osama!
E U's in peril
Bizarre tyrant dies
Will married Kate
T'was the year of two thousand e-lev-en

Happy New Year to all.

# Mayhem at the Mall

Holy Ho, Ho, Ho! What is happening with our youth? Have you heard about the riot at the Mall of America perpetrated amidst the throngs of mid-day returners, exchangers and bargain hunters on the day after Christmas?

Police received reports of dozens of out of control teens participating in up to ten separate fights. Chairs were flying in the Food Court. Displays were being smashed in the stores. Innocent bystanders were being pummeled.

Instead of sharing family time with visiting friends and relatives or even experiencing the adrenaline rush from exchanging the unwanted gift for the coveted one; these kids simply ran amok.

Apparently, it all started with the "rumor gone viral" that rappers Lil' Wayne and Drake were visiting the mall. First off let me admit that I have no clue as to who these guys are and I am equally in the dark as to why on earth their appearance in a mall would spark the violence and destruction we all witnessed thanks to all of those tweeters and texters posting the real time chaos.

Man alive, it was a war zone!

But this was not a strictly isolated incident; sadly not. There have been reports by the dozens, as of late, documenting gangs of teens causing random acts of malicious mayhem in countless stores throughout the country. Apparently a cyberspace message goes out as to where and when and hoards of kids show up to destroy displays, clear the shelves by smashing their contents to the floor and yes, taking what they want as their prize.

What I keep asking myself is why?

What in the world is going on...oh wait, could it actually have something to do with exactly that? Could what is going on in the world be feeding into and exacerbating the typical prank-like antics of youth?

Look at the world as these kids see it; remembering that they have no experience with the seemingly simpler, gentler world in which we all grew up. They've known nothing but war abroad and violence at home. They hear crude and often disgusting political rhetoric and see the shameful way many of our leaders behave. They witness religious hatred, have lived through devastating terrorist attacks and feel the very real dread of financial uncertainty. They are bombarded with violence wherever they look whether it be on T.V., at the movies or in their video games. Their parents, if they are lucky enough to have two, are both working leaving them to their own devises most of the time and they are under enormous pressure both peer, to be cool and parental/institutional, to be successful.

I am not excusing this despicable behavior. I only look for answers and yet they come not.

The Mall of America is reported to be the largest retail/entertainment complex in the U.S. Now another "largest" can be added to the list; one that I am sure is not wanted...the largest scene of Mall Mayhem.

# 2012

# The Glee of Resolutions

I have a personally embarrassing admission. I have never seen the T.V. show Glee. I have no excuse; just haven't tuned in. I doubt that I am alone in this. I'll bet there are lots of you out there that have not seen the show. The embarrassment comes from my complete, long term love affair with the genre of "musicals." I do not exaggerate when I unequivocally state that I love, love, love musicals. From the time, when in middle school, my Grandmother took me to New York to see three of them on Broadway; I have been hooked. I have performed in them in high school, have subscribed to various theatrical subscription series throughout the years, have advanced from memorizing lyrics off of 33 and 1/3 L.P.'s to CD's; I have even written a couple of musical productions myself. Strange, don't you think, that I have had no desire to watch the musical/comedy Glee?

So, why do I bring this perplexing quandary up? I find myself utterly intrigued with one of its stars.

Have you noticed that you cannot have the tube on without seeing a commercial featuring Jane Lynch? For those of you, like me who don't watch the show, she plays a warm-up suit wearing, snide remark slinging, !@#$% and I'm told is funny as all get out!

In her commercials, she sings and dances and mugs for the camera in a charmingly self-deprecating fashion poking fun at herself by adopting a kinda caricature of the character she plays on the show.

Not only is she on the series, she still does theatre, scads of commercials and she even hosted the Emmy Awards Show this past year.

The gal is everywhere!

I first became aware of her talents when she guest starred in a recurring role on Criminal Minds on CBS. She played the boy genius of the FBI Behavior Analysis team's mentally unstable mother. She was absolutely compelling and quite brilliant in the role.

My assessment at that time...gifted, serious actress.

So, what to make of all the attention she is receiving for musical comedy prowess? Well, it prompted me to look into her career to see what else she had done. I was stunned at the body of work she had amassed but even more taken by the quantity of comedic roles she has played. Silly me; I assumed that she was a dramatic actress who had recently punched a new notch in her genre belt with this musical/comedy role on Glee!

So What? "Get to the point" you might be saying by now.

O.K. here it is. As we embark on this New Year, an election year no less, I am making a resolution. I am going to strive to look for the backstory, not rely simply on that which I think I know, but do my homework into what is the reality.

So, what do you think? Wanna join me in this resolution?

# Mission Possible?

I haven't seen the new Mission Impossible movie but I am hearing that people really like it. Never having been a Tom Cruise fan, I must begrudgingly admit that the man does know how to make crowd pleasing movies. Honestly, what's not to like about intrigue, and suspense, huge explosions with matters of life and death hanging in the balance? These bigger than life extravaganzas have a pull, a hook that seems to capture the adventuresome spirit, those deeply hidden heroic virtues we like to believe reside in all of us.

Picture, if you will, a tinted windowed car, let's see ... make it a black Mercedes ... driving along a rather congested street in Iran. Out of a side street a motorcycle comes into view and weaves its way through traffic edging up alongside the car. As the two vehicles move in tandem, the cyclist pulls some sort of metal device from his leather jacket and attaches it magnetically to the speeding car's door. The motorcycle speeds away and KABOOM!!! The car seems to belch black smoke into the air and as it clears, all that remains is the burnt-out shell of the once quite beautiful vehicle and the charred remains of its occupant.

Could be a great opening scene for yet another Mission Impossible sequel, no? But this scene was not shot on a film set. It was not casted with actors and while it was most definitely scripted, the objective was not to create movie ticket sales. This scene was very real indeed and the occupant of that car was one of Iran's nuclear scientists.

Mostafa Ahmadi Roshan was in that car and is but the latest Iranian nuclear scientist to fall victim to an assassin's attack. Five Iranian scientists or engineers affiliated with their nuclear program have been killed and one other narrowly escaped an attempt in the past few years.

It is pretty much universally assumed that it was Israel's highly reputed and feared Mossad agents that have pulled off the picture perfect, precise and very lethal missions aimed at thwarting Iran's efforts to attain nuclear weaponry.

For its part, Israel is neither confirming nor denying having masterminded and executed the attacks yet those in the know can't help but see the hallmarks of an Israeli operation.

"This tactic is not a new one for Mossad," a former Mossad Officer stated. "It worked very effectively against Egypt's rocket program in the 1960's."

Secretary of State Hillary Clinton has emphatically denied any involvement by the U.S. in these attacks yet, not surprisingly, a poll indicates that on the streets of Tehran it is believed that these attacks are some kind of concerted effort between the U.S. and Israel.

I can't tell you how many times in the past several years friends have said to me that we shouldn't be worried about Iran's nuclear capabilities. They stated confidently that if Iran gets too close to having nukes, Israel will just "take 'em out."

I don't know ... could this be evidence of a "Mission Possible?"

# A Private Matter

I really love the game of football. This surprises many who know me ... why I am not sure, but it does. As an eleven year old, with two older brothers watching out for me, I was the quarterback in our neighborhood touch football games which took place in the vacant lot next to Chuckie O'Malley's house. The thought was that I was less likely to get hurt in that position, but in reality it was because I had a pretty good arm parlayed with an accurate eye.

I have been enthralled with the game ever since.

Even if you are not into the sport my guess is that you have heard some of the rumblings about the Denver Bronco's young quarterback Tim Tebow. He's the good looking kid who is an unabashedly devout Christian and displays that devotion by taking a knee after every game and crediting all of his prowess to his lord.

Much has been made of this in the media; some lauding his wholesomeness, while others poking fun at him. There are scads of people in both camps. Religion has become a big story on the sports' pages.

All of this made me think about another arena where religion has also become a player...politics. We have seen a dramatic rise over the past decade of religious beliefs playing a role in our political system. As with Tim Tebow, there are those on both sides of the question: is this a good thing or a bad thing?

Since time immemorial athletes have been crossing themselves before stepping up to the plate or free-throw line and thanking God for their win before saying "Hi!" to mom. Every baseball fan of an age remembers star pitcher Sandy Koufax refusing to pitch in a World Series game scheduled on Yom Kippur.

Likewise, politicians have always asked God to "bless America" and invoked His name in speeches. And let us not forget the question when JFK was running, whether he would be taking his marching orders from the Pope because he was Catholic.

But, what is happening now is different.

In these complex confusing times it seems appropriate for us to try to find meaning and purpose in our lives, ergo religious fervor. The question is shouldn't our faith be a personal thing, a private matter?

There have always been those who, for lack of a better word, flaunt their faith but they have never been considered main stream. I don't know about you, but I'm thinking that is rapidly changing.

For those athletes and politicians insisting that their faith somehow enables them to be more successful or better than those choosing not to vocalize their beliefs, there is a great quote from a church leader in Louisiana that I think they should take heed of.

When New Orleans first named their football team the Saints, he was asked if he thought that it was a bit presumptuous to which he replied "I think they should remember that all of the saints were martyrs!"

# Poetry, Prose and Politics

Did you watch the State of the Union Address last week? I thought it was a really well crafted, well delivered speech. While not agreeing with some of the policy parameters and noticing the President's neglect of several important issues facing us as a country, I gotta say I still think our President brought his "A game." Even Fox News political panelist Charles Krauthammer, an often virulent opponent of the President, acknowledged the speech as a good one (while of course disagreeing with the substance).

And the Republican "rebuttal" by our own Governor Mitch Daniels was also really quite good. Again, I was not in agreement with some of what he said, but he presented his criticism of the current administration and yes even a few compliments, in a well-organized (although less stylized than that of the President) competent manner. Even MSNBC political panelist Chris Matthews, himself an often virulent opponent of the Republican Party, acknowledged the speech as a good one (while of course disagreeing with the substance).

Just as a side note, how interesting that Mitch got the nod for the rebuttal. There are grumblings that with the Republican primary being viewed by many as a "Dumb and Dumber" sequel, the powers that be selected a calm, successful governor to present their case in the hope of garnering favor with the Independents out there who have been "scared off" by the antics of many of the republican candidates...oh but wait, Mitch isn't a candidate. Isn't selecting him just pointing out the shortcomings of those who are the candidates?

Anyway, what I took away from the two speeches was that the President is trying to once again stir-up the troops with that Yes We Can fervor of four years ago; his eloquence in delivery and quite lovely language complete with imagery, almost lulling us into forgetting that the reality of governance is quite different.

The Governor, on the other hand, using not the imagery of hope was predicting, in his own style of language and delivery, dire consequences if a change is not made in the White House. To my mind he was every bit as eloquent.

Whether waxing romantic or scaring the bageebers out of us, the political rhetoric from both men was definitely in campaign mode.

Many years ago, I had the pleasure of meeting Mario Cuomo, former Governor of New York, whom many considered to be not only a mesmerizing speaker but one of the truly masterful politicians of the 20th century. There is a wonderful quote of his that I believe to be "right on" in a presidential election year and one that we should all keep in mind when assessing what a candidate or even a party representative says during a campaign season.

"One campaigns in poetry but has to govern in prose."

# Can They Do That?

Why is it that just when you think you can relish the prospects of a new year, a clean slate, a fresh beginning you are pulled up short by the realization that before you know it you will have to tackle the ever perplexing, always annoying job of preparing your tax return?

Even every presidential candidate is proclaiming the need for broad sweeping tax reforms...aha one thing upon which they can agree. The problem is, of course, they disagree dramatically on what the reforms should be; but that is a tale for yet another time!

While sitting in a restaurant I could not help but overhear the conversation at the next table. Two very irritated, loudly vocal diners were expressing their discontentment with having to pay any taxes at all.

While I, like I am sure most of you, do see the necessity of paying taxes for the common good, one has to wonder why so much of what we pay in seems to be spent on a lot of gobbly-gook.

At this "almost Oscars time" I draw a reference to the wonderful movie Charlie Wilson's War wherein Tom Hanks played Congressman Wilson brilliantly. The movie documents Wilson's ability to get a pet project of his funded using tax payer dollars.

Did Congress believe in the merits of Wilson's proposed project for funding? No. He was able to procure mega-bucks from fellow legislators because it seemed everyone owed him favors. The funds were then used to arm and train the Afghani rebels fighting the Soviet Union. While successful in that initial goal, unfortunately it led to our training etc. of the very fighters that went on to become Al-Qaida! OOOPS!

If our tax dollars are/were being spent for purposes so obviously against the common good, I ask, is that even legal? Can we be taxed to support anything at all the Congress decides to fund? What exactly are the constitutional parameters of our government's ability to tax its citizenry and the usage of those tax dollars acquired?

I found that like so much in our constitution, the guidelines for taxation are stated quite simply, in the vaguest of terms.

Article 1, Section 8, Clause 1 (commonly referred to as the taxing and spending clause) states: "The Congress shall have the power to lay and collect taxes, duties, imposts and excises to pay the debts and provide for the common defense and general welfare of the United States; but all duties, imposts and excises shall be uniform throughout the United States."

That's it? That's all the Constitution states regarding the subject? Yep, I'm afraid so.
The argument is often made that the "wiggle room" that was intentionally written into the Constitution is the reason the document has served us well for lo these many years. The Founding Fathers had the foresight to allow for flexibility.

Personally, when I think of the ominous task of compliance with IRS requirements; I can only shake my head and wonder how such a simple concept as stated in the Constitution has morphed into the behemoth with which we now have to contend on an annual basis.

So, good-bye happy new year. Hello tax season!

# Alzheimer's Then and Now

At eight or nine years old I was very excited to be going to New York with my Grandmother. I had her all to myself...no brothers or cousins with whom I had to share her attention. Yippee!

Not so yippee, the trip included an excursion to a "mental hospital" where one of her cousins was doing some sort of research for a year before he had to return to Germany. It was a long drive through the city. It was dark; he could only see us in the evening. When we arrived we had to pass through locked gates where a uniformed man had to check his list to make sure we were expected and the gate clanged shut as the car passed through. I remember feeling very apprehensive and my Grandmother kept giving me reassuring looks.

The structure we pulled up to was gothic and looking back could have been the setting for any "B" horror movie. The cousin was very nice serving us cookies and tea. I was able to pick up from their conversation that he was studying people who had been normal but as they aged became kinda "crazy."

Fast forward to my early thirties, a time before the word Alzheimer's was in everyone's vocabulary, I was working with a client, a nursing home, on some radio ads to attract new residents. I was pretty comfortable with this particular client. We had worked together in the past. But my task this time was to effectively introduce a new service they were offering. They had opened up an "Alzheimer's" floor; the first such facility in the area.

Upon arrival at the "home" when the Administrator asked if I wanted to see the floor (there was tremendous pride in her voice) I of course said yes. We entered the elevator wherein she had to use a key instead of just pushing the button.

As the door opened, I was filled with horror. Around the nursing station, tied into wheelchairs, were the patients in various states of consciousness. They were obviously drugged and looked to have been totally ignored.

I literally ran from the place. Once in my car, I called Drew pleading with him, with tears running down my face, to shoot me rather than put me in a place like that.

Today there are over five million Americans suffering from the disease and that number is predicted to double by the year 2050. Everyone knows someone with Alzheimer's.

But there is hope. With heightened awareness and funding, great strides have been made in the development of medications to abate the mental deterioration. Earlier this month the government announced a boost in funding of fifty million dollars to look into the genetic underpinnings of the disease. And there are facilities designed to treat patients with respect and compassion.

We certainly have come a long way from those early memories of mine but as any family dealing with Alzheimer's will tell you; we still have so much farther to go.

# Rolling in the Deep

She was literally bouncing with excitement as the camera came in for a close-up. She had sky-rocketed to notoriety; first stop, video fame then on to singing with the back-up choir at last year's Oscar award's show and now in a Target commercial which ran several times during the Grammy Awards. And here she was in the spotlight, live this time, on Good Morning America. Her excitement was palpable as George Stephanopoulos asked the usual questions. Standing beside him, my guess, he was relieved to finally be interviewing someone who was shorter than himself...of course Denise Bestman, new shooting star of the music business, is only 11 years old. Sorry George, odds are she will outgrow you soon.

Here was this "little girl" on national T.V. self-consciously answering questions; her nerves apparent by the constant movement of her body. And the mike loomed, quite large and ominous next to her, as the camera moved out for the long shot. I could think of nothing else, could not hear a word of what she said. I could only murmur to myself; "Oh, please don't let her freeze up...please let her be great." And the moment came. She stepped to the mike and my heart clenched again when I realized she would be singing a cappella...no musical accompaniment, oh no! That is difficult even for seasoned professionals.

Her voice rang out powerfully, tone clear, notes hit easily with a crispness usually only present in a mature voice. "Rolling in the Deep...Rolling in the Deeeeeep." She sang the lyrics to one of the songs that made Adele the singing sensation of the year.

I breathed a sigh of relief. This little girl has IT and she proved it.

Ironically, the next segment of the show was reporting on Whitney Houston's death. It was ironic because she too was not even a teenager when her meteoric flight to stardom began. Like Denise, Whitney began by singing in choir. We all watched and loved "the voice" as Whitney would come to be known. We loved her songs. We were blown away by that amazing rendition of the Star Spangled Banner. We even loved her not so great attempts at acting just because she was Whitney. She seemed so grounded, grounded by her tight-knit family and by a spirituality that she was unashamed to make public.

Oh but then ... then her world seemed to crumble. Poor personal choices, public displays of bad behavior and all at once she went from glorious superstar to fodder for nighttime comedian jokes.

I couldn't help but think about the trap into which so many young, budding stars fall. They have such promise, so many possibilities but somehow the flames of the evil side of fame consume them leaving only embers of what could have been.

So Denise Bestman sang "Rolling in the Deep" on Good Morning America and sang it well. I looked up the meaning of the phrase and found it to be quite interesting. Rolling in the Deep is an old fashioned, poetic term for what boats do when they are far out to sea.

Will Denise Bestman fall victim to the rolling depths of fame or will she prove buoyant and smoothly ride the tide. Only time will tell.

# When You're Desperate...

I take great pride in the fact that I have refrained, up until now, from commenting on what has become the latest brouhaha in the presidential race. This whole religious freedom/birth control furor seems to be at the forefront of the media's attention.

When the story that the President enacted the policy mandating the provision of birth control in health care coverage provided by employers, the "Church" went ballistic.

All I was hearing from the media was what a mistake it was for the President to be roiling the waters; huge mistake to cut off potential supporters before his campaign is even in full swing. And true to form the Republicans jumped on this, thumping their chests and yelling about freedom of religion.

From the get go I thought it was a strategic move by the President. With Rick Santorum gaining steam in the Republican race and Mitt Romney jumping off a cliff to appease the far right of the party, I think the President formulated a calculated move, proving that, unlike his Republican adversaries, he has learned from the past.

The simple facts are that over 50% of voters in the last presidential election were women. Statistics also show that overwhelmingly voters are in favor of birth control. So it is only logical that all of those pro-birth control voters would be in favor of birth control options being a part of their healthcare plans.

And to make it worse for themselves, the Republicans framed the debate around freedom of religion. They made it a religious thing rather than a government interfering thing. Santorum has even brought up the whole question about the President's religion, again, by stating that the President has a "phony theology."

Paul Ryan, you know that smart kid from Wisconsin who is not running for president ... yet, gently nudged Santorum by suggesting that he went too far and should have framed his criticism around Obama's governance philosophy rather than his theology philosophy. He feels the better attack would be to point out that this is yet another example of bigger government interfering where it doesn't belong.

But no. They made it about religion and I personally think that the President bet that they would do just that. I think he knows that old saying: when you're desperate you forget what you've learned.

I think he felt that Republicans would remain true to form and go back to the tried and true, red meat social issues that have not worked for them in the past. Do they not remember?

And to add insult to injury, the congressional panel convened to examine all of this was comprised of all men. To quote Nancy Pelosi (not one of my favorite politicians but in this case she nailed it) "all men?" She moaned. "Not one woman on the panel? ... DUH!!!"

Come on Republican Party. Those of us who would love to see a viable candidate from you guys hereby remind you that one shouldn't react out of desperation:

When You're Desperate You Forget What You've Learned.
Of course that assumes that you have learned.

# Don't Mess With "Bebe"

Anyone who thinks that Benjamin Netanyahu (Bebe) is someone you can bully or cajole is badly mistaken.
It was a time in his previous term as Prime Minister of Israel when Yasser Arafat was the iron fist of the PLO. A rash of suicide bombings had occurred injuring, maiming and killing dozens of innocents in Israel. Riots were breaking out in the Palestinian areas of Jerusalem. Arafat stuck to his script telling the world that he couldn't control the "fanatics."
It was early morning when Bebe picked up the phone and called Arafat. He gave him until five that evening to stop the riots and call off the "Jihad" (holy war). Arafat started reciting his denial of any complicity when Bebe cut him off saying that he was ordering tanks to deploy to Ramallah (Arafat's headquarters).Their sights would be set on Arafat's home, offices and administrative buildings and that he would give the fire command if the streets of Jerusalem were not calm by then and the violence not stopped. Arafat began to protest and Bebe hung up.

I was in a group of about 10 people when Bebe related that story to us. It was told not to brag but rather in a matter of fact way pointing out Israel's resolve and capabilities when provoked.

All I can say is that bold action ushered in one of the longest periods of calm in the Israeli/Palestinian conflict to date.

So, now we have an older, some would say wiser Bebe being confronted with the prospect of Iranian nuclear weaponry.

And we have a U.S. President entering an election campaign with the significant power of the pro-Israel vote threatening to jump ship due to a perceived lessening of U.S. support for Israel under the President's leadership.

Hmmmm. Very interesting dynamic.

It is pretty common knowledge that there is no love lost between these two leaders; yet, they came together on Monday to discuss the whole "Iranian nuclear problem."

Bebe came out of his meeting with the President spitting fire in a speech later that evening. He stated that he would never gamble with the security of Israel. That Israel, as a sovereign state, has the right to defend itself and be the master of her own fate. He pointed out that Israel has never asked for or received American boots on the ground and that they are not asking for that now.

Obama argued that our intelligence indicates that Iran is still at least a year away from nuclear weaponry and there is time before a military strike is necessary ... Ah, I don't mean to be too picky but we did have a bit of an "egg on the face" moment when we relied on intel regarding weapons of mass destruction in the past.

Bottom line: President Obama wants to wait and let diplomacy work.

Bebe gave his reasoning for not waiting. "We've waited for diplomacy to work. We've waited for sanctions to work. None of us can wait much longer."

With the use of the word "much" Bebe made it clear that Israel will not move militarily against Iran immediately but it was also clear that Bebe, as he stated, "will never let his people live under the shadow of annihilation."

Like those many years ago, I think that Bebe has just picked up that phone and not only the Iranians but the world better be listening.

History has taught us that you don't mess around with Bebe.

# Rebel with a Cause

What is it about those bad boys that capture our hearts? You know what I mean, those guys that push at the boundaries of appropriate behavior yet know instinctively when to stop before breaking through. We love those rebels without causes, those adorable little imps that make you turn your head so they won't see you smiling at their antics before you compose yourself to face them with the stern face of disciplinarian. They act with no malice. They have no evil in their hearts but rather they have an enviable joie de vivre, an intrinsic spirit of joy that those of us who are ruled by logic can only wonder at. Women adore them while men, even if secretly, applaud their daring.

As the soap opera of the British Royals played out over the past few decades, millions watched the fairytale wedding of Prince Charles and Lady Diana disintegrate into scenes from a bad "B" movie; we saw their youngest, fire haired, Prince Harry emerge as the one that you could count on to bring a smile to your face. He is viewed as the loveable bad boy prince.

While his destined to be king brother and now sister-in-law receive the lion's share of media attention, it was Harry this past week who stole the show on the international stage. In honor of his grandmother's 60th anniversary since ascending to the throne, it was Harry who was sent to the Caribbean for a Royal visit, his first solo, toe in the water of international diplomacy moment.

At age twenty-seven and third in line to the throne; Harry, officially this time, captured the hearts of the world.

In an interview I saw he was relaxed and quite charming when stating that his only desire for the trip was to make his grandmother proud. I could almost hear the maternal "awwww how sweet" gasped by ma's and grandmas 'roud the world! When asked about how accessible and genuine he seemed with the mobs of people coming out to see him, his answer was, "With all of the warmth I felt from the people I just had to give it back." Another awwww.

And he was very clear that with his position came responsibility and he has taken up many of the charitable causes that were dear to his mother and many that he feels strongly about on his own. C'mon ladies let's hear another awwww!

He hammed it up while feigning to race with the fastest man alive ... jumping the gun to everyone's delight in the audiences. He donned blue suede shoes at another event having some now calling him a fashion icon! He even gave and received a warm hug from the Prime Minister of Jamaica even though she had very publically threatened Jamaica's cutting all ties to England.

The boyish imp has blossomed into quite an accomplished face for the royal family.

It certainly appears that he is no longer a rebel without a cause!

# Bye-bye Blago

Did you see the "farewell" address Blago gave on the day before he left for prison? With a teary-eyed Patti by his side, the now infamous mop-top looking in dire need of a trim and that, excuse the expression, @#$%-eatin' grin we've all come to know, plastered on his face; He spoke to a small crowd of reporters and an even smaller crowd of people gathered in front of his house. Spouting a slew of "Blago-isms" and I must admit sounding, can it be, a bit humble; he rambled for quite some time, invoking a bit of a mea culpa demeanor.

But just when I was feeling a tad sorry for the guy, wouldn't you know it; the next morning there were pictures of him posing jovially with fellow flyers, signing autographs, grinning rather stupidly at the camera when having his full-body security scan and by all appearances, having a grand ole time while seated on the plane making his way to a Federal Penitentiary in Colorado.

Does this man never learn? For pity sake, put your head down, ignore any cameras, keep your mouth shut and quietly make your way to your punishment.

So, that night I was having dinner with friends and the conversation inevitably turned to the former Governor's plight.

At this point I need to back track for a moment. One of my friends in attendance suffered a truly tragic family event now 2 decades past. Her brother was car-jacked. While he didn't resist, offering up the keys without a fight; one of the 2 men threatening him at gun point simply blew his head off.

The two men, who were quickly caught, tried and convicted; ended up serving less than seven years. Unbelievable isn't it? Between the two of them, they served less than seven years for senselessly taking the life of a young stranger.

O.K. Now, back to Blago's incarceration. While none of us around that dinner table had much sympathy for the ex-Gov. but given the sentencing of those two murderers (a story with which we were all so familiar); does it seem fair that he received a 14 year sentence for basically being a foul mouthed huckster trying to personally cash in on his elected position while those other two thieving, murderers received less than seven years between them?

As much as it pains me to say it 'cause I do think he is a total sleaze; it does seem like Blago kinda got the shaft!

So, I looked to find out just how this disparity in sentencing could occur. The distinction is quite simple. Blago's was a Federal Court case while the murder of my friend's brother was a matter for the State Courts.

In Federal Court there are specific sentencing guidelines. The Judge has the say-so in how lenient to be within those guidelines. The judge in Blago's case was a tough, old-time punishment pronouncer who could not cotton to Blago's high profile, ludicrous antics. He seemed disgusted by not only the offence but the modus operandi as well; thus, the steep sentence.

I hate to repeat myself but honestly Blago, you shoulda just put you head down and kept your mouth shut!

# Tech Tom-foolery!

My e-mail was hacked into and I am not happy! I'm quite sure that those in my e-mail address book who received bogus communications from me aren't either. Fortunately, it was a "harmless" intrusion meant as a nuisance and nothing more. I have heard horror stories from friends of having entire contact lists and e-mail files deleted, lost out in cyberspace, never to be seen or heard from again.

I guess I should be grateful for that not being my case. I should feel lucky not to have to reconstruct my entire "e-mail life." But, I am not grateful. I do not feel lucky. I am teed off! I just don't get it. What was the point?

Several months ago, I wrote a column about the epidemic of computer crimes plaguing our society (http://wendylevenfeld.com/index.php/columns/199-cyber-security) It is appalling just how many people can and do invade the privacy of individuals and organizations on a minute to minute basis.

Nothing I can do about that so, back to my plight. I wanted to send out notification to all of my contacts letting them know what had occurred. I felt I needed to warn them.

But, wait! What's this error message I received?

Since a hacking occurred sending a mass e-mail from my account to my entire address book (which I reported and then completed all of the steps necessary to cleanse and reactivate my account) I was now being denied access to my own contacts list.

O.K. Now I was really getting angry. After several communications prompted from my provider's website, I was finally told that I would be able to send e-mails in a couple of hours but I had to divide up my contact list into groups of no more than twenty. No more mass e-mails from me would be accepted.

So the hacker could "shot-gun" his venom to my whole list while my efforts to notify them to potential hacking danger had to be batched in groups of twenty which literally took me over an hour to accomplish?

Then, to add insult to injury, later in the morning, thinking that all was well once again in my little techno-doofus world; I tried to access my account from my smartphone. Guess what? My smartphone told me that it wasn't so smart after all. I could not get into my e-mail.

I tried my new password. I tried my old password...NOPE!

I finally, got in the car and took a trip to Verizon where a really nice tech support guy who had short strawberry blonde hair, wore braces and looked to be no older than 12 years old, took a second and a half to get me back into business. Like it wasn't bad enough to waste my entire morning dealing with all of this; I had to be rescued by Opie Taylor!

I am now glad to report that I am back on line, plugged in, booted up and rarin' to go but, oh my word; what a hassle.

I certainly don't condone it but at least I can understand the motivation when some kind of personal gain is achieved by cybercrimes. But, this nonsensical, malicious, tech tom-foolery that serves no purpose except to frustrate and annoy the recipient; this I just don't get.

# New Realities

Mad Men is back for another season. I don't know if it is the familiarity of being transported for an hour a week back to the time of my youth or if it is just the compelling characters and storylines, but I have to admit; I love the show. It takes place in the environs of a Madison Avenue advertising agency in the early sixties complete with constant smoking and drinking and subtle (at times not so subtle) sexual innuendo and action. It was a time when ethnic and racial slurs made up a part of the humorous banter in the hallways. And this season heralds in the first-time hiring by the agency of an African-American and a Jew. Those were the realities in the workplace then.

Maybe part of the show's draw is being able to pat ourselves on the back acknowledging just how far we have come since that time.

Anyway, there was a great line in Sunday's episode. Roger Sterling, one of the main characters, after a discussion of the upheaval in the agency, a few words about life and death concerning a pending cancer diagnosis and an unsuccessful stab at getting the Rolling Stones to perform a jingle for the agency's client, Heinz Beans, he turns at the door before leaving and says, "When is everything going to get back to normal?"

Back to normal; made me start thinking.

There is a new book out "Going Solo" by Eric Klinenberg. It looks at the astonishing trend relating to single adults. To put his findings quite briefly, 22 percent of adults in the U.S. were single in 1950. Today it's more than 50 percent, and one out of every seven adults lives alone...one out of seven! That makes adults living alone larger percentagewise than any other domestic unit, including the nuclear family. Quite startling, no? And the U.S. is not an anomaly.  The trend is rising throughout the world. This demographic is a new reality and we better adjust to it.

So, what exactly are some other current realities to which we better start adjusting? We have a political system that doesn't seem to have a chance of working. We have our tax code, health care system, energy policy (or lack thereof) public education system and geopolitical threats, all of which are alarmingly ineffectual or even downright frightening and none of which were in the consciousness of those good ol' Mad Men.

Whether we like it or not, this is our new reality. It seems to me that we better recognize the "here and now" and come to grips with it. We have to stop moaning about the way things were and live with the way things are.

It's not easy. Oh, no it is not. In fact, as I sit here rereading these words I find myself wanting to open that office door on the set of Mad Men and as I depart through it, question with longing, "When is everything going to get back to normal?" And then have someone reply with a date!

# One Man One Vote

Have you heard of the National Popular Vote Movement? From a very unofficial poll I have conducted (those in line at drug stores, grocery stores and movie theaters!) I have yet to find anyone who has. I certainly do not consider myself an authority on the movement but let me give you a smattering of what it is all about.

It calls for the abolishment of the current Electoral College system. It would enable the presidential candidate receiving the most votes to win.

Wow, that's major and most of us haven't heard of it.

I don't know about you but it seems like a pretty good thing to me. After all, are we not the land of "one man, one vote?" Doesn't it seem that we are giving up some of that ideal when we put the power to elect our president in the hands of some amorphous group of delegates called the Electoral College?

Why not just have a simple, "he who gets the most votes in November is the President?"

Arguments against the movement include:

*Instituting this system would double or triple the cost of campaigning.
I guess candidates would be forced to effectively deal with their own campaign budget, making tough choices so they can actually pay attention to people living in non-swing-state locations.

*It would lead to massive law suits dealing with voter fraud or miscounts.
I don't have stats, but I have heard of very few lawsuits stemming from gubernatorial contests. The states seem to do a pretty good job of counting their votes and deciding on the candidate of their choice. (Uh, let's just not include Florida!)

The good news for those trying to advance this movement is that it does not take a constitutional amendment. It does not require an act of Congress.

We keep hearing about the "magic number" of electoral votes needed to become President of the United States. Well, there is another "magic number" dealing with electing a president. If states representing a majority of electoral votes (the magic number is 270) pass in their state legislatures the National Popular Vote policy; it will be instituted nationwide.

To date there are 8 states and the District of Columbia (representing 132 electoral votes) where it has passed. That means we are almost halfway there. halfway to totally changing the way we elect a president and yet, until very recently, I had never even heard of the movement and according to my "pollees" neither had they.

Kinda amazing, don't you think, that in an election year when we keep hearing about the desire to see less Federal Government in our lives, this tremendously impactful "States Rights" issue hasn't been brought to the attention of the American people in a big way?

Just sayin'!

(I wrote an article about how I would totally change the system during the 2008 presidential campaign which certainly still applies. If you are interested, you can find it at www.wendylevenfeld.com under the "Columns" heading: search Campaign Recipe.)

# How to Change the Game

I doubt that anyone would argue with the statement that the election of Barack Obama was a monumental event in our political, social, historical and just about every other "cal" aspect of our country. He spoke with eloquence. He ran a masterful campaign and his supporters assumed that mastery would translate into a masterfully run presidency.

So, three and a half years ago this man was elected. There was hope in the hearts of most, tears in the eyes of some and great optimism for our future in the air. Barack Obama proved that anything is possible in the United States of America.

While his opponent, John McCain, came up with his strategy of "game change;" Obama didn't need a game changing strategy he was the game changer.

But now three and a half years later, how exactly has the game changed?
In the early 1900's, college football had become the rage attracting tens of thousands of fans to games while major league baseball, at the time, was lucky to get a couple of thousand in the stands. This relatively new sport had stolen the hearts of the American people.

At the time, on the gridiron, no one had ever seen or even conceived of passing a football during a game. Nope. No passing, only running, tackling and the hope of scoring.

Risking being besieged by angry e-mails, it was not, as many believe, Notre Dame that first inserted the forward pass into the game. But that is a topic for another column. The point is that the idea to have the ball thrown down field gave birth to modern-day football.

Now, that was a game changer...or was it? There were still 100 yards that had to be covered. There was still the required number of men on the field. There were still referees and fifteen minute quarters and countless other aspects of the sport that remained the same. Football was still football.

And no matter how significant the election of Barack Obama was, no matter how broad reaching the movement behind him stretched; American politics is still American politics.

So, if even the election of Obama really changed very little, what could?

I think Hillary has an answer. During the campaign she got lambasted for addressing this very point.

A successful social movement needs two leaders with two very different, distinct sets of strengths. She pointed to the Civil Rights Movement as example and got slammed for it.

But, in my opinion, she was dead-on.

The Civil Rights Movement could not have succeeded on the strengths of Dr. King alone. It needed the political savvy of President Johnson to make it happen.

So, now it is three and a half years later and I have to believe that many lessons have been learned. A true social movement needs not only one figurehead with power. It needs both a leader that inspires people to action and a savvy politician that can get things done in Washington. Put those two things together and just watch how the game will change!

# Mouse Droppings in Government Cabinets

Ah, Spring! Tis the time to open the windows and air out the house, empty the cabinets and drawers for an annual deep cleaning and move the furniture to get at those places that have been ignored by the vacuum for far too long.

I think our government could use a few industrious women to pick up the brooms and dust rags. Yep, it is past time to do some spring cleaning!

As the seemingly weekly barrage of governmental scandals keeps right on coming, the exposure of the Secret Service's, not so secret anymore, exploits while on "advance team duty" in Columbia is rocking the airwaves.

C'mon boys, you are supposed to be the best of the best, the crème de la crème, the elite units charged with keeping those of greatest importance to our nation safe; instead you are acting like teenagers auditioning for a new reality show, "Boys Gone Wild!"

Where are the grown-ups? What happened to a simple code of ethics? What could make the young adults (and some not so young and in supervisory positions) on this detail ignore not only protocol, but common sense as well?

Beats me. To my mind, these men are simply idiots and idiocy can be dangerous.

Current reports indicate that "foreign nationals" (Don't you just love euphemisms?) were brought into the hotel which would host the President and perhaps into the very rooms where his entourage will be staying. I know very little about security procedures but even I can see that this lapse in judgment is not only quite serious but potentially deadly.

And if that weren't bad enough, there's the GSA scandal being talked about as well. Have you heard that the Agency Head received a report from the Inspector General citing serious spending abuses? I don't know about you but if I were the one receiving that report, I would make it a top priority to get to the bottom of it. So, what happened ... the report was totally ignored. That fact is now receiving national attention because at least one government employed, conference attendee (expensing his trip to the tax payers) posted pictures of his "lavish exploits" out there into cyber land.

Will men in positions of power or authority ever learn? It's bad enough to betray the trust of the American People but then to publicize it to the world?

Anyone who has ever taken on the task of spring cleaning knows; when you start to clean that cabinet and find a few mouse droppings, there is a more serious problem than the immediate clean-up will require. You can't just simply wipe down the cabinet.

I fear these latest scandals are just the tip of the preverbal iceberg. You know as well as I that the few droppings you find in that cabinet are merely a herald of the larger, much more serious problem.

EEEK ... we've got governmental mice in our cabinets!

O.K., so we have found those few droppings. This should convey the message, loudly and clearly to those responsible for keeping our house in order; somebody better do something about the obvious infestation hiding in the darkened corners!

# Microcosms

I had completed our assignment on time and was really not looking forward to the classroom discussion. A crazy, peg-legged whaling captain; oh, c'mon! And page after page of truly boring details about those mammoths of the sea ... who cares? O.K. I think I got some of the symbolism and the "at sea" narrative was pretty descriptive but on the whole it was a ginormous white whale waste of time. It wasn't until I was introduced to a word during my teacher's opening comments on the book that I found compelled to read Moby Dick again, in a different light. The word was microcosm.

Did you see any of the President's comments at the White House Correspondent's Dinner this past weekend? This dinner is traditionally a platform for our Commander in Chief to show off his comedic prowess; his ability to, with tongue-in-cheek, toss a few zingers; his poise in self-deprecation. Truth be known, I never really paid much attention to this annual event until it was George W. Bush's turn at the mike. Who knew W. could actually be funny ... intentionally?

Anyway, there was the President at the dinner closing with the comment that he had more to say but, looking at his watch, he had to cut it short so he could get the Secret Service guys back home before the newly implemented curfew. The cameras panned to the uproarious laughing in the audience and then to the unmistakably, glowering faces of the Secret Service detail on duty. OOPS!

When lauding the virtues of the President I haven't heard any left wing pundits mention enormous courage. C'mon, he's got to be really brave to poke fun at the guys who are charged with taking a bullet for him. I sure wouldn't want to make those guys mad if it was my back they had.

I felt kinda sorry for them standing there being made fun of. It made me start thinking that isn't the Secret Service just another one of those microcosms my Junior High teacher was describing far too many years ago to mention? Here was the President lampooning several of his detail who had nothing to do with the embarrassing Columbia fiasco.

And in the broader sense aren't the campaigns themselves microcosms including within the bad-boys, the funny guys, the devious guys and even the truly genuine, altruistic guys? Should any individual within a group have to take the blows deserved by others in the group?

As on that ship in the hunt for Moby Dick, the current presidential campaigns are manned by individuals with all of the limitations and foibles, admirable qualities and quirks of nature found within our society. I hope that the Reps and Dems recognize that this is true within both of their parties and cut each other a little slack.

We find ourselves with two Ahab's in this race steering their party ships in the hope of capturing the huge, elusive white prize. We can only hope that in the hunt for capturing the great white house, they don't forget that Ahab's goal was to kill the whale but in his blind obsession for the prize, the great white killed him.

# Relationships Are Hard

Our fascination with "celebrity couples" (I include political pairings as well in this category) goes back to the Branjolina of their day Adam and Eve - so, would they have been called "Adeve" or "Evdam" by People Magazine if it were in print back then? Just something to think about...please don't thank me!

From the studio system of decades past making couples out of movie stars to promote their films to celebrity couples making headlines even in the "reputable news media" of our day; we seem to have a hunger to get the details of the relationships of others.

I think we have all heard the stat that half of the marriages in our country end in divorce; so is this fascination some kind of search for the secret of a great relationship? Or, perhaps it is the validation we might receive by having celebrity couples exposed as being no better than we at making relationships work.

Some may shrug off the behavior of actors and media celebs as "you know, those kind of people" as if they are somehow different from us because of what they do for a living. Yes, the scandals in the entertainment industry are rampant and titillating. But, I need only catch a news bit on the testimony in the John Edward's trial to confirm that even a man seeking to become the most powerful man in the world is a blundering idiot (forget how sleazy and disgusting the whole ,excuse the pun, affair was) when it comes to personal relationships. Again, we can say that's the political, "I can do anything" mentality we find in so many of our representatives.

But relationships are hard whether you are a news worthy notable or not and we, as a result, quite often really screw them up.

I saw an interview with the actress Rita Wilson ... not a household name but she has been a working actress for almost three decades. If one knows her name at all it is probably because she has been married to Tom Hanks for more than twenty years. While no one can really know what goes on behind closed doors, all accounts indicate that they have a really good marriage.

In the interview she was promoting a career change. She is releasing a musical CD and of course the interviewer had to ask what Hanks thought about her change in professional focus. She answered that he was excited and would welcome becoming "Mr. Wilson" instead of her being Mrs. Hanks.

I loved that answer.

I am no expert but I have been married for thirty-seven years and like Ms Wilson in that interview, I have been asked, "What is the secret to a successful marriage?"

First of all ... really dumb question. If there was a fool-proof guide book we wouldn't have half of the marriages in this country fail!

But I can offer one tip. So often we go into a relationship with expectations, if not demands, of what our partner should be, do, or become. Like Rita Wilson indicated about her marriage, a major factor in the success of my thirty-seven year marriage is the absolute knowledge I have that Drew only wants for me what I want for myself and vice versa.

# Honor Thy Father

Ben-Zion Netanyahu father of Israeli Prime Minister Benjamin (Bebe) Netanyahu recently died at the age of 102. While the loss of a parent is often a life-altering event, the senior Netanyahu's death seems to be particularly relevant at this point not only in his son's Prime Ministry but in the history of Israel itself.

Ben-Zion pushed Bebe to always maintain a hardline stance. One of Bebe's friends was quoted, "Always in the back of Bebe's mind is Ben-Zion. He worries that his father will think he is weak."
The Prime Minister himself also cited his father in televised comments two years ago when he spoke about the "impossibility of compromise:"

"We are very simply in danger of extermination today. Not just existential danger, but truly in danger of extermination. They think the extermination, the Holocaust, is over, it isn't, it goes on all the time..." The elder Netanyahu was quoted as saying.

And his son's entire political career was shaped and formed by the views of the father.

With that in mind, it is not surprising that Bebe keeps shoring up Israel's military capabilities.

In recent days an event with long-term implications for Israel's security has all but escaped serious attention. Three new "Dolphin" submarines were added to Israel's naval force. While what little media focus this did attract seemed to deal with rumored "special tubes" supposedly capable of housing nuclear-tipped missiles, the real significance is the huge boost this purchase will give Israel's long-range strategic capabilities.

But, even with these "super-duper subs," the Israeli on the street believes that, and I quote Charles Krauthammer, "Israel is currently facing the greatest threat to their existence – nuclear weapons in the hands of apocalyptic mullahs publically pledged to Israel's annihilation." I think we can all relate to that fear as we too are targets.

But, within Israel, while these external forces once again threaten; Bebe found himself in the midst of a legislative struggle. He had to do something to break domestic gridlock and silence politically driven dissention to be able to effectively address international threats.

So, we come full circle back to the passing of Bebe's dad.

In the middle of the night of May seventh, Bebe shocked many by making the call, soon to be voted on in the Knesset for early elections, moot. He brought the main opposition party, Kadima into a newly formed "National Unity Government" by agreeing to open up discussions on many points and giving Shaul Mofaz, the new leader of Kadima, "political power perks" he would never have thought of yielding while his father was alive.

"The State of Israel needs stability," Bebe stated at a news conference after a long night of negotiations with Mofaz. "The new coalition is good for the security of Israel, good for the economy of Israel, good for the society of Israel and good for the people of Israel."

While Mr. Netanyahu's popularity was already sky high, broadening the coalition significantly consolidates his power. He now has 94 of the 120 members of Parliament officially on his team ... What would our President give for those numbers?

So, Bebe has lost his father. I certainly mean no disrespect. But, it does appear that the elder Netanyahu's voice in his son's head isn't quite as loud as it used to be.

# Baseball and Politics

Growing up, baseball was "The Sport" in our house. My mother's Uncle Freddie, being a South-sider, had box seats for the White Sox and would give us tickets for several games each season. We were there when Bill Veck's exploding scoreboard exploded for the first time; forever changing the capabilities and fan expectations of scoreboards throughout the world of sports. I remember my brother missing a foul ball because my mom, fearing for his safety, reached an arm out in protection resulting in the man behind him making the catch. My brother's ensuing snit of all snits lasted long after the final out was called.

As a young mother, living on the North side, I became a Cub's fan as well. Our family outings to Wrigley Field make up many of the most wonderful memories of the young Levenfeld family. And thanks to WGN's early entry into syndication, and America's love of an underdog, the Cubs are quite simply the favorite losing team in the nation.

But now the Cubs are garnering yet more national attention which has nothing to do with the game of baseball. It is all about the game of Politics.

Have you been reading or hearing about the whole Super PAC/Wrigley field renovation/ Family Ricketts brouhaha?

For those who haven't, here's my take in case you want to keep score.

The Starting line-up:

Joe Ricketts is "TD Ameritrade's" founder, multi-gazillionaire and politically conservative activist.

Tom Ricketts, Joe's son, is the current Chairman of the Cubs.

Chicago Mayor Rahm Emanuel is with whom Tom Ricketts has been working to obtain City, County and State funds for a public/private venture to bankroll a much needed and costly Wrigley Field renovation.

For those of you scoring this game, those are the players; now, onto the action.

Reports are that Joe Ricketts was funding a $10 million political action committee aimed at defeating the President. It has also been reported that some of the ads created with those funds are, let's see how shall I put this, pretty sleazy.

Strike one!

But hey, I can't say that I agree with the whole super PAC epidemic afflicting both political parties but it is legal so what's the big deal, one might ask? Hmmm, let's score my opinion as...

Ball one!

We cannot forget that Rahm, whom Joe's son Tom desperately needs to work out the Wrigley field deal, is arguably the most staunch Obama supporter on the planet not to mention the President's longtime friend and campaign honcho.

OOPS. Tom cannot be too thrilled with his dad right about now.

Strike two!

So, Joe has begun back peddling. The announcement that the ads will not run is evidence of just how upset Tom is with his father. And Tom has released press statements distancing himself from the whole issue hoping to salvage any kind of a relationship with Rahm. But, to date, Rahm won't even take his calls.

OOOH, just like my brother all those years ago, it looks like, because of parental interference, Tom is going home from the ballpark empty handed.

Strike three ...YEEEER OUT!

# The Artistic Crime of the Century

It was a warm August day in New York City; the year 1974. August in New York with its predictably humid, heavy air was true to form on that particular day; a day when the impossible became possible and the unimaginable turned into reality.

You probably don't know the name Philippe Petit. I certainly didn't until I read a wonderful, bestselling book "Let the Great World Spin." Authored by Colum McCann, which has been described as a sweeping, radical, social novel. I personally prefer to categorize it as a really interesting, good read! But, all of that aside, the backdrop and almost a character of the book is the now very famous, fabulous crime committed by Philippe Petit. Petit was an adventurous young man when he strung a wire, 110 stories up, between the twin towers of the World Trade Center and proceeded to walk across. Eyewitness accounts confirm that he not only walked it, he scurried, hopped and at one point skipped across. His feat took over forty-five minutes which gave ample time for the word to spread and the masses to congregate below in awed silence.

As Manhattan seemed to stand still, with all eyes pointed upward, Monsieur Petit mesmerized and delighted, shocked and deliciously terrorized the thousands watching from below and through high-rise windows in the immediate area.

Coincidentally, or if you believe that there are no coincidences, ironically; having recently read the book; purely by chance, I stumbled upon a program Philippe Petit gave. HMMM, just read the book; then watched his program; was this some kind of message meant for me?

I figured I had better write about it!

Let me start by saying this man, now well into his middle aged years, is charming, witty, poised (no surprise there!) and amazingly inspirational. He is a gifted storyteller spinning his personal trials and tribulations into a wondrous tapestry. He embraced his audience and delightfully ushered them into his world while effortlessly relating valuable life lessons.

He identified six essential ingredients to which he attributes both his success and achievements: passion, tenacity, intuition, faith, improvisation and inspiration. He interestingly demonstrated how these six touchstones molded and shaped a six year old little boy who wanted to be a magician into the man that was able to conquer that thin wire 110 stories up delighting and inspiring not only a city and the nation but the entire world.

One of the characters in McCann's book is the judge who was given the ominous task of sentencing Petit for his crime... quite a dilemma, since the city whole-heartedly embraced the daring young man whose amazing "stroll across a Manhattan street" has come to be known as the Artistic Crime of the Century.

I prefer to think of that act of daring do, that moment in history, not as a crime but as a call to us all to become a bit more daring, a bit more self-fulfilled, a bit more intuitive. Rather than remembered as a crime, I will always consider that walk as Philippe Petit's gift to us all.

# A Brief Respite From Politics

I am a self-confessed political junkie. Those of you who read my column regularly (and I thank you very much) already know this. While I am tempted to write about Mitt's finally getting the numbers needed to officially be the Republican Presidential Candidate; I shall refrain.

Today, I take a respite from the world of politics and delve into another one of my passions—music.

I have never been a fan of Madonna's music. Don't ask me to name any of her songs except "Material Girl" and I only know that title because she is often referred to by that moniker. What I have most definitely been is a fan of her almost uncanny business sense. She has that non-learnable, indefinable, instinctive sense of what sells in the music industry and exactly how to sell it. For decades Madonna has morphed into new personas giving her millions of fans exactly what they want before they even know they want it.

But, now she has some competition from the self-described "biggest Madonna fan;" Lady Gaga. Again, don't test me on Gaga's hits... couldn't name a one but I could tell you about the infamous "meat-dress" she wore, the famous "egg entrance" to an awards show she made and the Christian groups in Korea wanting her concert cancelled for fear that she will spread homosexuality among their youth.

Despite imitation famously reputed to be the best form of flattery, apparently Madonna isn't too pleased with Gaga's emulation of her signature long blonde pony-tail concert hair or her costume cloned pointy, futuristic bras and especially Gaga's pilfering of the chord progressions in her famous "Born This Way" mega hit.

Madonna's "Express Yourself" was released in 1989 and just last year Gaga's "Born This Way" soared to super platinum sales. Immediately comparisons within the industry were made. On the Tonight Show Gaga told Leno that she received an email from Madonna's team "sending me their love and complete support," when rumors of a feud brewing surfaced.

I hadn't heard anything about a new multi-country tour by Madonna beginning this past weekend until last week when a rehearsal clip was released and went viral. Madonna apparently inserted verses from Gaga's "Born This Way" into her rendition of "Express Yourself." All at once Madonna's jab at Gaga was a story on most of the news shows, albeit a minor segment.

But, once again, the Material Girl brought herself into not only the entertainment world spotlight but put herself on the international news radar as well just before her concert tour began. How does she get it right, commercially, almost every time? Whether calculated or purely instinctive, the gal's got a gift!

Man, wouldn't either one of our Presidential candidates love to have her secret formula for self-promotion and giving the people what they want ... oh wait, whenever a political candidate "morphs" in order to capture voter support they are called a flip-flopper! Not good in politics! O.K. so maybe Madonna isn't such a great role model.

Darn! There went my respite from politics!

# Brothers in Politics

"Morning Joe" was broadcasting from Chicago this morning (Monday) and they couldn't have ordered a more beautiful day. Positioned in a plaza on North Michigan Avenue with the cameras pointed west, Joe and Mika were backdropped by what I think is the most beautiful skyline in the world. I hate to give the devil his due but "the Donald" did himself proud by erecting the architecturally stunning Trump Tower which shimmered silver behind them reaching up into the cloudless blue sky.

Joining them in the discussion was Bill Daley former Obama Chief of Staff and Presidential Cabinet Secretary during Bill Clinton's tenure as President. The talk was about Jeb Bush's' statements yesterday regarding the current state of the Republican Party.

The former Governor of Florida had been groomed to be President; was expected to make a run for it; had a really great chance of being the second "President Bush" by most accounts. He is a fiscal conservative, and proved to be somewhat moderate on social issues during his very successful tenure as Florida's top elected official. Most polls show that those are exactly the positions held by most Americans today.

Then, seemingly out of nowhere came W. surprising most by winning the Governor's mansion in Texas, and then usurping his brother's claim to the Presidency. Many books have been written documenting the fact that within the Bush family, around the dinner table so to speak, it was Jeb not W. who was supposed to be the brother sitting in the Oval Office. But we all know how that turned out!

So, what did Jeb have to say ... plenty! He basically lambasted the current "trend" in the Republican Party for not allowing disagreement or compromise. He evoked the memory of Ronald Reagan and his father as examples of Republican Presidents who worked with Congress to get things done. He pulled out the stops and squashed any rumors that he was a possible candidate for the Vice Presidency, not that Mitt would ask.

Bill Daley (and one couldn't be more Democratic than a Chicago Daley) actually praised Jeb for the job he did in Florida and the statements that he made yesterday. Certainly no stranger to sibling professional rivalry, Daley and his brother Richie seemed to have come to an understanding long ago to divvy up the family political pie; Richie taking the city while Bill took on D.C.

One can only imagine how different things might have been if the Bush Boys would have done similarly. Just think if the second President Bush had been the brother with a bit more moderate ideology and the nature to execute a bit more common sense approaches to policy making; well one can only speculate but it doesn't take a rocket scientist to know the current state of our country and that of the Republican Party would be very different.

Bill Daley almost sounded regretful when he said that because of the Bush name and the "anti-dynastic" sentiments of the American people, there is little likely hood that we will ever see another Bush in the White ... as least from this generation.

Looking at the two sets of brothers, the Daley's and the Bush's, one can only imagine what might have been if Jeb and W could have been a bit more like Richie and Bill.

# Reagan-itis

In modern political campaign rhetoric, most candidates, presidential and congressional are now, at some point, invoking the name of Ronald Reagan implying that they embody in some way his ideals and his absolute conservative convictions. Surprisingly it is not only Republicans but many Democrats jumping on the Reagan bandwagon as well. How on earth did that happen?

Awhile back I saw an excellent documentary on President Reagan. It was very well researched and quite long as I recall. The interviewees were very impressive. Reagan's official biographer Edmund Morris who spent 14 years with the Reagan's and had access to the president for all 8 years of his Presidency; Reagan's Chief of Staff, James Baker; Pat Buchannan, his Communication's Director; and a multitude of other Reagan biographers and members of the Reagan family all spoke candidly and not always flatteringly about a President whose "creds" seem to be continually growing.

The fact of the matter is, under Reagan, the size of government grew substantially. Running a national deficit became acceptable when it tripled in size under his stewardship. He increased taxes eleven times. Man, if this stalwart of American Conservatism was the incumbent running today on his record with members of the far right wing of the Republican Party to deal with; one has to wonder if he wouldn't be facing a challenge from within his own party for the Oval Office!

And one also has to wonder if all of the candidates genuflecting to the myth of Reagan have forgotten the "Arms for Hostages" scandal which took place on his watch? Or how 'bout the "Iran Contra Affair?" That was a good one. There we armed and trained the very same men who would turn our arms and training against us. The huge scandals resulting from these illegal activities taking place in the White House created a new moniker for the President. He became "the Teflon President" because none of the blame for all of the wrongdoing ever stuck to him.

And, finally, let us not forget his huge "flip-flop" going from union super-supporting democrat to union busting, big business backing republican ... can you imagine how that would play in this election climate?

But, hey, having said all of that, I have to admit, we Levenfeld's did very well economically during President Reagan's tenure. And, let's not minimize the importance of the elegance and style which seemed to come so naturally to Nancy and which, let's face it, was a welcomed relief from the somewhat dowdy Rosalind Carter. And then there's Reagan himself with his horse riding, fence mending, rancher rugged good looks, his ability to turn a phrase (and look great doing it) and the much publicized and very apparent "love affair" between he and Nancy; he was the man every man wanted to be and every woman wanted in her life. But the perplexing question is, with all that he really was then, was he really the "Conservative God" that everyone seems to make him out to be now?

# Character, Values and Birthday Parties

The phone rang at 3:30 in the morning. Groggy and astounded, Drew and I listened as our son-in-law announced that our fourth grandchild had been born ... in the car, on the shoulder of the highway, on the way to the Birthing Center. Not to worry, our beautiful baby girl and her mom are great and we are all feeling very blessed.

Coming almost three weeks early, all of our planning went out the window.

We dropped everything and boarded a plane to Boston to welcome her into the family and the world. It is almost indescribable that feeling of having your own little girl give birth to a little girl of her own. Memories come flooding back, birthday parties and special occasions of yore bringing smiles of joy.

During our visit, I saw a report on the growing trend of young parents spending absolute fortunes on their children's birthday parties. The stimulus for the report was the recent, way over the top, party Tori Spelling threw for her daughter Stella's fourth birthday.

Tori said that Stella (mind you, she is four) gave her strict orders to throw a pink and purple tea event that would be fit for a princess. And Tori did just that. The outdoor extravaganza was resplendent with huge balloon sculptures (pink and purple of course) spectacular pink and purple floral arrangements with matching dishes and tea cups and Disney characters including Belle and Cinderella in attendance walking around greeting the guests.

Granted we are talking about the Spellings, but even so, what were they thinking?

Apparently they were thinking what many other young couples are thinking: how to outdo the parents of their children's friends. Lavish, expensive children's birthday parties are not just for television royalty or movie stars anymore. It is a growing and I think disturbing trend in our country. To punctuate the point there is even a new reality show titled "Outrageous Kid's Parties" documenting the planning of such parties for "just average people!" One mother justified the $32,000.00 price tag for her daughter's party by stating that it was worth it because the party "really put my child on the map." What freaking map! Are the patients running the asylum? $32,000.00 on a kid's birthday party?

There is just so much wrong with this story, especially in light of this period of economic trouble. But, even more troubling than the idiotic waste of money is what this is teaching these children. What life lessons and personal value system is this outlandish homage to excess instilling? My God, How will these children ever learn anything about the realities of life?

What once could be dismissed as, you know "Main Stream" for those celebrities throwing those parties, now seems to be going "Main Street."

But I just can't think about all of that right now for I choose instead to sit cradling our precious new gift, this beautiful little girl and remembering what now would be considered the cheap birthday parties we threw for her Mother, where the laughter and joy was priceless.

# I Think I Love Aaron Sorkin!

The American President is one of my all-time favorite movies. If you haven't seen it, rent it; no buy it!

Because we are in the middle of a hugely contentious, extremely divisive Presidential Campaign (which I see as an analogy for the contentious, divisive climate permeating so many aspects of American life today) the movie conveys what I think to be a multitude of essential messages for us all.

That movie was so well written and conveyed so many truths; I was prompted to take a closer look at Aaron Sorkin, the man who wrote it. When I learned that he had also written "The West Wing" T.V. series, which I had never seen, I began watching the reruns. Episode after episode I was totally hooked on the, albeit fictional, workings of the Executive Branch of our government. Evidenced by the ratings and awards garnered by the show, I expect that I am one of the few people in this country who had never seen even one of the Prime Time broadcasts.

Jed Bartlett, wow, now he was a president! Watching the reruns, I was filled with the hope that government could truly function for the betterment of the people and not just for the betterment of the politicians.

This Aaron Sorkin guy could really write!

So, I was not going to miss his new HBO series "Newsroom" which takes a look at the inner workings of a cable news network. Given the enormous effect the people working within newsrooms today have on the thoughts and attitudes of the American people, I couldn't wait to see how Sorkin handled this new show.

Two episodes in, critics have pretty much panned it. I love it!

Imagine a prime time news show that is endeavoring to take personal opinion and bias out of the reporting and actually providing the facts instead, allowing the viewers, once informed, to make up their own minds.

In many columns and even more conversations I have fretted about what most now consider journalism and here is a very entertaining show that is addressing just that problem.

But, much like Shakespeare's Old English, Sorkin's writing takes a bit of getting used to. His characters are really smart and talk really fast. There's a rhythm to his style; it's almost poetical. After a few moments of getting used to it, one can then concentrate on the meaningful messages conveyed through his words.

My take away is there is a similar thread running through both "The American President" and "Newsroom." They both convey the principle that whether it's politics or journalism it should all be about character, integrity, truth; not playing for ratings or endorsements or votes but crediting the American people with the intelligence to hear the truth, understand the truth and then to react responsibly to the truth, no matter what the issue.

Oh, that Aaron Sorkin!

But alas, since I am very happily married and he is dating Charlotte from "Sex in the City," I know there is no future for us ... still, I think I love the guy!

# Rich? Sorry You Can't Run!

I hope you all had a wonderful 4th spending time with family and friends, enjoying all of the summer activities you love in spite of or because of the brutal heat. News reports show that Mitt did just that. Beautiful family vacation pictures are being used as fodder for a new wave of personal attacks.

Come on, all of you political vultures out there (from both parties) cut it out! As I wrote in a column defending President Obama's right to take a vacation with his family, I am now supporting Mitt's right as well.

With all of the problems this country is facing, why is anyone making hay out of a vacation? Oh wait; there's also Mitt's shell corp. in Bermuda and his Swiss Bank account and something in the Caiman's.

Hello! Mitt is rich.

He doesn't deny that. He has submitted all of the financial disclosure forms and tax returns required for the Presidential bid.

Mitt is rich.

He ran a very successful FOR PROFIT company where it was his job to make a profit and he did just that making lots of money for himself and others. Before his bid for the Governor's mansion in Massachusetts, he transferred many if not all of his assets to his wife, a fact which is also getting some play in the media and which, I have been given to understand, is pretty common practice for politicians.

None of the above is illegal. Let me repeat that, none of the above is illegal.

Money begets more money. Strategic investments and planning...that is what rich people do.

Mitt is rich...get over it!

There are so many other issues we all should be debating before we vote in November; this stuff is hooey. Should we be negating a person's character and right to be President because he/she is rich?

Let's take a look at who would never have been President if that was the case.

In today's dollars FDR was worth $60 mil. LBJ: $98 mil. Jefferson: $212 mil. And the great father of our country George Washington a whopping $525Mil. But it is JFK at $1 billion, that holds the title; not solely due to his family money but also because Jackie was an oil heiress in her own right.

There you have just a few examples and there were many more multi-millionaire Presidents that I just didn't have the space to list. How very different would our country be if the rich couldn't run?

So let's stop with all of the nonsense and get down to the very serious business of electing a President. I'm so very tired of both parties sniping at each other and the candidates' "spokespeople" dwelling on the insignificant.

In the second column I wrote for this paper, while in the midst of Obama's first run for President, I suggested a "new recipe" for Presidential campaigning. If you would like to read it go to www.wendylevenfeld.com  select the "columns" option and search at the upper right of the page for (type in) "recipe." I think what I wrote then still holds true. Let me know what you think?

# Political Animals

In 1989 I had a truly amazing experience. Drew and I took a trip to Nepal and spent several days atop elephants traversing the surprisingly diverse terrain of the tiny country.

This was when I fell in love with elephants. Though huge and powerful they are gentle and friendly. We fed them and helped to bathe them during the trip and marveled at their playfulness. They have a firm sense of family and both protect and nurture all the young in their extended herd.

Now, I ask that you bear with me here. I promise to come back to the elephants!

Did you see the premiere of "Political Animals" this past weekend? It is but the latest entry in the behind the scenes, fiction based on fact, look at the workings of the White House. Its focus is to illuminate the lasting effects experienced by the individuals toiling within the "office with no corners" and their families.

USA Network bills the show as "a limited series event" (not quite sure how limited it is but hey this hype will appeal to those not wanting to get invested in a long running series) and has cast a heavy-hitting team of veteran actors and rising young stars.

In the hope, I am sure, of preventing law suits and protecting the innocent (are there any innocents in politics?) the names, of course, have been changed and a few spicy storyline elements and characters have been added.

As if we couldn't identify who the lead characters are based on....well let's just test it and see:

We have the former President who was a southern governor. He had a brilliant, ambitious wife who stuck by her man as his womanizing tarnished his presidential legacy. She then ran for President and lost but now serves as Secretary of State reporting to the man who defeated her.

Anyone out there have any doubts which political couple this is based on?

Anyway, while not blown away, I have to say I did enjoy this first episode. I especially liked the tense dynamic between the Madam Secretary, "Elaine Barrish," played beautifully by Sigourney Weaver and a new face to me, Carla Gugino as "Susan Berg" a Pulitzer Prize winning journalist who made her name by publishing scathing columns about the then first family.

By the end of the episode, these two strong, professional, capable women, after an hour of verbally battling it out; quite miraculously (only in Hollywood) end up late at night on a bench at the zoo talking while quasi bonding. Then, in a character defining moment, "Secretary Barrish" tells the young reporter why she loves elephants.

Besides their obvious majesty, it's because they are mighty and yet gentle and thrive in a totally structured, Matriarchal Society where, and this is important, the bull members of the family are ousted when they reach puberty!

After leaving the zoo Secretary Barrish announces to her Secret Service Officer her decision to run again for President of the United States.

Maybe the "old boy's club" better watch out if Hillary, like the fictional Barrish, starts to take the example of my beloved elephants seriously.

# Is "Legal" Enough?

Penn State, in an attempt to salvage some iota of its former good name, hired the Freeh Group, run by former FBI Director Louis Freeh, to get at the facts and provide a report on the who, what, where, and when of the horrific sexual abuse charges leveled at former assistant football coach Jerry Sandusky. With the release of Freeh's scathing report and Sandusky being found guilty of 45 counts of sexual abuse, the reputation of not only Penn State, but its once thought to be, sainted Head Coach, Joe Paterno has "bit the dust."

On Monday the NCAA weighed in by issuing punishments that will all but fatally cripple the university's football program for decades. In addition, they stripped the recently deceased Paterno of all of his official NCAA records. But perhaps the most heartbreaking symbol of "The Coach's" fall came when university officials removed the statue of Paterno from outside the playing field.

While I haven't heard any accusations that Paterno committed any actual crime, his actions and inaction, as sited and substantiated in the Freeh report, are undeniably egregious.

All of this made me start thinking about one of my recent columns. It dealt with the brouhaha over Mitt's financial dealing and the fervent call made by many for him to release more of his tax returns.

While I am certainly not equating the magnitude or the resulting human suffering of the two situations, it does seem to me to beg the question: is doing only the minimum of what's legal enough? Should we have the right to demand more from our public figures?

Since there appears to be no evidence that Mitt Romney violated any laws, is it fair to hold him to a higher standard? And if indeed there is no evidence of illegal activity in Mitt's tax returns (and I personally would be surprised if there were) why doesn't he just release them?

There is some speculation that they will show that, due to perfectly legal tax planning etc. he didn't owe or pay any taxes in one or more years and that is why he is so reticent for them to be made public.

Mitt, Mitt, Mitt, you're running for president. If the speculation is true you should have disclosed it months, maybe years ago, and taken the hit and put it past you.

If I were ever to run for office (and there is no chance in hell that I ever would!) at my candidacy announcement I would distribute a list of every single little thing that I have done that might impact negatively on my run. My speech would then include the statement that that's all of the stuff I am not proud of... have at it and then let me concentrate on dealing with the real problems confronting our nation.

I don't know about you, but I do think that if you choose to put yourself in a high profile position, whether it be politics or sports, you do have an obligation to live up to the trust and admiration of the people supporting you.

# Olympics – The Greatest

As I have noted in the past, we were a family of sports enthusiasts. With athletic parents and two older, very athletic brothers, I think it is safe to say that sports are just a part of our familial DNA. So, I guess it is not surprising that I love the Olympics! When else can one O.D. on watching the best young athletes in the world compete in not just one sport but a whole slew of them?

The year was 1960 and the Olympics were being held in Rome. Now, many who know me have a hard time believing that I was then and still am a fan of boxing.

Though not quite nine years old at the time; I quickly became intrigued by a young American fighter, Cassius Clay. His style was different than anything I had ever seen and the mouth on that kid; well they didn't nickname him "The Louisville Lip" for nothing! To say that I was thrilled for him to win the light-heavyweight gold medal in Rome is more than putting it mildly.

Fast forward...The Year was 1964 and Clay, now fighting as a heavyweight, had somehow snagged a title fight with the hugely favored champion, Sonny Liston. The odds were 7 to 1 against him. My brothers, thinking that they were once again going to take advantage of their ridiculously stupid little sister, made a bet with me on the outcome of that fight and were so proud of themselves when I agreed to take the underdog.

Well, do I need to tell you the outcome? My "float like a butterfly" hero, of course, did not let me down and while they protested that, had they won, they would not have collected, I pled my case to the ultimate authority, our dad, and ended up not only beating them on the bet but in the "father presiding, sibling court" as well. SWEEEEET!

Almost 20 years ago my nephew, the son of one of those ever tormenting older brothers of mine, was visiting us and we went to a restaurant in New Buffalo for dinner. You'll never guess who was dining (or trying to) at the table next to us...you got it Muhammad Ali (AKA Cassius Clay).

He was surrounded by kids, and while evidence of his recently reported Parkinson's disease was apparent, it didn't stop him from making them laugh, joking around with them and even sketching a drawing on a napkin for my nephew depicting one of his knock-outs in the ring.

Then in 1996 I was thrilled to witness that unforgettable moment when a physically ravaged Ali lit the Olympic torch in Atlanta to wild and deafening applause.

And now to the present. Did you see any of the Opening Ceremony of these 2012 Olympics? Have you been hearing or reading any of the opinions about it? It appears that most doing the talking didn't really care much for it.

I disagree. My heart was pumping, the emphasis on the up-and coming athletes brought tears to my eyes and when the Olympic Flag was carried around the field and they once more honored Ali by having him touch it ... it was, well, dare I say it ... The Greatest!

## Politics and Movies Trying to Sell a Remake

We went to see the new Batman movie over the weekend and was treated to what seemed like a never ending string of previews of the "Blockbuster" movies to come. There is a new spin on The Wizard of Oz focusing on the character of the Wizard ala Wicked's focusing on the two witches. There is a new spin on the Bourne franchise which apparently, due to Matt Damon's age, now has a new, younger "programmed to kill" hero. And there is a new Superman machination coming our way, as if we haven't had enough of those.

Finally, the movie began.

To put it bluntly, I thought it was really bad (save your money). The script was lame. The special effects weren't special and the villain was actually comical looking rather than menacing. To add insult to injury, it was so long that the man in front of me actually woke after a two hour respite and groggily asked his wife

"Isn't it over yet!"

Are there no new ideas for "blockbuster" films in Hollywood? Are the studio execs too afraid of failure to risk a bold initiative rather than rehashing the ideas of the past?

Hmmm, made me think of the Presidential campaigns we are currently enduring.

While coming at it from very different angles, aren't both candidates trying to sell a remake? They are trying to present their own versions of "reviving the good old days." And aren't their scripts really pretty lame? Neither is truly hitting home with the voters. And aren't they both drawing their opponent as the arch villain using fear inducing threats to our way of life as their theme when in fact they both seem like essentially nice guys?

And isn't this campaign, as are all in my view, just too damn long leaving us all saying "Isn't it over yet?"

What ... did the crafters of this movie choreograph both of these campaigns as well? If so, they should do the candidates a favor and take a look at the previews running before their movie. While there is nothing they can do to help the Batman Movie at this point, as they say it's "already in the can," there is certainly something that can be done by the candidates before their efforts land one of them in "the can."

I don't want a mere remake of past political policies. Do you?

The Wizard of Oz doesn't need reshaping. Damon's Bourne shouldn't get kicked to the curb by a younger wannabe and who can think that we need yet another Superman? Let's remember how good the originals were but not try to mess with them. Rather, let's create the next generation of "blockbuster classics."

I think it's time for our candidates to take a chance, make some bold moves and create some "original blockbusters" of their own. Otherwise, and I 'm afraid I am not alone, all I have to say is "isn't it over yet?"

# Mitt's Three M'S

So, I was watching Morning Joe when Joe and Mika's guests included Chris Matthews. For those who don't know, Mika Brzezinski is an ardent Democrat whose father Zbingniew was President Carter's National Security Advisor. Joe Scarborough is a former Reaganite Republican Congressman from Florida. They host at their table in the morning, people representing varied points of view that have credibility and experience. Needless to say, the discussions are often heated but the two of them set the tenor ... they are never personally cruel or petty. I think their show represents the best that T.V. political journalism has to offer at this time.

Anyway, I was somewhat surprised with Chris Matthew's recent performance on the show.
Just a sidebar: You may know that I have had the opportunity to meet Chris on two separate occasions when he appeared in LaPorte County at the Forum and I have had intermittent correspondence with him ever since.

The public has come to know Chris as the hard hitting, ever interrupting, flaming liberal that they see on his show "Hardball." Which is why I was surprised that he left that T.V. persona of his behind when he appeared on Morning Joe. For a persona it is. In reality, he is an amazingly bright political historian in addition to being a popular (with mega-liberals) T.V. personality.
In a rather quiet discussion, he and Joe detailed the three M'S that in their view Mitt should forcefully addressed in light of some of the attacks against him.

Mormonism. He shouldn't shy away from it. He should make a powerful statement detailing his beliefs. The basic tenets of charity and kindness and his personal grounding because of those tenets which have made him a devoted husband and the father of 5 (by all appearances) terrific sons.

Money. He should come out firmly stating that he made his money legally, has paid all of the taxes that were legally required of him and he has a right to spend that money as he chooses ... isn't that part of our inalienable rights? He shouldn't have shied away from his wife's "dancing horse" at the Olympics. He should have been in the front row cheering it on.

Massachusetts. He won the Governorship of arguably the most liberal State in the Nation ... Ted Kennedy's State for goodness sake! And by garnering bi-partisan support (isn't the country hungering for a president who can unite the parties?) he was able to do some really good things for his constituency; the best of which might very well be his healthcare reform plan. He is shying away from that accomplishment due to the thought that His plan was a blueprint for the President's healthcare plan. Mitt, embrace it! Frame it as a States' Rights issue. States should have the right to formulate effective plans for their own constituencies without expanding Federal Government intervention. It's a great case for limiting the size of the Federal Government.

Well there you have it; advice for Mitt as Election Day draws closer. Think there is any chance he takes the advice of Chris Matthews?

# What Was He Thinking?

I have just returned from a visit to Israel—the Holy Land. I was going to write about a true gem of Christendom located in the "Old City" section of Jerusalem which receives little attention, if any, on most tour itineraries.

The Old City, for those who haven't been there is the location of the remains of King David's Temple and its environs. This area contains Holy Sites revered by all three of the world's great religions. Excavations throughout the decades have uncovered archeological treasures and have unearthed many features of the ancient city. One can now walk the actual "streets" surrounding the Temple and see the Temple steps from which the common man entered this Holy Place revered by Christians and Jews alike.

I was going to write about one other such Holy Place that most visitors to Jerusalem don't see but, alas, that column will have to wait.

For over the weekend an astonishing disclosure was revealed regarding another trip to Israel. This trip involved a group of 20 freshman lawmakers, some of their family members and aides. Expensed as a fact-finding tour, we the taxpayers footed the bill for the almost unbelievable, totally disrespectful, colossally stupid escapades of these "should be representatives of the United States of America."

According to reports, the group was reveling on the shores of Lake Kinneret. Admittedly drunken and obviously unruly, one of the Congressmen removed his clothes and went for a bare-bottomed bathe...in the Sea of Galilee.

In the Sea of Galilee! Where Jesus was reported to have walked on water? Where tens of thousands of pilgrims a year make their way as part of their spiritual journey;

this place which is held sacred by Christians all over the world...Skinny dipping, really? Congressman Yoder, are you kidding me? Skinny dipping!

How many times must we the people have to say "What were you thinking" to our elected officials?

During every trip I have made to Israel, and the number is approaching twenty, I have sought and found a new experience sparking a deeper regard for the place; a more awesome (and I use that term as it should be used...something truly inspiring awe) sense of faith.

On several occasions we have been to Lake Kinneret; the Sea of Galilee. While one might not expect a nice Jewish girl to have been moved spiritually by the location, I can state unequivocally that I was. For I feel that spirituality, true faith has not the restrictions and requirements of institutionalized religion. To me faith is not bound by facts or specific dates or memorized dogma, but rather it is intangible, inspirational, individually heartfelt. And so standing on the shore of that Holy Christian place I relished, no basked in the "spiritual significance" of the sea.

So, as an American tax payer I am (and I would imagine you are too) outraged at the behavior of this Congressional Delegation; this abuse of tax payer dollars and this embarrassment to our country. And as a spiritual person I am appalled at the total lack of judgment displayed and the egregiously offensive disregard for a truly holy site.

# The Eagle Has Landed

I'll bet that you remember where you were when the words "the eagle has landed" were broadcast across the airwaves signaling that the first spaceship ever had landed safely on the moon. Were you like me? Though only 8 years old, I remember so very clearly sitting transfixed, staring at the television as Neil Armstrong made that historic, no inconceivable, first step onto the surface of the moon. My parents and I were huddled together viewing the impossible and yet seeing it for ourselves. Spontaneously we burst into applause when we saw him step out of his landing craft. And we instinctively knew that the world would never be quite the same again.

My son is an "aeronautical junkie." He majored in aeronautical engineering at Purdue wanting to know everything about space travel, air travel and the vehicles making it all possible. Fate or destiny or some might say luck, took his career in another direction when he moved to Israel. Now a counter-terrorism expert, his fascination with all things that fly has become a beloved hobby rather than a career.

A couple of years ago Rory received orders to prepare for a "big shot" coming from the United States. This VIP and his wife would be sightseeing for several days and then their visit would culminate in his delivering a speech.

Rory received a ton of information except who it was that was coming. After being informed that this man would be flying himself around the country in a helicopter; my son's level of curiosity peaked ... but to no avail. He was not told who the guest would be.

Finally, on his last call to the office he said, "Look I'm here at the airport, my men are here at the airport. Who is this guy?" The response shocked him. "Oh, some guy named Neil Armstrong; whoever that is."

"Neil Armstrong!" He yelled. "THE NEIL ARMSTRONG? One small step for man one giant leap for mankind Neil Armstrong?" He was incredulous that the name apparently meant nothing to the other person!

It took him less than five minutes to dismiss the personal "body guard" he had assigned and slate himself in his place.

So, for several days my son was at Neil Armstrong's side ... and in his own personal glory.

Neil Armstrong and those original astronauts sparked the imagination of the country. We were a "we can do anything" nation and they were the impetus for countless young people to reach for the stars literally and figuratively.

Professionally, the man was a hero. Personally, he was a hero as well. Humble, quiet, subtle sense of humor; he felt guilty that so much attention was being cast his way due to the "moon walk" because its success had been dependent upon hundreds of people, that no one ever heard about, doing their jobs well.

We lost a true American Hero this past weekend. Neil Armstrong passed away from complications he experienced after having open heart surgery at age 82.

The Eagle Has Landed and I say thank you and God Bless.

# A Little Seen Treasure

It stood on a hill, and the remains still do. The mighty wall surrounded in tribute, a stronghold of faith and power. It stood on a hill for all to see; for all to admire for all to revere. It was the Temple of the faithful, the home of the pious. It was King David's Temple in Jerusalem.

The streets around the Temple still wind in a tangle of dust and scents and commotion; for like centuries ago; crowds, hundreds of people, flow, at all times of day, through the maze of stone that make up what is now called "the Old City."

Back then there were shops with spices coloring the air in scents of exotic flavorings from places so far away that no one had even heard of their names. And there were skins and sweets and birds and eggs and crafts that could certainly not have been bought by the average pilgrim. Of course then, like now, the rich could buy all that they chose not to make

Now, most of the stalls carved into the rock of the hill centuries ago, display anything a tourist might like to buy. And yet, there is the occasional expert local craftsman displaying his wares or the jewelry maker showcasing unique designs, precious stones and gems; the potter with a Yemenite style of artistry or an Egyptian cotton merchant carrying the finest linen to be found.

Within the walled city is the Church of the Holy Sepulcher, where Jesus was reported to have been crucified and the Dome of the Rock, where Mohammad was reported to have risen to heaven and the Wailing Wall where it is believed that prayers made there have a direct route to God's ears.

There is oh so much to see in the Old City of Jerusalem.

But, there is also a place there that most tours leave out. This is not because it lacks significance, but simply because it is located at a remote corner of the Old City, upon a rather steep incline, difficult to reach.

I had heard of this small, round, basilica, seen by few yet truly significant. The Basilica of the Assumption (or Dormition) is where the Virgin Mary is said to have gone to die.

I wanted to see it.

It was a hot, hot day as we made our way weaving through the city streets. Cobblestones and time hardened sand comprised the incline making it quite difficult to walk as we made our way upward. The farther we walked the higher we climbed the fewer the people crossing our path.

And then it was there in front of us and upon entering, we were rewarded for all of our efforts.
It is truly a holy place. It is simple by most standards yet exudes a spiritual aura. It has a beautiful mosaic pavement, in the center of which are three intersecting circles, symbolizing the Holy trinity. In the vaulting of the apse is a mosaic of the Virgin and Child. In the center of the crypt is a finely detailed sculpture of the Dormition (the Virgin on her death bed).

The frescos, statuary ornamentation and stained glass somehow seem simple and pure. There is a serenity, a calming presence to the place. It felt holy.

Should you venture to Jerusalem, you might think seeing it worth the difficulty it takes to get there. I certainly did.

# The Political Conventions

So James Taylor walked out onto the Democratic Convention stage. Oh, Oh, Oh, I do remember Sweet Baby James! He was ruggedly handsome with a deep tanned complexion and a manly swagger. And, when he sang; I knew I had a friend, I knew about fire and rain and I went to Carolina in my mind! He was tall, lanky, had a full head of very manly long dark hair and he was the heartthrob of my late teen years.

As he walked out onto the convention stage, he still had the stride, but his pallor was ashen, face wrinkled and he is bald! Yet, when he began to sing and play his guitar; I closed my eyes and I was once again 17 and he was just totally "far out!"

I opened them again and, alas, I was 61 years old and he, even older, was BALD!

So Clint Eastwood walked out onto the Republican Convention stage. Having seen him age through the years, his appearance was not a shock. I'll bet you could ask anyone on the street and they would have a Clint Eastwood favorite movie and probably one for both his acting and his directing.

As he walked out onto the convention stage and began to speak, I thought he was doing an impression of Jimmy Stewart; stammering and stalling. I was amused. But then it became obvious that he was not doing an impression. He was launching into a "stand-up comedy routine." As with so many comics of today it was filled with foul language, spoken and implied and insulting personal jabs; sort of Don Rickles meets Chris Rock. I became uncomfortable. I do not agree with many that say he is an 82 year old that is "losing it." I think his shtick was actually well crafted and in his own way well delivered. Rather I thought it was simply in bad taste, inappropriate for prime time viewing and even more inappropriate for a political convention.

It might be a stretch, but I think I can make a case that in some ways these two performances sort of represented elements of their respective conventions.

The Republicans presented a string of speakers, like Clint's routine, who delivered well-crafted speeches. They were good speeches but had almost nothing to do with the Romney/Ryan ticket. They delivered their "self-aggrandizing" spiels detailing what they have done. I feel, as with, Clint, this was totally inappropriate for the occasion and did the Party Ticket a great disservice.

The Democrats brought out the big gun in political oratory, Bubba Clinton to decimate the arguments lodged against the President during the Republican Convention. And as with James Taylor, if you closed your eyes you might have been transported back by his words and delivery, back before the man took sexual advantage of a young intern in the Oval Office, lied to Congress, lost his law license and was impeached. But, as with Sweet Baby James, Bubba's problem is one cannot keep one's eyes closed forever.

I really enjoyed both conventions. I thought each had strengths and weaknesses. Yet, I very much doubt if either changed many minds one way or the other.

# September Eleventh: This Is Not Good

Just when I thought that I had reached my limit of frustration and fear for the future brought on by the festering, fetid fighting within our political system; September 11th arrived and once again brought the horror and loss caused by terrorist attacks flooding back like one of those petrifying, recurring nightmares that just won't let you sleep. But unlike past anniversaries of that tragic day over a decade ago, this year the fanatics got us again.

The tragic, fatal actions against the American Consulate in Libya killed four Americans including our Ambassador. Unfortunately, the attack in Libya was not the climax of the violence; but rather the herald of violent protests to come waged against the United States that are still going on. Virulent hatred of America and Americans is currently being expressed in the streets in over 20 countries and I gotta be honest; it scares the hell out of me.

Salman Rushdie has a new book out; "Joseph Anton" a memoir this time rather than his usual fictional offerings. You remember Rushdie? Back over twenty years ago he wrote "The Satanic Verses" a novel which inflamed the Islamic fanatics to the point of apoplexy! The Ayatollah Khomeini (yes, that guy that over threw the Shah and held our Embassy employees hostage in Iran) put out a "Fatwa" calling on Muslims, worldwide, to kill Rushdie.

In the new book, Rushdie chronicles that period in his life where fear, not only for himself but for his family and anyone associated with "The Satanic Verses," altered every aspect of his existence and he was forced to recognize that his life as a "free man" would never be the same.

And it hasn't been!

In an interview I saw, Rushdie spoke about the attack on the American Consulate in Libya and the other violent uprisings against America worldwide by Islamic fanatics. He described the relationship these attacks have to his situation back then, by creating a film analogy. He used the Alfred Hitchcock classic horror film "the Birds" in his analogy. Rushdie contends that back all those years ago, the "Fatwa" issued against him was the first bird that attacked in the movie. If you recall, the rest of the film was filled with hundreds, thousands more pecking, screeching, really creepy avian attacks. Using this analogy, with the birds being the Islamic fanatics, we are currently smack dab in the midst of those attacking birds.

If we take the case made by Salmon Rushdie and extrapolate out even further, perhaps it will tell us something about our future. Like the Fatwa for Rushdie, 9/11/01 changed all of our lives forever. It was our "first bird attack." And just as in the movie, the dark menace keeps swooping down, encircling us, creating dizzying havoc only to retreat until the next flapping, screeching, sometimes fatal barrage. This is not good!

I think that most who know me consider me to be a generally optimistic kinda gal. I approach life thinking that there is a logical solution to problems; a way to fix whatever it is that is broken. But I have to tell you, I have this nagging feeling in the pit of my stomach about all of this that just refuses to go away.

Not a rosy outlook, huh?

Having said that, when I truly take the time to think this through, I do manage to remember that Salman Rushdie is still among the living and he is going strong ...

So is the United States of America!

# "Homeland" Security

So, the Emmy's were held on Sunday night and though I didn't watch them I was really pleased to learn that a Showtime series, "Homeland," took the honors for Best Drama Series. Claire Danes won for her role in the series as well. For those who are not familiar with "Homeland," in brief, it follows the life of a CIA agent specializing in the Middle East who is haunted by her inability to have stopped the 9/11 attacks and is determined not to "miss anything" again. She is in pursuit of a "turned U.S. POW" whom one of her Arab operatives on the ground told her is a potential threat to Americans on American soil.

It is very heady stuff and scary as hell.

Also on Sunday evening, David Gergen spoke at the Purdue North Central Sinai Forum and when asked about the Israel/Iran nuclear weaponry situation he gave a very sobering answer. With his extensive contacts throughout the world garnered by his serving four American Presidents as a Policy Advisor, he was able to tell the audience that all of those contacts are predicting an Israeli strike against the Iranian nuclear facility within six months.

Also, very heady and scary stuff.

This week at the United Nations I'm sure that Ahmadinejab will rail against Israel in specific and "the West" in general and Netanyahu will continue to make the Israeli case for why they cannot wait much longer before launching a pre-emptive strike against the Iranian nuclear facility. And, meanwhile, the U.S. and Allies will continue to caution patience citing intelligence reports indicating there is still time for sanctions and diplomacy to work.

To which I say, "oh, yeah?" Like our collective intelligence has really served us well in the past!

Let's see now, no one put the pieces together to avert 9/11. And where oh where are those WMD"s? Surely, you remember those weapons of mass destruction identified by both American and British Intelligence Services as existing in Iraq?

Netanyahu cites Israeli intelligence, which has a far better reputation than ours, as indicating that there is not a lot of time. And there can be no doubt as to what Iran will do once they have nuclear capability.

Ahmadinejab has unequivocally stated that Israel should be wiped off the face of the Earth.

But would Iran actually use nukes? Let's not forget that in destroying Israel in that way they will have to destroy many of the holiest shrines and sites in the Islamic faith. And the nuclear fallout could very possibly draft back upon their own people.

O.K. sorry about that last point; they have already shown that they think there is no value to human life especially when martyrdom is so glorious.

But really would they launch an attack if they could? And can Israel afford to rely on U.S. intelligence rather than their own?

I'll bet Netanyahu would feel very invested in and sympathetic toward Danes' character in "Homeland," if he were to watch the show, for they are both eminently aware of what is at stake. And they both share the huge challenge of getting true "intel," interpreting it properly and acting accordingly before it is too late.

Heady stuff and very scary!

# Andy Williams, the Osmonds, and Mitt

Twenty years ago Drew and I met a woman who had been raised in the home where Johnnie Mercer wrote "Moon River." How cool was that; Moon River written in her childhood home. The Moon River, sung by Andy Williams with his smooth, clear voice floating through the notes as effortlessly as the cool water babbling down the river itself. I was envious.

With the recent passing of Andy Williams, that less than six degrees of separation was enough to make me personally feel the loss. His rendition of Moon River propelled him to stardom and into the home of millions with his "Andy William's Show."

I remember watching that show with my family. I remember all of the singing stars of old; Bing, Judy, Tony and the stars of the day like The Beach Boys singing along with him. I clearly remember watching a young singing family, the Osmond's, being introduced to the Nation.

The Osmond's were the first Mormon's I had ever seen. I didn't really know what the religion was about and quite frankly didn't care because Donnie was such a doll!

Years later, I took a business trip to Salt Lake City, Utah. At the time I was working at the American Hospital Association and we were introducing a new computerized information system for children's hospitals. My task was to meet with the CEO of the health care system there and introduce him to AHA's program.

When I arrived in Salt Lake the taxi ride from the airport took me past the Mormon Tabernacle and I was awed by its splendor. It stood tall with a perfect azure backdrop and shimmered in the sunlight. I hadn't thought about the Osmond's in years but that sight sparked the memory.

The entire city was clean; it was so clean! There were actually young people cleaning the streets...remember I hailed from Chicago, pre-clean-up, dirty, gritty; the REAL Mayor Daley's Chicago!

That night in the hotel restaurant, all at once, I was struck by the fact that all of "the help" looked like Donny & Marie! Chambermaids, busboys, wait staff all were freshly scrubbed, apple-cheeked, bright smiling, beautiful young clones of Donnie & Marie. In fact, all of those young people I had seen earlier in the day cleaning the streets looked exactly the same way.

I shook it off before going to bed convincing myself I was being silly. But, the next day at my meeting I noticed again that all of the non-medical support staff in the hospital had that same look...all of them young and beautiful!

What the ....?

It was then I learned that the Mormon Church owned the hotel, the hospitals, the major bank and what seemed to be most every other important business in the city. It was explained that the young people of the Church had to give, I think it was, a year of service to the Church during their teen years.

So that was it! All those Donnie & Marie employees were doing their required service to the Church. And they did it happily, respectfully.

The city was really impressive and so were those young people.

I hadn't thought about all of this until another Mormon entered the spotlight...you know who I mean! And I began to wonder if he might not build on his own Church experience to propose a mandatory year of service by our 18 year olds...not necessarily military but public service of some kind. If those young people I saw in Salt Lake those many years ago are any indication, it would do our kids a world of good.

Just a thought for a "specific" Mitt could bring up at the Debate Wednesday!

# Debate Tweeters and Twitterers

It was 1988 when Jim Lehrer moderated his first presidential debate. In the ensuing years he has moderated 11 more of them. The man is a highly regarded, award winning television journalist. But, since last Wednesday's debate, the twittersphere has gone wild. He has been called an "old man that should have hung up his moderating shoes years ago", "an inept moderator with an agenda of his own" and too many other lewd and obnoxious comments on his performance to include herein.

We are living in an age where one can get "lit up" instantly on twitter by anonymous sources. And Jim Lehrer certainly did.

If I had the luxury of merely being an observer to the techno mania of our current culture instead of being a part of it; I would truly find it all very fascinating. Instead I find it truly disturbing. Not even waiting until the debate was over; the twitterer's were tweeting up a storm. (Please don't e-mail me to tell me that people who tweet are called tweeters not twitterers. While admitting to very little knowledge of the whole twitter world, I do know that much. I call those that tweet under a cutsie name not their own, "twitterers." It has the "you can't take it all that seriously" sound to it that I feel applies here.)

In light of all of this, I feel that I must rise to Lehrer's defense. For the record, the Commission on Presidential Debates (CPD) was established in 1987 (one year before Lehrer's first moderating job) as a not-for-profit, non-partisan organization whose mission includes "providing the best possible information to the viewers and listeners." It was the CPD that established the parameters and format for this debate.

If you saw "Game Change" with its primer on debate prep, you saw how a candidate can intentionally flip to anything other than the answer to the question within the old format. The CPD decided to do some tweaking (not to be confused with tweeting) to the traditional debate format. The thought was to have a more open exchange of positions instead of a strict 2-3 minute allotment of time to answer a specific question.

In this debate format it was decided by the CPD not Jim Lehrer that the candidates would have to face each other mano-a-mano and debate the real merits of their individual plans.

In this format Mr. Lehrer's job was to "let it run." He was to put the topic out there and then "stay out of the way" until the segment time allotment had expired.

And he did just that.

It was not his job to "call" either candidate on the truth of their statements. It was not his job to "make sure" either of them or both of them effectively expressed their plans. That was the candidates' job. His job was to throw out the topic and let them at each other. Both campaigns were aware of this format. They agreed to it.

If you didn't like the outcome...don't shoot the messenger.

For all of those twitterers out there who feel that the instant airing of their personal views are of the utmost importance, at least be "tweeter enough" to put your own name on your tweets.

What? Are you afraid that someone might hold you accountable?

# The Truth Isn't Always "Good"

1972: In a creative writing class in college, I fulfilled a short story writing assignment by penning the details of "The Woolworth Caper." The story chronicled my life altering, ill-conceived, first and only foray into a life of thievery. Growing up, down the street from us, lived my older cousin who often took me under her wing and provided much of the education I wouldn't receive in school or over the dinner table. Other relatives were never shy about stating that her middle name should be "the little devil." At the age of nine, instead of prompting me to avoid her, this moniker only served to make any time I was able to spend with her seem not only desirable but, well, exciting!

So, when she let me in on her plot to "lift" ankle bracelets from the five and dime store my initial trepidations were easily whisked away by her self-styled logic and reasoning.

In my short story I attempted to humorously relate exactly what occurred. Without revealing any more detail just in case I decide to rewrite it in its entirety someday, let me just say my professor was not impressed. When he expressed incredulity at the sequence of events I replied,
"But, that's what happened. It's the truth!"

I was totally expecting the statement to override his criticism. To my chagrin he sharply replied, "Just because there's an interesting plot and the story's true, doesn't make it good."

1979: The American Embassy in Iran was seized during the Islamic revolution and overthrow of the Shah's regime. 52 members of the American Diplomatic Service stationed there were being held captive. Those of us of a certain age remember well a nightly update by a young Ted Koppel with "the days held captive count" glowing in large numerals behind him. That is how ABC's Nightline got its start.

The presidency of Jimmy Carter, which had already begun to falter, received the final blow when an attempted rescue of those hostages failed. It was so much more than a disappointment and a blow to our national pride; it broke our hearts.

2012: Have you heard about a new movie entitled, Argo? There is tremendous hype circulating about it and I for one can't wait to see it. The plot revolves around another rescue attempt carried out at that time. Reportedly, in the movie, several US Embassy employees manage to elude the Iranian siege and make it to the Canadian Ambassador's residence.

In what I consider to be the ultimate sating of my duel obsessions of politics and the movies; Argo, details their rescue which includes having the U.S. Embassy staff members pose as a movie crew that had been shooting in Iran. The film is being touted as a masterful merger of the business of politics and the business of making movies.

OMG! Could it get any better than that; movies and politics rolled into one?

Oh wait, yes it can. It's based on a true story!

I'm thinkin' this might, just might, hit my all-time favorite movie list ...

Uh oh ... what's this? I better hold off on revising that list for I'm being harkened back, all those years ago, to my college professor's admonition. "Just because there's an interesting plot and the story's true, doesn't make it good."

# It's An Allergy Epidemic

I don't know about you but I am amazed at how many people have begun complaining about allergies. It used to be that you knew of a few people that suffered from "hay fever" every year. (Can someone tell me why is it called hay fever when the people suffering are not now nor ever have been within a hundred miles of any hay...just askin'?) Anyway, there were also those that had a specific allergy; you know pet hair or mold, but thinking back to my youth, I can't even remember one of my friends in that category. Whereas now; I can't think of any of my friends that haven't complained of the cold-like symptoms that they refer to as allergies.

I am not a scientist, an ecologist or even (I am embarrassed to admit) much of a re-cyclist. But I gotta say, I think all of these relatively new allergies are our own fault.

I think that we have, unknowingly for the most part, screwed up our planet to the point that our environment is becoming toxic to our systems. As a result, we are sneezing and coughing more, suffering headaches and sore throats more and don't even get me started on the "plague of cancers" with which we are now forced to deal.

All of this was in the back of my mind when Drew and I were discussing an article he read about the planet Jupiter.

For those of you, like me, who know very little about Jupiter; let me tell you some of what I discovered after that discussion.

Jupiter's mass is 318 times greater than that of Earth. Jupiter's volume is large enough to contain 1,300 planets the size of Earth and rotates faster than any other planet in the solar system ... it is one huge, fast son of a gun!

There is a great red spot visible on the planet which is a storm that has been raging for 300 years. It has a ring encircling it like Saturn and Neptune and there are surface clouds which consistently hover over the planet.

What caught my attention is that scientists have noted a significant change in the color of those hovering clouds recently.

Got me thinking. Is it possible? Could it be that maybe, just maybe, our messing with our own atmosphere has begun to mess with the atmospheres of other planets?

O.K. so maybe that is a stretch especially since scientists are speculating that the change in Jupiter's cloud color is due to radioactivity on the planet. It is widely known in scientific, planetary circles that Jupiter sends out strong radio radiation; so strong it can be detected on Earth.

Still, I think my concerns about our role in diminishing our environment are not unwarranted. Whether politicians want to acknowledge it or not, there are serious problems resulting from our treatment of our world and we better take heed and do something about it.

But hey, look on the bright side. Just think of all of the industries benefitting from our new found allergy epidemic. We're using huge amounts of tissues, buying billions of dollars' worth of over the counter drugs (yes that billions with a B) and literally gilding that huge horn in the Ricola commercials with solid gold.
So, scientists agree that the cloud color changes over Jupiter are not our fault ... yet!

# Along Came Hurricane Sandy

Just when I was totally fed-up with all of the presidential polling predictions dominating most every political discussion and ready to bury my head under my pillow in an attempt to escape the incessant white noise of numbers; along came Hurricane Sandy. All at once political commentators on various networks began predicting (did they do a poll?) that due to the power outages caused by the massive storm it could be 4 or 5 days before national polling organizations would be up and running again. Oh the horror of it all. No polling numbers for several days; what will they have to talk about? How will they fill their 24/7 "news cycle" without the numbers to analyze and debate? This, my friends, truly is a disaster!

Forget the lives already lost and the people uprooted from their homes. Forget the massive destruction and the explosions of power stations and transformers that will keep huge areas in darkness for ... only Mother Nature knows how long. Even forget the fact that Letterman and Kimmel had to perform their late-night shows Monday night with no audience members in attendance.

There will be no new national polling numbers! (Huge sigh of despair)

To be honest, the whole polling frenzy and the increased emphasis the campaigns are placing on poll numbers is a bit baffling to me. Historically, polls just aren't that accurate. And the methodology is all over the map varying from polling organization to polling organization. Some poll likely voters. Some poll registered voters. Some use alarmingly small samples. Some use "scientific sampling" models while others admittedly "adjust" the results based on demographic criteria. Yet each camp uses the polls of their choice to spin the advantage their candidate has over the other.

How is anyone supposed to truly understand what all of the numbers mean if the methodology is so dramatically different from poll to poll?

So Sandy has given us a respite, if but a brief one, from the infernal analysis of the latest numbers. But how oh how will the pundits fill the void that is left?

Hey cable guys, here's an idea. Why not rationally and calmly discuss the very real differences between our two candidates? No yelling or slandering, no screaming or name-calling; just the laying out of positions. Even without many policy specifics being offered by either candidate, there are some very significant and far reaching differences in the way the two candidates' view how our government should work and what the role of government truly is. So why not have a civilized discussion of their hugely differing points of view? And in light of this devastating storm, isn't this a great opportunity to examine the candidates' views on the role of state governance versus that of the Feds?

Just a thought!

I'm sure that Hurricane Sandy will be remembered and talked about for years to come and my heart and prayers go out to all of those affected by it. But, for this political junkie, there was one good thing to come out of this tragic storm. I got a brief respite from the numbers numskulls.

# Car and Election Problems

I'm out for a drive minding my own business trying very hard not to think about the whole election cycle. I, along with apparently hundreds of thousands of others (if the media can be trusted... big HUGE if?) voted early so all that is left for me to do in this season of endless, obscenely costly campaigns is watch Tuesday night to see who wins. Of course by the time you read this we will already know but trust me that will not have an impact on this column.

So, I am driving along really enjoying the tunes being played on the radio when out of the blue, an odd sound catches my attention. Not really discordant, almost melodic in its rhythm; I focus on the radio wondering why the songwriter would include such a strange noise in the score. Being of an age, I have often shaken my head at some of what now passes for music, but this was different. The song had really been quite pleasing.

Don't you just hate when you think everything is going along quite well and in one brief moment you are shocked into the reality of a pending problem? Uh oh. What I thought to be merely a strange choice of sound to be included within the score is in reality, a terribly annoying and utterly dread producing problem.

I check the dials, lights, gauges and mystery indicators, of which I know nothing, to see if I can discover a clue. Lo and behold, the clock contained in the "audio system thingy" is reading 4:30 PM when it is actually 8:30 AM.

OK. The clock. How could a problem with the clock be much of a problem at all? Oh, but I can't forget the noise which continues as I drive. This is not good.

Listen, I begin my internal rationalization. I don't expect much from my vehicle. I want to turn the key and have the engine start. I require only relative comfort be able to get where I need to go. I don't require the clock to display the time accurately, though it is really nice that it usually does.

Are these things too much to ask? Man, I wish I knew more about auto mechanics!
And then crazy me, I begin to think about the election once again.

Should we all know more about the political mechanics? Do we need to know the details of the gadgetry, gauges and mystery indicators of politics? Don't we deserve responsible leadership to turn the key to start our economic engine once again? Is it too much to ask that our representatives maintain our country in working order so that we may reach our collective destinations in relative comfort? Shouldn't we expect that they accurately, "give us the time of day" as to their proposed policies and priorities?

So, off I go to the service department of the auto dealership, confident that they will be able to fix my car. If only I had the same confidence in our elected officials' ability to fix the problems of the country.

# Sex and Spies

Like millions of other people over the weekend, I went to see the new James Bond movie, Skyfall. Perhaps I should confess, upfront, that I am one of the multitudes of 007 fans. While at age twelve, a bit too young to really appreciate the first James Bond movie Dr. No; my fascination with all things "spy" was sparked and I have to admit, that fascination still exists.

I'm thrilled to tell you that the franchise has, to my mind, passed the difficult bar of continued cinematic success by smoothly aging and changing with the times. Daniel Craig is great as a somewhat older "Bond...James Bond." But, it's the plot that struck me as the real achievement of the movie. While paying homage to the classic standards of past Bond capers, its tech-dependent storyline brings it into the twenty-first century.

Another indication that 007 has come of age is while there are beautiful women in 007's path and we do get a hint of the old Bond sexual prowess; the major, explicit subplot of the steamy, seductive, rather titillating leading lady simply isn't there.

Yep, you heard me; not there from the start, there at the end, stereotypical Bond girl in Skyfall. Yet there is nonetheless that sexy undercurrent, that whole Sex and Spies thing that, as in Bond movies past, is palpable.

Also this weekend the whole Petraeus Affair (no pun intended) continued to unfold. I'm sure most of you have heard the same details that I have. Jealous lover threatens perceived rival who then goes to the FBI with the scary e-mails.

Upon investigation, it's discovered that the highly honored, well respected, retired General David Petraeus, currently our nation's "Spy-in-chief," is at the center of the whole mess. In fact, Petraeus is so well respected, the FBI, after finding steamy e-mails between he and his lover, thought his e-mail account must have been hacked for they couldn't believe that he had written such things in e-mails.

Oh, there's seems to be no escaping that dynamic duo...Sex and Spies!

But, what truly amazes me is that our Spy-in-Chief got busted by e-mail.

I realize that "Q" is just a character in the Bond movies but surely we have our own CIA equivalents. We have to have a whole cadre of techno-geeks coming up with the latest and greatest "spying gadgetry." One would think that our Spy-in-Chief would have access to the latest communication technologies available to his agents. But yet, he apparently doesn't know how vulnerable any data contained in e-mail is? Really? He put incriminating stuff into e-mail and sent it out into cyberspace?

How many embarrassing indiscretions have to go viral before powerful men in our government get it?

Actually, come to think of it, this could be a working plot line for the next 007 offering! Or wait, even better; I have an idea. Let's create an all new spy hero and let's see...shall we call him "DOUBLE O WHAT WERE YOU THINKING?"

# Gaza Again!

In trying to decide how to comment on what is happening now between Israel and the Hamas led Palestinians in Gaza, I just keep coming back to Reagan's famous line from one of his presidential debates where with head shaking he said, "There you go again!"

Well, here they go again.

I feel compelled to provide some history. In 2005 Israeli Prime Minister Ariel Sharon ordered the evacuation of all Israelis from Gaza. This was not a popular decision but in the hope of promoting peace, Sharon made the difficult call. In the end it meant IDF troops (Israeli Defense Forces – their Army) forcibly evicting 17,000 residents from their homes and businesses. My son was one of those soldiers. I can tell you from personal experience that it was heart wrenching for the soldiers as well as the residents. But as in the past, Israel had taken the first, albeit painful, step in trying to establish peace.

For the first time, in 2006, there were free elections, closely monitored democratic elections, in Gaza. The people elected Hamas a universally acknowledged terrorist organization to be their leaders. That was the last semblance of democracy the people of Gaza have seen since.

I don't think most people realize that Gaza has a Mediterranean Coast; the same type of natural Mediterranean beaches as France, Italy and Monaco. Gaza could have been developed into a thriving, self-functioning community. With that coastline Gaza could have become a tourist attraction creating economic stability. Hamas could have built a self-sufficiency that provided their populous with employment, education and a greatly improved quality of life.

But instead Hamas built an estimated 800 illegal tunnels through which approximately 47,000 Iranian supplied rockets have been smuggled in from Egypt. Instead of building a life for their people the Hamas leadership has fired over 8,000 rockets on Israel in the ensuing years ... over 8,000 rockets fired on Israel in those 7 years of Hamas rule. That's more than 1,000 rocket strikes a year! Can you imagine what our response would be if we had only 1 rocket fired on U.S. soil?

None of this is really new. What is new is that Iran has now supplied Hamas with rockets that have the capability to hit Jerusalem and Tel Aviv.

So, Prime Minister Netanyahu's Cabinet gave him authority to launch "Pillar of Defense." The Cabinet's statement regarding this action was simple:
1. Remove the threat
2. This action is not limited in time or in scope

As a side note, isn't it interesting that this Iranian backed barrage orchestrated, ostensibly, to show Israel how much more powerful Gaza has become, has in effect halted all international attention on Iran's nuclear capability progress?

Just sayin'!

But, however this current conflict ends however long it takes; in regard to Israel the messages of Hamas and Iran are crystal clear. They say what they mean and mean what they say. They want to destroy Israel and drive the Jews into the sea. Ironic isn't it that it is the same sea they could be utilizing to build a thriving community for their people.

# Tony Bennett—Mentoring

I saw an interview with Tony Bennett who is currently promoting his new duets CD. You gotta just love the guy. He's so incredibly humble and given the fact that Sinatra himself said that Bennett was the best voice he ever heard, that's saying something. And he is really savvy. Releasing several duet albums he has joined with many of the "younger" popular talents of the day to produce top of the charts sellers.

In the interview he sang (no pun intended) the praises of such mega-stars as Lady Gaga, Christina Aguilera, Josh Grogan and Sheryl Crow, just to name a few, and subtly conveyed the sense that he had gently sprinkled upon them drops of wisdom he had acquired through his 6 decades in the business. Don't get me wrong, the man is shrewd. By pairing up with young talent he has been able to keep his musical career going, now appealing to a new generation of CD purchaser; but still, how great that he is "mentoring" these young entertainers.

Made me start thinking about the whole mentoring thing.

We live in such a volatile, scary world. Live shots of actual war, real people being maimed and killed is nightly fare. Our evening newscasts would be rated "R" if they were movies yet they are broadcast into our homes for our young people to see daily.

I think that video games, graphic novels and even advertising cast such a warped perspective, not only on society and lifestyles but on human nature itself; how can our children not be negatively affected by it all? And don't even get me started on the whole moral/sexual desensitization that makes me fear our young people won't ever be able to experience true loving relations due to the acceptance of "sex" as just another after school activity!

They hardly have a chance to be kids; innocent, trusting, compassionate, hopeful children.

Now more than ever, they need mentoring. With the economy almost mandating that both parents work to stay economically afloat and so many single parent homes, too many of our children are not getting the hands on, teaching by example experiences derived from mentoring relationships with adults. It's not that parents today love their children any less or that they want anything other than the very best for them; it's a matter of that hackneyed phrase "quality time" becoming all too rare.

We of the baby-boom generation have been given so much, experienced so much, have so much to offer and yet more and more I keep hearing about how bad things are from my fellows of a certain age. Isn't it time we stop complaining about every little thing and start doing something about it?

We need to take a page out of Tony Bennett's playbook. He doesn't harp on the demise of good music; he has embraced the young talent and in doing so has kept himself vital.

Instead of lamenting and moaning about what is wrong with this young generation, we should take the time to spend some time sharing our knowledge.

And it isn't just for the kids that I am advocating. If we give of ourselves I think that we just might have our faith in human nature restored and add some much needed vitality to this next phase of our lives.

# Walking on Wind

I saw an interview with a man that "blew me away." His engineering as art creations literally walk on the wind.

For thirteen years Theo Jansen, a Dutch artist, has been refining his designs of what he calls "Strand Beasts" which are gorgeous, intricate, wind propelled, animal-like works of art designed to walk majestically on beaches. His lifelike kinetic sculptures are a masterful fusion of art and engineering. In fact, when I saw his working design drawings, they immediately brought to my mind the schematic working drawings of Leonardo Di Vinci.

Pretty amazing stuff!

Over time and constant tweaking, Jansen has created hundreds of different Strand Beast designs. His goal was to not only make them beautiful but to have them become better and better at surviving the elements.

Jansen experimented with a slew of materials including wood and cardboard before deciding upon PVC plastic tubing for the major pieces of construction needed for the skeletal features of his creatures. He has invented bottle-like storage containers for wind which he calls "stomachs" to be used for propulsion on windless days. His pipedream (excuse the pun) is to "put these animals out in herds on the beaches, so they will be able to independently live their own lives" being totally self-sufficient.

He likens his process to that of child rearing. He takes his creation and nurtures it, doing all that he can for its development and will someday release it out into the world to survive on its own.

O.K. I'll admit that part is a bit Twilight Zone-ish; but there is nothing unbelievable or smirk producing about the beauty of his creations themselves. With their piping and wood skeletal bodies and wing-like sails capturing the wind; they are breath taking. And, when you see them walking along the beach; they are nothing short of magnificent.

We find ourselves in a world, a point in history when we rarely take the time to really look at very much of anything; yet there I sat mesmerized with wonder and awe relishing the feelings these manmade creatures evoked. How lovely it was to actually feel enchanted if only for a brief moment.

Theo Jansen is currently in negotiations to bring a major exhibit of his Strand Beasts to the United States next year. I can tell you for certain, if that show does come to pass and he lets his "beasts" loose on the sands of Lake Michigan, I for one will be there.

# Call Me Old Fashioned

Call me cynical. Call me passé. Call me old-fashioned...hell, just call me old; but I saw an ad for a new type of credit card today that raised a red flag – did I say red flag?...it actually raised my hackles!

For those of you under the age of 50, let me assure you that you read me correctly. I said it raised my hackles. Great old expression never used anymore, hmm, I wonder why not? Anyway, hackles are those hyper sensitive little hairs on the back of one's neck that were reported to tingle and bristle when something seemed rotten in Denmark in decades past. If all of the presidential pollsters that are now scurrying around for topics to poll, now that the election is over, were to poll "young people" asking if they know what that expression means, I'll bet my bottom dollar their percentage of "don't have a clue" responses would be even higher than Hillary's chances for the 2016 presidential nomination. And that is saying something!

Raise one's hackles, something rotten in Denmark, bet my bottom dollar; I fear I have truly digressed from the subject of this column into the world of mostly forgotten descriptive phrases!

Anyway, this credit card that was advertised seemed truly amazing, revolutionary, quite fantastic ... until I began thinking about it.

So here's the deal. You use this card to make all of your purchases. You then post your purchases online and the issuing bank's program automatically scans the product you bought to see if any store is offering it at a lower price. Honestly, how cool is that? And, if that isn't cool enough; if they find the same item at a lower price, they automatically give you the difference back. No more going from store to store price shopping (Oops, showing my age again.) I mean website to website comparing prices. They do all of the work for you!

Wow, is that a great cost saving tool or what?

Or what? Wait a minute. All I have to do is post all of my purchases online to get the service? All of my purchases? Online in one place?

Wait a minute. Hold on a second here. Let's just think about this.

How much money I am spending and exactly what I am spending it on will now be available in one tidy little bundle out there somewhere in cyberland?

Whoa!

After all of the scandals resulting from idiots thinking that what they send via e-mail, or Facebook, or text messaging is private, am I to believe that all of this personal data about my spending habits (not to mention what can then be deduced about my life) is safe in the marketplace of seemingly unlimited data retrieval capabilities?

I remember a conversation I had with a security expert and how shocked I was to hear him say that he could find anything out about anyone, given some time. Well, apparently he will now need no time at all. He and most everybody else will be able to go one stop shopping for heretofore difficult, personal information.

I may be old fashioned but you can bet your bottom dollar that my hackles are indeed raised because there is definitely something rotten in Denmark when it comes to the hidden risks of this great new innovation in charge cards.

# Lots of Blame to Go Around

Early in our marriage while watching a movie, I began to cry. I don't remember what prompted it but later when Drew asked me about it I answered that I think I have a "tear quota" and when that quota hasn't been met, I cry at what normally would not produce that salt-watery effect. Some tears are just inexplicably shed but the tears I am shedding now are for our babies; certainly for the babies and adults so senselessly, brutally murdered in the nonsensical murderous rampage in Connecticut, but also for all of our babies.

We are beginning to get a few details about the shooter, about his mental problems, about his family life, about what happened. We are also hearing of the selfless heroism of teachers and staff whose only concern was the protection of the students. And we are hearing of the lives of the fallen, lives not lost to war (though that grief is not any less tragic) but in what should have been the safety of their classrooms.

Babies, and those trying to protect them, gunned down.

And the tears keep flowing.

It is hard not to think about, almost hear, the rapid fire of an assault rifle and the pop pop pop of a semi-automatic as round after round was discharged in mere seconds.

So, the cry is being heard that it is ineffective gun control that is to blame.

And the first victim of this rampage was the boy's mother. A woman who legally obtained these weapons yet she kept them where this disturbed child, this boy that she knew had mental problems, for whom she had sought help; had access to them.

Some are saying that her irresponsibility is to blame.

And the tears still flow.

When the Mental Hospitals were unilaterally shut down the deal was supposed to be that the patients would be cared for in "half-way houses." Our consciences were clear we had come up with a solution to the deplorable conditions in the Mental Hospitals and the patients would receive the help they needed in an acceptable environment...except it was not acceptable. No community wanted such a place in their neighborhood so thousands, perhaps hundreds of thousands of sick people needing help, simply had nowhere to go. One such person was our shooter.

Many are saying that a broken mental health system is to blame.

And we've learned that this boy was an avid gamer spending hours creating mayhem and perpetrating violence in his virtual world. But on Friday he brought that virtual world of his into reality with such tragic results.

Now, the cry is for restrictions to the amount and degree of violence to which our young people are exposed. Violent content, whether it be in the form of video games or movies or song lyrics should be regulated.

And still the tears keep flowing.

I'm hearing about 2nd Amendment rights and 1st Amendment rights and the difficulty and fear surrounding any action that might be taken. After all it is our very freedom that is at stake. But, I agree with those who say that "freedom isn't free." There is always a cost. This is just too high a price to pay for it.

Yes, there is plenty of blame to go around and I know that my quota of tears has long since been met; yet the tears keep flowing.

# Twelve Stories of 2012
(To be sung to the Twelve Days of Christmas)

1. It's the end of the year so it's time to look on back
T'was the year of two thousand and twelve

2. We learned that a sure bet doesn't always work
Facebook's IPO's an oh no
T'was the year of two thousand and twelve

3. Will and his Kate shared their secret with the world
The royals are expecting
The IPO's an oh no
T'was the year of two thousand and twelve

4. Petraeus' medals took on a sleazy tint
When will these men learn?
The royals are expecting
The IPO's an oh no
T'was the year of two thousand and twelve

5. Republicans mourn for a chance that was lost
Obama's still the Man
When will these men learn?
The royals are expecting
The IPO's an oh no
T'was the year of two thousand and twelve

6. We heard once again from a vengeful Mother Nature
Sandy slammed the Coast
Obama's still the Man
When will these men learn?
The royals are expecting
The IPO's an oh no
T'was the year of two thousand and twelve

7. Shows called reality continue to confound
What's a Honey Boo Boo?
Sandy slammed the Coast
Obama's still the Man
When will these men learn?

The royals are expecting
The IPO's an oh no
T'was the year of two thousand and twelve

8. Roberts shocked the Right in a ruling quite "Supreme"
Obama Care's upheld
What's a Honey Boo Boo?
Sandy slammed the Coast
Obama's still the Man
When will these men learn?
The royals are expecting
The IPO's an oh no
T'was the year of two thousand and twelve

9. The Nation still teeters upon the Fiscal Cliff
C'mon you stubborn bastards
Obama Care's upheld
What's a Honey Boo Boo?
Sandy slammed the Coast
Obama's still the Man
When will these men learn?
The royals are expecting
The IPO's an oh no
T'was the year of two thousand and twelve

10. Security was breached and we seek to know the truth
Benghazi facts are "hazy."
C'mon you stubborn bastards
Obama Care's upheld
What's a Honey Boo Boo?
Sandy slammed the Coast
Obama's still the Man
When will these men learn
The royals are expecting
The IPO's an oh no
T'was the year of two thousand and twelve

11. Whitney is gone but not forgotten is that voice
Houston definitely had a problem
Benghazi facts are "hazy."

C'mon you stubborn bastards
Obama Care's upheld
What's a Honey Boo Boo?
Sandy slammed the Coast
Obama's still the Man
When will these men learn?
The royals are expecting
The IPO's an oh no
T'was the year of two thousand and twelve

12. We mourn for the deaths caused by needless
senseless violence
God bless their souls
Houston definitely had a problem
Benghazi facts are "hazy."
C'mon you stubborn bastards
Obama Care's upheld
What's a Honey Boo Boo?
Sandy slammed the Coast
Obama's still the Man
When will these men learn?
The royals are expecting
The IPO's an oh no
T'was the year of two thousand and twelve

Merry Christmas and Happy New Year to all.

# Les Miz

I have written about my love for musical theater, my love for all theater. I have written about my love of the cinema and I have written about my love of all genres of literature. And now it has finally happened. After years of not even realizing I had been patiently waiting; it has occurred ... the perfect, Wendy's ideal, creative storm. It is as if the skies have opened above and cascades of glorious sparkling sunlight have flooded down, crashing upon me, casting me in total luminescence and I am swept away in its tide.

O.K. so maybe that's a bit over the top. But I have to tell you I received the best Christmas present from Hollywood this year and even better than that, you can all have it too! Of course I am talking about the greatly hyped, much anticipated, new musical movie version of Les Miserable which opened on Christmas Day.

In high school I was entranced by Victor Hugo's masterful work; so much so I even read it in the original French! At age seventeen, my heart broke for Fantine. As I turned the pages I mourned her death, feared for her beautiful child, rooted for Valjean to find peace and hated Inspector Javert. I was impassioned by the young revolutionaries and even fell a bit in love with Marius. He and his compatriots were my age; they were fighting for their beliefs just as my friends and I were marching in protest over the U.S. involvement in Vietnam.

I felt I knew these characters Hugo had created and I loved them.

The musical version of the beloved book actually began as a French Pop Album in 1980 being performed for the first time in a French Sports Stadium. In 1985, revised into English, it was presented to visionary producer Cameron Mackentosh and the rest as they say is history.

Les Miz was adapted by the "Cats" team for Broadway, garnered drop dead reviews, drew standing room only crowds and changed the American musical theater forever. While in New York in 1987, the year it opened there, I was privileged enough to see the original production of Les Miz on Broadway.

So, what did I think of the Broadway production? It was great! Great, great, great, great, great! While straying some from the Hugo novel, the musical captured the basic story and tone in wonderful song and inspired staging. I saw the show twice more when it played in Chicago and each time I was transported, beguiled, I laughed and cried and applauded and was self-affirmed once again that this was and still is the very best a musical show can be.

Fast forward to now ... it's a movie! And if that isn't good enough it stars hunky Hugh as Valjean and angelic Anne as Fantine and rotten Russell as Javert ... Ohhh, be still my heart!
So what did I think of it you might ask?

As the lyrics of my favorite song from the show states: "I dreamed a dream in time gone by when hopes were high and life worth living"... that such a movie would be made and this year it was!

# The Debt Ceiling...Again!

The latest round of legislative ineptitude has ended with even the President quoting that great sage, that master of advanced thinking, Yogi Berra, when he expressed his frustration by uttering, "it's déjà vu all over again." So, while we still teeter on the precipice of the "fiscal cliff," legislative attention will now be turned, once again, to the impending debt ceiling crisis.

Surely, you remember the debt ceiling crisis of just last summer? The one where a temporary agreement was reached to kick the can on down the road but with the promise of a "Super Committee" comprised of Dems and Reps who would hammer out a solution once and for all? You know that historic compromise made by true statesmen seeking only what was good for the country with no regard for their own political future. You remember that stunning example of our system of government at its finest, don't you?

Hah! So, here we are gearing up for a debt ceiling battle yet again.

I couldn't help but notice that in all of the bickering, haggling and basically doing of nothing this past year of "the ceiling debate;" one essential fact kept/keeps getting glazed over. The expansion of the debt ceiling was/is not for future allocations but to pay the ones we have already incurred!

So, let's get this straight. The same people that approved the expenditures in the first place are now fighting over whether or not they should allow the payment of those bills coming due?

And yet another interesting question is why have we not heard anything about this whole debt ceiling thing being a problem in other countries?

Well, guess what? Other countries don't have a debt ceiling limit. Say What? Nope they don't. Doesn't that beg the question, why do we?

Congress has to appropriate all spending, why do we need a debt ceiling limit? It is their job (or should be) not to spend more money than we have coming in. If we have overspent, it is congress's fault for passing the spending bills and now they want the U.S. to just renege on its commitments.

I don't know about you, but this just seems so wrong to me.

So, what can we do about this whole Congressional runaway spending epidemic? After all, if we didn't have the deficit dilemma we wouldn't have a debt ceiling dilemma.

Well, we could take the advice of The Sage of Omaha: "I could end the deficit in 5 minutes," Warren Buffett told Becky Quick of CNBC. "You just pass a law that says that anytime there is a deficit of more than 3% of GDP, all sitting members of Congress are ineligible for re-election."

I would add one more thing. All of their life-long benefits would be cancelled as well!
And if those last couple of paragraphs sound familiar it's because it is exactly how I closed my column on the debt ceiling this past summer.

As the man said, "It is déjà vu all over again."

# 2013

# Politics and Acting - Natural Bedfellows?

So the Golden Globes Show was Monday night and it struck me that we are now in the Presidential Primary Season of the entertainment industry ... it is Award season time. You know, that time when the seemingly endless airing of award shows, those "always a bridesmaid never the bride" competitors of the always the bride, Oscars do their best to seem meaningful.

Traditionally more fun than the Oscars, perhaps due to the fact that the audience sits at tables supplied with drinks, lots of drinks; the Globes is sort of the black sheep of the Award show family notorious for being a bit embarrassing on occasion (need I point out the similarity in this respect to the Republicans' Candidates debates?).

Hosted by the brilliantly funny, best friend team of comedienne's exemplar Tiny Fey and Amy Poehler, this year's broadcast didn't disappoint. In fact, I think that it is time for Oscar to take a lesson from Globe. No lengthy musical dance numbers, adherence to time constraints; it actually ended on time in spite of including numerous television categories while Oscar always runs late even though it gives up to a dozen fewer awards.

Anyone paying attention out there at the Academy of Motion Picture Arts and Sciences? Just sayin'.

Oh, and the gorgeous gals in their gowns and the hunks in tuxes and ... OMG former President William Jefferson Clinton even made a surprise appearance! (Just as a side note, this was a really gutsy move by the producer considering Bubba has been known to extend (putting it mildly) his allotted speech making time). But, after receiving a lengthy standing ovation, Clinton was a good boy and kept his introduction of the nominated film "Lincoln" brief.

But Bubba was not the only interjection of politics into the show. The actual CIA agent upon whom the winning film Argo was based took a shaky turn at the microphone ... apparently facing a crowd of celebs is a bit more intimidating than facing down terrorists. And former governor (now disgraced philanderer) Arnold Schwarzenegger was a presenter. Oh, and Julianne Moore won for her great performance as vice presidential candidate, Sarah Palin in the movie Game Change, as did the brilliant Daniel Day-Lewis for his masterful portrayal of President Lincoln.

Amy Poehler, in what I thought was one of the most amusing shticks, gushed over actually seeing Hillary Clinton's husband! Thus the Secretary of State was, in a way, brought onto the premises.

I can't remember a season when so many political based storylines including my personal cable fave, the very addicting Homeland, have been produced. I think this begs several questions. Have current politics now been relegated to fodder for the entertainment industry? And, is it just me or are the lines between acting and politics getting really blurry?

Actor Ronald Reagan certainly made the switch effectively but we are now seeing the reverse movement. Politicians now seem compelled to appear in the entertainment media or risk losing the very important "hip factor."

Could it be that politics and acting have always been natural bedfellows and we are just now acknowledging that truth?

All I know is that with super movie star Clint Eastwood, famously, or infamously, making an appearance at the Republican Convention earlier this year and equally famous super political star Bill Clinton appearing at the Globes, it's just getting very confusing!

# The Evolution of the Presidency

The History Channel concluded its miniseries "The Ultimate Guide to the Presidents" on Friday last week. (It is being re-run at various times this week as well) The timing of the series couldn't have been better. President Obama took his second oath of office on Monday thus he once again holds the most powerful, influential position in the world.

While not having seen the series in its entirety, I did see parts of several episodes and viewed several interviews with the writer. I was totally fascinated by the snippets he shared from the programs. The eight hour miniseries is billed as showing "... the ebbs and flows of Presidential power as each man deals with the events, expectations and challenges of his time."

Great anecdotes are also included. Don't you just love the little personal shtick?

Apparently, George Washington really didn't like to be touched so he was very torn about eliminating all examples of "royal" deference" toward the fledgling country's new leader as without it he would have to shake hands ... a lot of hands!

When an assassin shot twice at Andrew Jackson missing both times, the President lunged at him and almost killed him with his own "Presidential bare hands!"

And in Lincoln's time, the Oval Office was still open to anyone wishing to see the president. That policy changed after the assassination of Garfield.

It was Teddy Roosevelt who expanded the powers of the Presidency on the domestic policy making front.

When told by an opponent that he couldn't do what he had proposed, Teddy stated that "I have read the Constitution, show me where it says I can't do this!"

The ever appealing example of the hearty American outdoors man; Teddy Roosevelt also survived an assassination attempt when just before delivering a speech a shot hit him, on target, right at his heart. Only the folded copy of his very long speech in his breast pocket, saved his life as the bullet had to pass thorough the wad of paper. Though injured and bleeding quite profusely, ever the He-Man, the President delivered his speech before allowing himself to be taken to the hospital.

Yet, even with all of those obvious security problems, people were still able to picnic on the lawn of the White House up until WWII.

Woodrow Wilson broadened Presidential power on the foreign policy front, much like Teddy did domestically. And FDR certainly continued to broaden Presidential power even further.

It was the cold war that redefined the Presidency once again and forged the mold of the modern-day office holders. With the threat of nuclear weaponry, war became institutionalized. We now live in a world of "permanent war" requiring a totally different Chief Executive mindset.

So, now as Barack Obama, the newest member of the most elite group in the world (Presidents of the United States of America) begins his second term; how fitting it is to have a definitive, historical series highlighting just how the modern day Presidency evolved into the office we know today.

# Advertising for Advertising –
# Campaigning for Campaigning

So, the Super Bowl is nearly upon us. True confession time: although I am a football fan, since neither the Bears nor the Colts are participating this year, I am really not all that interested. However, I am very interested in something that is new this year. The much anticipated, sometimes great, sometimes very disappointing Super Bowl ads have a new marketing strategy of their own; "advertising for advertising."

Many of the companies spending millions on a 30 or 60 second spot have decided to optimize the popularity of their advertising by releasing previews of the ads they will run. I'm not altogether sure this is a smart idea. Already I have heard a slew of negative comments.

And, there seems to be something very new on the political front that I am not so sure is a good idea either.

Did you see the 60 Minute's joint interview on Sunday evening with the President and the Secretary of State? I have to wonder if O & Hil are taking a page from the Super Bowl advertiser's playbook by beginning to "campaign for Hillary's 2016 presidential campaign."

My reasoning? It seemed a most unusual step for the President to share the spotlight of a one-on-one interview with 60 Minutes, still the most watched news show on the planet, especially with the ambitious second term agenda his inauguration speech suggested.

So, what gives?

While they dodged the "is Hil running or isn't Hil running?" questions; one has to wonder, since no State Department announcements were made, no new national policy agendas of any kind disclosed or detailed; why would the President do this?

Well, many pundits assert that it was Bill Clinton's "coming to the rescue" at the tail end of the President's campaign that put him over the top. Many also feel that by Hillary accepting the Secretary of State position; it cemented a unified Democratic party, which was quite essential for President Obama to have any hopes for success.

Could this be payback?

Just a brief look at the polling numbers tells us that Hillary has a really high approval rating as does President Obama. By anyone's standards they are a dynamic duo. And they seemed so friendly, in sync, and comfortable with each other in the interview; it even prompted "Morning Joe" co-hosts, Joe Scarborough and Mika Brzezinski, to comment that they might be out of a job if O and Hil wanted to fill their chairs!

But all of this begs the question, what about V.P. Joe Biden's presidential ambitions? He has got to be teed off by this; after all over the past few months he has been the President's go-to-guy, his MVP for reaching any kind of agreement between the parties in Congress. And here is the President seemingly endorsing the Secretary of State's bid for the Oval Office?

Joe's gotta be thinkin' "say it ain't so, O!"

Like it or not, we now have advertising for advertising and campaigning for campaigning; new strategies to be sure.

Forgive me for playing on a quote from Hogan's' Heroes' Sgt. Schultz, "very interesting...but it is it stupid?" Only time will tell.

# Warriors

Did you see the Super Bowl on Sunday? Wow what a game! It really had it all; stellar athleticism, family drama and entertainment so electric – the power grid blew! And of course there were the much anticipated, to my mind pretty disappointing, obscenely expensive Super Bowl ads. And new this year was the recognition that the mood of the nation is changing toward the sport because of the now documented, tremendously devastating physical dangers of playing what has become America's Game. Anyone who thinks that the game will remain the same need only look at the issue of drunk drivers and what happened when the moms of this country got "MADD."

On Sunday night there was something for everyone from the passionate fan to the blasé observer.

I've never made a secret of my love for the game. From being a child raised in a "Chicago Bear's fan family" to becoming a mom that missed not one game in which her son played; football brought me joy.

I must confess that my passion for the game has waned proportionately to the replacing of my dark brown hair with grey. But, Sunday night it all came back to me...well all but the brown hair!

The hugely satisfying emotions associated with watching worthy athletic warriors battle it out for victory were with me once more.

There is another story in the news about a noble warrior which elicits a very different, even more intense emotion. Chris Kyle, former Navy Seal, recipient of seven medals for his service during his four tours of duty in Iraq, was murdered. He authored a book "American Sniper," which documents his service to our nation and the struggles he overcame trying to adjust, once more, to civilian life.

Husband, father of two, bona fide war hero; this man who struggled with his own demons upon his return from war was selflessly mentoring other returning vets when apparently one of the men he was trying to help shot him at point blank range. It is frustrating and oftentimes useless to try to figure out why a person would do such a thing, especially to someone who is trying to help.

At times we all feel we have to fight in our lives. We all have personal battles, some more dangerous than others. But, it's the senseless taking of human life, the acts in which no kind of logic plays a role; these are the acts that darken the soul of humanity.

So today I mourn the loss of one heroic warrior and exalt in the triumph of two teams of warriors.

What a game Super Bowl 47 was. What a spectacle the entire evening turned out to be. I thank the San Francisco Forty-niners and the Baltimore Ravens who were able to excite us, renew our faith in the competitive spirit. They fought valiantly and buoyed us all with their ability to triumph over the unexpected.

And I'm thankful for the all too brief moments of watching those men on the football field that allowed me to forget, albeit if only for a moment, the true horrors of actual combat and its aftermath that our dedicated military warriors must endure.

Yes, a game, that game and its warriors were great but I can't seem to get the loss of one truly heroic warrior out of my mind...Chris Kyle.

# What is, What Could Be, What Might Have Been

I spent two hours last week with Former Vice President Al Gore...OK, so there were several hundred other people there as well but I did get a chance to have a conversation with him.

I'm sure that many of you have seen him of late making the talk show circuit promoting his new book "The Future: Six Drivers of Global Change." Upon learning of my meeting with him, the first thing many have asked me is "he has gained a ton of weight; how did he look in person?" I have to agree that on the tube he looks like a former athlete whose body has gone to seed. He seems to have expanded into the equivalent, girth-wise, of the later day Orson Wells; but in person he simply looks like a middle-aged man that could lose twenty pounds.

Now that that is out of the way, the first thing I said to Drew when Gore's talk was over was, "if he had spoken like that throughout his presidential campaign, things would have been very different."

He was eloquent, funny and at times communicated very technical information understandably without coming off stiff or arrogant. He was at ease, relaxed and showed none of the mechanical aspects of delivery which plagued him during his presidential campaign. He literally commanded the room; and with no notes. He instinctively knew exactly when to insert some humor to lighten the mood of his audience. He was charming, honestly self-deprecating on occasion and came off just really likeable.

His book, in a nutshell, lays out his opinion of the six biggest challenges confronting us for the future. He touched on three of them in his talk.

The first is "the Global Economy." He went into some detail about how the trend of outsourcing is and will lead to more and more Robo-sourcing; that is the use of robotics in the broad sense of the word, to replace human workers. He also cited the levels of economic inequality in our country as a huge challenge and stated that we are more economically inequitable than both Egypt and Tunisia. Not sure what his source material is for that statement but the man said it.

The second is "the Global Mind." Techware has totally changed how we organize our businesses, our social lives and even our thinking. The volume of information flow makes us virtually "alone together." And, we are developing a stalker economy where every time we put a "buzzword" in an electronic communication of any kind it can be tagged for potential marketing by some company who has paid for the information (not to mention government's access as well)...this is scary!

The third is "Life Sciences." With seemingly minute to minute advances in nanotechnology and genomics, we have and will continue to improve on our ability to literally alter the fabric of our lives. Maybe "improve" was not the best word choice for me to use. Those of us afraid of the negatives these technological advancements might produce need only remember that Alfred Nobel was so horrified by how his discovery of dynamite was used; he endowed the Nobel Prizes in personal penance!

Anyway, there was a lot of really thought provoking stuff in his talk. Mr. Gore was truly interesting and surprisingly good given his pretty bad rep as an orator.

I have to say I am anxious to read the book.

# Groundhog Day and Our Government

I wonder if you've heard people referring to our current governmental situation, you know the constant replaying of "crisis, quick fix then on to next crisis," as reminiscent of the hit movie of years past, Groundhog Day; but I certainly have.

You probably don't know the name Danny Rubin. I spent a weekend at a workshop many years ago at which he was one of my instructors. Danny had penned a screenplay entitled Groundhog Day. He was young. It was his first script to be bought by a studio for production. His movie had been released the previous year to pretty unimpressive box office receipts but the critics loved it and it was beginning to take off with viewers as well.

He told us the story of how the movie, came to be produced. He had written it as a sort of "Graduate-esque" comedy/drama about a young man, fresh out of college, unsure of his future who somehow gets stuck reliving the same day over and over. And OMG a studio liked it and wanted to buy the rights. Being a true novice he went to the meeting signed the contract and thought himself to be the luckiest man alive ... until he read in Variety that Bill Murray, a middle aged comedian, had been cast in the lead. He was stunned. His protagonist was young, unsure of himself, seeking understanding about love and life.

When he contacted the studio and a lawyer (word to the wise, contact a lawyer before you sign a contract not after!) he was informed that he no longer had any say in the script. They were revising it and in fact, if his actual words accounted for only a small percentage of the final script, he wouldn't even be listed in the credits.

He convinced them that if they insisted on revision, he should be the one to work on it. And they agreed.

So, the movie was a hit. And because of its success he has a career. His voice got very quiet as he went on to tell us that not one day has gone by that he doesn't regret not being able to make his movie.

The story stayed with me all these years as a cautionary tale of life. Decisions, while at the moment seem to be right, could have serious consequences down the road. It also begs the question, how do we determine what we are willing to sacrifice for a secure future?

These governmental impasses we have all had to endure are indeed reminiscent of the basic plotline of Groundhog Day. The déjà vu crisis scenario keeps popping up and no one from either side of the isle seems willing, as Danny Rubin was, to rewrite the script. It's time someone has the courage or common sense to say "a rewrite has to happen I'll give in and do it."

Just as a note: I watched a recent interview with Danny and sat shocked as he told a completely different, much more glowing account of how Groundhog Day, the movie, came about. He obviously no longer regrets not making his original concept but relishes the outcome of the produced version. Hello Washington- think of Danny. Compromise might not turn out to be so bad!

# Sandra Day O'Connor: a Woman for History

Did you know that March is Women's History Month? Don't feel badly if you didn't...until I saw an interview with Sandra Day O'Connor, I didn't know it either! How pathetic is it that we need a Women's History Month to highlight the achievements of women such as the former Justice of the Supreme Court. We don't need to have a Men's History Month; it's every month!

Much like all successful grass root movements, this idea of honoring the accomplishments of women has evolved and grown through the years. In 1911 March 8th was declared International Women's Day. In 1978 Women's History Week was born. Then, in 1981 Congress made it all legit by passing a resolution declaring Women's History Week which led to 1987 when celebrations of National Women's History Month began.

From day, to week, to month; now, much larger than just our country's acknowledgment, we find ourselves in the celebration of International Women's History Month.

So, this week I think it only fitting to take a look at an exceptional role model for our young women; one truly worthy of recognition; Sandra Day O'Connor.

As mentioned earlier, I saw an interview with her during which she came off not like the 83 year old grandmother that she is, but like the highly respected, truly intelligent and still oh so savvy woman who was appointed to the Supreme Court by Ronald Reagan in 1981 as the first woman Justice.

She has a new book coming out this week entitled "Out of Order" so should you want to see and hear her yourself, network interviews with her most assuredly will abound as part of her book tour promotion.

A self-proclaimed "cowgirl" born in Texas, raised in Arizona, educated at Stanford; she excelled, reaching the highest pinnacle in the totally male dominated world of "the law."

Named to the Supreme Court before ideological litmus tests began being applied to nominees, and in a time when the role of Justice was to rule only on the constitutionality of an issue; she was often the "tie-breaker" on important issues making her regarded by many as the most powerful Justice of her tenure.

During the interview, she pulled a pocket sized copy of the Constitution from her jacket. Amazing Charley Rose, she said that she carries a copy with her always, and gave it to him, as a gift, stating that when she was on the bench "this is what we were concerned with!"

Now, that's a woman to be admired not only during Women's History Month but every month of the year.

Every month of the year: yeah. Now, how to make that happen? I know, how 'bout taking all of the resources spent on these commemorations and spending them on revising all of our historical texts. If the history books accurately reflected the accomplishments of all people there would be no need for this hoopla. We shouldn't have to designate a month for the recognition of great women of the world.

In all history classes, every day, every month should be Women's History Month. History isn't gender specific. Why should the teaching of it be?

# "Amazing" Spider Goats

Have you heard about spider goats? Well, I hadn't until recently and what I heard made me take a closer look at spiders, those oh so creepy crawlers, and the silk construction of the webs they weave. What I found out was "amazing." The fragile looking spider silk that appears in the nooks and crannies of our homes in such intricate, delicately woven patterns (which can only truly be appreciated when sunlight streams through them) are in reality not fragile or delicate at all; far from it. Here are some facts about Spider Silk. It's...

- Five times stronger (weight for weight) than steel
- Can be stretched by a factor of up to 40% without snapping or losing integrity
- Does not decay, dry out or become brittle over time
- Is completely immune to microbial and fungal degradation
- Is completely waterproof
- Is lightweight in relation to its strength
- And, is compatible with the human body in terms of the reproduction of biological tissues.

One scientist stated that "creating spider silk has been the Holy Grail of material science." The products and of course the profits to be made from spider silk seem limitless; unfortunately the supply of the "more valuable than gold," thread is indeed limited.

So, now enter genetic scientists who have developed a way to incorporate spider DNA into goat embryos thus engineering the hybrid "Spider Goats." The milk from the Spider Goat offspring will give scientists the capability to produce the huge quantities of the "spidey stuff" necessary for mass production of the silk.

Why, one might ask, don't they just get the silk from the spiders themselves? Why invest tons of time and treasure creating these, I gotta say, conceptually creepy creatures? The answer might, just might, scare you as much as it scares me.

Spiders are crazily territorial. When spider farms were created to harvest the silk from large quantities of the little web weavers, they devoured each other. Yep, the masters of such artistry, the creators of the lace-like wisps of silk that all of us have seen flutter gently in the breeze, turn on each other in impulsive, instinctive, self-preservation frenzies. They kill.

I don't know. Do we really want goats multiplying with even a few of the genetically engineered characteristics of spiders, those creatures that by nature and instinct turn on their own; kill their own if they sense an infringement on their territory? What other "side effects" will we discover after the fact?

The spider goo that transformed the Amazing Spiderman into the super hero, created the means by which the character could use super-human powers for the good of mankind. And that is an "amazing" concept.

But, this whole spider goat thing...hummmm, I think might not end up being quite so "amazing."

I have never been much of an "Amazing Spiderman" fan. Never read the comics but I have seen the movies ... nope, really not much of a fan.  It probably has something to do with the fact that the original movies starred Tobey Maguire whom I have never been able to warm up to as an actor. However, in the 2012 version of the superhero saga, Andrew Garfield starred. I first became aware of his talents watching his stellar performance in "The Social Network." But, as Spidey, even though Garfield was adorable and, holy goat, really flexible; alas, I still was not all that enamored.

Having spider gunk in your body, even if the powers it produced were "amazing" was just too ucky for me.

# What's In a Name?

Juliet: "What's in a name? That which we call a rose by any other name would smell sweet."
Thus spoke Juliet Capulet to her beloved Romeo Montague in William Shakespeare's immortal "The Tragedy of Romeo and Juliet." This was Juliet's attempt to convince Romeo that a name is merely an artificial and meaningless convention; that she loved the person called Montague not the Montague name or family.

Can we apply maiden Juliet's wisdom to modern times? Rather than the rose being the focus of name recognition today; it is the "Bush" that is garnering the buzz on the current American political front.

Jeb Bush has been making the political talk show circuit (5 this past weekend alone!) promoting the release of his new book. Since he is no longer empathically denying a run for the presidency in 2016, it seems these appearances are also a way for him to put his toe in the water to check the temperature of the nation. How high is the fever and how painful is the suffering we are still experiencing from our almost fatal case of "W-itis?" You know "W-itis" that nasty viral infection with which Jeb's big brother infected us during his tenure as president?

The sixty-four thousand dollar question is how will the legacy of his brother (and less so, that of his father) affect his chances for the presidency?

You gotta give the man credit for not throwing his brother under the bus in those interviews. Instead he stated again and again that he didn't feel there was any "Bush name baggage" and that, "History will be kind to George W. Bush."

I don't know about history, but in all of the polls taken that I've seen, W is consistently rated as one of the six worst United States presidents ever and he only beat out Richard Nixon as the worst president in modern times.

So, the pundits are saying poor Jeb doesn't have a chance with that albatross of a name hanging from his neck, but I wonder if they aren't underestimating the American people. I for one would not want to be judged by the actions of my siblings...would you?

Also, is there any truth to the "inside Washington rumors" that there's major Republican money, money earmarked for Jeb, just waiting to be shelled out if he throws his hat into the race?
And, let's not forget that with all of this "re-branding" hoopla that the Reps are spouting, here is a proven leader that works well with others and is not ideologically tunnel visioned.

I don't know Jeb sounds to me like a more viable presidential candidate than all of the 2012 republican contenders combined!

So, it seems to keep coming back to the name. Will enough time pass? Does he have to do a one-eighty and denounce his brother's job performance to have a chance?

Important questions but the one really needing to be answered is:

If a rose is a rose is a rose, is a Bush a Bush a Bush?

# The Sequester

With the Papal Conclave garnering lots of attention, not to mention air time, in the recent weeks and the whole "automatic budgetary cuts" and new budget submission stories clogging up the remaining commentary time; the word sequester keeps popping up when talking about both situations. Do you find that to be as odd as I do? The application of this word in such completely differing settings, seeming to describe such diverse situations just doesn't make sense to me.

I totally understand it being used in the Conclave context. The Cardinals are indeed sequestered; locked behind closed doors, unable to leave the premises until they complete their charge of electing a new pope. But used as a noun, the sequester, labeling the automatic budget cuts (you know those cuts that no one from either party thought would ever be enacted) well, it makes no sense to me. Oh wait, how much sense was utilized when, in their empirical wisdom our representatives devised the proposal to begin with? They thought it to be so extreme and arbitrary it would never, ever be enacted and then because they couldn't get their, you know what together, they let the seemingly impossible indeed become not only possible but a reality!

Still, the word itself being used as it is, for some reason, irks me. So I looked up the meaning trying to get some clarification. Here's what the dictionary says:

se·ques·ter
verb (used with object)
1. To remove or withdraw into solitude or retirement; seclude.
2. To remove or separate.
3. Law. To remove (property) temporarily from the possession of the owner; seize and hold, as the property and income of a debtor, until legal claims are satisfied.

4. International Law. to requisition, hold, and control (enemy property).

Alas. Nope. Not much clarification there as to why in the world "the sequester" is the label attached to the automatic cuts that have been and will be made.

I do however; have a solution to that problem. I have a way that would have the sequester, in our current budgetary context, actually mean what it is supposed to mean.

Do you remember the former wrestling star turned Governor of Minnesota, Jesse Ventura? Well, he's a huge hulk of a man who, when no progress was being made on budget discussion in the Minnesota legislature, locked the doors and stood in front of them with mammoth arms crossed on his chest telling the warring factions that anyone wanting to leave before an agreement was reached would have to go through him. Hmmmmm, very interesting.

And, I am told that the Cardinals, who by all accounts live quite comfortably if not luxuriously in their respective residences and are accustomed to dining equally as well; while in sequester, have minimal comforts and what many have described as quite terrible food for the duration of their deliberations. While not quite as dramatic as Mr. Ventura, it does seem to add to the urgency of coming to a decision.

Our representatives obviously felt no such urgency attached to their task and thus totally dropped the ball. Perhaps we should hire Mr. Ventura to conduct a sequester intervention, and let's throw in really bad food to boot...think that would finally get something done?

# Cheney According to Cheney

We have hit an ominous milestone. We have been at war in Iraq for ten years and it has cost the U.S. tax payers $2.2 Trillion. But even an amount of money that obscenely high doesn't come close to the obscenity of losing 4,488 U.S. service men and women. And that doesn't take into account the 134,000 Iraqi civilians that have been killed. Mind-boggling numbers for any war casualty list made even more so by the fact that when asked "has it been worth it," I think the vast majority of Americans would answer no; this war certainly wasn't necessary.

Not necessary, that is, unless your name is Dick Cheney.

There is a new two hour documentary currently airing on Showtime entitled "The World According to Dick Cheney." It was created by the very well reputed documentarian, R.J. Cutler featuring an interview with the VEEP interspersed with historical facts and commentary from various other high level players in the scenarios discussed.
***Spoiler Alert***
(I am going to be quoting a few of the answers Mr. Cheney gave so if you want to hear them first from the horse's mouth (or the horse's other end!) you might want to stop reading and watch the documentary.)

I should also warn you that 2 hours is a long time to sit still especially given Cheney's never wavering, unapologetic, black or white telling of event remembrances delivered in his characteristically monotone drone...I was fascinated!

While I was fascinated, Cheney according to Cheney was always right.

When asked how he felt about the negative comments and accusations throw at him throughout his political life he responded, "I don't lie awake at night thinking, 'gee, what are they going to say about me?'"

In answer to another question about his unpopularity he quipped "if you want to be liked you should be an actor."

As entertaining as his attitude and answers were I found the "meat of the show" to be really good. Did you know that Cheney was the first Veep to ever head-up the transition team? He staffed the White House with his choices passing over W's staffers. He gave himself an "all access pass" which allowed him to sit in on any meetings that were being held so while W was sayin' "thank ya Dick for takin' care of that fer me"... Cheney had created clear passage for himself to maneuver through every aspect of Executive Branch activity. And being the novice, W yielded to the pro's expertise allowing Cheney to become the most powerful Vice President in the history of this country.There was a reason the Secret Service called Cheney "Back Seat" as in back seat driver!

Cheney justifies all of his actions (including but certainly not limited to the infamous implementation of warrantless wire-tapping and facilitating this now ten year war) by saying that he did what was necessary to prevent another terrorist attack on American soil.

When asked if he has any regrets, he said simply, "no." When Cutler waited for more, Cheney, looking almost exasperated by having to elaborate said, "If I had it to do over again, I'd do it over in a minute." He nonchalantly stated with a slight shrug of the shoulder, "I did what I did, it's all on the public record, and, um, I feel very good about it."

Yes Mr. Cheney, it is all on the public record.

# Cyber Attack a Virtual Whack-a mole

Did you know that one of the largest cyber-attacks in history occurred last week? Our super-duper information highway experienced a traffic jam that affected millions of users and shut down countless servers. The cyber highway was so gnarled and tangled horns were blaring all around the globe. O.K. so there were no horns but if our computers had horns they would have been blasting forth with the frustrations of internet users from here to Timbuktu.

Gee, and to think, I didn't even notice; did you?

Notice or not it did spark my interest; made me want to know "so what gives?"

Apparently there are two warring factions of computer whiz kids creating havoc for the rest of us who only want our internet service to do what it is supposed to do. A gladiatorial battle of the brainiacs is being waged not in the confines of an old time Roman arena but out in the limitless world of cyberland. Just think of it; hummmm let's see...I picture McGee from NCIS going head-to-head with Garcia from Criminal minds - whoa, now that would be fierce!

But, what is this real feud all about?

On one side we have the internet service providers (ISP) and web hosts who look the other way, not asking any questions of their clients who host spam and other destructive, malicious code. BOOOOO, HISSSSSS!

One the other side are groups that try to name and shame the spammers and stop them from infiltrating your inbox or worse, your bank's server! As Eli Lake (Senior National Security Correspondent for Newsweek) put it, "This side is engaged in a massive game of virtual Whack-a-mole..." They slam down fast and hard whenever the other side raises their malicious heads. YEAAAAAH, RAAAAAH.

So, what happened this time?

Sorry to say those mighty, white hatted good guys just weren't fast enough. The spammers got the better of them. The bad guys were actually able to shut down servers and slow the entire internet down to what must have seemed like a snail's pace to those who live with a need for speed.

As one who doesn't expect much speed (I remember all too well the ancient dial up modem and that incessant, chills down the spine screech it made as it took its own sweet, sloooow time to connect) I didn't have a clue my computer was running any slower than usual. But whether or not I realized the loss of speed; it's the implications to be drawn from the breaches in security that are truly frightening. If they (meaning the bad guys) have the ability to shut down unsuspecting servers, who must have state of the art security measures in place, what are the limits of how much damage and mayhem can be foisted on just average users?

We need McGee and Garcia to play for our side in this Whack-a-mole cyber battle and the inevitable ones to come in the future!

But sadly, while Whack-a-mole is fun; this is no joke.

There is a reason why cyber terrorism is now considered by many experts to be the number one concern to our national security. This is no game; no futuristic avatar battle. This is our new reality and we better get a handle on it.

# #42 Jackie Robinson

Have you seen the movie #42? It opened this weekend to lots of hype and media attention. The movie chronicles the events and the personalities responsible for the racial integration of "America's favorite pastime" major league baseball. It is the story of Branch Rickey's bold, dangerous and some say heroic decision to sign Jackie Robinson to the roster of the Brooklyn Dodgers as the first "negro" player in major league history.

I had seen numerous interviews with Rachel Robinson (Jackie's widow and consultant on the film), Harrison Ford (he plays Branch Rickey) and Chadwick Boseman (who plays Jackie Robinson) so I was pretty psyched to see the movie. Having been a baseball fan all of my life, I thought I knew the story of Jackie Robinson's emergence onto the major league stage. But, like so many times in life when you think that you know something, I was pulled up short after seeing the movie; I truly had no idea!

Did you know that Jackie had played ball for and graduated from U.C.L.A.? Me neither!

Did you know that a key factor in Branch selecting Jackie over other "more talented black players" was that Jackie had played with white players at U.C.L.A. and was therefore already exposed to some of the challenges he would have to face? Me neither!

Could you ever imagine that Jackie would receive file folders full of death threats, hundreds of them, and some were against his wife, his newborn son and that Branch would have to have the FBI and local police safeguarding Jackie at every city to which he traveled? Me neither!

Could you have imagined not only the players, but the coaches from opposing teams hurling a constant barrage of racial obscenities at him every time he entered the batter's box and some of his own teammates signing a petition stating that they would not play with him? Me neither!

Rachel Robinson put it in perspective historically saying that Jackie was always acutely aware of the bigger picture of what he was accomplishing. He knew he had to rein in his own feelings, his own tendency of impatience with the ignorance of others. And, as Branch Rickey told him, he had to fight back by showing them all what he was made of on the field...and that is what he did, and did so well.

So much more than an historical statement of what it was like back then, this is a story of two men and a woman who together changed the course of history. Branch Rickey had the power of money and morality behind him. Jackie Robinson had the power of exceptional talent, resolve and almost god-like patience. And, Rachel Robinson had the power of unfaltering love, instinctual savvy and granite-like faith.

Putting them together brought the first real progress in the civil rights movement since the Civil War. The world as we knew it shifted.

#42 is the only number in professional baseball to be retired by the league and Monday was the annual tribute to Jackie Robinson observed by every team...every year all of the players wear #42.

So, Drew and I went to see the movie "42" over the weekend along with more people than have ever attended the opening of a "baseball" movie in history. Chalk just one more history making milestone up to the legendary Jackie Robinson.

# Rats Get a Reprieve

I had to be in New York on business. It was a last minute trip, no avoiding it. This was a time in my life, when I had to travel quite often for my job. All of my friends were jealous thinking that business travel was glamorous; after all, I got paid to go to really great places and had an expense account to boot! What they didn't realize was that all I experienced was business meetings and room service. In the late seventies a woman unaccompanied would never eat in a restaurant let alone go to a show. Nope, out on the town, out of town; out of the question!

So, on this particular trip, I found myself in a hotel room literally no bigger than a good sized closet. The twin bed was wedged into a corner making room for a small three drawer chest. One could only open the drawers if seated cross-legged on the bed.

The shower stall couldn't have measured larger than 3' X 3' and the shower head dangled from the ceiling. Yes siree, I was really living the glamorous life!

While sitting on the bed watching the miniscule T.V. that was perched atop the chest of drawers, one of the news magazine shows came on with a segment about rats. Just the word, rats, brings a scowl to most faces. I can't think of one thing about rats that isn't offensive. They are dirty and disgusting and carry deadly diseases.

In 1348 – 1351 the Black Plague swept through Europe killing, by some estimates, 2/3 of the population. 2/3 of the population; just think of that. And, rats were the culprit. All because of those black menaces with the beady little eyes and pointy noses perched over those vampire-esque sharp little teeth; UGH, rats; makes me shutter just to think about them.

And yet there I sat mesmerized, and then terrified by the report that New York City sewer's had such an infestation of the wretched little beasts, they were actually escaping the sewers by coming up through toilets. I swiftly turned my head to see that the toilet seat lid was indeed down but a sweep of panic coursed through me as I realized that the lid rendered little protection.

I slept fitfully, hoping that I could go without using the facilities until I was out of the city.
Rats, so creepy, so dirty, so responsible for horrid diseases.

But now, lo these many years later, due to the advancements in forensic science (don't you just love the CSI shows?) the rats have gotten a reprieve. That's right. They have been proven not to be responsible for all of those deaths, all of those diseases.

But, is this a reason to breathe a sigh of relief? While the rats might have gotten off the hook in regard to the Black Death; their creepy factor has not diminished in my mind. In fact, once in a while I can't help but approach a toilet with a very skeptical eye!

# Is Character The Thing?

Do you remember that heart thumping, patriotism confirming, amazingly well written scene at the end of the movie An American President when President Michael Douglas (or whatever his character's name was) emphatically states in a press conference that "the Presidency is all about character?" In the context of the movie the concept of character was a theme that threaded masterfully throughout the film and built dramatically to that climactic moment when anyone watching just had to agree with President Douglas (Shoulda looked up the character's name...sorry!) that the Presidency is all about character.

Last Thursday the four living former Presidents of the United States and the current President assembled for the dedication of the newly constructed George W. Bush Presidential Library and Museum. There was a flurry of promotional appearances and a ton of print, tweets and social media blather available for all to see and hear.

As I combed through several articles about "W's" legacy, one point was repeated over and over; that character is the historical measure of a Presidency and that "W" has plenty of that.

Beloved friend and valued advisor Karl Rove, began his defense of "W's" Presidency by stating; "I'm obligated to state the obvious, which is that George W. Bush is hardly flawless....." going on he basically said that the really important thing is that "W" has character.

I found seven other articles about the "W" legacy which pointed out a slew of reasons why "W" is one of the bottom three least admired Presidents in history; but ended with his "strong character."

The legacies of Ike and Harry Truman seem to be the ones most cited in these articles as examples of Presidents, who when leaving office, were regarded as having done a pretty bad job; but, who through the passing of time and the publishing of well researched biographies, have substantially gained in popularity in the eyes of not only the historians but of the American people as well. They pointed out that like Ike and Harry; only time will tell what "W's" true legacy will be.

The more I read about his character the more the words of my favorite bard kept creeping into my mind "Thou dost protest too much!"

The other favorite highlight on the "W's greatest hits reel" the authors of these articles all seem to have reviewed is that he kept America safe after 9/11.

O.K. Until the tragedy in Boston that was indeed true. But, what about....well I know I don't have to list all of the things "W" did and didn't do to get him that low standing in public opinion.

Don't get me wrong, I too think that character is an important criterion for judging a President but, I don't know about you, I gotta believe that actions and consequences speak louder than intentions.

I don't pretend to know how history will judge George W. Bush's Presidency but I have to ask, is character really the thing?

# The Kim Jongs

Note:   Kim Jong Il, now deceased, was the leader of
North Korea

        Kim Jong Un (Il's son) is the current leader of
North Korea

I'm sure that you have heard that tensions are
escalating over North Korea flexing its nuclear muscles.
They do have nukes but are unable to make them small
enough to be placed into missiles for launching...yet.
None the less, Kim Jong Un seems to be issuing what
some consider to be "over-the-top" threats on a daily
basis. Apparently, the "over-the-top" descriptive runs in
the Kim Jong family.

I wrote two columns in the past describing Un's dad Il
and his strange behavior. In a somewhat joking manner
I described him as "that crazy little man." His bizarre
antics were just too whacky to resist making fun of.
But, what is happening now is no joke and that "crazy
little man" is proving to have raised an even crazier heir.

Before his death, Il greased the skids for Un to easily
slide into control of the North Korean Government. By all
accounts Un is an inexperienced, sheltered child of
privilege determined to prove his power by instigating
some kind of military conflict with someone.

The latest report is that North Korea has moved a
missile to its east coast, seemingly to back up Un's
threat that he will nuke the U.S.  South Korea,
immediately issued a statement that the missile in
question isn't capable of reaching the United States.

Does that make you feel any better?

In response to this report, last Wednesday, the U.S.
deployed an advanced missile defense system to Guam
as a precaution.

O.K. so now I do feel a bit better.

But the situation is truly dicey. Even China, probably North Korea's last ally, voiced "serious concern" over Un's latest rhetoric and action.

So, what does all of this mean? What could really happen?

By all reports, the North Korean military though massive in number is undertrained and ill-equipped. If a conventional battle were to break out, any one of their possible opponents would find victory in short order. The fear is that with defeat an almost given, the decision to use weapons of mass destruction would be made.

So, what can be done?

It appears that China is finally coming to realize that a viable nuclear North Korea would be incredibly bad for their self-interest. They have to know that if North Korea has operational nukes, then South Korea will want them and Japan will want them and Taiwan will want them and Laos will want them ... man, with all of those wants; the last thing China needs is to be surrounded by nuclear powers.

So, with this latest statement, it appears that China is starting to make a move and that's good because Un needs to be reined in. Since North Korea's economy relies heavily on China, they might be the only nation that can get through to Un.

I never thought I would say that I miss Il and his whacky hair, egocentric behavior and international attention seeking stunts; but his heir, this current Kim Jong, seems to be exhibiting much more dangerous lunacy. This "crazy little man" is no joke.

# The Language of Texting

As I find myself being dragged further and further into the 21st century, current technology continues to baffle me. Look around you. At any time, any day, any place, someone (usually many someones) will be texting. And, if the loss of what I consider to be vital to humanity, namely actual voice to voice contact not to mention person to person contact, isn't enough to make me hate the medium; those seeming to be professional texters are brutally mangling the written word as well.

Come on. Admit it. If you receive a text from someone under the age of 30, don't you spend more time trying to figure out what all of the cockamamie abbreviations mean than it would have taken them to write an entire essay using the genuine English language which you could have easily read in a minute and a half?

And all of our young people are doing it all of the time. I don't know about you, but I am worried that they will lose the ability to communicate with the beauty of imagery, the power of irony, and even more tragic; I fear that one day they will have gotten to a place where they will never know, never experience the magic of beautiful writing.

Just when I thought that all was lost ... enter John McWhorter.

McWhorter is a highly credentialed, very well respected linguist and author. And, guess what? He says that texting is not only a natural progression of our communication skills but it is actually a really good thing; of great benefit to our youth. Rather than a nasty mutation of our language he calls texting "fingered speech."

A wonderful speaker (and it didn't hurt that he is a real "cutie patootie" as well) I was captivated by the logic of what he said. Backing up his assertions with historical references and comprehensive studies; he methodically, and quite entertainingly, supported his premise that texting is not the ruination of our language but rather it is just another stepping stone in our ability to communicate effectively.

According to McWhorter, the "language of texting" is evolving. And, much to my relief, he contends that "fingered speech" is not replacing traditional language at all. No, indeed; rather than diminishing our youth's language skills, utilizing the language of texting has instead been found to have the same benefits as if they were becoming bilingual. They are utilizing their ability to do two things at once, learn two things at once. So, like bilingual individuals, those creating, utilizing and confusing old folks like me with this "fingered speech," are actually reaping cognitive benefits equal to those of bilingual individuals.

Wow. Who knew? And here I thought ...well you know what I thought.

Is it possible that texting is a good thing? Are there really cognitive benefits to be derived from the incessant thumbing of those teeny, tiny keys as a teen plows into you on the sidewalk, so absorbed that he is not looking where he is going?

I'm not so sure...

BTW text me wy.02 (translation: by the way, text me with your two cents worth)

# Hacking and Getting Away With It

Those nefarious, devious cowards hiding behind their computer screens have been at it again. For the third time in so many years my email was hacked. The previous two times the act, which I think should have mandatory jail time if perpetrators are caught, appeared to be simply a prank. You know one of those harmless antics the presumably young, mischievous computer geek foists upon us just because he can. But while causing no damage, so to speak, no "crime" perpetrated; I still had to spend considerable time sorting out the mess.

And though it was no fault of mine, the guilt factor was huge. All of my contacts had to be alerted and if they had unknowingly opened the bogus email from me, they too were then infected. OY the guilt!

After changing my password, following other suggested advice and having been reassured that there was nothing left to be done; I notified all of my contacts apologizing profusely and warning of the potential problem to their email.

That was then.

This latest hacking was much more sinister and actually criminal. I first became aware that there was a problem when I received error notices saying that emails I had sent were undeliverable. Since it was first thing in the morning and I had sent no emails yet, my first thought was, "this is odd." But, it took no time at all for the realization to set in that, oh yes; I had been hacked...again! When I attempted to open an email which was sent from a friend, I'm sure notifying me that I had been hacked; the email was deleted as soon as I clicked to open it. I tried one more email and again it was instantly deleted. I couldn't access my emails.

I then went to my contact list to notify everyone not to open the infected email... guess what? My entire contact list had been deleted. I had no way of letting everyone know.

I had gone from aggravated to irate in a matter of moments.

After hours (and I do mean multiple hours) of time trying to sort out the mess; my email account was scrubbed, my contacts were once again accessible and all was right with the world.

I later learned that the hacking was a scam designed to get people to send money to help me out of a terrible situation abroad. The hacker quite ingeniously then made it impossible for me to access my contacts to let them know it was all a con.

I doubt very seriously that any one on my contact list would have fallen for the scam...it is after all an oldie but not a goodie and anyone who knows me knows that I would never send such an email; but just opening it left them all vulnerable to a similar hacking fate.

So, once again I am informing all in every medium I can, that you should never open an email from me (or anyone) that does not have a specific, recognizable subject line applicable to the sender of the email.

Never, ever, ever!

So, my latest brush with the seedier side of modern technology is over but surly not forgotten. What really bothers me is that this was not a prank. This was no geeky kid flexing his computer-skill muscles. This was a skilled con man, breaking the law and getting away with it.

# Crises—Wasted Moments

When BP leaked (what am I talking about leaked, BP gushed) its oil in the Gulf; the attention of the world was captured. There were days, weeks, months of hand-wringing, moaning and reams upon reams of columns, articles, speeches and editorials calling for a comprehensive energy plan; a wide-ranging plan, a big, bold plan that would not only address the issue of alternative sources of energy but tackle the entire environmental problem facing us today and in the future.

While this environmental catastrophe was still fresh in our minds what better time to really come together and get something done?

Yes, the beginning dialogue was sharp and intense and many were optimistic. Sadly, the optimism was very short lived. We have seen no big, bold plan.

We learned nothing from Columbine and so many other tragedies of gun violence leading up to the horrific massacre at Sandy Hook. But, it seemed that this time it was different. There were sharp, clear voices being heard through the heart-wrenching keening of the nation for that loss of too many, too young. Unexpected voices joined the call for something to be done.

Over 90% of the nation wanted big, bold gun reforms put into place. While the tragedy was still fresh in our minds, still breaking our hearts, what better time to really get something done?

But, Washington can't even pass an impotent bill that doesn't have a chance in hell of reducing gun violence.

Now, enter the current IRS scandal. The charges of IRS abuse of power are confirmed. The acting head guy has been fired and a whole slew of governmental investigations have begun. Though many instances of this politicizing the powers of the agency have occurred in the past under both Republican and Democratic administration; no excuses can be made for the egregious acts.

Accusations, vitriolic verbiage abound. But, there are many cooler minds talking about the need for sweeping changes to the entire IRS system. Many are asking for a big, bold "start from the beginning" revision of the entire tax code. While this abuse is still fresh in our minds, what better time to really get something meaningful done?

Our history is replete with instances of brave, bold leaders rising like the Phoenix of myth from the ashes of catastrophe; men and women who were willing to put self aside and do what was best for the future of this country. Visionaries who propelled our growth with bold imaginings then turned into workable solutions to problems.

Do you see anyone in Washington like that today? Does anyone have the backbone to crush the special interest groups, enact campaign funding reform and create a governmental system that will take us forward into this the 21st century instead of keeping us mired in the past and the ways things "have always been done?"

I was taught to position myself, whether through education or other experience, to be ready for opportunity when it presents itself. A pretty vague concept I admit but one that has served me well.

What a shame that there seems to be no one positioned to take the bold initiatives, imagine the better ways, do something meaningful to address the truly dire problems facing our nation.
So many opportunities wasted.

# It's Fitzgerald's Turn

The biographers of F. Scott Fitzgerald (that's Francis Scott Keys Fitzgerald...I'd use the initial and drop the Keys too!) and Ernest Hemingway can't seem to agree on what exactly the relationship was between the two men. As the two most famous American authors of their time and some would argue the best American authors ever; there was of course a rivalry. Both reached fame and notoriety in their lifetimes and both were characters "bigger than life." They led the kind of lives that most people only read about...probably reading about in the novels penned by the two men!

They were expats in Paris together and with their spouses (two of Hemingway's Four) it is agreed that they certainly socialized regularly. What it is also agreed upon is that they had a fierce rivalry.

For the past several years Papa Hemingway has experienced a revival on the bookshelves of America. Several books reached best seller status about his wives and the lives they lived courted by and married to the great man. An award winning movie was also made about his tumultuous affair and then marriage to his third wife, foreign correspondent Martha Gellhorn. Papa was peaking in the consciousness of a new generation of Americans.

But now, fueling the flames of that previously neglected fire of rivalry between the two great authors; Fitzgerald is rising to prominence once again. And like Papa, the major focus is on his wife. While married only once, Fitzgerald's wife Zelda is being immortalized in four new books. The tortured, talented, beautiful, fun- loving, outrageously behaving southern bell, who was the muse of many of Fitzgerald's works, is now speculated to have been suffering from bipolar disorder which transformed the "it girl" of the 20's into a sick, middle-aged woman who ended her once charmed life in a mental institution.

If new literary publications about the men and their wives are the gauge for the current competition between them, one would have to judge it pretty much a tie.

But wait ... enter the new remake of Fitzgerald's immortal work The Great Gatsby and I'm afraid even all of you Hemingway rooters out there will admit, Fitzgerald has significantly pulled out in front.

Being a huge Gatsby fan I was greatly anticipating the new version's release. I am also a huge fan of its director, Baz Luhrmann; thus my wait for the movie's opening was almost unbearable. In preparation I reread the book discovering once again the power and majesty of lavish yet terse descriptions and character development needing only a sentence or two to expose the depth and breadth of their individual natures and struggles. It is truly a stunning piece of fiction.

And in my opinion, the movie is a stunning piece of cinema. As only Lerhman can, the money and the glitz and the opulence and the needless waste by the rich of the time is portrayed in all of its haunting, garish, over the top, gory glory. No nudity or explicit sex scenes are required to expose the obscenity of the era.

The acting is good. The script is very sympathetic to the original novel. And the overall, heart wrenching themes of love and loss, the haves vs. the have nots and the tragedy that can result by trying to recreate the past still holds up, still rings true.

Alas poor Papa; you're recent sojourn into the limelight is officially over. Make way. For now it is Fitzgerald's turn.

# The New Star Trek Movie, or Is It?

Have you seen the new Star Trek? It is filled with new faces portraying the much loved original television series favorites. Those TV actors had "beamed themselves up," to appear in a series of movies depicting the voyages of the Starship Enterprise on the silver screen once the TV. series had ended its very long run. But now we have a new cast filling the roles of Kirk, Spock, Uhura and their crewmates on the familiar starship bridge.

While not having the ooph of the original Uhura, Nichelle Nichols' or the straight-spine (in every sense of the term) of Spock portrayed by Leonard Nimoy and certainly not the kitsch of William Shatner's Kirk, for those die hard trekkies; it is something.

Oh wait. Hold on a minute. Something is not "balancing" up on the Bridge. It isn't the new Star Trek movie which was recently released. Oh no, it's not the multi-million dollar, special-effects packed, view it in the 3D IMAX format so you can literally be surrounded by the action and feel the shaking of your seats as you are propelled into that last frontier of space.

No siree; it is a training video produced by the IRS for one of its employee conferences. That's right. The IRS! Who knew that the stereo-typical straight laced, stogie, nit-picky IRS agent even knew who/what "Spock" was!

The existence of this video was uncovered by the investigation into the IRS's purely political policies of targeting not-for-profits of the Conservative/Republican persuasion. It seems that the already beleaguered agency can now, in my opinion, add the obscene use of agency funds to produce this spoof of the Star Trek franchise for training purposes, to its list of misdeeds.

The investigations have found that included in the tens of millions of dollars the IRS spent over the past several years on employee conferences in general, this training film and one spoofing the TV series Gilligan Island cost the agency, and by extension you and me, over $60,000. That's $60,000 for a training video.

I gotta tell you that I have produced literally hundreds of training videos for clients throughout my career as a marketing consultant and I have never come anywhere close to charging that kind of money.

How could they have run up a bill of that size for a training video, you might ask?

Well, there was the starship set, a very convincing replica of the original Enterprise Bridge appearing to be accurately reproduced. In addition, they rented the actual costumes worn by Kirk and crew, which seemed, at the time of the original show, to be futuristic back in the sixties, but now just look like pajamas.

And that cost $60,000? They didn't even use professional actors rather opting for employees playing the roles. Forgive me. I just don't get it.

If you haven't seen the actual video yet, you gotta Google it or YouTube it or Bing it, or whatever … judge for yourself. I think it's a hoot!

But, all kidding aside, let there be no mistake. Yet another blatant misuse of funds by a federal agency is anything but a hoot.

# At a Loss for Words

Drew and I were at a restaurant the other night. Across the room sat a grandfather, a father and a son. The distance between our table and theirs was such that I couldn't hear a word that was spoken. While we ate and talked; I periodically looked over at the three generations across from me. At first I was unaware that I had been glancing their way at all and then I realized that I had become fascinated with the scenario in front of me. The show unfolding before me was certainly not unique and yet I hadn't really thought about what I was witnessing in the way in which I was now seeing what was happening.

The grandfather and the father were conversing with each other for the entirety of the meal. Sometimes laughing, other times seeming to be seriously discussing something of importance. The son in the meantime was thumbing out messages and reading others on his phone the entire time...and I mean the entire time! He never looked up and only glanced quickly at his fork when stabbing a morsel of food to place into his mouth. He never once looked at, let alone engaged in the conversation with, the two adults at the table. Oblivious to all around him, his concentration was so utterly fixed on the screen of his phone, he didn't even notice when having finished his meal he was still absentmindedly stabbing at the empty plate for another bite.

And there I sat thinking, how will this obsession with technology that our young people are experiencing affect them in the future?

I remember selective conversations from my childhood family dinners. I clearly remember my children's participation in our own family's "round the table discussions." And what I know for a fact is that even when I, and especially when my children, couldn't have cared less about what "the grown-ups were saying" around our table, we were nonetheless exposed to the conversation. Even if unaware of it, we were absorbing the language if not the actual content of the discussion. Whether it was sports, or school or the weather or mindless banter; we all were exposed to every word shared. This is how we learned vocabulary, phraseology; communication skills that last a lifetime. This is where we learned to formulate ideas and opinions and in my household with two older brothers, I learned the art of "fighting with my words."

With our busy schedules and pressing obligations I mourn the loss of the every-night family dinner. And as I watched that other table I realized that it is not only the loss of the family dinner we need to worry about, it is the loss of our children's participation even when we do all sit around a table together.

Far be it from me to try to squash any forms of communication, but forgive the cliché: "there is a time and a place for everything" and I just don't think that having dinner is the time or the place for texting.

# Domestic Spying

Are you as perplexed as I am about this huge story of our governmental policies regarding domestic spying? I'm sure you must have heard about it; the story of our own government's abilities to spy on average Joe's - you and me?

I have heard opinions ranging from; this is nothing new, to this is nothing to be concerned about, to this heralds the demise of American freedom.

All this is the result of the exposure of a National Security Agency (NSA) data mining program that is set up to identify terrorist networks through telephone-log patterns and the details of a program code-named "Prism." (Just have to say, that is a really cool name!)

The telephone thing isn't getting all that much traction because apparently the government has been monitoring phone records in one way or another for years. Gees, all you have to do is watch one of the myriad of crime shows on T.V. to know that!

But, Prism is another thing altogether. Prism allows the NSA access to information garnered from 9 of the largest internet providers; Google, Microsoft, Yahoo and AOL being among them. And we're talking not just the ability to identify patterns but to read all of the actual communications being scanned.

Does that seem creepy to anyone else but me? Can they really do that? And here I thought that hackers were the baddies of internet privacy invasion!

Before I really get riled it must be noted; we are told that Prism is currently utilized to intercept the emails of non-U.S. citizens residing outside of the United States. But, that's not to say it can't and won't and hasn't been used in the past on you, me and our next door neighbors.

Gen. Michael Hayden, a former Director of the NSA and former CIA Director, told NPR's Weekend Edition Sunday that "the government's acquisition of phone records and surveillance of Internet activity is lawful and justified by the changing nature of the war on terrorism...and an accurate reflection of balancing our security and our privacy."

In an interview on PBS with Charlie Rose, President Obama indicated that the important issue here is not should we be doing this but rather are there proper checks and balances in place to afford the American people the confidence that the program is being used properly.

Most seem to agree with the President and the former "spy-in-chief" that what is being done is legal. The vast majority of questions being raised deal with the much more difficult issues of are these programs necessary and if so, are they being appropriately monitored?

Charles Krauthammer summed it up this way, "The problem here is not constitutionality. It's practicality. Legally this is fairly straight forward. But between intent and execution lies a shadow – the human factor, the possibility of abuse. And because of the scope and power of the NSA, any abuse would have major consequences for civil liberties."

So, should our Government have the right? Do you trust the government, after reading it, will take your comments into consideration!

# Being a Good Governor Makes Good Politics

In July 2011, I wrote a column about the news making, relatively newly elected governor of New Jersey, Chris Christie. At the time, here in the Midwest, we were just starting to hear about his bold measures, actions which seemed to offend everyone residing in New Jersey in order to balance his state's budget without raising taxes; a campaign promise he had made. Imagine, a politician actually keeping campaign promises!

And from that point on the larger than life (and not just figuratively) Christie has become a fixture in the political landscape of the country. He not only holds a 70% approval rating in his state, he also polls second in favored, possible republican candidates for the presidency in 2016.

But now, many consummate, ultra-conservative members of the Republican Party are methodically disparaging the Gov hoping to waylay a Christie Republican presidential candidacy in 2016.

After the dismal showing in the past two presidential elections, one would think that the party would be thrilled to have such a popular potential candidate especially one whose record on the issues is pretty much always conservative hard line.

So, what gives?

That's simple ... collusion with the enemy!

After all, who could forget the photo-ops featuring Christie with the President in the immediate aftermath of Hurricane Sandy. Not only did he welcome Obama, he praised him for the attention and efforts of the federal government in assisting New Jersey residents affected by the massive storm.

And, recently he was conspicuously absent from this year's Faith & Freedom Coalition Conference in Washington. This conference of conservatives gathered, among other things, to hear from the Republican Party's potential 2016 presidential contenders. And if Christie's absence wasn't slight enough, he appeared instead in Chicago at the Clinton Global Initiative, joining a panel to discuss crisis management seeking ways to better serve New Jersey residents in the future.

These two actions have pundits wondering if Christie truly understands what it takes to win a Republican nomination at this point in time.

What the pundits don't seem to get is that apparently the Gov doesn't care and they certainly don't seem to get that by doing what is best for his New Jersey constituents, he just might be speaking to a nation looking for that kind of leader for our country.

He wasn't afraid for his political future when he "made everyone in his state angry with him" for keeping his campaign promise and balancing the budget without raising taxes. And what happened next? His approval rating soared. He wasn't afraid of diminishing his chances for a presidential run when he angered the Republican hard liners by working with President Obama for the benefit of his state. And what happened next? His approval rating both statewide and nationally soared.

I think it is time for politicians from both parties to be less concerned with their political futures and more concerned with serving their constituents if they want the kind of approval ratings Chris Christie enjoys. They should heed the words of the governor from New Jersey,

"My only job is to do my job."

# The One Person Difference

Picture an eleven-year-old pretty little girl, the daughter of newly divorced parents suddenly being moved, from the only home she knew in West Warwick, Rhode Island to the tumbleweed town of Fort Worth in the tumbleweed state of Texas. One of four children, she was raised by a single mother who had only a sixth grade education and received no child support.

The child began working at age 14 and by 18 was married and had a pretty little girl child of her own. One year later she was divorced and like her mother before her, found herself to be a single mother, on her own.

Now picture a precocious little boy whose tribal name colloquially translates as "troublemaker," born on a distant continent almost a half century earlier and thousands of miles away from Fort Worth, Texas in a country whose poor was ravaged not only by disease but by institutionalized racism and poverty. Though descended from tribal royalty, both of his parents were illiterate and the boy grew up in the dirt-poor village of Qunu South Africa where as a child he tended herds as a "cattle-boy."

What could these two culturally, racially, gender and generationally dissimilar individuals possibly have in common?

They exemplify the time honored concept which drives the democratic spirit – that one person can make a difference.

The woman in my tale is Wendy Davis a state Congress "person" in Texas and the man is Nelson Mandela revered civil rights activist and former president of South Africa.

We left Davis struggling with a child to support and seemingly no good options and yet she managed to put herself through junior college and then went on to get her law degree from Harvard. No doubt you have heard of Davis' stand last week; and I mean that literally as she filibustered the Texas Statehouse for 11 hours in opposition to a vote that would, for all intent and purposes, ban access to health care and legal abortions for the vast majority of Texan women. As the hours passed and she stood her ground, thousands rallied to the Statehouse to show their support of not only the issue but of her sheer tenacity. Whether you agree or not with her political stance, to my mind you must agree with her right to make that stand.

On the other side of the world, the "troublemaker" little boy was sent to a local Methodist school where his was given the name Nelson and he developed a love affair with African history and listening to tales told by elder visitors, both of which helped him to begin his journey for justice. We hear of Mandela's failing health (by the time this goes to press he might very well have passed) and are reminded of his personal struggles which never deterred him from his mission of freeing South Africa from the shackles of the racist Apartheid system of government under which so many suffered so severely for so very long.

My tale is of two inspirational individuals.

## Egyptian Greatness; Stone by Stone

The year was 1995. It was June and the weather was hotter than I had ever experienced. Drew, the children, my mom and her friend journeyed with me when first I traveled to the Middle East on an adventure that, unbeknownst to us all at the time, would change our lives forever. The nightly weather report told us that it had been 115 degrees in the shade that day where upon I turned to Drew and asked "What shade? There is no shade!" The dry desert heat was so oppressive that we each drank liter's-full of water all day long and never had to stop on our journey to pee!

The immense spectacle of artistry and innovation encompassing all that we experienced was almost staggering. Yes, like you, we had all seen the pictures of the Pyramids and the Sphinx; learned of the seemingly impossible engineering feats necessary to construct those and so many other Egyptian monuments but none of that prepared me for the humbling awe that coursed through me as I stood at the entrance to the Temple of Ramses II at Abu Simbel, generally considered the grandest and most beautiful of the temples in all of Egypt.

I thought what an amazing legacy was left by the ancestors of the truly friendly and welcoming people of modern-day Egypt.

Over this past weekend, reports of what is being called a massacre in Cairo are flooding the newswires. The official death count is being reported at over forty. But, no other confirmed details are known at this point about this latest chapter in Egypt's struggle for self-governance.

This latest wave of violence and protest was prompted by the military ouster of Mohammed Morsi, democratically elected president representing the victorious Muslim Brotherhood party who, upon taking office, undemocratically rammed through a constitution sending Egyptians back into Islamic Orthodoxy and igniting the flames of the current protests.

Christopher Dickey and Mike Giglio wrote in a Daily Beast article what I think is an apt summary of the problem of getting to the bottom of what is happening, what has happened and the situation in general.

"...in the Middle East...the first casualty of violence like this is truth, not just because it is hard to ascertain the facts even if you are in the middle of the confused and frantic action, but because people will believe what they want to believe."

The hope was for a working democracy to bloom forth from Egypt's Arab Spring. Maybe the only truth to be gleaned at this point is that a democratic election does not ensure a democracy.

Yet, I choose to believe that the uncertainty and fear that Egyptians are struggling with today will not destroy their potential for future greatness. After all, they have a history of adapting to progress. In 1968, Abu Simbel was painstakingly moved in its entirety, stone by stone, to its current location in order to make way for the Aswan Dam project the Egyptian Government had undertaken.

Taking a cue from the past, an Egyptian democracy can be built but it won't be an easy task. The people will have to do some "heavy lifting." Just like with the moving of Abu Simbel, Egyptian democracy will have to be constructed stone by stone.

# An Oldie But A Goodie

My first County Fair was shared with my children, Drew and his parents. Grandpa, being raised on a farm in Michigan, was appalled that I had never attended one and so we had a family outing to the Fair of his youth. It was a day of wonderful memories that none of the Levenfeld household will ever forget.

Our children, being raised in the Lincoln Park neighborhood of Chicago, were totally enthralled. As we wandered through the various exhibits we ate the most unhealthy food we could find and with noses crinkled from the odors, watched the animals trying unsuccessfully to comfort themselves in the beastly (excuse the pun) heat.

We bought a ton of over-priced fair paraphernalia and a straw cowboy hat airbrushed glistening silver for Mari Jae which she proceeded to wear every day for the rest of the summer.  It was great fun...and then some!

When we moved to LaPorte County and began attending the County Fairs here, our love affair with the experiences to be had at the Fair became a time honored, family tradition. Now, with Mari Jae's family in Boston and Rory's family in Jerusalem, while being a bit bittersweet to be attending without them, Drew and I never miss a year to soak in the magic of the LaPorte County Fair.

Did you know that our fair, begun in 1845, is the oldest County Fair in all of Indiana?

The Fair website states, "As we were essentially an agricultural society in the early days, special emphasis was on promoting quality farm products. Later, traditional domestic projects were added such as food preparation, canning, sewing, craft, fine arts and painting.

Events such as horse racing, stage shows and carnival attractions were later added."

And the additions keep coming. My all-time favorite is the Pioneer Village. Watching the young families joyfully sharing the experiences of our past is nothing short of heartwarming. And in this age of high-tech this and super-sonic that; a reminder of simple pleasures is a welcomed relief.

The rides are amazing. I held my breath as a small, tow-headed little girl squealed with delight while bungee jumping and marveled at the funky, somewhat trite booths of the mid-way.

And if all of that wasn't enough, Willie Nelson headlined the entertainment this year. Yes, "Momma's don't let your babies grow up to be cowboys" Willie Nelson! I'll tell ya, it doesn't get much better than that.

We went Saturday evening for our last good-bye to the LaPorte County Fair 2013 and to our great pleasure; the sky was clear and the temperature perfect with nary a hint of humidity. We strolled past the food and novelty kiosks, bumped into old friends, visited the additions to Pioneer Land and totally pigged out on...well pig; enjoying BBQ ribs and pork chops.

So, another Fair has ended; well attended and I am sure very well enjoyed. But I would be very remiss if I didn't acknowledge the scores of volunteers necessary to make it all possible. Without their dedicated attention to every detail none of us would be able to have the pleasures inherent in attending our Fair.

If you haven't attended, you really have no idea what you are missing. The Laporte County Fair; an oldie but truly a goodie!

# A New Politics of Problem Solving

Apparently the heat wave that we have been enduring has begun to create a slight thaw in the Ice Age of partisan politics which has held our country frozen, captive to legislative dysfunction for far too long.

Or is it a group of legislators creating the slight cracks in the massive bergs with a bi-partisan ice pick?

Have you heard of "No Labels?"

Don't feel bad if you haven't, I hadn't either until I heard a passing mention of it on one of the morning news shows and it peeked my interest; so I looked it up and here is what I found on their website:

"No Labels is a movement of Democrats, Republicans and everyone in between dedicated to promoting a new politics of problem solving. While many powerful interest groups in Washington wield influence that effectively pulls leaders and the political parties apart, No Labels' mission is different -- it's about fixing, not fighting. The goal of No Labels is to provide a forum to create solutions to our nation's problems. Bringing a refreshing attitude of collaboration, instead of alienation, No Labels' members in Congress are committed to working together respectfully and thoughtfully to make Washington work. This new attitude drives the No Labels platform. "

O.K. sounds good in concept, but how to make it work?

Seek and ye shall find. As I read further my question was answered.

"In January 2013, No Labels unveiled the Problem Solvers: a group of House and Senate members who have agreed to meet regularly to build trust across the aisle. This group is unlike anything that has existed on Capitol Hill, where there is no forum for large groups of

Democrats and Republicans to actually meet together to work through problems. Each party has its own weekly meetings, but there is no opportunity to hear from or reason with the other side. The Problem Solvers offers a new way forward. The Problem Solvers are committed to regular across-the-aisle meetings, embracing the new attitude of problem solving and being real leaders."

Can this be? Is it true? There is actually a group of legislators who are more interested in serving the people than their party's interests?

Yes, yes, yes! 81 members from both houses have come on board. These members from both parties meet regularly. They establish relationships with the "opposition" promoting constructive dialogue rather than destructive strategies.

And guess what? It's working. Compromises have been struck. 17 bills emanating from this bi-partisan group have been passed so far.

I anxiously scrolled through the list of members wanting to see all of those names representing our state. I anticipated a goodly number after all, these "Problem Solvers" sound like just what the majority of Hoosiers want from our Representatives and Congressmen.

So, I scrolled. And I scrolled. And I scrolled. Our State has one ... yes only one person who has joined the group. Todd Young a Representative from the 9th District.

So I ask and I hope you will too; where are the others?

# New Phone Madness

I had to buy a new cell phone. Please make note of the words "had to" for I did not "want to" buy a phone. After using my smart phone for 2 years, I had come to grips with the fact that either it was not as smart as it was supposed to be or it was me who wasn't smart enough.

Either way I had at least grown accustomed to the nuances, the idiosyncratic personality traits of the device and (dare I say it) I had become rather used to what the phone could and couldn't do. There is a certain degree of comfort in knowing what to expect.

Of course you know where I am going with this tale...

All at once my smart phone started acting funny. The battery seemed to need a charge more often than usual. At first, of course, I thought that I was doing something differently, wrongly. But I couldn't for the life of me figure out what it was. So, finally after having to charge the thing three times a day; I took it in for service hoping to find out what was wrong. I assumed that the worst case scenario was that I would have to buy a new battery and then go on my merry way.

But no! While I did indeed need a new battery, guess what? No one carries replacement batteries or even makes the batteries for my phone anymore.

Can you believe it? The phone was only 2 years old, and they no longer make/carry replacement batteries?

The geniuses of the tech industries, with their eyes to profit and their planned obsolescence had me by the parts of the male anatomy women don't possess, and I was not happy. And to make matters even worse, the 11-year-old salesperson behind the counter began gushing about improvements and the awesome capabilities of the new phones--none of which, in my wildest imagination, could I ever see myself wanting or having any inclination toward learning how to use.

When I stated that I just wanted the phone closest to the model that I had, and I truly needed no new gizmos, no upgrades, she literally stood gaping at me for a beat.

"But you'll have 4G instead of 3G capability!" she almost squealed with delight, adding a bunch of what sounded like mumbo jumbo but was apparently other features which she felt were sure to impress me.

Please! Do I care if the phone has 3G or 4G capability? What is "G" capability anyway? And why would I want a crisper image for TV and video viewing when I have no intention of watching a TV show or video on a 4"X 2" hand held device when I have a real, person-sized television at home?

I wanted a phone that stores a contact list and that lets me check my email and do occasional internet searches. Having my calendar on hand is also great but all the other upgrades, to my mind, is just more stuff that can go wrong.

Aha! Now I have it. The more stuff that can go wrong means the more new phones we all have to purchase. Alas, to paraphrase my old friend Bill Shakespeare, "there is a method to all of this madness!"

# Herod the Great

Memories of fun with family filled days and magnificently brilliant star filled evening skies are already residing in my mind though it has only been a few hours since departing Tel Aviv for the long journey home from our annual trip to Israel. With our son and his family living there and having made the trip almost more times than I can remember, there's never much sight-seeing on our agenda when we go. But, we made a point of visiting the Israel Museum to see the new exhibit of archeological remains found and beautifully arrayed documenting the life and accomplishments of the utterly brilliant, sadistic, paranoid King of Judea, Herod.

Born in 73 B.C.E. and living to the age of 69, Herod ruled ancient Judea for 33 years and while most remembered for his actions recorded in the bible, he left an indelible mark on the landscape of what is now modern-day Israel. As I strolled through room after room of the exhibit, I found myself completely absorbed in the life and times of this incredibly complex, historically significant ancient King.

What I knew of Herod was his deception of the Magi and his brutal paranoia prompting him to order the death of all male children under the age of 2 in fear that the prophecy of Jesus' life would come true.

What I didn't know and what constitutes a far more favorable legacy is that he was a masterful visionary, creating cities of architectural splendor the remains of which constitute many of the significant points of interest to travelers visiting Israel today.

Probably most significant was his expansive and architecturally glorious rebuilding of Solomon's Temple in Jerusalem. This magnificent project on such a massive scale, incorporating styling and detail unseen before in Judea was completed in just 1 ½ years. Later destroyed in 70 A.D. the 4 retaining walls still remain constituting the perimeter of "the old city of Jerusalem."

He designed and built the fortress city of Masada, the largest man-made seaport of Caesarea and the city of Jericho. He designed water systems for his cities which were unheard of in the area before.

He allied with Cleopatra jointly owning the monopoly over the extraction of asphalt from the Dead Sea a hugely lucrative venture. And in a stroke of political genius, he journeyed to Rome when Marc Anthony was deposed and laid his crown at the feet of Augustus Caesar charming him into granting his continued rule as King of Judea.

But like many tragic geniuses, his life was consumed with obsession, fear of betrayal and jealousy. In fits of irrational ire he killed his wife and two eldest sons convinced that they were conspiring against him.

As further proof of his paranoia, fearing that no one would morn his death, he ordered the most distinguished men of the time be brought to Jericho. He then decreed that upon his death they be killed to insure that "appropriate" wails of mourning would be heard throughout the city. When he died, his surviving son and daughter rescinded the order.

An amazing story of a truly complex man brought to life in a spectacular exhibit; and yet another great trip for the Levenfelds with memories galore!

# "Just Walk Away, Rene"

Oh, Anthony, Anthony, Anthony: you're such a Weiner!

Oh, A-Rod, A-Rod, A-Rod;, you're such a...well "wiener!"

Now, I know that we are not New Yorkers so the trials and tribulations of New York politicians and sports figures really don't impact us but the most recent outrageous behavior of these two public figures points to what seems to be an ever increasing number of "notables gone wild."

What is it with these guys? Have they no shame?

Apparently not, for instead of just quietly retreating into the night as a shamed person should, they keep getting right up in our faces.

Here's what's currently up with these two jokers:

Anthony having made all of the right moves, exhibiting appropriate contrition when his "private-parts texting" was, forgive the pun, exposed; has now chosen to re-enter public life in a bid for the Mayor's office in New York. O.K. we Americans are very forgiving. But, in the last week alone, the idiot not only offends women by taking part in a very heated confrontation with an irate female constituent (where were his handlers, his own common sense; he should have been pulled away immediately) and then he attended an AARP Forum where he derogatorily called his opponent "Grandpa." Oh, and apparently he has continued his "sexting."

Hey Weiner, news flash, continuing bad behavior, offending women and seniors in one week, you can wave the mayor's office goodbye.

And then there's Alex Rodriguez arguably one of the best Major Leaguers of all time. Like his fellow New York scandal perpetrator, A-Rod is also once again rearing his "ugly head" (again, excuse the...well you know!). Here's the skinny on him. A-Rod, the highest paid player in Major League history gets accused of using performance enhancing drugs in the early 2000's. 2007 there is a public denial. 2009 he offers a shaky confession. Since then he has pulled other PR shenanigans: womanizing, partying and of course an occasional negative reaction to the famous N.Y. ridicule for bad performances on the field. Let's just say they don't like the guy in New York. Now at 38, he is facing another round of doping scandals from which he has earned himself a 211-game suspension which he is appealing. During the appeal process he has the option to continue to play and he is very vocally and to my mind stupidly exercising that option. The fans hate him. His fellow players are distancing themselves from him. Even the player's union is keeping him at arm's length. C'mon A-Rod, at 38 years old, with substantial, damning evidence against you, what are you doing?

It appears that in spite of the public's obvious distaste for these two men, a barrage of negative media attention and their own inability to stop tripping over their own lack of character; they blindly continue on their quest for restored glory.

I love how an article written for CBS News summed up their advice. "When you get caught tweeting pics of your naughty bits, or swinging a bat with a needle in your arm, just, well, don't do it again. And if you do, for the love of God at least pretend you're sorry."

I would add one more thing. There was a song from my youth whose title I feel to be great advice for these two guys. Any of you out there remember: "Just Walk Away Rene!"

# The Eagle of the Arabs

There are posters on the walls throughout the constructed landscape of Cairo bearing his name and formidable image declaring that "He is the one we can trust." In Egypt he is often compared with the ruthless and charismatic former Egyptian leader Gamal Abdul Nasser. He is the undisputed military leader having taken the post of Commander-in-Chief of the Egyptian Armed Forces as well as becoming Minister of Defense.

He is Abdel Fattah Saeed Hussein Khalil el-Sisi. Not surprisingly, given the length of his name, he is commonly known as General Sisi.

General Sisi played the leading role in the July 2013 military coup ousting democratically elected Egyptian President Mohamed Morsi. Yes, unlike others who are still refusing to call Morsi's ousting a coup, I can't see any other word for it. If it looks like a coup, acts like a coup, tastes like a coup...it's a coup! I am pretty confident that Morsi would agree.

So, it is General Sisi calling the shots. But what do we know about the man heading the largest army in the Arab world?

The truth is not all that much.

General Sisi was born in Cairo in 1954. He graduated from the Egyptian Military Academy and attended the prestigious and historic U.S. Army War College in Pennsylvania.

Under President Mubarak, the Egyptian military-industrial complex thrived and the very top officers allegedly made vast fortunes. But not our man Sisi who is generally (excuse the pun) thought to be clean.

He is quiet, avoids the press and has been successful in keeping his family and private life relatively private.

I was able to find an interview with Sherifa Zuhur a professor at the War College when Sisi was attending and I think that some of what she said about him sheds some light on the man, how he thinks, operates and perhaps even a bit about what we can expect from him in the future.

She described him as "always ready for a debate, but not aggressive. He could be angered but possessed a lot of self-control and would choose not to respond when others might do so. He was not quiet because he was passive but more contemplative, waiting, watching..."

While at the college he drafted an 11 page academic paper titled "Democracy in the Middle East." He stated that "Whereas Americans believe in life, liberty and the pursuit of happiness, Islamic cultures cling to principles of fairness, justice, equality, unity and charity." He later stated that "Muslims cherish the memory of the ancient caliphate. However, this does not mean a theocracy will be established. Rather it means a democracy will be established based on Islamic beliefs."

In a recent interview with the Washington Post (one of the few he has given since taking power) he made it very clear that he is unhappy with the U.S. for the "little support offered to Egypt when Morsi turned autocratic and the Muslim Brotherhood subverted the popular will." He went on to say "You turned your back on the Egyptians and they won't forget that."

If he sounded mad at us then, he has got to be really teed off now that U.S. aid to Egypt is being put on hold. This is really no sweat off his brow because the funds he has been promised by the Sunni Royals of the Gulf far exceed those the U.S. had committed but it still has to frost him a bit.

So, who is this guy and what will he do next...beats me. But in light of our deteriorating relationship, how ironic it is that our national symbol is an eagle and General Sisi is known as "the Eagle of the Arabs."

# A Tale of Two Alleged Atrocities

One of my favorite cable shows by one of my all-time favorite writers is back on the air for its second season. The Newsroom conceived and penned by Aaron Sorkin, while garnering mixed reviews in its maiden season (I personally loved it) has come out swinging for the fences in this season. Often lauded for his timely subject matter and current topics of interest, Sorkin, as he did so often in his weekly masterpiece The West Wing, has done it again. This season's Newsroom intrigue revolves around allegations that the US used sarin gas on a village of civilians to complete a rescue mission of captured Americans gone awry. Of course only our merry band of "news-folk" has gotten wind of the alleged war crime and their efforts toward discovering the truth, getting the scoop and coming to grips with the knowledge that the US actually did this horrific thing is the tread that holds this season together.

Unlike Sorkin's Newsroom, where the small cadre of reporters and producers are stunned and disbelieving that such a thing could be true; in real life Syria, there appears to be few who disbelieve that the pictures and reports the world is receiving detailing the mass murder of hundreds of Syrian citizens due to the release of chemical weapons by the Syrian military is absolutely true.

US intelligence reports confirmed that the Syrian Military has used small amounts of chemical weaponry against its rebels in the past. But the pictures of bodies upon bodies, draped in white sheets, lining the make-shift mortuary floor, many of which are obviously the bodies of children, is almost too horrific to believe.

Voices can now be heard from the International community demanding investigations into whether or not this atrocity really occurred. The Syrian government, not surprisingly, has denied responsibility for any chemical attacks. Russia, Syria's principal ally, again not surprisingly, has accused the opposition forces of staging last week's attack to discredit Syrian President Bashar al-Assad.

As the fact finding, the building up of the details of the terrible misdeed and subsequent cover-up comprises the Newsroom's weekly scripts; shouldn't we expect to see some reports of what actually happened in Syria? It's been days since the accusations were made. Surely some preliminary findings are available?

Ah...well... no.

Due to seemingly never ending airstrikes and the pummeling by artillery from those completely innocent Syrian forces, of the area where the alleged attack occurred, it has become virtually impossible to investigate the allegations. Thus, the prospect of finding more evidence of the attack is becoming less and less likely. Experts are speculating that there will never be a "smoking gun" found.

Reports this morning indicate that inspectors will be allowed at the site but unfortunately in all likelihood it will be a case of "too little too late."

And so in a way truth is mirroring fiction in this, my tale of two alleged atrocities. Two nations are accused of using chemical weaponry; but that is where the analogy ends.

No "spoiler alert" warning needed here for Sorkin structured his Newsroom season so we know from the opening episode that the US did not do this horrible thing. Sorkin's story is about how the news folks got it wrong. The much more terrifying Syrian story is of how they could have done it.

# It's only a Movie!

"History is gossip well told."

Early 20th Century American writer, artist and philosopher: Elbert Hubert

I went to see "Lee Daniel's The Butler" over the weekend. (Will someone please tell me why the director has to have his name in the title? I was already skeptical). But, it is a wonderful movie based on an article penned by Washington Post journalist, Wil Haygood. The article chronicled the life of Eugene Allen who began working at the Eisenhower White House in 1952 and retired during the Reagan White House in 1986. Those of us of an age, remember that time span as being seminal in our growing up years, shaping many of the ideals which we still hold today. It was a time of the burgeoning civil rights movement, the Camelot optimism of the JFK presidency and the defiance of our government's commitment in Vietnam.

The movie is beautifully well acted...I see Oscar nominations galore coming, and it is a compelling story of the American work ethic and complicated family dynamics all presented in front of the backdrop of the civil rights struggle which we, as a nation, are still "struggling with" all these many years later.

But it is only a movie!

The first literary work in the genre of "novel based on a true story" is credited to Truman Capote for his masterpiece "In Cold Blood." It's a genre with which I am very well acquainted. In it one changes the names, pulls the salient facts of actual people and events around which the story is constructed and then the author lets his/her imagination run wild with their own story. It is the same in creating "a movie based on a true story."

In "The Butler" we see only the bare bones of the skeleton of Eugene Allen's life; basically the years and

Presidential families served in the White House and the historical events encompassing the Civil Rights Movement. Unfortunately, many that go to the movies, when told that it's based on a true story, believe that everything in the movie actually happened.

Michael Reagan, eldest son of Ronald Reagan and first wife Jane Wyman, penned a scathing rebuke of the movie's portrayal of his father and ticked off many inconsistencies between the real butler's life and that shown on the screen. (You can find his editorial at www.newsmax.com)

I am torn in my feelings about Michael Reagan's reaction. On the one hand, were it my parent portrayed in a manner I found totally offensive, I too would be furious and want to set the record straight. But, on the other hand I am a firm believer in the creative process and creative license.

Man, this is a conundrum!

So what is the responsibility of the filmmaker/author when basing a work on a true story?

I happened upon an interview with Wil Haygood the author of the original article. I was interested in finding out his take on the movie and the significant differences between the real Eugene Allen and the character of Cecil Gaines. When pressed, he would only say that he felt that Eugene Allen's essence and soul had been captured in the character of Cecil Gaines.

Whether factually accurate or not (remember Daniel's has never implied that this is an historical biography) I think that the audience has a responsibility to remember that a movie theater is not a classroom.

It's only a movie.

# Purdue North Central Sinai Forum: Sixty Years of Greatness

The Purdue North Central Sinai Forum will present its 60th anniversary season beginning September 15th. I would like to tell you about some of the amazing people that have graced the Forum stage during my tenure as Executive Director; relating some of those oh so amazing moments during a program which provided the audience with "not to be received from any other source" information that makes attending the Forum such a rewarding experience. I will also throw in a few peeks into the personal side of some of our speakers.

I share these people and their stories with you in the hope that you will "check out the Forum" for yourself. For mine is not a unique experience. Everyone attending our programs comes away with stories of their own and experiences that will not soon be forgotten.

For those of you who have attended this LaPorte County gem know that our community has hosted a list of speakers that any speaker series in the world would be proud of. In fact I am told time and time again by speakers and agencies alike that there isn't another series like the Purdue North Central Sinai Forum. For a fee of $75.00 for the entire season our audience hears from and interacts with experts in the fields of interest to us all. And we are proud to admit for free, any student presenting a valid student ID.

This season will also mark my last as the Executive Director of the Forum. Looking back, these years have been both exciting and enriching. So, I ask that you join me for a brief trip through time to meet some of the amazing people who have graced the Forum stage. I hope that you will enjoy them as much as I have.

### Political Insights

*James Carville & Mary Matalin 1999*

It was before the 2000 Presidential Election when James Carville and Mary Matalin came to speak at the Forum. I was really excited about our season's opening speakers because the incongruous matching of these two political strategists from opposing parties, not to mention the matching of them in "real life" as husband and wife; had me anticipating a really spirited and informative program. Carville an ardent Democrat and equally ardent defender of Bill Clinton during the whole Monica Lewinsky affair and Matalin a staunch Republican and advisor to the likes of Dick Cheney and George W. Bush; proved that not only can some common ground be reached across party lines, but the American people can truly benefit from it.

Don't get me wrong, theirs was not a lovey-dovey program...not by a long shot. They strongly disagreed casting zings at each other's candidates across the stage. What was remarkable was that neither resorted to the "down and dirty" fighting we had and still have plaguing our political process. They had humor and charm and even though serious, they made their points without personally assaulting the other.

Each gave us their assessment of their candidate's worthiness for the position of President. Their assessments were well thought out and comprehensive and at times very amusing. They then proceeded, rather predictably, to entirely disagreeing with each other.

At the end of their time with us they agreed whole heartedly on one thing, and it was an amazing revelation for our audience. They were both convinced, from the research they had independently conducted on past elections, that the winner is simply always the man who effectively projected the most optimistic future for the country.

Many came up to me after the program saying they had never thought about voting for a president with that in mind. And perhaps that is exactly why such a simple formula is never really mentioned when analyzing presidential campaigns. It is intrinsic. It is visceral. It encapsulates the essence of our country. And Carville and Matalin made us all think about it; probably for the first time.

(I learned that Mary's folks live here in Indiana and that James is an unabashed dog lover when the two of them had dinner at my house before the program. So relaxed and at ease with himself, James fell asleep before dinner on our couch with our black lab, Spike, nestled on his chest. )

*Sam Donaldson 2007*

The country was already in the throngs of the 2008 presidential campaign. By all standards of measuring such things, Hillary Clinton had the nomination sewn up. She had the momentum, she had already been "vetted" by the American people during her tenure as First Lady and most importantly; she had the money...gobs and gobs of money. As White House Correspondent for more years than he chose to mention, host of various political television shows and guest panelist on numerous political roundtables; Donaldson spoke about the "inside stories" of presidential campaigning. He also gave us amazing insight into the nature of then President George W Bush.

Since Donaldson also hails from West Texas, his perspective was really interesting. He told us that no one who knows anything about West Texans could be surprised at George W's style of governing.

"See, West Texans, when confronted by a rattle snake don't convene a panel to discuss what to do. They don't take a poll to see what the country thinks...no they just shoot the sucker and then eat it for dinner!"

All in all Mr. Donaldson was not only informative but really funny.

It wasn't until the end of his program that he made a rather shocking prediction. He stood at the podium and cautioned us not to be so quick to assume that Clinton would be the Democratic candidate. He suggested that we watch the Junior Senator from Illinois, Barack Obama.

Now you have to remember, at that time, the vast majority of the country had never even heard of Barack Obama. But, Donaldson waited out the murmurs and even a bit of tittering laughter from the crowd and simply ended with "You just wait and see."

After the program several people remarked to me that they enjoyed the program but what in the world was he talking about at the end? Hillary not the nominee? Barack who?

But good old Sam nailed it and I'm thinking that many in the audience that night, myself included, watched that junior Senator from Illinois' numbers rise during that campaign with renewed respect for Sam Donaldson.

(In all of my years dealing with and I might add driving around our speakers, I had never before or since run into a speaker quite like Sam Donaldson. Now I need to take a slight detour here because it is important to this story. I am very territorial when it comes to my car. Only under emergency circumstances do I even let Drew drive it. So you can imagine my dilemma when Donaldson INSISTED on driving from the pre-program dinner to the auditorium. Taken aback but realizing that before a program was not the time to rile the speaker, I tried cautiously but in vain to keep my car out of the hands of this stranger. Whether a raging chauvinist or simply a chivalrous southerner; Sam Donaldson was surely something alright. And I might add a pretty good driver!)

### Important, Personal Stories

*Elie Wiesel 2000*

Auschwitz survivor, acclaimed author and Nobel Peace Prize recipient Elie Wiesel is a small man, has a rather ashen complexion and looks as if the burdens of the world are carried upon his shoulders. Though soft spoken, he has the capacity to generate an intensity that grabs you, holding you rapt in awe and then in the very next moment, with index finger to his cheek and a hint of a crooked smile appearing on his face; he has you joyfully laughing.

I got a sense of the man before the program when he came to my home for dinner. He spoke to me of having had his son later in his life and that now he was desperate to be a grandfather! When I asked if his son was a writer like his father, his face lit up as he told me that his son had mastered the kind of disciplines that he could not. His son was a financial whiz, a computer expert and the father spoke with such pride and obvious love. It was as if he were reveling in the knowledge that his son had grown up in the huge shadow that he cast and yet was able to step out of it and accomplish so much in his own light. It was quite a moment. It made me even more eager to hear what he would tell the Forum audience.

There was total silence in the auditorium for his entire program only interrupted by spurts of spontaneous laughter brought about by his subtle wit. He spoke of the nature of man, of the necessity to nurture the humanity within all of mankind. His quiet wisdom permeated his talk and made you feel as if that wisdom came from some ancient, sacred place.

He told us of a conversation that he had with then president Bill Clinton. He had called the President on the eve of Clinton's entering into peace talks between the Israelis and the Palestinians. As we all leaned in a bit closer not wanting to miss one word that he spoke he quite seriously said, "That's a perk that comes with winning the Nobel Peace Prize...Presidents take your call."

His voice low, his timing so perfect, it took a moment for what he said to register with the audience then all at once we were laughing as he stood shyly smiling. But all became serious again when he related what he had said.

He told the President that a 10 year moratorium on violence of any kind should be put into place with no conditions, no exceptions and that the issue of Jerusalem and borders be tabled for those ten years. During that time every Israeli child would spend one day a week in a Palestinian school and every Palestinian child would likewise spend one day a week in an Israeli school. Also during that time every Palestinian businessman would have lunch once a month with an Israeli businessman. And after the ten years, resume the talks and peace would be achieved.

Clinton replied that it couldn't be done to which Wiesel countered, "If both sides really want peace it could be done."

And all of us there in that auditorium believed that he had spoken the truth. There could be peace but only if both sides want it.

After his program people came up to him with tears in their eyes and wordlessly just hugged him. I heard people say that they had never been so moved. One woman told me that the program changed her life.

It was an amazing program presented by an amazing man.

*Irshad Manji 2006*

Irshad Manji is a most remarkable woman...young of years...old in wisdom. Tiny of build, she took on the Forum audience with her experience, insight and knowledge. An ever-questioning soul, she stands fearless amid a world of suppression and terror.

Irshad as a young child was ousted with her family from her homeland of Uganda when Idi Amin took power and declared Uganda to be a "Black Nation" expelling all non-black residents. Irshad's entire Muslim community was among those forced into exile.

And so Irshad found herself living in a multi-racial, multi-cultural community in British Columbia Canada. Her family, oppressive father, compliant yet loving mother, and two sisters were forced to start a new life. Nonetheless, her father insisted on holding firm to the strict Moslem disciplines of the past. So, she attended a Medrassa (a traditional Moslem school) in which the study of Koran was to be the essence of all education. There, in that stifling, oppressive, male-dominated environment, the Irshad Manji of today emerged.

Not yet a teenager, she dared to ask questions at school.

Hearing of her impertinence her father chased her around the house brandishing a knife and threatening to cut off her ear until she sought refuge on the roof of their building where the vastness of the sky and the mysteries of the stars inspired her to seek her own answers to all of the troubling questions in her mind. Several years later, with both ears still intact and many important questions never answered in school, she was finally expelled from the Medrassa and she began her journey of self-education, a journey in which she sought to understand her religion and one which she hoped would give her reason to remain in the Moslem faith.

It is this struggle to discover the truth of her religion, what the Koran actually says rather than blindly following the dictates of the fanatics who have established themselves as the champions of Islam, which is the basis of her amazing book, "The Trouble with Islam" in which she calls on the huge silent majority of moderate, non-Arab Moslems to rise up and take back their religion.

Irshad came to speak to the Forum audience about her book, and her life. She stood brave, declining the body guards offered to her since a "fatwa" was declared against her by several powerful Imams and Ayatollahs in the Arab world.

I, as I think most in the audience that evening, sat amazed and astounded listening to her impassioned words. People are still approaching me all these years later thanking me for signing her to speak at the Forum and expressing how glad they are to have been in attendance.

(She also had a wry, very cryptic sense of humor. On our drive over to the auditorium from the dinner; I had forgotten that my sunroof was opened a crack. And wouldn't you know it, it began to rain. Irshad looked over at me as rain dripped on her hair. She swiftly pulled some of her hair up into two spikes while she said with an ironic smile, "The Arab Moslem's call me a devil... might as well look the part!")

*Lisa Ling 2010*

Petite and really quite lovely, Lisa Ling strode across the Forum stage effortlessly in what appeared to be killer, six inch, stiletto heels. She came to us as a noted reporter of important stories often neglected by mainstream news organizations. Her career had taken her from panelist on "The View" to a highly respected television journalist courted by Oprah for her then new television network. But the program she presented was not about her media accomplishments. No, hers was a much more compelling story.

In 2009 Lisa's sister, also a journalist, was released after being falsely accused and then imprisoned as an American spy by the "Dear Leader" of North Korea, at the time, Kim Jung Il. She chronicled for us how she had worked through the agonizing weeks, months, years of bureaucratic and political red tape to finally secure her sister's release. She was totally engaging and held the audience rapt in her tale but as fascinating as that story was, what really intrigued me was her personal take on that bizarre, little, some say quite insane, North Korean leader; Kim Jung Il.

She told us of his obsession with being taken seriously and his craving for recognition on the international stage. His demand that Former President Clinton come personally to fetch her sister was predicated on the promise that he would have a photo op with Clinton so he'd have proof, to hang on his office wall so all could see, that a former President of the United States had come to him for a "favor." It was an amazing insight into the complex nature of that, wanting to be a major player on the world stage, tyrant. Only someone truly inside the situation could have brought that story to us and only by being in the Forum audience that evening would you have such a fascinating glimpse into the mind of such a complex historical figure.

Oh, and about those killer heels; her secret (advice given to her from Oprah herself) is to wear slippers to and from the venue only putting on the heels for the actual time of the event!

Wonderful memories of terrific Forum programs. I hope that you will attend the Purdue North Central Sinai Forum so you can have stories of your own.

Information about the Purdue North Central Sinai Forum can be viewed at www.sinaiforum.org including how and where tickets can be purchased for the 60th anniversary season beginning September 15th.

# Do We Need to Know?

Life was simpler when we didn't know so much. I realize that statement sounds so like just an "older person" lamenting about the past but I gotta say that doesn't make it any less true.

There have been a slew of books and films documenting (from found journals and personal letters) just how little the country knew about the lives of and reasons for the decisions made by many of our most respected presidents. There was Lincoln's invention of the lobbyist, sending out people to essentially buy votes in Congress and FDR's womanizing, actually keeping two lovers at once by his side, one as his secretary and one as, well, his companion. And don't get me started on JFK!

Back then the press used discretion. They allowed for presidential privacy. And I think that the vast majority of people were o.k. with sensing that "stuff was going on" not only behind the personal scenes but the political scenes as well. We didn't need to know. They would handle whatever needed handling in the best way possible for the country. Sounds pretty naïve but I think that most people really believed it and subconsciously we were quite content not to have to worry about it.

Ah, but now we have the demands for transparency. We have investigative reporting. We have whistle-blowers and security information leakers and 24/7 news reporting and social media, twitter and YouTube and everyone has a camera phone and video is streaming ...

And, the release of chemical weapons on the people of Syria.

If you are like me you're frustrated and numbed by the barrage of media attention being slathered on the "should we strike Syria or shouldn't we strike Syria" debate.

In an interview over the weekend, Assad contended that there is no evidence of his government releasing the deadly gas. It was the rebels that did it, he said. He talked about opinion poll results and American legislators' reluctance to get involved. He stated emphatically that Syria would retaliate if the U.S. strikes.

Well, duh! After two weeks of yammering followed by strongly asserting, then back peddling and finally asking permission of Congress by the administration; it's no surprise that Assad is emboldened. He's had all of this time to react and plug into all of the data that we have all been subjected to since the incident.

So there he sat with Charlie Rose looking smug; enjoying the quagmire in which we find ourselves.

At this point no matter what we do, America's reputation has been diminished.

I don't consider myself a hawk and God knows I certainly don't want to see our men and women of the armed services put in harm's way any more than they already are; but if we were going to do something, we should have done it...quickly, emphatically, surprising Assad and sending a message that we of the 21st century will not abide this atrocity.

I understand that no one wants to be involved in another conflict in the Middle East; but we are already involved, for history has shown that what happens there has a direct effect on what happens here and if we let the use of chemical weaponry go unchecked, it will be Americans who will be clamoring for gas masks.

Maybe if we knew a little less and our government acted a little more...and sooner; we wouldn't be in this mess.

# Michael Bloomberg

With Anthony Weiner's final, fingered farewell to the media on primary election night in New York, heralding his lose and hopefully the end of his obnoxious public behavior; it has finally begun to set in that Michael Bloomberg will indeed not be mayor of NYC very much longer. I have a confession; I think I love Michael Bloomberg. From strictly an outsider's viewpoint, he has been a terrific Mayor of New York.

As a political independent, a "gazillionaire" in his own right, he has been able to divorce himself from the "politics as usual" requirements most politicians are required to abide by for financing their campaigns and focus instead on making what he considers the right decisions for his city.

There is an example of one of those decisions which, like so many others he has made, has not gotten a whole lot of media attention. After all, it doesn't have blood and guts spilling in the streets, sleazy sex stuff or political bashing from one or the other side of the aisle. No, it just has the prospect of future growth and increased prestige for New York City...Yawn, how dull is that?

I saw an interview with Bloomberg when he announced a new initiative; a private/public endeavor forged between Cornell University, Technion (Israel's Institute of Technology) and the Big Apple. Together they will create an Applied Science and Engineering Campus on Roosevelt Island.

Bloomberg explained it this way:

"Today will be remembered as a defining moment," said the Mayor of New York Michael Bloomberg when he announced that the Cornell-Technion partnership had won the city's tender for an applied science graduate school and research campus. The NYC Tech Campus on

Roosevelt Island will combine the full spectrum of both institutions' academic strengths, entrepreneurial culture, and leadership in commercialization and technology transfer.

Over the next three decades some 600 spin-off companies are anticipated, Bloomberg predicted. Cornell President David J. Skorton outlined how technology is no longer just for the sake of technology but is technology in the service of business and industry. Technion President Peretz Lavie said that this undertaking is "something new that will energize the city."

The ultimate goal is to enable New York City to "take on" Silicon Valley as the premier location in the country to educate and employ the truly gifted technical thinkers of the next century. How cool is that?

Gotta just love Bloomberg eh? Perhaps it is time for an Independent candidate to run for President... I'm just sayin'!

# A Guide to the Moderate Man

Last week was really interesting on several political fronts. Being a former high school English teacher I took particular note of an event dealing with the selection, translation and usage of language in a very important, not to mention really interesting, news story occupying scads of print space and hours of broadcast time.

Enter Iran's new President Hassan Rouhani. Rouhani has been making lots of news trying to convince the western world that Iran is ready to talk. He is trying to portray himself as more moderate, someone with whom the West can negotiate; far removed ideologically from his Holocaust denying predecessor, you know that "I'm a dinner jacket" guy! Oh, sorry I mean Ahmadinejad.

Prior to his speech at the U.N. and several interviews, Rouhani tore up the twitter-sphere laying the groundwork for his entrance onto the international political stage in his new role as "a more moderate" President of Iran. I guess he missed the irony that he was utilizing (some have said abusing) technology forbidden to the Iranian people by his government. And are we supposed to forget that for more than three decades he has advised both the Ayatollah Khomeini and the current supreme leader Ayatollah Khamenei? Oh, and of course one can't even run for president in Iran without being judged "ideologically sound."

But it was the brouhaha over his interview with CNN that I found really interesting.

Do you remember the really funny old movie A Guide to the Married Man? It was a romp through several vignettes about the perils, trials and tribulations of married life. One of the truly memorable vignettes has the unexpected, unsuspecting wife returning home to find her husband in bed with another woman. Without a word the "other woman" scoots out of the room grabbing her discarded stuff and the husband casually makes the bed, dons his clothes and lights a pipe while sitting down, staring expectantly at his wife. When she begins her condemnation he looks innocently at her feigning surprise and explaining that what she saw wasn't what she saw at all.

"What woman in the bed? There was no woman here." This went on until exasperated and frustrated and even a bit unsure now of what she had seen; the wife gives up.

Anyway, in that interview with CNN's Christiane Amanpour (a Farsi speaking journalist) Rouhani acknowledged that the Holocaust did occur and acts against the Jews and so many others were pretty reprehensible. These are my words not exactly his but the meaning seemed clear. And there is the rub. Ah the words...

A radical news agency in Iran immediately picked up on the press Rouhani was getting about his moderate stance and slammed CNN for miss translating what he said.

Some might say President Rouhani got caught in bed, so to speak, with the infidels.
What is he saying to all of this? As of today Rouhani has stoically remaining silent on the subject of the "was it a miss-translation or wasn't it" question.

I think he has casually made the bed, seated himself comfortably, lit his pipe and is now looking at us all innocently.

# A Plague O' Both Your Houses

So our government has shut down.

I'm sure that you have heard the stories of children unable to get meds in drug trial programs and the perils of having our EPA inspections halted and the shutting down of one of our country's only sources of non-tax revenue – our National Park Services; the list of "what are they thinking?" shut downs goes on and on.

At the same time many non-essential personnel that had been furloughed have been reinstated and all of the rest have been granted full retroactive pay once the shutdown has ended. And let's not forget the millions of dollars it takes to not only shut down the government but to then start it up again.

Why in the world would our legislators do this; especially now when our fiscal condition is precarious at best?

All of this is because a small group of Republicans can not admit defeat...defeat of their efforts to defeat Obamacare.

And then there are many more Republicans who are so afraid of being "primaryed" in the next election thus suffering defeat to their Tea Party candidate opponents; they are going along or just not saying anything.

Man lots of "defeat stuff" causing lots of problems!

But if fear of defeat is motivating the silence of the conservatives willing to negotiate, why aren't the "Tea Party" stalwarts also afraid of the ramifications at the voting booths if they are seen as the perpetrators of this financial nightmare?

The answer is one word: Gerrymandering

In 1812 E. Gerry the governor of Massachusetts redistricted the state in an attempt to secure his party's majority in his state house. The resemblance of the map of Essex County to a salamander after the redistricting prompted the press to label the practice gerrymandering.

The current definition of gerrymandering is: dividing of a state, county, etc., into election districts so as to give one political party a majority in many districts while concentrating the voting strength of the other party into as few districts as possible.

And that is what both parties have been trying to do since the early nineteenth century in an attempt to secure their majority.

The most recent success of the gerrymandering process by Tea Party republicans makes their re-elections pretty much a given in their districts. Thus, they have achieved power within the party to such an extent that even though what they are doing is unpopular with the vast majority of Americans (per every major poll) they are standing firm assured of their reelections by their like thinking constituents.

Come on guys ... Obamacare is the law. It is being implemented. So, why not do the right thing for the country and stop this nonsense. You are not going to abolish Obamacare.

Plus, so far the roll out seems to be a bit of a nightmare.

Instead of making the Democrats face the consequences of its implementation you are turning the country against your ideological disregard for what is best for the country by keeping the government shut down.

I just don't get it. What is the plus side for anyone?

I don't know about you but my feelings in regard to Washington right now are summed up by good ol' Bill Shakespeare..."A Plague O' Both Your Houses."

# #Gravity

I love this time of year. Fall is in the air. Football season has begun and lest I forget ... the studios are beginning to release the really good movies!

After three quarters of a year filled with mediocre films with only a few exceptions; this is the time when films with "the sky's the limit" budgets, spectacular star power, and meteoric box office receipts soar into theaters near you. And leading this year's mission toward Oscar glory is the movie Gravity.

Drew and I saw it in IMAX 3D and let me just say: WOW WOW WOW WOW!

The plot is pretty simple. I won't give anything away that hasn't been appearing in the trailers for several weeks now by saying that Sandra Bullock, on her first mission into space, is teamed up with veteran astronaut George Clooney taking the Space Shuttle out to repair the Hubble Space Telescope. From the beginning of the movie things start to go wrong, very wrong. The rest of the plot answers the question, "does she survive and if so how?"

But as simple as the plot is, that is how extraordinarily complicated creating the splendor of Gravity was. The movie is nothing less than visually spectacular. No it's more than that; it is awesome, and I am using that word with the all but forgotten meaning of "truly awe inspiring."

Costing over $100 million to make, the gasp producing scenes of Bullock careening weightlessly about were created by the use of a 12 wire rig with carbon filtered harness that literally let the filmmakers become Bullock's puppeteers.

In addition to receiving a medal for letting herself be battered brutally about while wired like a marionette, I think that Sandra Bullock gives the performance of her career and George Clooney is...well...adorable George Clooney!

Having voiced my opinion, it seems that there are those that seriously don't agree with me. The twittersphere has been going nuts with banter between those thinking the movie is just unrealistic (I mean really with no gravity how does Bullock's hair stay put?) and those finding it totally believable and any technical inaccuracies to be well within the realm of creative license.
Hundreds of thousands of followers are clicking - #gravity – and putting their two cents worth into the discussion.

So, I decided to seek out an expert who is one of those commenting on the movie.
Astronaut Michael Massimino has logged 600 hours in space with 30 of them consisting of space walking and he said that the movie "made him feel like he was back among the stars." Adding, "I would say that it is a pretty accurate depiction...the Space Shuttle, the views from space and even the tools used were realistic." And he ought to know. He flew twice in the Space Shuttle Atlantis to upgrade the Hubble Space Telescope.

Oh, and by the way, Massimino is thought to be the astronaut upon whom Clooney's character is based. Gotta wonder; is he as adorable as Clooney?

Anyway, I suggest you see the movie and judge for yourself.

And to those hundreds of thousands in the tweeting frenzy I say:

#gravity – talk all you want about details and accuracy...Gravity is simply a glorious spectacle to behold.

# Obamacare, the Tea Party and Hezbollah

Oh my. Oh dear. Obamacare!

No one is arguing with the fact that there are huge problems with the rollout of the President's signature accomplishment thus far in his presidency. No one is arguing that millions of dollars seem to have been wasted in overage fees for the site to be up and running by the October 1st deadline. No one is saying that the rollout has been successful; to the contrary even the President himself in his speech earlier this week expressed his frustration and anger with the major problems experienced by those trying to access the site.

Most people, it seems, have realized that the Ted Cruz instigated shut down of the government, presumably to make a stand for defunding the Affordable Care Act, was certainly not the way to win over Americans to his cause. Most people, it seems, feel that a very small minority of the House of Representatives is running roughshod over their colleagues and being allowed to exert tremendous power. Most people, it seems, think that this "out of the mainstream minority" could be stopped from having such power and more importantly should be stopped.

I am pretty sure that you all think as I do that the over $24 Billion it cost all of us to shut down the government (with that number still rising as the cost of now starting it up again multiples) is ...
OBSCENE!

Yes I am mad enough to use shouty, capital letters!

Sunday, at breakfast with Drew I was shaking my head and bemoaning my complete incomprehension of the situation. I want to know what in the world the "Cruziacs" hoped to accomplish. Drew suggested that I read Thomas Friedman's editorial in the New York Times for some further insight.

(Just a note: whether you agree with TF or not politically, this Pulitzer Prize winning journalist and syndicated columnist is arguably one of the foremost authorities on the Middle East. And in this editorial he boldly points out the tactical similarities between the Tea Party and the terrorist group Hezbollah).

Here I quote from his editorial:

"It's striking how much the Tea Party wing of the G.O.P. has adopted the tactics of the P.O.G. — "Party of God" — better known as Hezbollah ... "Hezbollah's rule is: if we win, we rule, but if you win, you'll think you rule, but we will do anything and everything to hinder you, and then we rule."

The Tea Party... has legitimate concerns about debt, jobs and Obamacare. But what was not legitimate was the line it crossed. Rather than persuading a majority of Americans that its policies were right, and winning elections to enact the changes it sought — the essence of our democratic system — the Tea Party threatened to undermine our nation's credit rating if the Democrats would not agree to defund Obamacare. Had such strong-arm tactics worked, it would have meant that constitutionally enacted laws could be nullified if determined minorities opposed them. It would have meant Lebanon on the Potomac."

Now before all of you Tea Partiers out there start with the hate emails...No one, not even TF is suggesting that you all are terrorists. I am the first to defend your right to think, feel and say what you want. All I am saying is that TF's editorial really intrigued me and I am hoping that should you want to read more, you will read it in its entirety.

Problem is I am still shaking my head... but I can't shake the anger I feel at the nonsensical actions costing us all so very dearly.

# No Tricks, Only Treats

I grew up on a one block street in a northern suburb of Chicago. I was 11 months old when we moved into our home which would be my base, my safe haven until at nineteen; I got married. The street was only a gravel road back then and there were only five other houses on the block.

By the time I was five or six, our road had been paved, all 16 lots had been built upon and I was allowed to go out "trick or treating" with my two older brothers. Back then my parents waved goodbye at our front door and didn't see us again for a few hours.

Most of the houses on our block were occupied by families like mine; a couple or three children (oh the Lubie's were an exception - nine kids!) and in very short order on Halloween night, we all broke into our age specific little groups to ring door bells, fill our bags with goodies and solicit coins for UNICEF!

There was an elderly couple (well, I guess they were about the age I am now) living on the corner who gave out dollar bills and the widow next door to them made yummy taffy apples to hand out. In the middle of the block lived the Panos'. Mister Panos owned a Greek restaurant and always had Greek pastries, individually wrapped, to add to our stash. And at the other end of the block we could always count on caramel popcorn balls sometimes still warm and gooooeeee good which never made their way into our bags but straight into our mouths!

There were no tricks on my block only wonderful memories of all the treats.

My children don't have those kinds of memories of Halloween.

Of course now things are very different. Parents are afraid to let their children go out alone to roam the streets in search of the houses with the best treats. Kids are cautioned on the potential danger of eating anything that is homemade or not commercially wrapped.

Now parents (as Drew and I did) accompany their children and closely inspect everything before it gets dropped into the bag.

Don't get me wrong. We had great times with our kids trick or treating but looking back, it was another parent directed activity whereas my childhood memories are of the elation I felt at being "on my own," with my friends, laughing as our costumes or make-up disintegrated in a sudden rain or at an adult who answered our knocks in a silly costume.

Our world has changed. We have changed. And it saddens me to think that my children only hear tell of how Halloween was when Drew and I were kids and that in all likelihood our grandchildren won't even hear the stories let alone experience the jubilation of one night a year to be out after dark, dressed up...not ourselves but scavengers, adventurers seeking our very own treasures with no adult supervision and more importantly no fear.

I wish all of you and especially the children in our community a wonderful Halloween and a safe one...one with no tricks but only treats.

# Michael Jordan, Bigger Than Life

The year was 1993. Michael Jordan (his friends call him MJ) was in his heyday. The season, if the Bulls won it all, would mark an historic "Three-peat" accomplishment.

While basketball was never my favorite sport to watch growing up, being far overshadowed by my beloved football and baseball; you couldn't watch MJ (if I can be so bold as to call him that...oh what the heck I'm going for it!) play and not be totally smitten with the game.

A friend of mine had courtside seats at the old Chicago Stadium and wow, wow, wow, offered them to me for a game. While I was chomping at the bit to attend myself, I thought that our then 11 year old son would love to go with his dad.

If you have ever attended a game you know that the players warm up beforehand with drills and shot practice. In one drill the team lines up and one by one they shoot – follow up on their shot at the net and then toss the ball back to the next player so he can repeat the process.

As luck would have it, the player in front of MJ threw wild and the ball skidded across the floor right to my son. MJ then turned to Rory, waved a plea for him to throw the ball, so Rory then passed it back to Michael Jordan!

And it only got better from there. When MJ caught it he dashed to the basket, did a reverse dunk and then gave Rory a thumbs up sign with a huge smile.

OMG Rory had made an assist ... to Michael Jordan no less and would you believe that a news camera caught the whole thing and ran it the next day?

Needless to say, MJ became even more special to the Levenfeld's than he had been before.

Fast forward to what is going on today with my all-time favorite basketball player.

After living for almost two decades in an obscenely huge, over-the-top estate in Highland Park Illinois; Jordan has decided to sell it. Knowing people that live near the place, I had heard of it and knew that about a year ago it was put on the market with the staggering asking price of $29,000,000.00. Yes, that's 29 million for a house!

Of course it is 56,000 square feet under roof, 7 + acres of property with 150 trees forming a natural fence, 9 bedrooms and would you believe, 15 full baths! It also includes a full-sized NBA regulation basketball court and a PGA grade putting green just to mention a few of the amenities. Oh, and did I mention that the price also includes all of the furnishings?

SUCH A DEAL!

But seriously, when you think about it, how could a larger than life sport's figure like MJ live in anything but a larger than life abode? But who, pray tell, could fill his huge basketball shoes, not to mention his huge living space?

Apparently no one yet so, MJ has decided to auction the place off to the highest bidder on November 22nd.

Should you want an advanced peek before grabbing your check book on the 22nd, you can take a video tour of the place at www.conciergeauctions.com.

While all grown up now with a son almost the same age as he was at the time, I know that Rory remembers fondly that incredible moment so long ago at the Chicago Stadium when MJ proved himself to be a genuinely nice guy. And I wish only the best for one of the greatest sports figures of all time; someone who made my son feel very special; Michael Jordan.

# Rand Paul Defending His Honor

In all honesty I don't know that much about Rand Paul. From bits of speeches and several interviews I have heard where he has presented his positions on things; I strongly agree with some and equally strongly disagree with others. His name is often mentioned as a possible Republican Presidential nominee in 2016.

You might have heard that there was quite a flap last week about his apparent tendency to plagiarize lines and phrases in his speeches.

Had there not been such a feeding frenzy in the press over the debacle that is the roll out of the Affordable Care Act (Obamacare) I think the Rand Paul story might have had stronger legs. After all, more than two decades ago, then Presidential hopeful Joe Biden had his Oval Office hopes dashed by a plagiarism scandal of his own. Back then the reports were of phrases in a campaign speech Biden made closely mirroring a speech given by British politician Neal Kinnock (whoever he is/was) and Biden's opponent Michael Dukakis seized the moment creating an attack video that caused such a stir in the media; Biden was forced to exit the race paving the way for a Dukakis candidacy...and we all know how well Dukakis did as the Democratic candidate!

But there are countless other examples of plagiarism charges being made dating back to the inception of our government. In our recent history, both John McCain and Barack Obama have had the charges laid at them.

What has grabbed my attention about the Rand Paul incident is ...well...Rand Paul.

Over the weekend he appeared on several "Sunday Morning Political Koffee Klatches" wrapped in a cape of indignation and in the true style of a caped crusader stated that he only wished that dueling was still allowed in Kentucky for he would be throwing the gauntlet down to defend his honor.

I have to say, on this one; I agree totally with Senator Paul. He stance is that most of his speeches are extemporaneous and don't have the same footnote responsibility of an academic paper. Furthermore if he references say Wikipedia, as he has done, does he have the obligation to check to see if Wikipedia has referenced the originator or other news sources that might have used a similar phrase?

Oh, come on. It's enough already with the "we gotcha" journalism.

I ask; do you always know where you heard something; a phrase or description? And if remembered, you later find it to be relevant in a subsequent conversation do you even think to cite where you heard it originally? And even more ludicrous, do you check to see if there were previous sources to the one you heard it from that you should then cite?

Sorry if that was confusing but as far as I could tell from the interviews, that's the kind of nonsense Rand Paul is having to deal with over these reports.

Is this really what we should be focusing on?

So, I say Bravo to Rand! A duel? Really? How cool is that? Can I volunteer to be your second!

# The Best and the Brightest

It's been fifty years. Hard to believe but it is true. I was twelve years old, sitting in my Social Studies class when my best friend Becky Franklin came bursting into the room, much to my teacher Mrs. Stout's displeasure, and hugged me crying "the President's been shot" before sinking to the ground emitting low, pitiful, mournful sobs.

Every one of my generation has their own story of how they heard the news; the precise details of where they were, forever etched into their memory. Jack Kennedy had been shot; soon after to die in Dallas.

With the fiftieth anniversary of that tragedy upon us, the airwaves and bookstore shelves have been filled with JFK "product." Everything from made for cable movies, documentaries and biographies to alternative theories claiming to factually refute the findings of the Warren Commission regarding the assassination seem to be everywhere.

This fifty year milestone seems truly important because when the next "big one," seventy-five years having passed, takes place; the vast majority of us who were there, experiencing the horror and heartbreak of not only that day but the sobering days that followed; will no longer be around ourselves to remember.

Just when I thought I had seen and heard more than enough about that time, that presidency, I caught a special over the weekend. In a passing remark, mention was made of Nancy and Ronald Reagan's reaction and then actions following the assassination and my curiosity was peaked.

Did you know that Nancy, being heartsick for Jackie, reached out to her and a long-lasting friendship developed? Neither did I!

And when the Kennedy's were having trouble raising funds for the JFK Library, Jackie approached Ronald Reagan for help and he appeared at a fundraiser in the home of Teddy Kennedy to lend support and help raise funds.

The speech Reagan gave at the event was an elegant, heartfelt, beautifully written and of course beautifully delivered masterpiece of non-partisan humanity.

No matter one's political persuasion I don't think anyone could have seen that speech and not come away from it moved by the genuine emotion conveyed.

When asked about his decision to not only make the appearance but to actually fundraise for a Democrat, Reagan's answer was that our President had been struck down, the nation's President and the library was history, our history...our country.

Just think about that statement.

I'll tell you it really made me think about what is happening in Washington today and the kind of leaders we currently have "representing" us.

So, it has been fifty years but the memories are still vivid.

After the funeral procession, someone said "We'll never laugh again."
Patrick Moynahan answered "We'll laugh but we'll never be young again." And I think he was right. The event aged us, humbled us, made us aware of the fragility of life.

And I look at Jack Kennedy and Ronald Reagan arguably the two "rock stars" of their respective political parties and I can't help but think that they lived in a time and worked in a Washington where civility and yes even kindness were still acceptable. A time when statesmanship could still supersede partisanship. A time when not only the business of the country could get done but even some human kindness could be offered across the aisle.

I think that we need not only the best and the brightest in Washington but the civil and the compassionate as well.

# Who Do You Trust?

So, Secretary of State Kerry has reached an agreement with the Iranians. He was all over the Sunday morning news shows defining the parameters of the deal and trying to assuage skepticism.

My take was that the deal basically locks Iran's possibility to create nukes in place and marginally increases the amount of time it would take Iran to build "A Bomb." We will have daily access to their facilities to verify their adherence to the deal as well. But, they destroy nothing, dismantle nothing.

In return, we are lifting, to a small degree, some of the sanctions that have successfully thrown the Iranian economy in the tank. Well, not quite all of the economy. The upper crust by all accounts has not felt any of the economic pinch and the government has certainly not curbed its rapid progress toward becoming a nuclear power.

Not surprisingly, Israel is teed-off. The Saudi's are teed-off. Many members from both houses of Congress and from both parties are teed-off.

And I am genuinely at a loss.

On the one hand, isn't diplomacy always better than war?

Yet, why strike any kind of deal if the sanctions are causing unrest in the country and the possibility of dismantling the Iranian nuclear program could be a result of ramping up the sanctions rather than easing up on them?

However, isn't it a step toward negotiating a big deal?

But then do we really think that after spending trillions on their nuke program, the Iranians will just walk away from it?

Yet, could pressure from the other Gulf States and from their own people have a tempering effect on the Government?

I just don't know.

It is said that a good deal is when neither party is happy. Did you see the clips and pics of the Iranians rejoicing in the streets at news of the deal? Looks like one side is happy!

Even looking to history doesn't help. The Iranians have lied, deceived and broken every international resolution on the development of nuclear weapons. They finance horrific acts of terrorism around the world being very vocal about their desire to not only wipe Israel off of the map but the U.S. and other western nations a well.

And yet, do you remember back twenty years ago? Egypt and Israel, after having been arch enemies for longer than anyone living could remember, accomplished what no one thought possible. They came together and signed a peace treaty which is still in effect today. Could the recently elected Iranian president, Rouhani,(who looks sorta, kinda, to be more moderate) be the player we have needed to really make progress towards peace in the Gulf region? Could this deal be the beginning of a lasting "truce" with Iran?

Surely talking is a good thing...isn't it? It seems that the seven world leaders who signed this 6 month deal think so.

But I have a creepy feeling about all of this. And I have a big "what if" nagging at me. Call me cynical. But how do we really know that the facilities Iran has agreed to open up to our inspection are the only ones they have?

After all, at least one of the ones we know of was pretty well hidden in the mountains...aren't there a lot of other mountains into which facilities could be built? Just sayin'!

Honestly, who do you trust?

# Thanksgiving Good News

Drew and I have just returned from an extended Thanksgiving weekend visiting with our daughter's family in Massachusetts. I hope that all of you had a joyful holiday. We sure did with the traditional meal, grandchildren being absolutely adorable and a few precious moments of reflecting on all for which we have to be thankful.

In these days of international unrest, national disquietude and all of the pressures of this 21st century; it is not surprising that we may forget to give thanks. When I was very young I remember my grandmother telling me to take a couple of moments each and every morning, before getting out of bed, to think about all of my blessings. While I confess to not always adhering to her sage advice, when I do, the day just seems to be easier, lighter in some way starting out with such positive thoughts.

At this holiday season, besides our personal blessings for which to be thankful, there is some other good news that affects us all that I would like to share with you. Here are some great facts, Jack!

We can collectively pat ourselves on the back because the rate of high school degree conference is on the rise. According to a study conducted at Harvard, the percentage of kids graduating from high school has increased by 6% in the 21st century. According to an editorial in USA Today, high school dropouts account for about 75% of all crimes committed and earn less than $200,000.00 over their lifetime compared to high school graduates. The study attributes the increase in graduates to two other positive trends. Fewer kids are being arrested and fewer middle school and high school aged girls are getting pregnant; good news indeed for us all.

More good news on the energy front! The International Energy Agency predicts that the U.S. will surpass Saudi Arabia as the world's largest oil producer by the year 2016. And our natural gas reserves have grown so much that the ports built to import liquefied gas are now starting to export it. One result from all of this is that the increased supplies have helped to nudge gasoline prices down and have helped to fuel (sorry 'bout the pun) a modest rebound in U.S. manufacturing. Since 2010 526,000 manufacturing jobs have been created. O.K., O.K. so that doesn't seem like much of an increase, but it represents the first sustained uptick since we saw manufacturing jobs begin their slow decline in the 1970's.

Ready for some more good news?

The Department of Housing and Urban Development estimates that the U.S. homeless population is 4% less than it was in 2012 and 7% less than in 2007, when the economy was much stronger. The number of people actually living on the streets (as opposed to those living in shelters) has declined by a significantly greater amount ... 23% since 2007.

While we all wish that the number of high school graduates was higher and the number of homeless people was lower, and we of course want to eliminate our dependency on foreign oil; all of this news is really good, don't you think?

I hope that you agree with me that these statistics can be added to those blessings we should all count tomorrow morning upon waking up.

# Mandela

Picture a precocious little boy born in 1918, whose tribal name colloquially translates as "troublemaker," in a country whose poor was ravaged not only by disease but by institutionalized racism and poverty. Though descended from tribal royalty, both of his parents were illiterate and the boy grew up in the dirt-poor village of Qunu South Africa where as a child he tended herds as a "cattle-boy."

The "troublemaker" little boy was sent to a local Methodist school where his was given the name Nelson and he developed a love affair with African history and listening to tales told by elder visitors, both of which helped him to begin his journey for justice.

Of course, we all know him now as Nelson Mandela.

And today the world mourns his death but his legacy still lives and seems to be stronger than ever.

His funeral this morning (Tuesday) saw an assembly of world leaders, ex-United States Presidents, Mandela family members and tens of thousands of the people of South Africa who braved the truly nasty weather to pay their respects to one of the great men of our time...indeed perhaps of all time.

Since his death we have been reminded of his personal struggles which never deterred him from his mission of freeing South Africa from the shackles of the racist Apartheid system of government under which so many suffered so severely for so very long.

Much has been said and is being repeated about how this man as a young militant raged against the injustice in his beloved nation; a young man who had already laid down his weapons, instead choosing to continue his struggle on a non-violent path, when he was arrested.

Thinking that he would undoubtedly be executed; the surprise of "mere" imprisonment proved to strengthen his resolve to continue his struggle to not only better the conditions within South Africa but to better himself as a man and as a citizen of the world.

The last words he uttered before going into prison were "I fought against the domination of white people. I fought against the domination of black people." By the time he was released, he had come to realize all that he should be fighting for rather than what he had been fighting against.

While others are made bitter in prison, Mandela was made introspective. While others harbor anger and hatred, festering behind bars, Mandela honed his aspirations into a tolerant, forgiving resolve to rectify injustices.

Imagine being imprisoned for over two decades, surviving unimagined cruelty and yet having the forgiveness and grace to have his captors, his actual prison guards stand beside him as honored guests as he spoke after his release.

Just think about that one action. Think about what that says to the spirit of the man, the character of the man, the fortitude of the man.

He once said "I am not a saint unless you think of a saint as a sinner who keeps on trying." And keep on trying he most certainly did.

We mourn today the loss of a great man. We can only hope to be inspired by his example.

# Pivot to Asia

Those of us of a certain age remember the United Kingdom entering into a military conflict with Argentina over some obscure Island group in 1967. While war was never officially declared by either side it is known to all as the Falkland's War.

Wikipedia describes it this way. "The conflict was the result of a protracted historical confrontation regarding the sovereignty of the islands. Argentina has asserted that the Falkland Islands have been Argentinean territory since the 19th century...as such, the Argentine government characterized their 1967 invasion as the re-occupation of their own territory, whilst the British government saw it as an invasion of a British dependent territory."

O.K. You are probably thinking "so what?"

Well, it appears that now, this generation is witnessing another possible military conflict between Japan and China over yet another small Island group; this time in the East China Sea. But, unlike that battle 40 plus years ago, this one has our country smack dab in the middle of it.

There has been a long running dispute between China and Japan over which nation has the sovereign rights to the Islands known as Senkakus to the Japanese and Diaoyu to the Chinese.

China has now shot the proverbial "cannon over the bow" by establishing an "air-defense identification zone"(ADIZ) which requires foreign aircraft to notify China before flying over the islands and Japan is furious!

Before you ask, here is how we have gotten involved. We have a mutual defense treaty with Japan. We have aircraft carriers stationed in the East China Sea and Japan isn't our only ally impacted by the ADIZ.

So, what did we do in response to the AZID? We immediately violated it; I think more in symbolic protest, and as an act of solidarity with Japan, than for any other reason. But the heating up of the situation over an unoccupied, by all accounts desolate atoll had Secretary of State Kerry going to the region a couple of weeks ago.

So, why does anyone want such a place and be willing to risk an armed conflict over it?

A geological survey determined that the waters surrounding the islands likely contain vast deposits of oil and natural gas...oh I get it now; the old oil and gas thing!

No countries in the world are currently importing more fossil fuels than China and Japan. China needs this possible new influx of resources to sustain their exploding economic growth. And since the 2011 Fukushima nuclear disaster, Japan's almost total reliance on nuclear energy has come to a halt with the closure of all 50 nuclear reactors in the country, thus leaving them dependant on fossil fuels as well.

But what I find really scary is a totally non-energy related reason for the timing of this conflict.

Both China and Japan have new leaders of their countries. The scary part is that both men are considered "militaristic."

Xi Jinping is now China's President and Shinzo Abe has become the Prime Minister of Japan. Both men are anxious to assert their power and control in the increasingly tense Far East; Xi Jinping by establishing the ADZI and Shinzo Abe by calling for the rearming of Japan (this is a topic for another column as this call is in direct conflict with the agreements signed with Japan's surrender after WWII).

The result of the Falkland's War was that Argentina withdrew, basically with its tail between its legs. The two countries have since opted for the policy of agreeing to disagree about which country has sovereignty. But I don't see that happening in the East China Sea; not with the lure of vast quantities of oil and natural gas and the reputations of two militaristic leaders hanging in the balance.

Are you as creeped out as I am at the prospect of a military conflict in the Far East...one that we are honor-bound to be a part of? Shoot me an email and let me know your thoughts.

# Twelve Stories of 2013
### (To be sung to the Twelve Days of Christmas)

It's the end of the year so it's time to look on back
T'was the year of two thousand thirteen

We were rid of that Weiner but still he reappeared
Weiner causes indigestion
T'was the year of two thousand thirteen

Lance Armstrong 'fessed up to the lie heard 'round the world
Lance was major doping
Weiner causes indigestion
T'was the year of two thousand thirteen

Government was shut down as Congress stood on by
Fie on the Congress
Lance was major doping
Weiner causes indigestion
T'was the year of two thousand thirteen

Will 'n Kate gave the world a proper British heir
By "George" it's a boy
Fie on the Congress
Lance was major doping
Weiner causes indigestion
T'was the year of two thousand thirteen

Top secret revelations have Washington red faced
Snowden's now in Russia
By "George" it's a boy
Fie on the Congress
Lance was major doping
Weiner causes indigestion
T'was the year of two thousand thirteen

Miley Cyrus made waves with her tongue a hangin' out
What the heck is "twerking?"
Snowden's now in Russia
By "George" it's a boy

Fie on the Congress
Lance was major doping
Weiner causes indigestion
T'was the year of two thousand thirteen

The world lost a hero a giant of a man
Mandela is at peace
What the heck is twerking?
Snowden's now a Russian
By "George" it's a boy!
Fie on the Congress
Lance was major doping
Weiner causes indigestion
T'was the year of two thousand thirteen

The Affordable Care Act launched into cyberspace
O'care's a fiasco
Mandela is at peace
What the heck is twerking?
Snowden's now a Russian
By "George" it's a boy!
Fie on the Congress
Lance was major doping
Weiner causes indigestion
T'was the year of two thousand thirteen

The Cardinals selected a simple, pious man
Pope Francis really rocks
O'care's a fiasco
Mandela is at peace
What the heck is twerking?
Snowden's now in Russia
By "George" it's a boy!
Fie on the Congress
Lance was major doping
Weiner causes indigestion
T'was the year of two thousand thirteen

Reading Green Eggs and Ham Cruz droned on and on
and on
Eggs on face for Ted

Pope Francis really rocks
O'care's a fiasco
Mandela is at peace
What the heck is twerking
Snowden's now in Russia
By "George" It's a boy!
Fie on the Congress
Lance was major doping
Weiner causes indigestion
T'was the year of two thousand thirteen

The country mourned with Boston, a terrorist attack
Marathon explosions
Eggs on face for Ted
Pope Francis really rocks
O'care's a fiasco
Mandela is at peace
What the heck is twerking?
Snowden's now in Russia
By "George" it's a boy!
Fie on the Congress
Lance was major doping
Weiner causes indigestion
T'was the year of two thousand thirteen

George Zimmerman continues to wave his weapons
'round
Maniacs and guns
Marathon explosions
Eggs on face of Ted
Pope Francis really rocks
O'care's a fiasco
Mandela is at peace
What the heck is twerking?
Snowden's now in Russia
By "George" it's a boy?
Fie on the Congress
Lance was major doping
Weiner causes indigestion
T'was the year of two thousand thirteen

Merry Christmas and Happy New Year to all.

# Looking to 2014

Many years ago when I submitted my first Christmas column I began it with the statement "I love Christmas." All these years later I still hold that view. Being a Jew, that column surprised many. I received a slew of emails all supportive of my sentiment that regardless of religion I couldn't understand how anyone could argue with a holiday promoting peace on earth and good will toward men.

Christmas 2013 once again consisted of our own family ritual of a movie and Chinese food! Since it is the time of the year when all of the studios release their bids for Oscar contention, we went to see Martin Scorsese's latest flick the "Wolf of Wall Street" starring Leonardo DiCaprio.

I think a confession is in order here. I have never been a huge Leo fan. I mean really, how could anyone feel the passion between his Jack and Kate Winslet's Rose in "Titanic" when he looked more like her little brother than her lover? Having said that I am proclaiming now that I have become a convert. His portrayal of Jordan Belfort in this movie has to be one of the best performances that I have seen in recent memory. The movie, unfortunately is tooooo long, shame on you Scorcese; but the based on fact story of a con man whose investigation by the FBI exposed the AbScam scandal is a compelling one.

I could not help but notice the irony of this story of greed and abuse of every shape and size being released for viewing on Christmas day.

While all of that debauchery could have put a damper on my Christmas spirit, fortunately I had made a point of watching Pope Francis' first Christmas address from the Vatican.

I gotta say I love this guy! The new Pope stressed attention to the poor and aspiring for peace. He spoke of compassion and morality. And more than just words, in his short tenure as the religious leader of millions and an inspiration for millions more; his deeds back up the verbiage. He has shocked many by basically declaring a truce on the culture wars, while not changing the Vatican's stance on a variety of "hot button" issues, he has chosen to address the more basic problems facing us all in these times of turbulence, mistrust and violence. He is putting his "money where his mouth is" exemplifying tolerance and kindness.

Be you Jew, Moslem, Hindu, Christian, atheist, agnostic or alien creature, the Pope's message is one whose time has come.

Whether a call to each of us individually or to our institutions, our young people or our old, how can one dispute the everlasting truth that we all benefit, we all would be more contented if we were simply kinder, more compassionate, more respectful of one and other?

Isn't it time? Haven't we endured the mistrust, the vitriol, the violence long enough?

Daniel Day-Lewis won the Oscar for his portrayal of Abraham Lincoln in Steven Speilberg's "Lincoln" another one of the Levenfeld's Christmas outings of years past. That movie ended with an excerpt from one of the President's speeches ... "with malice toward none and charity toward all." Of course he was referring to the healing process that would be needed to bind the wounds of the Civil War, but unfortunately we still need a reminder of that basic sentiment lo these many years later.

So, my hope for the new year is that we will listen, take heed of the modern voice of this Pope and that voice from the President of the past and be kinder, more compassionate not only for the benefit of others but for ourselves as well.

# 2014

# Does Size Matter?

Were you among the millions of people who watched the premiere season of the Showtime series "Masters of Sex?" Since my absolute addiction to the Showtime series "Homeland " has been referred to in many of my columns, it should come as no surprise to you that I indeed stayed tuned for "Masters of Sex" which immediately followed the "Homeland" Sunday evening time slot this past season.

"Masters of Sex" fictionally chronicles the trials and tribulations of highly reputed physician William Masters and his research assistant Virginia Johnson as they dare to go where no one had gone before... conducting a scientific study of sex.

Hmm. Then throw into the mix the personal relationships of not only our two main characters, but many others on the hospital staff and you have one steamy nighttime soap opera.

Based loosely on the actual facts of Masters and Johnson's groundbreaking research, the show is so period specific, as viewers, we are treated to not only the look and feel of the fifties but the morals and mores of the era as well. Oh and did I mention that the acting is superb?

At one point, when Masters is trying to come up with a "hook" (a juicy tidbit which will insure his audience's attention at the first presentation he will make of his findings) he hits upon the age old question "does size matter?"

Coincidentally, I had just been reading about a minor controversy centering on whether or not One World Trade Center, the new tower constructed on the site of the September 11, 2001 tragedy due to be opening in 2014, is taller than Chicago's own Sears Tower.

O.K. O.K. I know it is now the Willis Tower but just like Cellular One Field is still Comiskey Park to me, so goes the Sears Tower!

It seems that some are concerned about Chicago losing status as home to the tallest building in the western hemisphere, and many are yelling foul on the way the height differential is being calculated.

The answers to such pressing questions as: 1.Should the height be determined by the number of floors? 2. Should the height be determined by the actual height in feet? 3. Do you include the antennae in the height calculation? 4. Do you only include antennae that constitute permanent fixtures?

Lofty concerns and questions indeed!

Honestly, does anyone, do you really care that with the opening of One World Trade Center, the Sears Tower will become the second tallest building in the western hemisphere instead of the first and the tenth tallest building in the world instead of the ninth? (Actually I do find the locations of the other nine structures very interesting...all except one are in Asia...what does that tell us?!)

And so here we are yet again pondering the question; does size matter?

Only time will tell if the down-grading from having the tallest to having the second tallest building in the western hemisphere will have any effect on Chicago at all, but in my humble opinion; nah, I don't think so. But let me end with Dr. Masters' conclusion on the "does size matter" question. His research indicated that size does not matter.

If you should want more details, you won't get them from me. You'll have to catch the episode On Demand where the good doctor explains his research and rationale.

Why won't I explain?

Because... well, it really doesn't matter!

# Israel's Last Best Chance for Peace with the Palestinians?

Ariel Sharon passed away on Saturday after a massive stroke left him languishing in a coma for 8 years. Drew and I had the privilege of receiving policy briefings directly from him during his tenure as Prime Minister of Israel (2001- 2006). A decorated military man, a Major-General in the Israeli Defense Force and considered to be a bona fide war hero by the Israeli people; he entered the political scene in 1973 known for never backing down; a man truly unafraid of breaking the rules.

We watched through the years as he grew from a skillful politician into a remarkable statesman; a statesman who had the ability to look at the very dangerous Israeli-Palestinian conflict and see that the best solution was a two state solution if Israel was to have any hope of being truly secure. At a time when that sentiment was very unpopular among his countrymen, Sharon almost singlehandedly moved Israeli consensus to a point where the value of peace and compromise superseded the value of land. He gambled his own political future on what turned out to be his last major initiative as Prime Minister; the unilateral disengagement from Gaza. This bold and decisive action on Sharon's part ceded Gaza and Northern Samaria over to Palestinian rule. This "first move" as part of the "U.S. road map" for a solution to the Israeli-Palestinian conflict was made, without any concessions on the part of the Palestinians, as an act of good faith.

Our son, while serving in the Israeli army at that time, was involved with the forced evacuation of those Israeli settlers living in Gaza who refused to move. I later wrote about that experience in a column for this newspaper. I have included excerpts from that column below hoping to show you what an emotionally difficult decision the disengagement must have been for Ariel Sharon to make.

605

I know the emotional toll it took on this mother of a young Israeli soldier but can only imagine the toll it took on the Israeli citizenry.

## A VERY PERSONAL LOOK AT THE DISENGAGEMENT OF GAZA

No Israeli wanted to oust other Israelis from their homes in Gaza and worse yet give that land that they toiled so hard to cultivate to their arch enemies. But to ensure the future of the state of Israel it was necessary.

I sat stunned, as I watched Israeli soldiers and Israeli "settlers" struggling with the horrific position in which they found themselves. Every major T.V. network was covering the story and yet the world didn't seem to understand the significance of what was happening.

To see these beautiful children (for most of the soldiers in the Israeli army are under the age of 25) and settlers alike shedding tears as families were being dragged from their homes, as S.W.A.T. teams evacuated synagogues and community centers, was heart wrenching.

The clearing of the Sinai of Jewish settlers so many years ago resulted in a peace accord with Egypt that lasts until this day. The hope was that peace with the Palestinians would also result from this similar action.

So, there I sat and watched as these children, following orders on one side, being forcibly evicted from their homes on the other; cried together, prayed together, perhaps neither side fully understanding the decisions of "the powers that be."

The political rationale for the action was certainly not foremost in my mind as the images on T.V. broke my heart. The emotional aspect of the decision seemed all that mattered.

I watched intently for a glimpse of my son, an Israeli soldier, hoping not to see him yet surveying the faces on the screen, desperate to catch sight of him. For months he and his fellow soldiers had strategy sessions, therapy sessions and various types of counseling to prepare them for this operation. But can one ever be prepared for such a thing? How could I have ever imagined that participating in such a military action would ever be my son's fate?

Of course we now know that the result of that action was not peace. But I have to wonder if only... if only Sharon had not suffered that stroke. If he instead was allowed to continue with his steadfast determination to find a peaceful solution to the conflict, could it by now have been long settled and truly behind us?

So, I mourn the loss of Ariel Sharon; the man, the warrior, the statesman and perhaps Israel's last best chance for peace with the Palestinians.

# Intelligence?

I have received many emails asking why I have not weighed in on the whole NSA personal data collection/retention stuff. To be quite honest about it, every time I thought to pen a column commenting on the hoopla ... well, I simply drew a blank. Yep, confession time. I just didn't know where to begin nor could I come up with what I thought to be an interesting angle.

Like many, I have really mixed feelings about the revelations concerning our government spying on we the people contained in Comrade Snowden's leaking of U.S. classified information. On the one hand; how dare they invade my privacy? On the other hand; I expect our government to do everything it can to protect us.

Now, finally I have been inspired.

The President on Friday stated his intention to revamp the no longer super-secret, formerly highly classified data gathering program known as Section 215 of The US Patriot Act.

One of the major points of his do-over is that the government will no longer house the data collected. Oh, it will still do the gathering but it will give up control of the data, no longer having quick access to it. Instead, all of that personal intel will be held by some private company (to be determined later) and will require court action to be retrieved.

What? Do you trust a private company any more than you trust the government to "warehouse" your phone calls and heaven knows what else? I don't care if it is a phone company or an internet conglomerate or Henrietta's Hat Boutique down the street, it's still my personal stuff; hands off!

I know, I know anyone and I mean anyone can get access to vast amounts of information on any one of us already but this is taking the intrusion even a step further...well actually I think it is taking it many, many steps further; my phone calls? Really?

And doesn't making it harder for the government to access all of this data, if they do determine a possible threat, defeat gathering it in the first place? I mean isn't time of the essence in countering terrorism?

So, there is this new TV show called Intelligence that just premiered a couple of weeks ago and the premise is that this government operative has some kind of genetic mutation that enabled the implantation of a chip into his body which allows him to be connected to all data sources (and I mean all of them – I gotta watch what I say about TV programming!) and virtually see any information that is "out there." There are these really cool visuals of what he sees and of course he has the sexy, female, Secret Service Agent assigned to protect him; he being our government's most valuable asset. I mean really, aren't all female Secret Service Officers sexy, witty and wise?

Anyway, all of the above has gotten me thinking about the word intelligence and two of its very distinct definitions.

Is it really so "smart" to collect all of this "information" if doing so opens up the possibility that our enemies (and even our friends – ask Ms. Merkel!) can have access to it? While I don't foresee a hunky, chip implanted government agent peering into my personal communications anytime soon; it does make me wonder. Are we really being "smart" in the long run to have this "information" warehoused in one place, whether governmental or private (or at all for that matter) making hacking into it all the easier? Intelligence ... hmmmm.

# Grammy's and Fame

Did you catch the Grammy's on Sunday? Truth be known, I haven't seen the award's show in a few years and, I hate to admit, I really don't know half of the "new bright stars" of the music world; but the show itself, to my mind, was dazzling. The staging and sets were really quite spectacular.

My fav moments were the production numbers pairing honored music legends with the rising stars on the scene today. The Chinese Liberace, Ling Ling (kinda sounds like the name for a panda don't you think?) accompanied, of all bands, Metallica in a breath-taking rendition of the band's "ONE." And there was Sara Bareilles joining my beloved sire of singer/song writers, Carole King, combining "Bareilles' "Brave" with King's "Beautiful." It was absolutely beautiful indeed. But, don't take my word for it, Google (or Bing or whatever) the 2014 Grammy Duets and you can see these for yourself and more.

Other than the oldsters, I hadn't a clue who most of the entertainers were nor what their music sounds like but surprisingly I really liked most of what I heard.

Oh, and lest I forget to mention, Ringo joined Sir Paul on stage performing the unmistakably McCartney penned new song to a standing ovation by the crowd.

Have you heard of "Lorde?" Neither had I but after seeing and hearing her at the Grammy's I will not be forgetting her soon. She's a 17 years old singer/songwriter and is the first New Zealand artist to ever hit number one on the Billboard charts. The song she performed Sunday night "Royals" won the best song of the year later in the evening. She was wonderful...and sooooo young!

But, another child singing/songwriting phenom, the now "all grown up 19 year old" Justin Bieber, was nowhere to be seen. Not surprisingly, the once darling of the Grammy's, you may have read, has been in a self-destructive, downward spiral for the past several years and has recently fled to Panama after his arrest for allegedly drag racing on the streets of Miami while intoxicated and high ... this coming on the heels of a stupid antic resulting in his neighbor suing him for $20,000 in damages for, of all things, egging his house.

Coincidentally, I had a conversation about U.S Ex-Pats in Panama just last week when an acquaintance mentioned that she was leaving the next day for her vacation home in the Central American nation. Panama it seems is coming into its own...and here I thought it was basically just the location of a canal!

Anyway, as I watched Lorde, this oh so talented teenager wow the crowd of the big shots of the music industry with her performance, I couldn't help but wonder what toll celebrity and unabashed adulation and all of the privileges afforded the famous will have on this child. How can anyone expect these young, seemingly very naive talents to deal with all that the media and 24/7 fans throw at them? They are dreamers and oh so gifted and all of that just adds the fuel to the flames of fame.

I fear for this child with whom I was so taken on Sunday evening. I hope she can keep all that awaits her in perspective...there are others who have. And I hope that she will one day visit Panama on vacation enjoying the beaches and acting her age, having fun in the sun and not because she is running away from the press due to foolish perhaps even criminal activities in the states. I hope so; Lorde I really do.

# A Tit for Tat

Note to Washington:
I'm past being frustrated, past throwing my hands up and pretending that I don't care anymore, past trying to see both sides and rationalizing to myself the Legislative and Executive Branches' idiocies; what I have to say to you all right now; Democrats, Republicans, Tea Partyers, Libertarians, oh, and Rand Paul, is grow up and do your jobs!"

Phew, while venting can be momentarily exhilarating, in reality it is rather fruitless. I just don't understand how Washington can't get their stuff together and...well, at the risk of repeating myself, grow up.

We have all had to learn the lessons, the realities of life, how things work. Granted, some of us have learned these things better than others. Whether we were lucky enough to have had "elders" available to help us figure it all out or if we got on the program of life all on our own; the vast majority of us understand that it can't always be our way. It can't always be exactly as we want it to be. We have learned that to not only live with each other but to get anything accomplished; it takes understanding, respect and COMPROMISE!

After watching the State of the Union Address I was once again stunned, when channel surfing the major news networks, by the diversity of "takes" on what exactly the President said and how the speech was perceived. Did they all really watch the same speech?

The seemingly intractable divisions within our government are not only mirrored within the media but are fueled by it 24/7/365.

And I heard nothing in the speech nor in the various commentaries afterward that led me to believe that anything is going to change anytime soon.

But, just what if the President had stood up there before Congress and the world and simply said: I know that there are issues we will never agree upon but what if...

1. I give you the Keystone Pipeline if you give me Natural Gas Retrofitting

2. I give you a simpler Tax Code if you give me the Minimum Wage increase

3. I give you no Social Security benefits for those under the age of 45 without definitive evidence of need if you give me my infrastructure projects?

I'll see you in the oval office tomorrow to discuss how we can make these things happen.

(Thank you to Former Congressman Harold Ford for these suggestions)

I know, I know. Ain't never gonna happen but something, someone has got to slap these amateurs up-side the head and tell them how things work, not only in government but in life.

It is obvious they cannot do any "big ideas" in this political climate but they should be able to chip away, like the one hopeful event occurring in this Congressional Session of the two year budget agreement worked out by (R) Paul Ryan and (D) Patty Murray.

So, to Washington I say:

C'mon you guys and gals; really, if Bubba could work with Newt and Reagan could work with Tipp don't tell me you all can't find some way to work together on something meaningful?

Do you not read the polls? (Actually, I can understand it if you don't) The American People ARE NOT HAPPY! The time has come and long past. Get it together. Didn't your parents or your grandmother or a teacher or someone tell you about how to get along in this world?

No? Well, there is an old expression my grandmother taught me and I am passing it on to you. Please become familiar with it...it's an old concept rarely referred to these days; a concept of exchange and fairness.

The expression is: A Tit for Tat. It is an English saying specifically meaning "equivalent retaliation."

Perhaps that definition (especially the retaliation part) might just make adhering to the principle a bit more palpable for our current congressional combatants!

# Movie and Music and Sports; Oh My

Movie:
A couple of years ago, in my search for Sinai Forum speakers, I happened upon a book, "The Monuments Men" by Robert Edsel. The true story of a group of middle-aged men on a dangerous treasure hunt near the end of WWII endeavoring to save the great art of the world was fascinating. When I looked into getting Edsel to speak, I was told (as a selling point by his agent) that George Clooney had bought the movie rights and would be directing it. Then when the star-studded cast (including Clooney) for the film was announced, I was very excited to see how "good ol' George" would do with this powerful story.

Music:
It was 1965 and I was no different than any other young teen – I was smitten with the Beatles. And, lo and behold, they were coming to perform a concert at Comiskey Park. After much pleading and more than a few shed tears, my parents agreed ... oh joy; if I could get my older brother to take me ... oh crap. Elation ... despair! Let's just say my brother (5 years older than I) was not my biggest fan. Actually, looking back now I wonder if my folks assumed that this condition they had insisted upon would lay the matter to rest because he would never agree to be seen with his totally embarrassing little sister out in public. But the Gods are good and his steady date at the time (now my sister-in-law for the past 45 years) wanted to go so I was able to tag along. Thank you Peggy! And, it was amazing; the concert and that evening with my brother which forged a new, much better, phase in our relationship.

Sports:
I ask you, who doesn't love the Olympics? Watching hundreds of beautiful young people fulfilling their life-long dream of Olympic competition; it's simply inspiring. Whether it's the Jamaican lugers, the Norwegian skiers or the USA ... well any sport; these young athletes have

given their all (and the all of their families as well) to get to this time, this place to strut their stuff. Win or lose they are simply awesome.

The Conundrum:
So, this past Sunday I found myself heading into quite a tsunami; a perfect storm of sorts pitting three of my passions smack dab against one and other. Do I go to the movie that I have been waiting to see for several years now? Do I watch what I was sure to be an amazing tribute to the Beatles on TV? Or, do I opt for being inspired by the great young athletes of our time?

MOVIE AND MUSIC AND SPORTS – OH MY! All at the same time!

But wait. Can it be? Yes.

The Solution:
Afternoon movie, prime time viewing of Sir Paul and Ringo, and recorded replay of the Olympics! Who said that you can't have your cake and eat it too? The tsunami skirted past without any damage at all!

After what seems to be months of the doldrums of this winter weather; what a day I had!
Don't we live in just wonderful times?

# The Right to Sue

39 years ago I married a lawyer and my father decided to sue the world! I admit to thinking that the incredulity on my dad's face when Drew kept telling him that he had no case was very amusing. But, believe me when I say it all got old very quickly. My dad's desire to be compensated for every little slight (and some not so little) while at the time seeming funny, marked the burgeoning awareness on my part of what a litigious society we had become and continue to be.

Have you heard that Senator Rand Paul is suing President Obama over the whole NSA's gathering of telephone megadata? Officially the suit is titled Rand Paul v Barack Obama but also charged in the suit are Director of National Intelligence James Clapper, NSA Director Keith Alexander, FBI Director James Comey, and my very elderly Aunt Betty. Ok Ok, of course my Aunt is not cited in the law suit ... sorry guys I couldn't resist.

The Senator has the right to bring the suit. We all have the right to have our day in court. Aren't our rights part of what makes our country great?

Whether it was a faint whisper from my dad, long departed, or simply curiosity; I began to look further into the law suit. I was quite surprised to find that there are already multiple, similar suits including one brought by the ACLU in the courts now. That seemed odd to me. If there are already lawsuits aimed at holding the government responsible for what many feel to be a violation of our constitutionally given rights; why bring yet another one? Is it a frivolous suit? Has the good senator been stricken with the "my son-in-law's an attorney so I'm suing" syndrome?"

I found that not to be the case at all. Paul's case is unique because he is trying to get it certified as a class action suit. Basically this means, should it thus be certified, anyone feeling impacted wrongfully by the NSA actions can potentially join in the suit.

I still found the question of why the senator is doing this interesting. Of course one can truly never know why someone else does anything but there is a theory flying around that might shed some light.

Apparently when one uses the internet to get the skinny on the suit, they are directed to several websites for information. Then, once linking to those websites, they have given Rand Paul's organization their direct contact information. A win for Senator Paul who now has a whole slew of potential supporters that he wouldn't otherwise have; some maybe even feeling a bit beholden to the senator for giving them a chance to address their grievances.

It is no secret that the senator is being talked about as a possible Republican candidate for the Presidency in 2016. Even, should he decide against that run for the White House; he still has a senatorial re-election bid to fund. Whether a motivation or simply a very advantageous side benefit to the senator's aspirations, he will now have a significant increase in his potential donor list.

Whatever the motive for the suit, I applaud Senator Paul if for nothing else, amazing ingenuity. I can't help but wonder if my dad were still alive; would he be tempted to check it out?

# There Are Bad Men (Part 1)

With the end of the Olympics, I think most of us are happy to breathe a sigh of relief that the reported terrorist attacks which were predicted never came to fruition. Between learning of the existence and the intention of the so called "black widows" (a group of young Islamic fanatical women believed to have perpetrated deadly attacks in the past) to target the games; the world watched with bated breath as the days passed without incident. Phew...Putin must be relieved.

But wait. Can it be? Is it true that he couldn't even enjoy his "victory" over terrorism on the world stage?

It is said that he had to continually interrupt his Olympic watching to deal with the "oh so pesky" problem of a major rebellion in Kiev. He even spoke with President Obama about the situation on at least one occasion during the Games. And the Kremlin has confirmed, to also being in communication with German Chancellor Angela Merkel about the situation as well.

What was so important you might ask, as did I?

Though geography has never been my strong suit, I do know that Kiev is the capital of Ukraine and Ukraine was one of the Soviet Republics comprising the USSR. Other than that I didn't really know much else; didn't pay too much attention to the country...until now.

Ukraine is a strategically located country of 46 million people, with an educated workforce, a significant industrial base and good natural resources including rich farmland and yet its economy is in tatters; verging on bankruptcy.

Oh, I forgot to mention that while the country was circling the drain, President Viktor Yanukovych was bestowing huge monetary favors on his cronies and spending millions on his own personal collections of finery including dozens of priceless antique cars and even a private zoo located on the grounds of his personal residence.

So, what's going on?

The country is divided politically between those wanting to "westernize" and affiliate with the European Union and those holding firm to their ties with Russia. An agreement with the European Union was on the table when Yanukovych unilaterally opted instead to receive a loan from Russia.

Protesters by the thousands took to the streets of Kiev expressing their displeasure; displeasure with their President's nixing of the EU deal and displeasure with his obscenely corrupt management of a country that should be prosperous. After three months, Yanukovych had worked out a truce with the opposition but unfortunately the truce fell apart last week. Renewed mass protests prompted Yanukovych to send in national Security Forces who entered the scene firing on the protesters and all hell broke loose. When the dust settled the opposition said that at least 70 and as many as 100 people had been killed, while municipal authorities put the death toll at 39.

Political cronies dropped Yanukovych like the proverbial hot potato; his own party placing total responsibility upon his head. He was forced to flee the country to parts unknown avoiding the wrath of the people. An interim government is in place and is reportedly in pursuit of the fallen leader who will face charges of mass murder and corruption.

But the future of Ukraine is still up in the air. Like other populace revolts, getting rid of a bad man alone does not always lead to the hoped for results.

Meanwhile, Putin's Olympic euphoria was disrupted because inclusion of Ukraine is important to his own self-expressed vision of restoring the "greatness" of the Former Soviet Union; not to mention that Russia has a huge naval installation in Southern Ukraine!

Yes indeed there are bad men in the world.

# There Are Bad Men (Part 2)

We are a competition driven world. We, to put it simply, just love a good competitive fight whether as participants ourselves or as spectators. It is in our DNA. We want not only to pick a winner; we want to be the winner. And the past few weeks have afforded the world an opportunity to partake of the ultimate competition in two of our most beloved pastimes: sports and movies – the Olympics and the Oscars. While I looked forward to writing about these two of my favorite events as I had done in columns past, I am unable to do so because of what some bad men in the world are doing at this time. I wanted to dedicate last week's column to the Olympics but felt compelled to write about one such bad man in my column labelling it "Part 1." I didn't think I would be penning a "Part 2" column this soon. No, I wanted to dedicate this week's column to the Oscars and the amazing slate of really good movies that the industry produced last year. But lo and behold, another bad man has made that impossible as well.

Ousted President Viktor Yanukovych of Ukraine (my bad man of last week's column) is comfortably settled into an apartment in Moscow watching his country's civil unrest being exacerbated by Russian President Vladimir Putin (my bad man of this column).

The complex situation in Ukraine and its southern territory Crimea, in particular, is changing very quickly and not for the better. As of now armed, masked, military uniformed forces (with no nationality identified) have taken over the Crimean airports and naval installations. Peaceful, unarmed demonstrators against this obvious Russian backed action are now being threatened with bodily harm by the invaders. Like those demonstrators mowed down last week by Yanukovych forces in the Ukrainian Capital of Kiev who were protesting the President's abuse of power and corrupt governance, these protestors want a more "western" society" rather than a government that is so obviously in

Russia's back pocket ... and Putin doesn't like the competition.

Putin has an unashamed, unabashed desire - actually it is much more than desire... let's call it obsession, to recreate the super power of the Cold War USSR. He has called the break-up of the former Soviet Union the "greatest geopolitical disaster of the 20th century."

On Monday, German Chancellor Angela Merkel, after speaking with Putin directly, described him as being "delusional."

In a statement reported on Tuesday, Putin declared that the "masked men" running rough shod over the area are not Russians but a "Crimean Militia" comprised of local Russian speaking patriots responding to ill treatment by the "progressive factions" in Crimea. It must be noted that there have been no reports of any ill treatment or discrimination of any kind from the region against their Russian speaking citizenry but a defensive Putin declared it to be so.

And now there is word that 2 Russian Battleships are making their way through the Black Sea toward the Crimean port. In response, the Ukrainian Navy's "flagship" Destroyer is following the 2 Russian ships close behind.

This does not look good...

Tsk,tsk,tsk; c'mon Vlad, your Mother Russia captured first place in the Olympic medal count ... you're a winner. The world acknowledges it. Did you really have to start another competition so soon?

But, unlike the Olympics or the Oscars this is one competition that we neither want to watch nor compete in.

# There Are Bad Men (Part 3)

With everything going on in Crimea you might have missed the fact that there was an election in North Korea. After the death of Kim Jong Il, his son Kim Jong Un ascended to ruling power. This North Korean "mini me" now reigns supreme over the demonically oppressive country. For whatever reason, Kim Jong Un has gone through the motions of finally having himself elected.

I have been presenting a book this year at book clubs entitled The Orphan Master's Son. Winner of the fiction category Pulitzer Prize in 2012 , it is at times horrifying yet at others funny and heartwarming. It takes place in NK during the rule of Kim Jong Il yet by all accounts the "spot on" descriptions of life in North Korea not only remain true today but some reports indicate that if anything, the quality of life for North Koreans is worsening. After reading and discussing the book with various groups, I have to say, it's hard to believe that conditions could actually be worsening.

The author, Adam Johnson, has visited North Korea twice and while there are very few people who have managed to defect from the country, Johnson was able to interview several of them in his research for the book. Daily loudspeaker announcements (every abode and workplace must have the speakers) blast propaganda. Hunger is so prevalent that families defy the law and curfew by scaling trees after dark to gather nuts or raid ponds for fish trying to survive, knowing that if they are caught they will be sent to labor camps if not publically executed as an example to others.

The protagonist of the book takes the reader on a journey that seems almost "Forest Gumpish" in his ability to be at the right place, to gather the right information, learning the skills he will need, to navigate the grotesquely roiling seas that constitute life in North Korea. I highly recommend the book. While a complex work, not an easy read by any definition, it is more than worth the effort to get at the essence of the despotic reign the Jong's have had over their people.

Growing up, Kim Jong Un was not the heir apparent. His older brother was to take over when Kim Jong Il died. But the elder opted to go and live in China for the freedoms and quality of life to be enjoyed there instead of staying in his homeland.

OK. So what does that tell us of the life in NK if China is viewed as a place of freedom?
Anyway, Kim Jong Un seems to be needing to prove himself worthy; needs to establish himself as indeed the supreme leader. Reports from NK indicate that he has had his Uncle and all of his associates publically executed as traitors accused of planning a military takeover of the government. Rumors say that he had them ripped apart in a public execution by a multitude of wild dogs...possibly, intentionally infected with rabies.

Hard to believe? Read the book!

So, now Kim Jong Un has had his election and guess what? He won! He even received 100% of the votes. Of course he ran unchallenged for who in their right mind would dare to oppose him?

# I Smell a Movie

Isn't the missing Malaysian Flight 370 story heart wrenching? I can't even imagine what the families of those on board are going through. There are so many questions, so few answers and so many intriguing mysteries. Iranian passengers using stolen passports, no locater pings from the plane's detection devices since contact was lost, the mystery of the actual flight trajectory, theories and speculation as to what actually happened changing daily; but the fact remains, the plane has simply disappeared.

Malaysia has recently released data (why this took so long is anyone's guess!) indicating the last transmission received from the plane before the transponders were presumably turned off, put the plane between Malaysian and Vietnamese tracking capabilities which seems to indicate intentional foul play by someone very experienced in and or knowledgeable about the workings of the aircraft and area airport capabilities.

Now, finally, the United States and European nations have been asked to join in the search for answers. Attention is at last being focused on the pilot and co-pilot while the possible search area has expanded to encompass five million square miles. Five million square miles!

Believe me; I am not diminishing the horror of this story. Can you imagine the families, in interviews over the weekend, expressing hopefulness in the latest theory that the plane was hijacked? How desperate they must be to cling to that scenario, that scary scenario, just to feel that their loved ones are still alive?

But as frustrating and horrifying as this story is, you gotta admit it has all of the elements and possibilities of an amazing movie. With all of the classic disaster movies, the against all odds rescue movies, not to mention the insanely popular TV series Lost; I have to think that someone is, as I write this column, penning a proposal. What am I thinking? There are probably hundreds of them being drafted!

And, speaking of movies, have you seen the new "Coke Mini" commercial? (Just wait for it...I will tie this in!)

I'm sure you will agree that most commercials, to be kind, are either boring or ridiculous. But, some are really clever and given the quality of most TV shows, more enjoyable than the primetime fare. Anyway...

Enter the Coke Mini ad.

So, Coke is touting its new smaller can option in this really good TV spot. As one who rarely finishes the standard size, the smaller can is good for me and I've got to say, a great marketing idea. But an even better marketing idea is the basis for the commercial...famous lines from classic movies.

Even for non-movie buffs, the lines featured in the ad are ones we have all heard a bazillion times; lines that have become part of the American lexicon. "I'm the king of the world" from, Titanic, "I'll have what she's having" from, When Harry Met Sally. "You lookin' at me?" from, Taxi Driver; to name a few.

The ad then brilliantly ends with Cuba Gooding Jr. parodying his famous (Oscar winning) line from Jerry McGuire, "Show me the "mini!" Very smart ad copy!

So what does all of this have to do with Flight 370?

I think you all join me in the sincere hope that the Malaysian flight 370 movie will be one of suspense and intrigue ending in the reuniting of the unharmed passengers with their families. And that what we all will remember in the future about the ordeal is a really great line from the film.

# Zombie Bees

Drew has often said that the very best insect repellent for him is to have me at his side. For some reason, I attract all of the pesky biting flyers and creepy crawly nippers leaving him unscathed to totally enjoy whatever outdoor activity we are attending. Lucky me!

With my obvious insect magnetism, I am a bit perplexed by the fact that there is one exception...I have never been stung by a bee; not wasp nor hornet either for that matter. The bugs of the buzzing variety just don't want to have anything to do with me. I repeat: lucky me!

While the sight and sound of the stinging villains usually sends people running, the production of honey from those same bees draws people into stores like flies...uh, well, you know what I mean. Who doesn't like honey? And who wouldn't like to have really fresh honey from the hive?

Apparently, I am not the only one thinking about this; but unlike me, there are many others who are acting on it. Between 1999 and 2012 there has been a 220% rise in beekeeping. And it is not only in rural, farm settings. A new trend has been documented...city apiaries. Young, health conscious urban dwellers are swarming to tend bees and thus gather their own honey. These "Eulee's" of the metropolis have set up hives on rooftops and porches, empty lots and backyards. The trend is spreading across the country.

Sounds great, no?

But wait. Can there be a downside to this seemingly win-win situation?

Enter the Mutant Zombie Bees. Yes, I did say zombie bees. Can it get much scarier than that? The walking dead incorporating that infernal buzzing and a stinger to boot!

It is deathly dark; not star nor moon to be seen. A faint noise wafts from the forest before me. I don't know where I am or what is producing that sound but it sends a shiver of fear coursing up my spine and as it reaches my brain the sound becomes familiar. The buzzing of bees? No, it's not the constant buzz of a bee yet it seems rather to be some maniacal "zzzing" of a distant tragedy waiting to happen; the hum of some ungodly species. And then I see them. Hoards of dirty, rag wrapped bees, man-sized creatures circling before me with "Star War" light sabers for stingers deadly glistening in the night....this is the stuff of nightmares!

But it is no nightmare, no science fiction plot; zombie bees are real and on the rise. First discovered on the West Coast, they have now been popping up in the Northeast as well. Can the Midwest be far behind?

They are called "the flying dead" and act like the ghoulish creatures of horror films. They fly at night which "normal bees" just don't do. Their flight is circular and methodically continues until they can fly no more and then they drop to the ground staggering, zombielike in the same circular pattern toward any light source until they die.

The mutation is thought to be caused by the fly, Apocephalus Borealis which latches onto European honeybees – common across the U.S. – and lays eggs in the bees that eventually hatch and wreak havoc on their systems leaving them by one scientist's definition "a combination of zombie and alien mixed together."

But, no need to go screaming into the night just yet. There doesn't appear to be any data suggesting these zombies are any more dangerous to humans than your run of the mill honeybees... just spookier.

Nonetheless, I'll keep my attractiveness to the flying bitters and be glad for it, if that is what is keeping the bees away from me...zombies or otherwise.

# The Inner Oort Cloud

Star Trek had been on the air for many seasons. Captain Kirk is clad in his iconic skin tight Star Fleet uniform though it is now bulging a bit, stretching over his no longer svelte middle. Honestly, did no one except me notice that the once built William Shatner had aged into an older, flabbier version of himself and required the uniform to be adapted to his new size and shape?

Anyway he stands, serious, in charge, at his command post on the bridge.

"Mr. Sulu, location update," he authoritatively requests.

"Captain, we are entering the 'Inner Oort Cloud,'" comes Sulu's immediate reply.

"Spock, any details on the object we spotted?" The Captain turns his attention to his First Officer.

"Captain," begins his pointy-eared compatriot. "It appears to be that new, recently discovered dwarf planet, 2012VP113."

"Specifics, Mr. Spock?"

"It is 7.5 billion miles away from Earth's sun in an area that is commonly referred to as 'the Badlands or Wasteland.' It's in a region of the Earth's solar system known as the Kuiper Belt," Spock drones on. "What's interesting, Jim, is that its orbit is elliptical which in all likelihood would indicate that the dwarf planet is composed of ice even though the surface appears to be reddish in color."

Pushing a few buttons on a handheld gadget, Spock continues. "And the surface temperature reading is at minus 432 degrees Fahrenheit.

Kirk appears to be pondering this information.

"Captain, shall I send our standard greeting in all of the languages known to us to see if any life forms respond?" asks Communication's Officer Uhura.

"Or perhaps we should beam a search party to its surface to explore further?" Sulu pipes in.

The Captain paces around his command chair in silent contemplation.

"What do you think, Bones?" He turns to Dr. McCoy who pauses for effect before answering.

"Jim, not much chance of any life forms at that temperature."

With confident determination, Kirk falls into his chair. "Take us out of here Mr. Sulu. After all, it's only a dwarf planet. Warp speed ahead!"

O.K. So maybe that was a bit hokey, but all of Mr. Spock's facts are true. Scientists have discovered a new dwarf planet in the Inner Oort Cloud, beyond Pluto.

Wow, recently demoted little dwarf planet Pluto has a new playmate!

What exactly constitutes a dwarf planet as opposed to a planet planet anyway?

To quote Chad Trujillo, co-discoverer of the new dwarf, "a bona fide planet is big enough that other objects will be sucked into it gravitationally. A dwarf planet is not big enough to become gravitationally dominant; it's too small to pull in objects in the area of its path."

Well, I'm glad we got that straightened out.

Now, let's get back to 2012VP113. While Captain Kirk might think it only to be a dwarf planet thus not needing further exploration; its discovery has scientists very excited. It opens up a "whole universe" of possibilities including better understanding of just how our solar system was formed and what else could be out there waiting to be discovered.

Oooh, you have to admit, new planets, new possibilities, the "Inner Oort Cloud;" it's way cool... and a bit "Star Trekkie," don't you think?"

# Alaska, Russia

Our right, our individual right, to petition the government is guaranteed by the 1st amendment of the Constitution. Did you know that if anyone can get 100,000 signatures on a petition and submits it to the White House it will be reviewed by government policy experts with the possibility of action on the issue by Congress? Neither did I ... how cool is that?

So, what kind of issues are we talking about? Well, there is one such petition circulating now that has an impressive 30,000 signatures so far. It demands that the United States give Alaska back to Russia. Yeah, they think that we should just give it back. Now, while I don't know their rationale for this, it does make me think of an interesting result if that were to happen.

Just imagine. If this petition gets legs and eventually ends up passing Congress (I know, I know, but just bear with me) instead of just being able to see Russia from her property, Sarah Palin would actually live in Russia. (For those of you who have been reading my columns from their inception - and I thank you for that! - You know that I was less than thrilled with John McCain's choice for Vice President. Should you want to read my thoughts on the former Governor of Alaska search "Sarah Palin" in the search box.)

Anyway, can you just imagine Palin's property becoming part of a Russian state; Sarah Palin living in Russia? Oh the fodder for Tina Fey's Saturday Night Live sketches would just be too good!

Now, now, for all of you Palin fans out there who are disgusted even angry at me for dissing Palin, come on, you have to admit, it would be funny. But what is really funny is there's not only noise coming from the United States side for ceding Alaska back to Russia but from the Russian side as well.

Apparently, the leader of Yakutsk, Aisen Nikolayer, wants to take back Spruce Island, one of the Aleutian Islands, claiming "historical justification" for the action. Yep, he wants to just take back Spruce Island, officially part of Alaska, from the United States.

Obviously, being spurred on by Russia's grab of Crimea, Nikolayer has been emboldened to make a grab of his own.

Oh yes, remember, not very long ago we were all inundated with reports of how Russia was on the brink of trying to re-institute the cold war? Crimea was said to be only the first step on Russia's ascension to the top of the Super Power ladder. Putin was on a path to reconstruct the Former Soviet Union through aggression and invasion of its former Soviet State neighbors. But that furor has died down (that is not to say that Putin has put his ambitions to bed) but now a little known politician from a little known region in eastern Russia seems to want his 30 minutes of fame by piggybacking on the international media frenzy surrounding the Crimea take-over.

Well, obviously there is little chance of Nikolayer attaining his goal …

But, what if?

Hey, I have an idea. Nikolayer and those 30,000 petitioners should get together. Form a PAC. Go to Las Vegas and meet with Sheldon Adelson in a casino parking lot … now we're getting serious.
Whoa, Sarah, better get those binoculars out. "The Russians Are Coming."

# Running Amok

When I heard of the latest killing spree at Fort Hood my first thought was, oh no not again! Incidents of mass killings in every demographic of modern life are becoming so commonplace, it seems that many of us are simply becoming numbed to the horror of them.

For some reason, the term "running amok" came to mind.

Have you ever mentally followed your own train of thought? You know, went through the unconscious progression of how a thought goes from one subject to another and then another until you end up mentally with something that had nothing whatsoever to do with the thought with which you started?

That is exactly how I found myself thinking about running amok. That was it. While beginning with the Fort Hood killings I ended up with how we seem to be in a society that is simply running amok. Now, not at all numbed, my attention became focused.

Running amok; what a strange phrase, one that all of a sudden seemed the perfect description for the craziness that seems to be so pervasive in our society today.

Coincidentally, a few days after the latest Fort Hood tragedy, I had lunch with a friend who is an anthropologist and I brought up "running amok" in our conversation. She told me that "amok" was a medically acknowledged condition, running amok an actual psychiatric diagnosis.

Who knew? So, I figured I'd better take a look at the expression.

"Running amok is considered a rare culture-bound syndrome by current psychiatric classification systems, but there is evidence that it occurs frequently in modern industrialized societies." So stated Manuel Saint Martin, M.D., J.D. in a paper published in 1999.

Apparently, except for psychiatrists, few in the medical community realize that running amok is a bona fide, albeit antiquated, psychiatric syndrome.

I didn't know that! I thought it was just one of those expression in our common lexicon. You know one of those expressions that we all just use. But, who knew it was an actual medical condition?

Now, back to Fort Hood. I can't remember combat veterans from WWII or even Vietnam committing seemingly senseless multiple murders after their return. I know that suicides and domestic violence are endemic, that PTSD is a very real and serious reality that we as a society, to date, haven't done enough about combatting. But, what I have learned about "running amok" puts it into a bit of a different light.

These mass murders, including those committed by recently returning vets, should be telling us that our society, current societal influences are part and parcel to answering the why of their happening so often now where there were so many fewer and farther between occurrences in the past.

The pervasiveness of violence, violence often perpetrated upon multiple victims, the abundance of uber violence on T.V., in movies, video games and even advertising is not only a disturbing commentary on who/what we are as a society but, according to what I read about "running amok," a contributing factor to the question: Why now? Why can't those of us of a certain age remember it ever being this bad?

We are all fast to blame mental illness, the stresses of combat, abusive upbringings and a plethora of other contributing factors but maybe it is time to think about our own complicity. Our communal "societal complicity."

# Look Again At Former Justice Stevens

Shortly after his appointment to the Supreme Court I had the opportunity to speak with Former Justice John Paul Stevens. During our conversation, I found him to be unassuming, rather glib in a funny way and really quite nice. His opinions on the Court proved him to be a moderate/liberal (although being appointed by a Republican President) and are public record. His decisions are noted for precision, elegance and common sense. His demeanor while on the Court remained true to the soft-spoken, always sporting his signature bowtie, and in truth kind of dull personality with whom I had spoken so many years ago.

The former "Supreme" has continued his low-key persona during his retirement, seldom being seen in public or making few if any public statements.

Not anymore!

His new book released April 22, 2014, "Six Amendments: How and Why We Should Change the Constitution" details changes he feels necessary to protect our democracy and the safety and wellbeing of American citizens.

In an interview with George Stephanopoulus, the former Supreme addressed 2 of his suggestions which are causing the greatest stir. And I mean STIR amongst not only the talking heads but throughout Washington.

1. He wants to add 5 words to the Second Amendment which would then grant the right to bear arms only to those "serving in a state militia." Thus eliminating any personal "Constitutional Right" to bear arms.

He contends that our Founding Father's intent for the 2nd amendment was to insure that a state has the ability to defend itself from "attack." He urged remembrance of the context in which the Constitution was written. The new nation was untested. He feels the 2nd amendment was merely a safeguard against military action against any given state.

2. He wants to add an amendment forbidding gerrymandering undertaken with the intent "to impose political power."

When pressed on how to determine gerrymandering he referred to the famous quote by Potter Stewart regarding pornography, "I know it when I see it."

WOW. Could he have chosen 2 more incendiary issues to break with his long standing reputation of quiet diligence?

Other additions/changes he is suggesting in the book deal with Anti-commandeering, Campaign Finance, Sovereign Immunity, and the "Death Penalty.

Already critics are calling his appeals for these changes ridiculous and totally unrealistic as to any possibility of passage. When Stephanopoulos cited those comments, the Supreme's response was that just because an issue is difficult does not mean they shouldn't be fought for. He went on to acknowledge that with the current political climate in Washington he does appreciate his critics' comments.

Another fact that came out of the interview which I found to be quite interesting is that Gerald Ford, near the end of his life, wrote that he considered appointing Stevens to the Court the action he was the most proud of during his presidency.

While nothing to do with the book, I found it interesting and hope you do too.
Anyway, I hope that Former Justice Steven's manifesto on how the Constitution needs to be changed will be, if nothing else, a catalyst for some serious examination

and discussion on how we can make our government work better.

Hate to be cynical but there is about as much chance of that happening as there is of getting Justice Stevens to ditch those bowties of his!

# Best Sellers and Banned Books

Last week was Banned Book Week. Betcha didn't know that! Well, don't feel badly, neither did I. Who knew that every year the State of America's Library releases a list of the books that have had the most challenges to their suitability for citizens to read with the recommendation of banning. Being a lover of books and a strong advocate for our right of freedom of speech, I found this very disturbing. Banning books...really?

So, I looked into it and what I found was absurd to the point of being comical. Novels making the list in the past include both Huckleberry Finn and Tom Sawyer, Gone With the Wind, The Grapes of Wrath, The Great Gatsby, For Whom the Bell Tolls and To Kill a Mockingbird; just to list a few. To many these titles and others on the list are considered modern day classics.

While I feel that one's taste in reading material is purely a personal matter, there is a book currently on the best seller list that has me baffled. At 696 pages, economist Thomas Picketty's "Capital in the 21st Century's" rise to best seller status surprised not only its publisher but the author as well. Personally, I would probably be more apt to use it as a doorstop than read it but what it deals with obviously is appealing to many.

Another newly released book, Elizabeth Warren's "A Fighting Chance" (at a mere 384 pages!) is also getting lots of hype...and sales. When I say it is getting hype, I mean it is getting HYPE. Senator Warren (representing the state of Massachusetts) has been making the rounds to promote it on any and all T.V. shows she can schedule and giving interviews to any and all print media outlets as well. This book could also be an adequate doorstop but Picketty has Warren beat by a mile!

What I find interesting is that a major portion of both books, I'm told, deals with the ever-growing state of wealth inequality. This problem is raising great concern for many here in the United States, as it should. The statement that "a country is only as strong as its middle class" has become a very "hot topic." If you don't believe me take a look at the numbers of people buying the senator and Picketty's books.

Adding fuel to the fire, concern about our diminishing middle class was reinforced by some newly released statistics. For the first time since such statistics have been compiled, the middle class in the United States is not ranked #1 in the world. Our neighbor to the north has usurped that status. Canada's middle class appears to be thriving in part because their tax structure (measurably higher than ours) allows the country to provide, among other things, healthcare and college tuition to its citizens free of charge. Apparently, Canadians feel that high tax rates are worth it if they can see the benefits.

U.S. tax rates are currently the lowest among the industrialized nations of the world. It is not surprising that many want to keep it that way. But economists are citing that fact as a contributing factor in our waning middle class. They suggest that raising the taxes of the 1% is not the only solution. Raising taxes across the board is suggested as a good start to addressing the problem.

OUCH! I wonder. Do you think that when next year's "banned books" list is released Dr. Picketty and Senator Warren's offerings will be included?

# To Kill or Not to Kill-Is that the Question?

Every so often something happens in that sterile room with invited witnesses in attendance behind the glass wall, that brings the controversy of should we as a nation have the death penalty as an option for punishment of convicted felons or not. While the numbers in favor of the death penalty are down in the polls, still the majority of Americans agree that we should have the option of killing perpetrators of heinous crimes.

In all honesty, I keep vacillating on the issue and here is why.

1. The advancement of DNA testing and other forensic science tools have identified many death row inmates and many of those already executed to have been innocent of the crimes for which they were sentenced to this irreversible punishment.

2. The death sentence is not carried out equally. Three times more people of color convicted of the exact same crimes as their white counterparts receive the sentence of death.

3. While I do value human life, I also believe that we have unrepentant monsters in this world and, to put it bluntly, I want them to die.

4. And on what some might consider a crass note, it is actually less expensive to house an inmate in prison for life than to, forgive the pun; "execute" the death penalty. Now before you write to tell me that that seems counterintuitive, it's the astronomical cost of all of the appeals required by law in death penalty cases that contributes to this fact.

While not a huge Stephen King fan, I can't help but think about his book/film, "The Green Mile" (which by the way if you have never seen the movie, rent it). In it some of my conflicted attitudes about the subject of capital punishment are exposed. There is a botched electric chair execution purposefully perpetrated by a sadistic guard. There is also the execution of an innocent, and I mean a really innocent man! Watch the film. You'll see why I stress his innocence.

But, back to real life...and death. We now have this whole botched execution in Oklahoma shining a light on these and the other troubling issues surrounding the death penalty controversy once again. Can someone please tell me why on every TV crime drama we see a virtual plethora of ways to commit murder by the injection of mass doses of something; say insulin or heroin just to name two, yet Oklahoma couldn't kill Clayton Lockett in a civil manner? (Please pardon the oxymoron!)

What in the world makes legal execution so much more difficult? Are "new and better" techniques only a pat on our collective backs in the name of progress or to assuage our consciences that it's ok to kill if it is done humanely? Has any real progress been made in civilizing the death penalty when the Guillotine was swift and seemingly painless?

There is just so much to be concerned about with this whole to kill or not to kill dilemma. I hope that you agree that if we are going to kill we should at least be sure that those convicted are indeed guilty. We should enforce this most drastic of sentences equally among the races and for Pete's sake, if we do kill; we should do it well.

## Do You Really Want to Boycott Israeli Products?

I am, and for 10 years have been, an unabashed fan of Grey's Anatomy. I wholeheartedly agreed that McDreamy was jaw-droppingly dreamy and that McSteamy was steamy indeed. While in all honesty there were low points in the plotlines through the years, I remained loyal and was subsequently rewarded with powerful character development and interesting medical solutions to oftentimes obscure ailments.

One of the mainstay characters is leaving the show after its decade run. Heart surgeon wunderkind; Christina Yang, played by the very talented Sandra Oh, is going to head up a too-good-to-be-true (but she is assured it really is that good) Swiss facility where futuristic dreams of medical technological advancements are actually being practiced.

We ardent fans, knowing Christina the way we do, understand that it would take something so profound, so incredible, so revolutionary to lure her away from her Grey's kinships; well it would be almost impossible. And yet, last week there it was: a holographic reproduction of a beating heart...the actual heart of the patient on the table, beating in real time.

With jaw having not recovered from its dropping at seeing the image, Christine listened as it was explained that the image can be manipulated by touch and even sliced open virtually, offering an unprecedented opportunity for guidance before taking the knife to the patient. The availability of such technology will significantly improve the success rates of not only heart surgery but virtually all surgery as well...and the best part is it is not science fiction created by the writing staff. It is real, conceived and designed in the small northern city of Yokneam in Israel.

Ever since Israel became a nation (actually even before) the Arab states have been calling for the world to boycott Israeli products. Through the years these boycotts have taken on various permutations and the parameters have expanded. Many academics have chosen not to attend conferences in Israel and not to invite Israeli scientists and innovators to their conferences. Products from Israel are on many "no buy" lists and some academic institutions have joined a "divestment" campaign eliminating Israeli companies from their endowment portfolios all as a show of support for the Palestinians in their conflict with Israel.

The boycott can be a very effective tool utilized by those feeling aggrieved. I firmly support anyone or any group in their right to utilize that tool. But I wonder if those supporting these boycotts realize that they can never buy another cell phone? If they should need kidney dialysis they cannot get it and should they or a loved one require intricate surgery, the cutting edge 3D holographic imaging device seen on Grey's Anatomy could not be used. Of course these are just three of the technologies that Israel has played an instrumental part in developing and producing.

When I am finished with this column I will be saving it to a USB flash drive, thumb drive "thingie" where I store all of my columns. Oh, sorry boycotters, yet another piece of technology you all can't have...

And so I ask: Do You Really Want to Boycott Israeli technology and products?

# Women in Journalism - Two Classy Broads

There are two stories in the news; one is all but over the other is still a brewin'. Both are examples of not only the role of women in journalism but of the larger conundrum of compensation disparity between men and women in the workplace. Of course I am referring to the retirement of Barbara Walters and the firing of New York Times executive editor, Jill Abramson.

When I was young I wanted to be Barbara Walters. There, I have said it. I watched every televised interview she conducted. I was glued to every special of hers that aired and I even interviewed my dog with hairbrush microphone in hand in mock "Walters' style."

Almost six decades ago, Ms. Walters began her T.V. journalism career in a world strictly controlled and populated by men. She "scratched and clawed" her way to becoming the person considered to be the most influential woman in the history of journalism. Most notably in her list of "firsts" is being the first woman to anchor a network nightly newscast and the first woman in journalism to earn that so well publicized million dollar salary.

She faced such blatant discrimination, with no one even questioning it; it is hard for young women of today to believe it could have taken place. When her cohost of the evening news demanded that she not be allowed to ask any of the "serious, hard hitting questions," instead of throwing a fit (which frankly I might have done) she persuaded the powers that be to let her conduct in-depth interviews...not in the studio. Thus her status of "The Interviewer" began and to this day she can still nab the must see interviews that other journalists only dream about.

She remains one classy broad!

One of the multitudes of women who should send Ms. Walters flowers on a monthly basis in thanks for paving the way in journalism for our sex is Jill Abramson. My guess is that you have heard about New York Times owner and CEO Arthur O Sulzberger's unceremonious firing last week of Ms. Abramson from her post as executive editor of the Times. As Ms. Abramson is not talking about the circumstances of her dismissal, lots of speculation has been flying around.

Mr. Sulzberger, on the other hand, has issued two statements which have raised many eyebrows. He denies the action was taken in response to her questioning whether or not her compensation package was equal to that of her predecessor, a theory allegedly supported by Ms. Abramson's meeting with an attorney to look into a possible discrimination action.

Jill Abramson is the first woman to hold the editorial reins at the Times and the only woman to be running a major newspaper. She is known industry-wide as a truth-telling, no nonsense professional with what some have called an abrasive management style. None of this was unknown to Sulzberger when he gave her the job. She had been working for him as both managing editor and bureau chief for 13 years prior to getting the executive editor's post. Yet these are the exact reasons he cited for justifying her dismissal. Uh, I don't know about you, but I'm not buying that those are the reasons she got the ax.

Abramson delivered the commencement address at Wake Forest College on Monday without going into any details of the whys and wherefores of her firing but rather telling the graduates that losing a job you love hurts. She went on to say that it was the honor of her life to lead the newsroom at the Times.

She remains one classy broad!

But her firing has highlighted once again a huge problem for women in the workforce. The compensation disparity between men and women is well-documented. Women still make only 57 cents to their male counterpart's earning of a dollar. In journalism women make only 83% of what the good old boys make for the same jobs.

So, now both of these women find themselves in the position of seeking a new reality for their future. Both have said that they look forward to new challenges. Both are inspirations. Both show that tenacity and smarts can prevail. Both are proof that discrimination in journalism is not a thing of the past, but like nationwide stats throughout all industries, still exists today.

And, both remain classy broads!

# Memorial Day Look at the VA

At age nineteen with one year of college under his belt, my father-in-law, Marv, was drafted and sent to an officer's training course. The Second World War was proceeding. With injuries and death tolls rising, he felt that he could better service his country as a PFC right away rather than continue training to become an officer. That was the kind of guy he was.

Handsome and funny, smart and compassionate, he was that man both women and men just wanted to be around. As an anti-tank gunner, he found himself in France approaching a town that had been taken by American troops. They were supposed to be holding the town. His Unit had not gotten the word that his fellow Americans had recently pulled out.

They were ambushed, the Unit commander killed and Marv was seriously injured. After being sent home, he entered the Veteran's Administration healthcare system. He was luckier than thousands of other soldiers. He lived.

After multiple surgeries, bone graphs and treatments, his only lasting physical consequence of the war was limited mobility in one arm, constant pain...and an addiction to painkillers and anti-depressants that he managed to hide so well, no one knew about.

He raised two terrific sons, always made a living that provided for his family's needs and died from his adult abuse of medication mixed with alcohol at age 56.

When Drew and I were helping to clean out the family home after his death, we found cases, multiple cases of the drugs hidden among the boxes lining the garage walls. They had been sent to him by the VA. When we asked the family doctor about them he was shocked. He had written prescriptions from time to time, through the years, for his friend Marv. After all, there were lasting effects from his ordeal. But, the Doc was totally unaware that the V.A. was sending Marv the drugs by the case.

At the time we didn't question the actions of the V.A. You just didn't do that back then. I am not blaming the V.A. for his drug abuse just for helping to make it so easy.

Now, we have this horrific scandal, apparently well documented, that our valiant, injured, returning military personnel are not only being mistreated but in some cases literally ignored to death.

Some are saying the unanticipated huge number of casualties and not enough funds are the culprits. But I'm told that Congress has allocated the equivalent of $30,000 per year per injured combatant. If the system is so overcrowded, why not give that money to the injured for them to procure their own insurance?

Or better yet, why not give that money to Medicare and have our returned heroes have their healthcare expenses paid as our retirees do, within a system that seems to be working?

This week of Memorial Day when we take time to honor our fighting men and women both who served in the past and are currently active, let us also take time to do whatever we can to insure that we take care of our injured returning heroes to the very best of our ability.

All those many years ago when my father-in-law was silently suffering, something was very wrong with the system and ours is just one story. Marv never recovered from his tour of duty. He never saw his grandchildren. Veterans today are needlessly dying. Surely we can do better.

# Edward Snowden: Traitor or Patriot?

Did you see the interview Brian Williams conducted with Edward Snowden last week? I must confess to not having seen the whole thing but those portions I did see left a lasting impression and a great deal of confusion.

Edward Snowden is a soon to be 33 year old computer professional born in North Carolina. Never completing high school due to illness, he received his GED from a local community college. By all accounts he is a really smart kid with a patchwork of community college and internet college credits never amounting to a degree in anything.

He enlisted in a program to fast track his entry into a Special Forces unit in the U.S. Army Reserves. He has stated that he broke both legs in training and was discharged. Army records only indicate that he was discharged. He says that from there he got a job as a security guard in a covert NSA facility at the U. of Maryland. The government says that the program was not NSA but a government / U. of Maryland partnership program in the Center for Advanced Study of Language and it was certainly not a classified facility.

He says he was a highly trained spy, the government says he was a low level system analyst.
Wow – will the real Edward Snowden please stand up!

Of his expertise in the field of cyber stuff there is no doubt. What is in doubt is exactly what his jobs with the CIA, DIA, NSA, Dell and Booz Allen Hamilton really entailed.

Everyone agrees that he held a consulting position with the NSA that allowed him access to classified information. He says when he realized that the rights of Americans were being trampled upon; he reported his concerns (before releasing any information to the public) through the proper, official channels and received nothing but dead-end responses. The NSA says that in Snowden's correspondence he did not "raise allegations or concerns about wrongdoing or abuse," according to the Office of the Director of National Intelligence.

When asked why he then leaked the documents he said, "The reality is, the situation determined that this needed to be told to the public." Snowden went on to say that a massive scaled violation of the rights guaranteed by the Constitution had occurred. Concluding that he was a patriot who broke the law in an act of civil disobedience and what is right isn't necessarily legal.

The government's position seems to be that he is simply a traitor.

Snowden has been charged under the Espionage Act about which I knew nothing. But, apparently those charges do not allow for a "whistle blowers" defense if he were to go to trial. To his mind this means that were he to come back to "face the music" as many are imploring him to do, he would spend the rest of his life in prison.

The Edward Snowden I saw in the interview was composed, presented himself as highly intelligent and articulate, seemed utterly sincere and quite frankly was believable. But if indeed he is a highly trained, covert-operations-trained spy, as he himself contends, wouldn't he have the skills to come across in just that way?

I think it is purely a matter of perception whether or not you believe his story or that of the government. But, in the end, does it really matter which Edward Snowden; traitor or patriot you feel him to be. The one thing not in contention is that he did indeed leak classified information. Even he admits that he did break the law. The only question seems to be, do the ends justify the means?

# The Bowe-Brody Connection

By the time you read this, I will be on vacation...WAHOO! The reason I am letting you know is that this column and the next will have been written a while before you read them. Just in case any major, new developments occur in the meantime you'll know why I have not taken them into account.

O.K. then...

So, we are now experiencing a huge brouhaha over the release by the Taliban of Sgt. Bowe Bergdahl, whom they have been holding for 5 years; in exchange for our releasing 5 Taliban bad guys that we have been holding in GITMO. Bowe has been taking a beating in the media, as has the President. The questions of the circumstances of Bowe's "capture" by the Taliban, the allegation that others lost their lives trying to find him, and the deal the President struck for his return are fueling very loud, very angry, and in my opinion very premature responses to the situation.

I don't know how he came to be captured. I don't know if he wandered into a capture or if he intended to "defect."

No one knows.

What we do know is that when he first disappeared, the report made by Military investigators stated that all of his comrades spoke highly of him. No mention of anything about his anti-American sentiments which are being so widely spread about now, appear in the report. And, there was no determination able to be reached as to what had actually happened to him.

Officials in the White House have stated that they had spoken several times of launching a rescue to bring him home but because Bowe had attempted to escape from the Taliban at least twice that we know of, his captors jacked up the manpower guarding him and were constantly moving him which made the logistics of a rescue impossible. Why is no one talking about Bowe's escape attempts? Does someone wanting to be with the Taliban keep trying to escape?

Well, if you watch as I do the Showtime series, Homeland, you might have some ideas. Homeland is based on an Israeli show. The Israeli writer/producer interviewed scads of returned POW's who had been held by fundamentalists, to be precise about how he portrayed the treatment of prisoners. Being the mother of a soldier who fought in 3 wars with the Israeli Army, I can tell you from personal accounts that the treatment of Showtime's "Brody" at the hands of his fundamentalist captors was spot on accurate.

Seeing the video that has been released of Bowe in captivity and listening closely to the accounts of those congress people viewing another video not yet released to the public, makes me think that this is a man who was tortured, drugged and God knows what else.

Whether he was captured or went to the Taliban of his own freewill; they were holding and mistreating an American soldier. We do not leave anyone of our fighting forces behind.

Only time will tell if we ever learn what really happened. But to my mind, however it turns out; we had to bring him home. If it makes those already having tried and convicted him feel any better; bringing him home was the only way to have him stand trial if offences were committed.

As I sat watching the steady breaking down of Brody by his captors, Sunday night after Sunday night, my heart was breaking right along with Brody's spirit. We can only hope that art has not imitated life in Bowe's case.

# The G-7, Normandy and Love Actually

The G-7 had a meeting in France. Before the leaders of the member countries adjourned to make the trip to Normandy for the commemoration ceremonies of the D-Day invasion; President Obama and the Prime Minister of England, David Cameron, held a joint press conference. I watched most of it but in all honesty my mind kept drifting back to the movie "Love Actually."

In it the newly elected British Prime Minister, played by the adorable Hugh Grant, is meeting with the lecherous U.S. President, played by Billie Bob Thornton. Much to the objections of his advisors, the Prime Minister has decided to be totally conciliatory in his dealings with the American President.

But when the Clinton-esque President puts a move on the Prime Minister's love interest (who happens to be a Monica look-alike...yeah that Monica!) all bets are off. Grant's character pulls the rug out from under Thornton's character at their joint press conference totally blind-siding him; much to the surprise of the assembled press corps and the Prime Minister's own staff as well.

But there were no such news worthy surprises on the part of either head of state at this "actual" press conference.

What was interesting however, was the speculation on how the newly ousted from the then G-8, Russian President Vlad Putin would be treated at the Normandy festivities to which he was invited.

With Europe's utter dependence on Russian oil, Prime Minister Cameron et al must walk a very fine line with Vlad vis-a-vis our President's call for more stringent sanctions on Russia in response to Vlad's annexation of Crimea and interference in Ukraine.

So, the question was: how would this tricky situation be handled?

Well, just leave it to the French!

The President of France arranged for a "Thanksgiving dinner schedule allowing the families of both of the newlywed couple to be appeased." President Obama was invited to dinner while Vlad was invited to a later in the evening supper.

O.K. one problem solved, but what about the placement of the heads of state in the obligatory photo of all of the attendees in Normandy?

Well, you can be the judge of how that turned out. Our President was positioned, front row next to the Queen of England just to the left of the center. Vlad was several people further off to the right of center next to...who was that woman...Oh yes, the Queen of Norway.

And then there was poor Angela Merkel (why she was there is a mystery to me given that Germany was the enemy of the D-Day invasion). She was relegated to the very back row.

Do you think a statement was being made?

Anyway, back to the Press Conference...

While David Cameron is no Hugh Grant and President Obama is far from his Clinton-esque counterpart in "Love Actually;" I was hoping to hear something less predictable from one of them at the press conference. Come on guys, couldn't you give us something? What about a jab at Vlad regarding his ousting from the G-8? Or how about a real zinger aimed at the disgraceful slaughter in Syria? Nothing? Really? Nada?

Maybe the drama of world politics needs a new screenwriter. What do you think? I wonder if the writers of "Love Actually" are available.

# Our Children's World

I missed my annual Father's Day column because I was very busy being "hands on Grandma" to two of my grandchildren who live very far away. While I feel badly about the column...Uh well, actually I don't feel too badly as I had almost two full, glorious weeks spoiling, cuddling and yes even gently scolding my two and four year old angels. While Skype is great there is nothing that can compare to that in person hug with the whispered "I love you Omi."

Why they call me Omi is for another column!

So, Father's Day has passed but I did see a Father's Day news snippet that caught my eye.

When I was running the Purdue North Central Sinai Forum my dream speaker was the future King of England: Prince William. All interviewers or Executive Directors of speakers' series for that matter yearn to snag that elusive, international figure about whom most everyone is curious. During my tenure William went from adorable child to motherless teen to Air Force Pilot to husband and now to father of Prince George.

And this Father's Day...Prince George walked!

Yes, the first born heir of the future King of England (and an exact "Mini Me" of William) was on the news walking, kicking at a soccer ball, grabbing hold of a polo mallet and simply enchanting the cameras at a charity event held on Father's Day. As I held two members of the future generation in my arms, I was watching yet another member of it teetering about on the "telly."

Simple pleasure for sure.

But then there were the constant news reports about the total disintegration of any kind of peace in Iraq at which I managed to cast cursory glances and my great joy in the prospect of the future for these babies became replaced by an ominous foreboding. Try as I might, I still find it creeping into my thoughts.

What a mess! There is certainly enough blame to go around in this situation and to be honest the questions so far out way the answers; only frustration comes when I try to sort it out in my mind.

Most seem to agree that the U.S. should do something but what in the world that something should be is up for grabs. Yes we are war weary and any of you that have read my columns on the subject of war (any war) know that I never want to "put boots on the ground" again. But are there situations that call for the risking of our precious children's lives? And more importantly, is this one such situation?

I think not.

The President of Iraq is a Shiite thug. As I type, our Secretary of State is meeting with him to try to convince him that he must form a more inclusive government in which the Sunni's need to be represented. Excuse my cynicism but really? Does anyone think this discussion will result in any real change? These factions and others have been fighting in the region for centuries. And the radical sects within all of them answer to no government whatsoever so how does Sec. Kerry think anyone will be able to enforce any kind of agreement if one could be reached?

There is no good option for us but I think a very good question (which I heard Rand Paul ask over the weekend). Why should we send our sons and daughters to fight for a country that the Iraqis themselves are refusing to fight for? Iraqi soldiers are shedding their uniforms and refusing to fight so why should our young men and women don theirs for this cause?

As I think of my baby grandchildren, yes and even of Prince William's little George; I can't help but wonder about the kind of world we have brought them into. I desperately want to be optimistic and yet...oh no...that ominous, foreboding cloud has begun hovering once again.

# How Are They Spending Our Money

You're busy. I'm busy. If you're like me you have lists upon lists, whether written or confined to the deep recesses of you mind, containing all of the calls you should make, all of the odds and ends around the house you should take care of and the countless requirements of the job and family or both that nag at you until attended to.

We are all busy.

And I'll bet, like me, you have a tendency to accept, even relish any of that "stuff" that can be handled by someone else. In fact we pay for others to handle things for us that we either don't have the time, inclination or expertise to handle for ourselves.

That's how I feel about paying my taxes. It's one of the rationalizations I employ when sighing over the withholding tax amount on my paycheck, writing the check for our property taxes and mentally adding the sales tax onto the price of items I am contemplating buying. I, like you, pay taxes so others, our government representatives, can just handle the things they handle for us. Like our accountant or our lawyer (I know a great lawyer if you are interested) we expect those who we pay for services to do their job and do it well.

We pay our taxes with the expectation that we will receive quality service in return. Yet all too often, especially lately, there seems to be more and more stories of just how horribly our money is being managed.

Did you see "60 Minutes" on Sunday? There was a fascinating, albeit quite disturbing, segment on the Social Security Administration's Disability Insurance Program. Of all of the government programs, this one is at greatest risk of insolvency.

The program was set up in 1956 with a very specific requirement for participation. It basically says that if there is any kind of job you can perform, you are not eligible for disability compensation. It was meant for only the "truly disabled."

Yet there are now 12 million individuals on disability, up 20% in just the past few years which will calculate out to be 135 billion dollars to fund...and the numbers are still rising.

Senator Tom Coburn representing Oklahoma (who is also a medical doctor) began looking into this in 2012. In a random sampling of disability recipients, his staff found 25% of the cases never should have been approved and another 20% were highly questionable. That's almost half of the current recipients of government disability payments, that we pay for, probably shouldn't be receiving it or at the very least should be investigated.

I'm feelin' kinda used here! How 'bout you?

Then there's this threatened lawsuit. Do you know that John Boehner wants to sue the President?

I don't know if there is merit to the suit or not. What confounds me is that we the tax payers will have to foot the legal bills...for both sides! That's right we will be "paying to fight with ourselves" and we have no say in the matter. The decision to sue or not to sue is not ours.

And please don't get me started on the fact that Congress will only be in session 26 days in the last 5 months of this year...26 days!

I don't know about you, but I'm not thinking my money is being spent very wisely.

Unlike an accountant or a lawyer we can't just fire these guys. What really troubles me is that come election time

when we can withhold our votes, will any replacements
do any better for us?

# My Mood Is My Business

Did you see fireworks on the fourth? I love fireworks - always have. Maybe it's the eruption of vibrant color in motion back-dropped by the enormity of the black sky or the spontaneous oohs and aahs signaling the total abandonment of self-consciousness they elicit. Or perhaps it is simply the delight of feeling once again the joy of a not forgotten youthful pleasure. Whatever it is, it's wonderful. Forgotten are the cares of the day – of life; replaced by exciting, instantly mood-altering pleasure.

Not trying to be obvious, I nonetheless obviously brought us to the "sorta scandal" being talked about involving Facebook. What's up with Zuckerberg et al at Facebook? Have you heard about it? During the year 2012, Facebook conducted a mood altering experiment on almost 700,000 of its service users...without specific notification or permission. Not being a true "Facebook person" (I only have an account so I can view the photos my daughter-in-law posts of my grandchildren who live in Israel) I am not fully invested in the whole Facebook culture but I do have lots of family and friends who are and I have to say that I really, really object to them unknowingly becoming lab rats in this experiment.

So here's the deal. Apparently, Facebook runs news feeds each morning for it subscribers (or whatever they call these unwitting lab specimens). But for those nearly 700,000 people in 2012, the content of the news feeds were altered. Some days the reports were heavily slanted to the positive news items while other days toward the negative. They also admit to altering other posts, information, etc. viewed by those users in addition to the news feeds. They then monitored the posts of those users that day to see if the abundance of negative or positive stories had influenced the mood they conveyed in their subsequent posts.

You might be asking, "Say what? Is that legal?"

Well, my guess is that they were totally within their rights to do this because every time we hit "Accept" on a program or service we are basically giving away all of our rights! And, apparently by accepting Facebook's terms, the company becomes one of your Facebook friends and is thereby granted access to your posts.

What's the old saying about "with friends like that...?"

But whether legal or not, it is just plain wrong...not to mention disturbingly creepy.

I thought Facebook was supposed to be fun, a computer-age way of keeping up with people in our lives.

While I'll admit that I personally don't get the attraction of continual, oftentimes trivial communications with "hundreds of friends," I do strongly feel that there is no justification for this un-specifically-consented-to experimentation with the moods of its users.

News flash: Yo Facebook! If I want my mood to be altered I will take the responsibility for it on my own...

I can listen to our National Anthem and get those goose-bumpy shivers up my spine. Or I'll call a real friend or loved one for just one of those nonsensical talks. Or maybe if I'm lucky I can experience our legal form of "bombs bursting in air" and see a fireworks show.

Come on Facebook; don't mess with my moods. You may think so, but I'm telling you my moods are none of your business.

So, that was my 300th Column – 300! As I said in my very first column, I want to thank you for taking a look at one woman's world each week. And thank you for sending so many e-mails to let me know what you think. It has been a pleasure regularly sharing a few moments of your time and I hope to share many more in the future.

# Acknowledgements

I was lucky enough to be given free rein as to subject matter about which to write from my editors. For that I will be forever grateful.

I would also like to acknowledge and thank those readers who have sent me several thousand emails. These people, whom I'm sure are very busy, as we all are, have taken the time to write to me and while we do not always agree on matters of the world, their correspondence is truly appreciated.

Finally, I would be very remiss if I didn't thank my family. To my grandmother and my mother whose wisdom and common sense have influenced me every day, I owe a huge thank you for I have referenced them both in so many of my columns. They were always supportive of whatever I did and I miss them more than I can express. To my children who provided (unwittingly) so much fodder for many of the columns; you are truly my inspiration. And to Drew who wants for me and expects from me only what I want and expect for myself, our forty-two years together have been the true blessing of my life.

Made in the USA
Lexington, KY
14 October 2017